THE ROMANESQUE ARCHITECTURE
OF THE ORDER OF CLUNY

AMS PRESS

NEW YORK

Vézelay, Yonne. The Façade of the Narthex before restoration.

From a lithograph by Émile Sagot.

THE
ROMANESQUE ARCHITECTURE
OF THE
ORDER OF CLUNY

by

JOAN EVANS

D.Litt., D.Lit., F.S.A.

Honorary Fellow of St. Hugh's College, Oxford
Sometime Susette Taylor Fellow of
Lady Margaret Hall

CAMBRIDGE
AT THE UNIVERSITY PRESS
1938

Reprinted from the edition of 1938, Cambridge
First AMS EDITION published 1971
Manufactured in the United States of America

International Standard Book Number: 0-404-02358-4

Library of Congress Catalog Number: 75-136385

AMS PRESS INC.
NEW YORK, N.Y. 10003

To

Those who have travelled with me in search of

Cluniac Architecture:

E. M. H., H. D. B., N. C. C., E. E. S. P., R. M. DE V., C. H.,
E. H., E. H. H., O. D. B.

*"C'est souvent sur les grands chemins que la vérité
apparaît aux chercheurs, ainsi qu'aux croyants."*
COURAJOD

PREFACE

I first visited Cluny in 1925, and was at once impressed by its outstanding importance. In subsequent years I travelled much in France, and gradually came to realize how many of the great Romanesque churches of France had been connected with its Order. In 1927 I began to work systematically at the subject. From the first time that we met at Cluny in 1928 onwards, Professor Kenneth Conant, the Director of the Researches carried out there by the Mediaeval Academy of America, has given me the most generous and friendly encouragement and help, culminating in the gift of the restorations and plans reproduced in figs. 9, 13*a* and *b*, 38*b*, 68, 82, 104, 147 and 206. For this encouragement, without which I should hardly have proceeded with my work, and for this material, largely unpublished, without which my account of the churches at Cluny could not have been complete, I can only offer him my sincere and profound thanks.

I am greatly indebted, for the completion of this work, to the Council of Lady Margaret Hall, Oxford, who by electing me to the Susette Taylor Travelling Fellowship for two years, from October 1933, have enabled me to travel in France at a time when the unfavourable exchange made such researches as mine matters of difficulty.

Finally, my thanks are due to the friends, to whom this book is dedicated, who by their cheerful companionship and unwearying patience have made the search for Cluniac architecture a delightful pursuit; and to others, notably Mlle Jeanne Vielliard of the Archives Nationales, M. Léon Kern, Archivist of the Swiss Republic, Miss E. M. Jamison of Lady Margaret Hall and Miss E. A. Francis and Miss E. E. S. Procter of St Hugh's College, who have helped me on points of detail. To Mrs Ward I owe the privilege of examining the monastic buildings at Much Wenlock at a moment when the alterations in progress made their investigation particularly revealing. Mr W. H. Godfrey has kindly allowed me to reproduce his plan of Lewes.

J. E.

1938

ERRATA

Page 95, line 25. *For* (Fig. 78) *read* (Fig. 82),

96, legend to illustration. *For* Fig. 78 *read* Fig. 82.

97, line 17. *For* (Fig. 82) *read* (Fig. 79),
and for (Fig. 81) *read* (Fig. 78).

CONTENTS

ARCHITECTURE

PART I: ABBEY & PRIORY CHURCHES

PART II: MONASTIC BUILDINGS

ILLUSTRATIONS

All the illustrations are at the end of the book, before the index, except the
frontispiece and those marked *.

MAPS (AT END)

BIBLIOGRAPHY

Books preceded by an asterisk are not (1936) in the Bibliothèque Nationale or the British Museum, and I have been unable to consult them.

I. EXTENT AND HISTORY OF THE ORDER

ALBERS, DOM B. *Consuetudines Monasticae:* I. *Consuetudines Farfenses.* Stuttgart, 1900. II. *Consuetudines Cluniacenses.* Monte Cassino, 1905.
— "Le plus ancien coutumier de Cluny." *Revue Bénédictine,* XX, 1903, p. 17. Maredsous.

ANGER, DOM D. "Le nombre des moines de Cluny." *Revue Bénédictine,* XXXVI, 1924, p. 267. Maredsous.

ARBOIS DE JUBAINVILLE, H. DE. "Les monastères de l'Ordre de Saint-Benoît en Lorraine et dans les trois évêchés de Metz, Toul, et Verdun, avant 1789." *Mémoires de l'Académie de Stanislas,* 5th series, V, 1887, p. 23. Nancy, 1888.

BEAUNIER, DOM and BESSE, DOM J. M. *Abbayes et Prieurés de l'ancienne France.* (In progress, continued by other hands.) Ligugé and Paris, 1905.

BÉNET, A. and BAZIN, J. L. *Archives de l'Abbaye de Cluny. Inventaire général.* Mâcon, 1884.

BERLIÈRE, DOM U. *L'Ordre monastique des origines au XIIe siècle.* Paris and Abbey of Maredsous, 1921.
— "Les monastères de l'Ordre de Cluny du XIIIe au XVe siècle." *Revue Bénédictine,* X, 1893, p. 97. Maredsous.
— "Die Kluniacenser in England." *Studien und Mittheilungen a. d. Bened. Ord.* 1890, p. 414.

BERNARD, A. and BRUEL, A. *Recueil des Chartes de l'Abbaye de Cluny.* 6 vols. Paris, 1876–1903.

BESSE, DOM J. M. "L'Ordre de Cluny et son gouvernement." *Revue Mabillon,* I, 1905, p. 5. Ligugé and Paris.

BRUEL, A. "Visites des Monastères de l'Ordre de Cluny de la province d'Auvergne en 1286 et 1310." *Bibliothèque de l'École des Chartes,* XXXVIII, 1877, p. 114.
— "Les Chapitres généraux de l'Ordre de Cluny depuis le XIIIe jusqu'au XVIIIe siècle." *Ibid.* XXXIV, 1873, p. 542.
— "Visites des Monastères de l'Ordre de Cluny de la province d'Auvergne au XIIIe et XIVe siècles." *Ibid.* new series, LII, 1891, p. 64.

[BRUGELÈS.] *Le grand Pouillé des bénéfices de France....* 1626.

CHAGNY, A. *Cluny et son Empire.* Lyons and Paris, n.d. (after 1931).

CHAMPLY, H. *Histoire de l'Abbaye de Cluny.* 2nd ed. Cluny, n.d. (1878).

CHARMASSE, A. DE. "Origine des paroisses rurales dans le département de Saône-et-Loire." *Mém. de la Société Éduenne,* XXXVII, 1909, p. 33.

CHAUME, ABBÉ. *Les origines du duché de Bourgogne.* Dijon, 1925.

CHAUMONT, L. *Histoire de Cluny depuis les origines jusqu'à la ruine de l'Abbaye.* 2nd ed., enlarged. Paris, 1911.

CUCHERAT, F. *Cluny au onzième siècle: son influence religieuse, intellectuelle et politique.* Lyons and Paris, 1851.

DAVID, DOM L. *Les grandes abbayes de l'Occident.* Lille, 1907.

DELACOURT, M. PEIGNÉ. *Monasticon Gallicanum* (Reprint.) 2 vols. Paris, 1877.

DELOCHE, M. *Cartulaire de l'Abbaye de Beaulieu (en Limousin).* (Documents inédits de l'histoire de France.) Paris, 1859.

DUCKETT, G. F. *Charters and Records of Cluni.* 2 vols. London, 1888.
— *Visitations and Chapters General of the Order of Cluni, in respect of Alsace and Lorraine, etc.* 1269–1529. London, 1893.

EGGER, DOM P. BONAVENTURA. "Die Schweizerischen Cluniacenserklöster zur Zeit ihrer Blüte." *Millénaire,* I, 374.
— *Geschichte der Cluniacenser Klöster in der Westschweiz bis zum Auftreten der Cisterzienser.* Freiburg, 1907.

EVANS, JOAN. *Monastic Life at Cluny, 910–1157.* Oxford, 1931.

GOIFFON, E. *Bullaire de l'Abbaye de Saint-Gilles.* Nîmes, 1882.

GRAHAM, ROSE. *English Ecclesiastical Studies.* London, 1928.
— "The Relation of Cluny to some other movements of monastic reform." *Journal of Theological Studies,* XV, 1913–14, p. 179.

GUÉRARD, M. *Collection des Cartulaires de France.* Tome III: *Cartulaire de l'Abbaye de Saint-Bertin.* (Documents inédits de l'histoire de France.) Paris, 1840.

GUILLOREAU, DOM L. "Les prieurés anglais de l'Ordre de Cluny." *Millénaire*, I, 291.

HEIMBUCHER, M. *Die Orden und Kongregationen der Katholischen Kirche*. 2nd ed. Paderborn, 1907.

HELYOT, P. and BULLOT, M. *Histoire des Ordres religieux*. Vol. V. Paris, 1792.

HERRGOT. *Vetus disciplina monastica*. Paris, 1726.

INGOLD, A. M. P. *Nouvelle Contribution à l'histoire des Prieurés clunisiens en Alsace*. Colmar, 1893.

LACROIX, F. "L'Abbaye de Saint-Chaffre-du-Monastier et ses rapports avec Cluny." *Annales de l'Académie de Mâcon*, 2nd series, X, 1892, p. 8. Mâcon.

LAVERGNE, A. "Les Couvents de Cluny en Gascogne." *Revue de Gascogne*, XVIII, 1877, p. 438. Auch.

LECESTRE, L. *Abbayes, Prieurés et Couvents d'hommes en France. Liste générale d'après les papiers de la Commission des Réguliers en 1768*. 2nd ed. Paris, 1902.

LONGUEVAL, J. *Histoire de l'église gallicane*, VIII, 1734, p. 228. Paris.

LORAIN, M. P. *Essai historique sur l'abbaye de Cluny*. Dijon, 1839.
— *Histoire de l'Abbaye de Cluny*. 2nd ed. Paris, 1845.

LUCE, S. "Visite par les Prieurs de Barbezieux et de Saint-Sauveur-de-Nevers des monastères de la Congrégation de Cluny situés dans la province de Poitou, 1292." *Bibliothèque de l'École des Chartes*, XX, 1859, p. 237.

MABILLON, DOM J. *Annales Ordinis Sancti Benedicti*, V, 1713, p. 252. Paris.

MARRIER, DOM M. and DUCHESNE, A. *Bibliotheca Cluniacensis*. Paris, 1614. Reprinted, Protat frères, Mâcon, 1915.

MIGNE, ABBÉ J. P. *Troisième et dernière Encyclopédie Théologique*. Vol. XVI. *Dictionnaire des abbayes et des monastères*. Paris, 1856.

MORAND, F. "Chapitre général de 1323." *Mélanges historiques*, new series, I, 1873, p. 89.

MÜLLER, E. *Le Prieuré de Saint-Leu-d'Esserent. Cartulaire*, 1080–1150. (Société Historique du Vexin.) Pontoise, 1900.

NANGLARD, ABBÉ J. "Pouillé historique du diocèse d'Angoulême. Abbaye de Saint-Cybard." *Bull. et Mém. de la soc. arch. et hist. de la Charente*, 6th series, III, 1893, p. 105.

OMONT, H. "Deux nouveaux Cartulaires de Cluny à la Bibliothèque Nationale." *Millénaire*, I, 130.

PELARGUS, C. *Geschichte der Abtei Cluny*. Tübingen, 1858.

PIGNOT, J. H. *Histoire de l'Ordre de Cluny depuis la fondation de l'Abbaye jusqu'à la mort de Pierre le Vénérable*. 3 vols. Autun and Paris, 1868.

PLANCHER, U. *Histoire générale et particulière de la Bourgogne*. Dijon, 1739, 1741, 1748 and 1781.

PROU, M. *Raoul Glaber: les cinq livres de ses histoires*. (Collection de textes pour servir à l'étude et à l'enseignement de l'histoire.) Paris, 1886.

REDET, R. "Cartulaire de l'Abbaye de Saint-Cyprien-de-Poitiers." *Archives historiques du Poitou*, III, 1874. Poitiers.
— "Visites des monastères de l'Ordre de Cluni situés dans la province de Poitou." *Ibid.* IV, 1875, p. 407.

ROBERT, U. "État des monastères franc-comtois de l'Ordre de Cluny aux XIIIe–XVe siècles." *Mém. de la Soc. d'émulation du Jura*, 2nd series, III, 1882, p. 3. Lons-le-Saunier.

ROBERT, U. and FITA, F. "État des monastères espagnols de l'Ordre de Cluny." *Boletín de la Real Academia de la Historia*, XX, 1892, p. 321. Madrid.

ROMAN, J. "Visites faites dans les prieurés de l'Ordre de Cluny du Dauphiné de 1280 à 1303." *Bulletin d'histoire ecclésiastique et d'archéologie religieuse des diocèses de Valence, Digne, Gap, Grenoble et Viviers*, IV, 1883–4, pp. 45, 85.

SACKUR, E. *Die Cluniacenser in ihrer kirchlichen und allgemeingeschichtlichen Wirksamkeit bis zur Mitte des elften Jahrhunderts*. 2 vols. Halle, 1892.

SAINTE MARTHE, D. *Gallia Christiana in Provincias ecclesiasticas distributa*: vetus, 1656, IV, 271, 966; nova, 1728, IV, 1117.

SCHREIBER, G. *Kurie und Kloster im XII. Jahrhundert*. 2 vols. Stuttgart, 1910.

SIMON, P. *Bullarium Sacri Ordinis Cluniacensis*. Lyons, 1690.

SMITH, L. M. *The Early History of the Monastery of Cluny*. Oxford, 1920.
— *Cluny in the Eleventh and Twelfth Centuries*. London, 1930.

UDALRIC. "Antiquiores Consuetudines Cluniacensis Monasterii." Migne, *Patrologia Latina*, CXLIX, col. 635.

VALOUS, G. DE. *Le monachisme clunisien des origines au XVe siècle*. (Archives de la France monastique, vols. XXXIX, XL, XLI.) Ligugé and Paris, 1936.
— "Le couvent et la bibliothèque de Cluny vers le milieu du XIe siècle." *Revue Mabillon*, XI, 1921, p. 89.

WILMART, DOM A. "Les établissements de l'Ordre de Cluny à la fin du Moyen Âge." *Annales de l'Académie de Mâcon*, 3rd series, XXIII, 1922–3, p. 375. Mâcon.

II. ARCHITECTURE

(a) GENERAL

AUBERT, M. "Les clochers romans bourguignons." *Bull. Mon.* LXXX, 1921, p. 38.
— "Les plus anciennes croisés d'ogives." *Ibid.* XCIII, 1934, pp. 5, 137.

BAER, C. H. *Die Hirsauer Bauschule.* Freiburg and Leipzig, 1897.

BAUDOT, A. DE and PERRAULT-DABOT, A. *Archives de la Commission des monuments historiques.* 5 vols. Paris, n.d. (*c.* 1900).

BREHIER, L. "Les origines de l'architecture romane en Auvergne." *Revue Mabillon*, XIII, 1923, p. 8. Ligugé and Paris.
— *L'art en France, des invasions barbares à l'époque romane.* Paris, n.d. (1930).

BRUNE, P. "Les églises romanes du Jura." *Cong. Arch.* LVIII, 1891, p. 152.

CHALVET DE ROCHEMONTEIX, A. DE. *Les Églises romanes de la Haute-Auvergne.* Clermont Ferrand, 1902.

COULTON, G. G. *Art and the Reformation.* Oxford, 1928.

DESHOULIÈRES, L. "Essai sur les bases romanes." *Bull. Mon.* LXXV, 1911, p. 77.
— *Au début de l'Art roman: les églises de l'XIe siècle en France.* Paris, n.d. (1929).

DICKSON, M. and C. *Les églises romanes de l'ancien diocèse de Chalon. Cluny et sa région.* Mâcon, 1935.

DION, A. DE. "Notes sur quelques églises de la Corrèze." *Bull. Mon.* VI, 1890, p. 103.

DURAND, G. *Églises romanes des Vosges.* (Revue de l'art chrétien, Supplément II.) Paris and Lille, 1913.

ENLART, C. *Manuel d'Archéologie française. Première partie: Architecture religieuse.* Tome I. 3rd ed. Paris, 1927.
— *Monuments religieux de l'architecture romane . . . dans la région picarde.* Amiens and Paris, 1895.

FRANCKL, P. *Die frühmittelalterliche und romanische Baukunst.* Potsdam, 1926.

GUÉRIN-BOUTARD, J. G. and A. *Les églises romanes de l'ancien diocèse d'Angoulême.* Paris, 1928.

JULLIEN, A. *Le Nièvre à travers le passé: topographie historique de ses principales villes.* Paris, 1883.

KAUTSCH. "Werdende Gotik und Antike in der burgundischen Baukunst des 12. Jahrhunderts." *Vorträge 1924, 1925 von Bibliothek Warburg*, p. 331. 1927.

LABANDE, L. H. *Études d'histoire et d'archéologie romane. Provence et Bas-Languedoc.* Avignon and Paris, 1902.

LABOUCHÈRE, G. C. *Compositie en Dispositie der Fransche Kerktorens in de 11de en 12de eeuw.* Utrecht, 1927.

LAHONDÈS, J. DE. *Les monuments de Toulouse.* Toulouse, 1920.

LAMBERT, E. "L'architecture bourguignonne et la Cathédrale d'Avila." *Bull. Mon.* LXXXIII, 1924, p. 263.

LASTEYRIE, R. DE. *L'architecture religieuse en France à l'époque romane.* 2nd ed., ed. M. Aubert. Paris, 1929.

LEFÈVRE-PONTALIS, E. *L'architecture religieuse dans l'ancien diocèse de Soissons au XIe et au XIIe siècle.* 2 vols. Paris, 1894.
— "Les niches d'autel du XIIe siècle dans le Soissonnais." *Cong. Arch.* LXXVIII, Pt 2, 1911, p. 138.
— "Les plans des Églises romanes Bénédictines." *Bull. Mon.* LXXVI, 1919, p. 439.
— "Répertoire des architectes, maçons, sculpteurs, charpentiers et ouvriers français au XIe et au XIIe siècle." *Bull. Mon.* LXXV, 1911, p. 422.

LENOIR, A. *Architecture monastique.* 2 vols. Paris, 1852.
— *Statistique monumentale de Paris.* 1867.

LÜCKEN, G. VON. *Die Anfänge der burgundischen Schule.* Basle, 1922.

Mâcon, Académie de. *Millénnaire de Cluny.* Congrès d'histoire et d'archéologie tenu à Cluny les 10, 11, 12 septembre 1910. 2 vols. Mâcon, 1910.

MALO, C. "Les églises romanes de l'ancien diocèse de Chalon." *Bull. Mon.* XC, 1931, p. 371.

METTLER, A. *Kloster Hirsau.* Augsburg, 1928.

MORELLET, J. N., BARAT, S. B. F., and BUSSIÈRE, E. *Le Nivernois: Album historique et pittoresque.* 2 vols. Nevers, 1838–42.

MORTET, V. *Recueil de Textes relatifs à l'histoire de l'architecture . . . en France au Moyen Âge.* Vol. I, 1911; vol. II, 1929.

OURSEL, C. "Cluny and Paray-le-Monial; the school of Cluny." *Art Studies, Mediaeval, Renaissance and Modern.* Harvard, 1926.
— *L'art roman de Bourgogne, études d'histoire et d'archéologie.* Dijon and Boston, 1928.

PORTER, A. KINGSLEY. *The Construction of Lombard and Gothic Vaults*. New Haven, London and Oxford, 1911.

PUIG Y CADAFALCH, J. *Le premier art roman*. Paris, 1928.

— *La géographie et les origines du premier art roman*. Paris, 1935.

RAHN, H. *Geschichte der bildenden Kunste in der Schweiz*. Zurich, 1876.

RANQUET, H. and E. DU. "Origine française du berceau roman." *Bull. Mon.* XC, 1931, p. 35.

REINHARDT, H. "Hypothèse sur l'origine des premiers déambulatoires en Picardie." *Bull. Mon.* LXXXVIII, 1929, p. 269.

REINHART, C. *Die Cluniacenser Architektur in der Schweiz vom X. bis XIII. Jahrhundert*. Zurich, 1904.

RHEIN, A. "Étude sur les voûtes des Déambulatoires." *Bull. Mon.* LXXXII, 1923, p. 254.

RICCI, C. *Romanesque Architecture in Italy*. London, 1925.

RIVOIRA, G. T. *Lombardic Architecture: its origin, development and derivatives*. Translated by G. McN. Rushforth. Oxford, 1910. 2nd ed. 1934.

ROSE, H. *Die Baukunst der Cisterzianer*. Munich, 1916.

SAINT-PAUL, A. "L'archéologie nationale au Salon de 1876." *Bull. Mon.* XLIII, 1877, p. 143.

SCHLOSSER, J. *Die abendländische Klosteranlage des früheren Mittelalters*. Vienna, 1889.

SWARTWOUT, R. E. *The Monastic Craftsman*. Cambridge, 1932.

THIOLLIER, F. and N. *Art et archéologie dans le Département de la Loire*. Saint-Étienne, 1898.

— *L'Architecture religieuse à l'époque romane dans l'ancien diocèse du Puy*. Le Puy, n.d. (1900).

THOLIN, G. *Études sur l'architecture religieuse de l'Agenais.... Agen* and Paris, 1874.

TRUCHIS, P. DE. "Les influences orientales dans l'architecture romane de la Bourgogne." *Cong. Arch.* LXXIV, 1907, p. 459.

— "L'architecture de la Bourgogne française sous Robert le Pieux." *Bull. Mon.* LXXX, 1921, p. 5.

— "L'œuvre architecturale de Cluny, au premier temps de la Renaissance romane." *Mém. de la Commission des Antiquités de la Côte d'Or*, XVIII, 1922–6, p. 253. Dijon, 1926.

VALLERY-RADOT, J. "Notes sur les chapelles hautes dédiées à Saint-Michel." *Bull. Mon.* LXXXVIII, 1929, p. 453.

— *Églises romanes: filiations et échanges d'influences*. Paris, n.d. (1931).

VIREY, J. *Les églises romanes de l'ancien diocèse de Mâcon: Cluny et sa région*. 2nd ed. Mâcon, 1935.

— "Les édifices religieux de l'époque romane en Saône-et-Loire." *Cong. Arch.* LXVI, 1899, p. 237.

WOILLEZ, E. J. *Archéologie des monuments religieux de l'ancien Beauvoisis pendant la métamorphose romane*. Paris, 1839–49.

(b) PARTICULAR

(1) FRANCE

Cluny

AMÉ, E. "Grille de l'abbaye de Cluny." *Annales Archéologiques*, XIV, 1854, p. 309.

AUBERT, M. "Le chœur de l'église de Cluny au début du XIXe siècle, d'après une aquarelle de la collection de M. le Comte de Rambuteau." *Bull. Mon.* XCIV, 1935, p. 376.

*BARTHÉLEMY, A. *Essai sur l'histoire monumentale de l'Abbaye de Cluny*. Cluny, 1842.[1]

BERNARD, A. "Abbaye de Cluny. Note sur les anciens Bâtiments aujourd'hui détruits." *Cabinet historique*, p. 226. Paris, 1863.

BOUCHÉ DE LA BERTILIÈRE, PHILIPPE. Paris, Bibliothèque Nationale, MS. nouv. acq. français 4336. *Description Historique et Chronologique de la Ville Abbaye et banlieue de Cluny.* (Written between November and May 1798.)

BRUEL, F. L. *Cluni, 910–1910: Album historique et archéologique précédé d'une étude résumée et d'une notice des planches*. Mâcon, 1910.

CHAVOT, T. *Destruction de l'abbaye de Cluny et ses causes*. Mâcon, n.d. (c. 1868).

CONANT, K. J. "La Chapelle Saint-Gabriel à Cluny." *Bull. Mon.* LXXXVII, 1928, p. 55.

— "Les fouilles de Cluny." *Ibid.* LXXXVIII, 1929, p. 109.

— "Mediaeval Academy. Excavations at Cluny: the season of 1928." *Speculum, a Journal of Mediaeval Studies*, IV, 1929, pp. 3, 168, 291, 443.

— "Mediaeval Academy. Excavations at Cluny: the season of 1929." *Ibid.* VI, 1931, p. 3.

— "The Apse at Cluny." *Ibid.* VII, 1932, p. 23.

[1] This was published in an edition of twenty-five copies and I have not been able to consult it.

CONANT, K. J. "Five old Prints of the Abbey Church of Cluny." *Ibid.* III, 1928, p. 401.
— "Cluny." *Liturgical Arts*, June 1935, p. 4.
DESHOULIÈRES, L. "Le rôle de Cluny." *Bull. Mon.* XCIV, 1935, p. 413.
GRAHAM, ROSE and CLAPHAM, A. W. "The Monastery of Cluny, 910–1155." *Archaeologia*, LXXX, 1930, p. 143. Oxford.
GUILHERMY. Paris, Bibliothèque Nationale. MS. nouv. acq. français 6099. *Papiers de Guilhermy. Description des localités; Cluny.*
LLOYD, R. W. and CONANT, K. J. "Cluny Epigraphy." *Speculum*, VII, 1932, p. 336.
MABILLON, DOM J. "Itinerarium Burgundicum." *Ouvrages posthumes de Dom Jean Mabillon et de Dom Thierri Ruinart*, ed. Dom Vincent Thuillier. 3 vols. Paris, 1717–24.
— In *Annales Ordinis Sancti Benedicti*, V, 1740, p. 235. Paris.
METTLER, A. "Die zweite Kirche in Cluni und die Kirchen in Hirsau nach den 'Gewohnheiten' des XI. Jahrhunderts." *Zeitschrift für Geschichte der Architektur*, III, 1910, p. 273; IV, 1911, p. 1. Heidelberg.
PENJON, A. *Cluny, la Ville et l'Abbaye.* Cluny, 1872.
VERDIER, A. Album de Cluny, 1852. No. 8 of *Catalogue de la Bibliothèque de la Commission des Monuments historiques*. Paris, 1875.
VIREY, J. *L'Abbaye de Cluny.* (Petites monographics.) Paris, 1927.
— "Un ancien plan de l'Abbaye de Cluny." *Millénaire*, II, 231.
— "Cluny." *Cong. Arch.* LXXX, 1913, p. 65.

Airaines
AUBERT, M. "Airaines." *Cong. Arch.* XCIX, 1937, p. 459.
MARCHAND, ABBÉ A. "Notes pour servir à l'histoire d'Airaines. Prieuré de Notre-Dame-d'Airaines." *Mém. de la Soc. d'émulation d'Abbeville*, XXII, 1909, p. 54. Abbeville.

Arles-sur-Tech
*GIBRAT, ABBÉ M. *Aperçu historique sur l'Abbaye d'Arles-sur-Tech.* Céret, 1922.

Aubigny-sur-Loire
GÉNERMONT, M. "L'église d'Aubigny." *Bull. de la Soc. d'émulation du Bourbonnais*, 1929, p. 265. Moulins.

Auch, Saint-Orens
CANETO, ABBÉ F. "Souvenirs archéologiques de Saint-Orens-d'Auch. Rapport par M. Guirondet." *Bull. arch. et hist...de la Soc. arch. de Tarn-et-Garonne*, V, 1877, p. 27. Montauban.

*SARREMEJEAN, —. *Étude sur le monastère de Saint-Orens.* Tarbes, 1913.

Auxerre, Saint-Germain
Bib. Nat. MS. français 18693. *Abrégé de l'Histoire de l'Abbaye de Saint-Germain-d'Auxerre, dressé l'an 1682 et copié l'an 1684.*
TILLET, J. "L'Abbaye de Saint-Germain-d'Auxerre." *Cong. Arch.* LXXIV, 1907, p. 627.

Baume-les-Messieurs
ROY, L. A. *L'Abbaye de Baume-les-Messieurs.* Baume-les-Messieurs, 1928.

Beaulieu
DELOCHE, M. *Cartulaire de l'Abbaye de Beaulieu en Limousin.* Paris, 1859.
LEFÈVRE-PONTALIS, E. "À quelle école faut-il rattacher l'église de Beaulieu, Corrèze?" *Bull. Mon.* LXXVIII, 1914, p. 58.
— "Beaulieu." *Cong. Arch.* LXXXIV, 1923, p. 366.
POULBRIÈRE, J. B. "L'église de Beaulieu et son portail sculpté." *Bull. de la Soc. arch. et hist. du Limousin*, XXI, 1872, p. 41. Limoges.
— "L'église et le portail de Beaulieu, Corrèze." *Cong. Arch.* XLIV, 1877, p. 582.

Bellegarde-du-Loiret
DESHOULIÈRES, L. "Bellegarde." *Cong. Arch.* XCIII, 1931, p. 178. (Orléans.)
PILLON, E. "Étude sur le château et l'église de Bellegarde." *Bull. de la Soc. arch. de l'Orléanais*, II, 1854–8, p. 343.
TARTARIN, E. *Études historiques sur Bellegarde-en-Gâtinais.* Orléans, 1888. 2nd ed. 1908.

Bersol
Compte-rendu des travaux de la Commission des monuments...historiques...de la Gironde, XV, 1853–4, p. 5.

Berzé-la-Ville
VIREY, J. "Saint-Hugues et la Chapelle de Berzé-la-Ville." *Annales de l'Académie de Mâcon*, XXV, 1926–7, p. 445. Mâcon.
F. MERCIER and M. AUBERT. "Berzé la Ville." In *Cong. Arch.* XCVIII, 1935, p. 485.

Binson
LUCOT, P. "L'église de Binson et Sainte-Posenne." *Mém. de la Soc. d'agriculture...du Département de la Marne*, 1880–1, p. 125. Châlons-sur-Marne.

Boulogne-sur-Mer, Saint-Wulmer
ENLART, C. "Les Grandes Abbayes." *Boulogne-sur-Mer et la région boulonnaise.* Boulogne, 1899.

Bourbon-Lancy

PERRAULT-DABOT, A. *L'ancienne église Saint-Nazaire à Bourbon-Lancy.* Paris, n.d. (1905).
DE TRUCHIS, P. In *Mém. de la Société Éduenne*, XXXV, 1907, p. 293. Autun.

Brancion

VIREY, J. "L'église de Brancion." *Bull. Mon.* LXXIII, 1909, p. 275.

Bredons

*BOUFFET, —. *Le prieuré de Bredons.* Aurillac, 1908.

Carennac

LEFÈVRE-PONTALIS, E. "Église et plaques de chancel à Carennac." *Bull. de la Soc. nat. des Antiquaires de France*, 1921, p. 259.
— "Carennac." *Cong. Arch.* LXXXIV, 1923, p. 420.

Cénac

BANCHEREAU, J. "Cénac." *Cong. Arch.* XC, 1927, p. 243.
BOYSSON, R. and RUPIN, E. "Église et prieuré de Notre-Dame-de-Cénac." *Bull. de la Soc. scient., hist. et arch. de la Corrèze*, XIX. Brive, 1897.

Chambon

LABORDERIE, A. DE. "L'église de Chambon-Sainte-Valerie." *Mém. de la Soc. des Sciences naturelles et archéologiques de la Creuse*, XXIII, 1925, p. 333.

Charlieu

BARBAT, DR. *Charlieu, ses monuments, son Abbaye.* Charlieu, 1925 (1st ed. 1907).
— *Charlieu pendant la Révolution.* Roanne, 1913.
DESEVELINGES, J. B. *Histoire de la ville de Charlieu.* Roanne and Lyons, 1856.
JEANNEZ, E. "La colonnade romane de l'Abbaye de Charlieu et le jeu du cerceau dans les Cloîtres Bénédictins." *Bull. de la Société de la Diana*, VI, 1891–2, p. 55. Montbrison.
— "Les fortifications de l'Abbaye et de la ville fermée de Charlieu-en-Lyonnais." *Ibid.* II, 1884, p. 445. Montbrison.
*MONOT, H. *Charlieu.* Paris, 1934.
RHEIN, A. "Charlieu." *Cong. Arch.* LXXX, 1913, p. 242.
— "Charlieu." *Cong. Arch.*, XCVIII, 1935, p. 442.
THIOLLIER, F. *L'art roman à Charlieu et dans les régions voisines.* Montbrison, 1894.
VALLERY-RADOT, J. "Les analogies des Églises Saint-Fortunat de Charlieu et d'Anzy-le-Duc. Églises bourguignonnes voûtées d'arêtes." *Bull. Mon.* LXXXVIII, 1929, p. 243.

Châtelmontagne

LEFÈVRE-PONTALIS, E. "L'église de Chatel-Montagne." *Bull. Mon.* LXIX, 1905, p. 506.

Coincy

ANDRY, A. "Coincy à travers le passé." *Annales de la Soc. hist. et arch. de Château-Thierry*, XLVI, 1912, p. 1. Château-Thierry.

Domène

*PERRIER, L. *Histoire de Domène.* Grenoble, 1921.

Doullens

DURAND, G. "Église Saint-Pierre de Doullens." *Mém. de la Soc. des Antiquaires de Picardie*, 3rd series, IX, 1887, p. 571. Amiens.
LEFÈVRE, T. "Prieuré de Saint-Pierre de Doullens." *Bull. de la Soc. d'émulation d'Abbeville*, I, 1890, p. 332. Abbeville.

Esnandes

BARTHÉLEMY, H. "Note sur l'église d'Esnandes, (Charente-Inférieure)." *Bull. Mon.* I, 1843, p. 173.

Felletin

LABORDERIE, A. DE. "Les églises de Felletin." *Mém. de la Soc. des Sciences naturelles et archéologiques de la Creuse*, 1928.

Fons

*ALLEMAND, A. *Fons-en-Quercy.* Avignon, 1923.

Ganagobie

AGNEL, A DE. "Notice archéologique sur le prieuré de Ganagobie (Basses-Alpes): église et cloître du XIIe siècle." *Bull. Arch.* 1910, p. 314.
BERNARD, C. "Notice historique sur Ganagobie." *Bull. de la Soc. scientifique et littéraire des Basses-Alpes*, XIV, 1909–10, pp. 76, 132. Digne.

Saint-André-de-Gap

GUILLAUME, P. "Notice historique et documents inédits sur le Prieuré de Saint-André-de-Gap." *Bull. d'hist. ecclésiastique et d'arch. religieuse des diocèses de Valence, Digne, Gap, Grenoble et Viviers*, II, 1881–2, p. 249. Romans.

Gassicourt

LEFÈVRE-PONTALIS, E. "Église de Gassicourt." *Cong. Arch.* LXXXII, 1919, p. 227.

Gigny

GASPARD, B. *Histoire de Gigny.* Chalon-sur-Saône, 1843.
— *Supplément à l'histoire de Gigny.* Chalon-sur-Saône, 1858.

Gourdon

MOREUX, C. "L'église de Gourdon." *Bull. Mon.* LXXXI, 1922, p. 361.

Innimont

JOLY, L. "Le prieuré de Saint-Pierre-d'Innimont." *Bull. de la Société Gorini*, X, 1913, pp. 15, 164. Bourg.

La Charité-sur-Loire

BEAUSSART, P. *L'église Bénédictine de la Charité-sur-Loire, fille aînée de Cluny.* La Charité, 1929.

BEZOLD, G. VON. "La Charité-sur-Loire." *Centralblatt der Bauverwaltung*, nos. 28, 29. Berlin, 1886.

LEBŒUF, L. *Histoire de La Charité.* La Charité, 1897.

DE LESPINASSE, R. *Cartulaire du prieuré de La Charité-sur-Loire.* Nevers and Paris, 1887.

PHILIPPE, A. "L'église de La Charité-sur-Loire." *Bull. Mon.* LXIX, 1905, p. 469.

SERBAT, L. "La Charité." *Cong. Arch.* LXXX, 1913, p. 374.

Le Bourget-du-Lac

BARUT, J. "Le Château-Prieuré du Bourget-du-Lac." *Mém. et documents publiés par la Société Savoisienne d'histoire et d'archéologie*, LII, 1912, p. 505. Chambéry.

Saint-Honoré-de-Lérins

MORIS, H. *L'Abbaye de Lérins.* Paris, 1909 and 1935.

Saint-Martial-de-Limoges

ARBELLOT, ABBÉ F. "Dissertation sur l'Apostolat de Saint-Martial." *Bull. de la Soc. arch. et hist. du Limousin*, IV, 1852, p. 209. Limoges.

DUPLÈS-AGIER, H. *Chroniques de Saint-Martial-de-Limoges.* (Société de l'histoire de France.) Paris, 1874.

LASTEYRIE, C. DE. *L'Abbaye de Saint-Martial-de-Limoges.* Paris, 1901.

ROSTAND, A. "Un dessin inédit du clocher de Saint-Martial-de-Limoges." *Bull. Mon.* LXXXIII, 1924, p. 172.

Longpont

VALLERY-RADOT, J. "L'église de Notre-Dame-de-Longpont." *Bull. Mon.* LXXIX, 1920, p. 65.

Longueville

LE CACHEUX, P. *Chartes du prieuré de Longueville.* Rouen and Paris, 1934.

LE VERDIER, P. *Notes sur le dernier état et les derniers jours du prieuré de Longueville.* Évreux, 1893.

Lons-le-Saunier

DUHEM, M. "L'église Saint-Desiré à Lons-le-Saulnier." *Bull. Mon.* XCIV, 1935, p. 51.

Lubersac

VALON, L. DE. "Monographie de l'église de Lubersac." *Bull. de la Soc. scient., hist. et arch. de la Corrèze*, III, n.s. 1891, p. 162. Brive.

Maillezais

BERTHELÉ, J. *La date de l'église abbatiale de Maillezais.* Vannes, n.d.

LACURIE, ABBÉ J. L. *Histoire de l'abbaye de Maillezais.* Fontenay-le-Comte and Saintes, 1852.

Marcigny

Bibliothèque de Dijon. MS. Fonds Baudot 1018, No. 7, p. 111. *Mémoires concernant les antiquités du prieuré de Marsigny (sic).* Eighteenth century.

Marcilhac

ALBE, E. *Quelques notes sur l'Abbaye de Marcilhac.* Cahors, 1901.

— and VIRÉ. *Histoire de l'Abbaye de Saint-Pierre-de-Marcilhac.* Paris, 1924.

Marolles

PERRAULT-DABOT, A. *L'église de Marolles-en-Brie.* Paris, 1898.

Meymac

FAGE, R. "L'église de Meymac et les singularités de son plan." *Bull. Mon.* LXXXIII, 1924, p. 69.

MAYEUX, A. "L'irrégularité de plan de Meymac." *Ibid.* LXXXII, 1923, p. 193.

Moirax

*DUBOURG, —. *Histoire du doyenné de Moyrax.* Agen, 1908.

SERRET, E. G. *Monographie de l'église Notre-Dame-de-Moirax.* Tonneins, 1889.

Moissac

ANGLÈS, A. *L'Abbaye de Moissac.* (Petites Monographies.) Paris, 1926.

AUBERT, M. "Moissac." *Cong. Arch.* XCII, 1929, p. 494. (Toulouse.)

LAGRÈZE-FOSSAT, A. *Études historiques sur Moissac.* Paris, 1870-4.

MARION, J. "L'Abbaye de Moissac." *Bibliothèque de l'École des Chartes*, 1849, p. 89.

RUPIN, E. "Durand, Abbé de Moissac et évêque de Toulouse, 1047-1071." *Rev. de l'art chrét.* XLII, 1892, p. 455.

— *L'Abbaye et les Cloîtres de Moissac.* Paris, 1897.

Montbron

BEAUMONT, C. DE. "L'église de Montbron, Charente." *Cong. Arch.* LXXIX, 1912, p. 270.

Montmartre

DESHOULIÈRES, F. "L'église Saint-Pierre-de-Montmartre." *Bull. Mon.* LXXVII, 1913, p. 5.

Mont-Saint-Vincent

BULLIOT, J. S. "Mémoire sur l'église de Mont-Saint-Vincent." *Mém. de la Société Éduenne*, XXI, 1893, p. 412. Autun.

CONTENSON, L. DE. "L'église de Mont-Saint-Vincent." *Bull. Mon.* LXXIV, 1910, p. 286.

Morlaas, Sainte-Foy

BOURDENAVE-D'ABÈVE, M. DE. *Morlaas et sa Basilique.* Morlaas and Pau, 1877.

CANETO, F. "Morlaas", in "Les églises romanes de la Gascogne." *Revue de Gascogne*, XII, 1871, p. 49. Auch.

CARRIÉ, C. *Courte notice sur la Basilique Sainte-Foy-de-Morlaas.* Tours, 1911.

LAPLACE, L. P. *Notice historique et archéologique sur Sainte-Foy-de-Morlaas.* Pau, 1865.

Mouchan

CANETO, F. "Mouchan", in "Les églises romanes de la Gascogne." *Revue de Gascogne*, XI, 1870, p. 493. Auch.

MARBONTIN, J. R. "L'église de Mouchan." *Bull. de la Soc. arch. du Gers*, XI, 1910, p. 56. Auch.

Moutier-d'Ahun

DESHOULIÈRES, L. "Le Moûtier-d'Ahun." *Cong. Arch.* LXXXIV, 1921, p. 132.

Mozac

GOBINOT, H. *Histoire de l'abbaye royale de Mozat.* Paris, 1872.

LUZUY, ABBÉ. "Mozac." *Cong. Arch.* LXXX, 1913, p. 124.

RANQUET, H. DU. "Fouilles de Mozac." *Revue d'Auvergne*, XX, 1903, p. 210.

Nantua

ARÈNE, J. *La sœur aînée de Cluny.* Nantua, 1910.

SMITH, M. VALENTIN. "Considérations sur l'histoire de la Ville et de l'Abbaye de Nantua." *Revue du Lyonnais*, XVIII, 1859, p. 365. Lyons.

Nevers, Saint-Étienne

BOUCHACOURT, M. "Le Prieuré Saint-Étienne à Nevers." *Bull. de la Société Nivernaise*, XXVI, 1922, p. 52. Nevers.

CROSNIER, ABBÉ A. J. *Notice historique sur l'église et le Prieuré de Saint-Étienne-de-Nevers.* Nevers, 1853.

RANQUET, H. DU. "Influences auvergnates dans l'église de Saint-Étienne-de-Nevers." *Revue d'Auvergne*, XXXVI, 1919, p. 102.

SERBAT, L. "Nevers: Saint-Étienne, Saint-Sauveur." *Cong. Arch.* LXXX, 1913, p. 300.

Noël-Saint-Martin

LEFÈVRE-PONTALIS, E. *Noël-Saint-Martin.* Senlis, 1886.

— "Notice archéologique sur l'église de Noël-Saint-Martin." *Comptes rendus et mémoires du Comité archéologique de Senlis*, 2nd series, X, 1885, p. 59.

Notre-Dame-de-Bethléem

SALLUSTIEN-JOSEPH, FRÈRE. "Quelques églises romanes du Gard." *Cong. Arch.* LXIV, 1897, p. 917.

Paray-le-Monial

CHEVALIER, U. "Chartularium Beatae Mariae de Paredo Monachorum." *Mém. de la Soc. hist. et arch. de Chalon-sur-Saône.* Montbéliard, 1891.

LEFÈVRE-PONTALIS, E. "Paray-le-Monial." *Cong. Arch.* LXXX, 1913, p. 53.

VIREY, J. *Paray-le-Monial et les églises du Brionnais.* (Petites monographies.) Paris, 1926.

Paris, Saint-Martin-des-Champs

ALINOT, P. "Église de Saint-Martin-des-Champs." *Journal de l'Union syndicale des Architectes*, 1914, pp. 819, 919.

LEBEUF, ABBÉ J. *Histoire de la ville et de tout le diocèse de Paris*, vol. II, ed. H. Cocheris. Paris, 1864.

LEFÈVRE-PONTALIS, E. "Étude sur le chœur de l'église de Saint-Martin-des-Champs à Paris." *Bibliothèque de l'École des Chartes*, XLVII, 1886, p. 345.

— "Saint-Martin-des-Champs." *Cong. Arch.* LXXXII, 1919, p. 106.

NORMAND, C. "Le Prieuré de Saint-Martin-des-Champs, ou le conservatoire des Arts et Métiers." *Bull. de la Soc. des amis des monuments parisiens*, IV, 1890, p. 65.

PERRAULT-DABOT, A. "Note sur la restauration de l'église de Saint-Martin-des-Champs." *Bull. de la Soc. de l'Histoire de Paris*, XLII, 1915, p. 58.

Peyrissas

DEDIEU, J. "Le Prieuré de Peyrissas en 1402." *Revue de Comminges*, XXVIII, 1913, p. 65. Saint-Gaudens.

Pommevic

THOLIN, G. "Notes sur les églises de Goudourville et de Pommevic." *Bull. arch. et hist....de la Soc. arch. de Tarn-et-Garonne*, VI, 1878, p. 193. Montauban.

Pont-aux-Moines

JARRY, E. "Le Prieuré de Pont-aux-Moines près Orléans." *Bull. de la Soc. arch. et hist. de l'Orléanais*, XIV, 1907, p. 579. Orléans.

Rabastens

GUITARD, E. "Rabastens d'Albigeois." *Cong. Arch.* XCII, 1929, p. 346. (Toulouse.)

Relanges

DURAND, G. "Église de Relanges." *Mém. de la Soc. arch. de Lorraine*, 3rd series, XIII, 1885, p. 229. Nancy.

Retaud

MUSSET, G. "Les églises romanes de Rioux et de Retaud." *Bull. Mon.* LXX, 1906, p. 271.

Rosiers

DURAND, V. and VACHEZ, A. "Étude archéologique et historique sur le Prieuré de Rosiers." *Recueil de mém. et doc. sur le Forez publiés par la Société de la Diana*, V, 1879, p. 299. Montbrison.

Ruffec

HUBERT, J. and BARGE, J. "Le Prieuré de Ruffec-en-Berry." *Bull. Mon.* LXXXVIII, 1929, p. 205.

Sagnac

CESSAC, J. DE. "L'église de Sagnac." *Mém. de la Soc. des sciences naturelles et archéologiques de la Creuse*, 2nd series, II, 1888, p. 91.

Saint-Béat

GOURDON, M. "Monographie de Saint-Béat et ses environs." *Bull. de la soc. Ramond*, XIX, 1884, p. 99. Paris.

Saint-Bertin

P. HÉLIOT. "Abbaye de Saint-Bertin." *Cong. Arch.* XCIX, 1937, p. 517.

Saint-Eutrope-de-Saintes

BESNARD, C. H. "Note sur les voûtes de Saint-Eutrope-de-Saintes." *Cong. Arch.* LXXIX, 1912, p. 195.
DANGIBEAUD, C. "Le plan primitif de Saint-Eutrope-de-Saintes." *Bull. Mon.* LXXI, 1907, p. 13.

Saint-Gengoux

RAFFIN, L. and CONTENSON, L. DE. "L'église et le doyenné clunisien de Saint-Gengoux-le-National." *Millénaire*, II, 59.

Saint-Gilles

M. AUBERT. "Les dates de la façade de Saint-Gilles." *Bull. Mon.* XCV, 1936, p. 369.
EVERLANGE, ABBÉ P. E. DE. *Histoire de Saint-Gilles.* Avignon, 1885.
FLICHE, A. *Aigues Mortes et Saint-Gilles.* (Petites monographies.) Paris, n.d.
GOIFFON, E. *Saint-Gilles, son abbaye, son grand prieuré, sa paroisse.* Nîmes, 1881.
— *Bullaire de Saint-Gilles.* Paris, 1882.
LABANDE, L. H. "Saint-Gilles." *Cong. Arch.* LXXVI, 1909. (Avignon.)
NICOLAS, C. *Notes de M. Delmas sur l'église de Saint-Gilles*, 1843. (Extr. des Mémoires de l'Académie de Nîmes.) Nîmes, 1903.

Saint-Leu-d'Esserent

FOSSARD, A. *Le prieuré de Saint-Leu-d'Esserent*, 1934.
LAMBIN, E. "L'église de Saint-Leu-d'Esserent." *Gazette des Beaux Arts*, 3rd series, XXV, Jan.–June 1901, p. 305.
LEFÈVRE-PONTALIS, E. "Saint-Leu-d'Esserent." *Cong. Arch.* LXXII, 1905, p. 121. Beauvais.
MULLER, E. *Le Prieuré de Saint-Leu-d'Esserent, Cartulaire.* Pontoise (Société historique du Vexin), 1900–1.

Saint-Marcel-lès-Chalon

CAZET, ABBÉ. "Notice historique et archéologique sur l'église et l'Abbaye de Saint-Marcel." *Mém. de la Soc. hist. et arch. de Chalon-sur-Saône*, I, 1844–6, p. 139. Chalon-sur-Saône.

Saint-Marcel-lès-Sauzet

DESHOULIÈRES, L. "Saint-Marcel de Sauzet." *Cong. Arch.* LXXXVI, 1925, p. 261.

Saint-Pierre-le-Moûtier

LEFÈVRE-PONTALIS, E. "Saint-Pierre-le-Moûtier." *Cong. Arch.* LXXX, 1913, p. 292.

Saint-Pons-de-Thomières

SAHUC, J. "L'art roman à Saint-Pons-de-Thomières." *Mém. de la Soc. archéologique de Montpellier*, 2nd series, IV, 1911, p. 5. Montpellier.

Salles

MÉHU, E. *Salles-en-Beaujolais.* Villefranche-sur-Saône, 1910.
J. VALLERY-RADOT. "Salles." . *Cong Arch.* XCVIII, 1935, p. 334.

Semelay

MARTRAY, COLONEL DU. "Semelay, église, prieuré, paroisse." *Mém. de la Société Éduenne*, XLII, 1914, p. 1; XLIII, 1919, p. 133. Autun.

Semur-en-Brionnais

RHEIN, A. "L'église de Semur-en-Brionnais." *Bull. Mon.* LXXIX, 1920, p. 183.
— "Semur-en-Brionnais." *Cong. Arch.*, XCVIII, 1935, p. 437.

Souvigny

AUCOUTURIER, H. *Souvigny: son église.* Moulins, 1922.
BRÉHIER, L. "L'église romane de Souvigny et les dates de sa construction." *Revue Mabillon*, Jan. 1922.
DESHOULIÈRES, F. "Souvigny." *Cong. Arch.* LXXX, 1913, p. 182. (Moulins and Nevers.)
— "Les fouilles de l'église de Souvigny, Allier." *Bull. Mon.* LXXXIII, 1924, p. 160.
— *Souvigny et Bourbon l'Archambault.* (Petites monographies.) Paris (n.d.).
— "Saint-Pierre de Souvigny. Fouilles et restaurations." *Bull. Mon.* XCII, 1933, p. 479.
— "Les deux transepts de l'Église de Souvigny." *Bull. de la Soc. nat. des antiquaires de France.* 18 Oct. 1916.
— "Les dates de l'église de Souvigny." *Revue Mabillon.* April–July 1922.
LIMAGNE, A. *Souvigny, son histoire, son abbaye.* Paris, 1904.
MARCAILLE, F. S. *Antiquités du prieuré de Souvigny.* Moulins, 1610.

Tain

BELLET, C. F. "Histoire de la ville de Tain." *Bull. de la Soc. départementale d'archéologie et de statistique de la Drôme*, XXXIX, 1905, p. 1.

Talmont

DIGARD, J. *L'église Sainte-Radegonde de Talmont-sur-Gironde.* Paris, 1934.

Taluyers

BÉGULE, L. *Antiquités et richesses d'art du Département du Rhône*, 1925, p. 141. Lyon.

Tayac

CASTELNAU, L. DE. "Tayac." *Bull. de la Soc. hist et arch. du Périgord*, IV, 1877.

Ternay

THIOLLIER, F. and N. "L'église de Ternay, Isère." *Bull. Arch.* 1902, p. 257.

Thierenbach

GASSER, A. "Le pèlerinage de Thierenbach." *Revue d'Alsace*, LXXI, 1924, pp. 114, 304, 424, 502.

Touget

DUFFOUR, J. "L'ancien prieuré de Touget." *Revue de Gascogne*, X, 1910, pp. 462, 505, 566; XI, 1911, pp. 80, 122, 182. Auch.

Toulouse, La Daurade

DUMAS DE RAULY, C. "Détails historiques sur le prieuré bénédictin de Notre-Dame de la Daurade de Toulouse." *Mém. de la Soc. arch. du Midi*, XIII, 1883–5, p. 94. Toulouse.
J. DE LAHONDÈS. *Les Monuments de Toulouse.* Toulouse, 1920.
J. DE MALEFOSSE. "L'ancienne église de la Daurade." In *Études et notes d'archéologie.* Toulouse, 1898, p. 69.
R. REY. "La Daurade." *Cong. Arch.* XCII, 1929, p. 105.

Trémolat

DESHOULIÈRES, L. "Trémolat." *Cong. Arch.* XC, 1927, p. 128.
MAUDIN, J. "Trémolat." *Journal de la Dordogne*, 24 Aug. 1899.

Uzerche

MAYEUX, A. "Uzerche." *Cong. Arch.* LXXXIV, 1921, p. 292.
PRADEL DE LAMASE, M. DE. *Uzerche et ses Sénéchaux.* Brive, 1929.

Varennes-l'Arconce

J. VIREY. "Varennes-l'Arconce." *Cong. Arch.* XCVIII, 1935, p. 443.

Vézelay

DESPINEY, CHANOINE. *Guide-Album de Vézelay.* Vézelay, 1930.
GALLY, CHANOINE. *Voyage dans l'Avallonais; Vézelai monastique.* Tonnerre, 1887.
GRAHAM, ROSE. *An Abbot of Vézelay.* London, 1918.
PORÉE, C. *L'Abbaye de Vézelay.* (Petites monographies.) Paris, n.d.
SALET, F. "La Madeleine de Vézelay et ses dates de construction." *Bull. Mon.* XCV, 1936, p. 5.
VIOLLET-LE-DUC, E.-E. *Monographie de l'ancienne église abbatiale de Vézelay.* 1873.

Vicq

DESHOULIÈRES, L. "Vicq." *Cong. Arch.* LXXX, 1913, p. 95.

Vigeois

LABORDERIE, A. DE. "L'église de Vigeois." *Bull. de la Soc. scient., hist. et arch. de la Corrèze*, 1932.

Visan

MALBOIS, E. "Histoire de Visan avant 1344." *Mém. de l'Académie de Vaucluse*, XXV, 1925, p. 85. Vaison.

Le Wast

ENLART, C. "L'église du Wast-en-Boulonnais et son portail arabe." *Gazette des Beaux Arts*, 5th series, XVI, July 1927, p. 1.

HÉLIOT, P. "Le Wast." *Cong. Arch.* XCIX, 1937, p. 468.

(2) SWITZERLAND

Grandson

RAHN, J. R. "Grandson und zwei Cluniacenserbauten in der Westschweiz." *Mittheilungen der antiquarischen Gesellschaft in Zürich*, XVII, Heft 2. Zurich, 1870.

Payerne

BOSSET, L. and REYMOND, M. *Payerne*. Payerne, 1928.

BURMEISTER, A. *Payerne*. Payerne, 1930.

RAHN, J. R. *L'église abbatiale de Payerne*. Traduit de l'allemand par William Cart. (Société de l'histoire de la Suisse romande.) Lausanne, 1893.

Romainmôtier

CHARRIÈRE, F. DE. "Recherches sur le Couvent de Romainmôtier." *Mémoires et documents*

publiées par la Société de l'histoire de la Suisse romande, III. Lausanne, 1841.

GAUTHIER, J. "L'église de Romain-môtier au canton de Vaud (Suisse)." *Bull. arch.* 1902, p. 265.

MEYMIER, J. *Le Prieuré de Romainmôtier dans le pays de Vaud et en Franche-Comté*. Besançon, 1899.

NAEF, A. "Les dates de construction de l'église de Romainmôtier." *Bull. Mon.* LXX, 1906, p. 425.

— *Guide à l'église de Romainmôtier*. Lausanne, 1916.

BRODTBECK, S. "Les voûtes romanes de l'église de Romainmôtier." *Bull. Mon.* XCV, 1936, p. 473.

ZEMP, J. "Die Kirche von Romainmôtier." *Zeitschrift für Geschichte der Architektur*, I, 1907–8, p. 89. Heidelberg.

(3) BELGIUM

GENERAL

BERLIÈRE, DOM U. "Documents concernant les prieurés cluniens en Belgique." *Compte rendu des séances de la Commission royale d'Histoire*, 4th series, XVII, 1890, p. 134. Brussels.

PARTICULAR

Saint-Séverin-en-Condroz

HALKIN, J. "Documents concernant le prieuré de Saint-Séverin-en-Condroz, de l'Ordre de

Cluny." *Compte rendu des séances de la Commission royale d'Histoire*, 5th series, III, 1893, p. 165. Brussels.

LEMAIRE, R. *Les origines du style gothique en Brabant*. Vol. I, p. 55. Brussels, 1906.

ROUSSEAU, H. "Deux églises romanes aux environs de Liége." *Bulletin des Commissions royales d'art et d'archéologie*, XXXI, 1892, p. 320. Brussels.

SCHELLEKENS, P. "L'église de l'ancien prieuré de Saint-Séverin-en-Condroz. *Rev. de l'art chrét.* LVI, 1906, p. 85.

(4) ITALY

PORTER, A. KINGSLEY. *Lombard Architecture*. Vols. II, III. 1916.

(5) ENGLAND

GENERAL

CLAPHAM, A. W. *English Romanesque Architecture after the Conquest*. Oxford, 1934.

CRANAGE, D. H. S. *The Home of the Monk*. Cambridge, 1926.

PRIOR, E. S. *Eight Chapters on English Mediaeval Art* (chap. III). Cambridge, 1922.

PARTICULAR

Bermondsey

GRAHAM, ROSE. "The Priory of La Charité-sur-Loire and the Monastery of Bermondsey." *Journal of the British Archaeological Association*, XXXII, 1926, p. 157.

Bermondsey (cont.)

MARTIN, A. R. "On the Topography of the Cluniac Abbey of Bermondsey." *Journal of the British Archaeological Association*, XXXII, 1926, p. 192.

Castleacre

FAIRWEATHER, F. H. In Ingleby's *Supplement to Blomfield's Norfolk*, 1929, p. 318.

HOPE, W. ST JOHN. "Castleacre Priory." *Norfolk Archaeology*, XII, 1895, p. 105. Norwich.

Crossraguel

MORRIS, J. A. "Charters of the Abbey of Crossraguel." *Archaeological Collections of Ayrshire and Galloway*, vol. II. Edinburgh, 1886.

Lewes

HOPE, W. ST JOHN. "The architectural history of the Cluniac Priory of Saint Pancras at Lewes." *Arch. Journ.* XLI, 1884, p. 1.

— "The architectural history of the Cluniac Priory of Saint Pancras at Lewes." *Sussex Archaeological Collections*, XXXIV, 1886, p. 71. Lewes.

— "The Cluniac Priory of Saint Pancras at Lewes." *Ibid.* XLIX, 1906, p. 66. Lewes.

SALZMAN, L. F. "The Chartulary of the Priory of Saint Pancras of Lewes." *Sussex Record Society*, vol. XXXVIII, pt 1, 1932; vol. XL, pt 2, 1934. Lewes.

VALLERY-RADOT, J. *Bull. de la Soc. nat. des Antiquaires de France*, 1929.

Monkbretton

WALKER, J. W. "Abstracts of the Chartularies of the Priory of Monkbretton." *Yorkshire Archaeological Society*, Record Series, LXVI, 1924.

Monkton Farleigh

BRAKSPEAR, A. "Excavations at some Wiltshire Monasteries." *Archaeologia*, LXXIII, 1922, p. 235.

Monk's Horton

GODFREY, W. A. "Monk's Horton." *Archaeological Journal*, LXXXVI, 1929, p. 315.

Montacute

Somerset Record Society. *Two Cartularies of the Augustinian Priory of Bruton and the Cluniac Priory of Montacute* (vol. VIII), 1894.

Much Wenlock

CRANAGE, D. H. S. "The Monastery of Saint Milburge of Much Wenlock." *Archaeologia*, LXXII, 1921, p. 105.

Northampton (Saint Andrew's)

Journal of the Northants Natural History Society Field Club, XIII, p. 79.

Prittlewell

(ANON.) *Prittlewell Priory and Museum. History and Guide.* n.d. (? c. 1920).

Thetford

FAIRWEATHER, F. H. In Ingleby's *Supplement to Blomfield's Norfolk*, 1929, p. 334.

INTRODUCTION

INTRODUCTION

ROMANESQUE ARCHITECTURE was created and developed in the service
of Benedictine monasticism; it is as unhistorical to study it in any other context as it
would be to study Gothic architecture apart from the cathedrals. But this approach
to its study has been made difficult by the lack of historical data and by the prejudices
of past controversies. Few would now assume, as Viollet-le-Duc assumed, that the
monks themselves built and carved the great monastic churches in Romanesque style;
but in our turn we have our prejudices, and we are too apt to conclude that if the monks
did not build them they had no influence on their planning and their decoration[1].
Yet we are realizing more and more clearly that in the arts that directly serve human
needs the public plays a part almost as important as that of the artist; that the Parthenon
owes almost as much to the common civilization of fifth-century Attica as it does to
Ictinus and Phidias, and that Versailles is as much the creation of the court of Louis XIV
as it is of Le Brun. We can, therefore, hardly deny a part in Romanesque monastic
architecture to the monks themselves.

Nor is this the only prejudice we inherit in reaction from past theory. Viollet-le-Duc
put forward the hypothesis[2] that Cluny provided Western Europe with architects as
she did with monastic reformers, scholars and statesmen; and that to her must be ascribed
the chief part in the creation of Romanesque architecture. No doubt his theories lacked
sufficient proof; but since Anthyme Saint Paul in 1867[3] demonstrated the invalidity of
his arguments, it has become a habit to assume that, while there may be a Cistercian
style in early Gothic, there is not a Cluniac style in Romanesque architecture[4]. Yet

---

[1] Professor Coulton, who has done more than any man to disprove the existence of "moines
cimentiers" in any number, is wise and learned enough to admit monastic influence. (*Art and the
Reformation*, p. 48. Oxford, 1928.) Similarly M. André Michel writes in his *Histoire de l'Art*
(I, 636): "Il n'y a plus à réfuter l'erreur, ou plutôt l'exagération, de Viollet le Duc faisant honneur
à l'abbaye de Cluny, de la création et de la propagation d'un style d'architecture et de sculpture.
Mais s'il n'y ait pas une école d'art clunisienne, il y eut certainement ce qu'on pourrait appeler
une puissance, une action clunisienne; il n'est pas de province où les traces ne s'en fassent sentir,
et dans les plus beaux monuments."

[2] *Dictionnaire raisonnée de l'architecture*, I, 108, s.v. *architecte*, and p. 130; and *Annuaire de l'archéologue*,
1877, p. 60.

[3] *Bull. Mon.*, 1867, p. 143; *Revue de l'art chrétien*, XXVI, 250; *À travers les monuments historiques*,
I, 25; and in *Viollet le Duc, ses travaux*, 1st ed. 1879; 2nd ed. 1881, p. 173.

[4] E.g. Virey, *L'architecture romane en l'ancien diocèse de Mâcon*, p. 21. Rivoira talked of a "school
of Cluny", but only in an attempt to show its want of originality compared with Lombard builders.
I am happy to see that M. Charles Oursel in his *Art roman en Bourgogne* (1928), p. 91, takes a juster
view of Cluniac architecture.

everyone who approaches the study of Romanesque art in a dispassionate spirit must find—as M. Mâle found—that "sur tout plane l'ombre de Cluny". And M. Mâle, accomplished stylist that he is, rightly uses "ombre" in preference to any more definite word, for until lately definition has been everywhere lacking. Of the abbey church at Cluny only a transept and a few capitals remained; of the history of the Order much was unknown or forgotten; its extent some would have set at 2000 houses and some would have made but a few hundred. Now, further light is everywhere being cast upon the scene; the excavations at Cluny itself have made possible fuller and more accurate reconstructions of the abbey and a more exact dating of its sculptures; and the publication of many of the surviving monuments has made the materials for the history of the Order more accessible. It is at last possible to compile a list of its dependent houses that we may hope to be both fairly accurate and reasonably complete[1]. The time has come for us to forget our prejudices and to consider the whole problem afresh.

We must first draw a clear distinction between Benedictine and Cluniac monasticism. Both followed the Rule of Saint Benedict, but by a process of evolution their organization became functionally different. The Benedictine monastery was originally, and remained, autonomous and independent. Thus each Benedictine abbey was built in the local style of architecture: Notre-Dame-de-Jumièges and Saint-Étienne-de-Caen are typically Norman; Fontgombault and Charroux, Poitevin; Sainte-Foy-de-Conques, Auvergnat.

Though Cluny was originally founded as an ordinary Benedictine monastery, it gradually developed into the Mother House of an Order. Its establishment in this position dates from the time of Odilo, who became abbot in 994. Like his predecessors[2], he reformed many monasteries; but unlike them he tended to make these monasteries subject to Cluny[3]. He substituted for the Benedictine idea of monastic autonomy the conception of a congregation of monasteries all owing allegiance to a single abbey, their government all ultimately controlled by its abbot.

To those he reformed were added other new foundations, and in his time the Order greatly increased: Saint-Victor-de-Genève, La Voulte, Paray-le-Monial, Saint-André-de-Gap, Malaucène, Nantua, Saint-Flour and the great abbey of Vézelay were added

[1] It is necessary to distinguish between the houses that definitely formed part of the Order and those that accepted its customs but remained outside it. Sackur, concerned as he is with the great movement of Benedictine reform rather than with the history of the Cluniac Order, does not sufficiently stress this point in his otherwise admirable book. (Halle, 1892, 2 vols.) Even M. Mâle (*Art rel. du XIIe siècle*, p. 419) is not infallible.

[2] Odo, abbot from 926 and 944, reformed Fleury (Saint-Benoît-sur-Loire), *c.* 938, Saint-Géraud-d'Aurillac, San Paolo fuori le mure at Rome and Sant' Agostino at Pavia, Saint-Austremoine- (or Allyre-) de-Clermont, Saint-Sauveur-de-Sarlat, Tulle, and Saint-Julien-de-Tours; and his successor Mayeul Sant' Apollinare in Classe at Ravenna (in 971) and San Pietro in Ciel d'Oro at Pavia. Saint-Pierre-le-Vif at Sens was once reformed by Odo and once by Mayeul, but it never became Cluniac.

[3] There are certain exceptions, e.g. the convent of nuns at Saint-André-le-Haut, Vienne, Isère, which he reformed, but which was never in the Order. Sackur, II, 76.

to the existing dependencies of Cluny—Romainmôtier, Payerne, Sauxillanges, Charlieu and Saint-Jean and Saint-Martin at Mâcon.

His successor Hugh of Semur consolidated the establishment of the Order as an Order[1], reducing many subject abbeys to the rank of priories and imposing upon all strict subordination to the Mother House and a uniform discipline. He also secured official recognition of the Order from the Cluniac Pope Urban II. His was the time both of great new foundations, of La-Charité-sur-Loire, founded in 1052, of Montierneuf, of Saint-Étienne-de-Nevers, of the nunnery of Marcigny, and of the inclusion of great and ancient abbeys in the Order: Saint-Pierre-de-Moissac, Saint-Martial-de-Limoges, Saint-Eutrope-de-Saintes, Saint-Saulve-de-Valenciennes, Saint-Sauveur-de-Figeac, Saint-Orens-d'Auch, Saint-Pierre-de-Beaulieu, Saint-Alban-de-Bâle, Saint-Wulmer-d'Unicourt, Sainte-Marie-de-la-Daurade at Toulouse, Sainte-Foy-de-Morlaas, and Saint-Martin-des-Champs. Mozat, one of the most ancient abbeys in France, was affiliated to Cluny in 1095, and in 1100 Saint-Germain-d'Auxerre and Saint-Bertin near Terouanne were added to the dependencies[2].

The Order came to have dependencies in England[3], Lombardy and Spain; and even the troubled abbatiate of Hugh's successor Pons de Melgueil could not break the strength of the Order, though it brought an end to its vigorous growth[4]. The wisdom and energy of Peter the Venerable could only maintain its scheme and reform its administration[5]; and with the new statutes issued by Hugh V in 1200 the great period of Cluniac history ends.

The size of these houses varied considerably. The traditional Benedictine twelve was probably the starting point of most of them, and the lesser houses were probably built with this number in view. Many, however, greatly exceeded it. Marrier's fifteenth-century list[6] gives over forty as having, or having had, more than this number[7]. Cluny

[1] See Evans, *Monastic Life at Cluny*, Oxford, 1931, p. 26.

[2] In 1100 Pascal II confirmed and sanctioned the Cluniac practice of reducing subject abbeys to the status of priories, except for eleven which, because of their ancient glory, were to keep the title of abbey: Vézelay, Saint-Gilles, Saint-Jean-d'Angely, Saint-Pierre-de-Moissac, Maillezais, Saint-Martial-de-Limoges, Saint-Cyprien-de-Poitiers (Montierneuf), Saint-Sauveur-de-Figeac, Saint-Germain-d'Auxerre, Saint-Austremoine-de-Mozat, and Saint-Bertin-de-Lille. *Bull. sacr. ord. Clun.* p. 32.

[3] The best available list of the Cluniac houses and their estates in England is that given by Dom Léon Guilloreau in *Millénaire*, I, 291.

[4] During his abbatiate the priories of Hautepierre and Vaucluse, in the diocese of Besançon, were the only additions of any importance.

[5] Under him Dompierre, Montdidier, Clunizet and the nunnery of Lavenne were added. Santa Saba on the Aventine was submitted to him by Pope Lucius II, but its monks refused to admit the cession. Pignot, III, 302.   [6] See Appendix A.

[7] Cluny itself, Charlieu, Paray-le-Monial, Nantua, Saint-Marcel-lès-Chalon, Saint-Vivant-de-Vergy, Beaulieu-en-Argonne, La Charité, Saint-Martin-des-Champs, Coincy, Lihons-en-Santerre, Abbeville, Saint-Leu-d'Esserent, Gaye, Longpont, Nogent-le-Rotrou, Saint-Saulve, Sainte-Foy-

held the record with 460 monks in 1144[1]; La Charité about 1080 had 200[2]. In 1342 the numbers had sunk to 260 at Cluny and eighty at La Charité, and these were further diminished by the ravages of the Black Death. Even more houses sank below the traditional twelve. The most striking feature of Marrier's list is the number of small houses with a prior and four or fewer monks to inhabit them. Over seventy had only one monk[3]; Grosbois had a prior alone. It must have been a strange life at such a house as Moirax, or Châtelmontagne, with a great priory church, and only four monks to serve it and maintain the essentials of conventual life; and in some of the remote houses of the Jura, Auvergne and the Rhône valley, containing a prior and one monk, even the semblance of that life must have been maintained with difficulty. The convents of nuns were, by comparison, large: Marcigny kept its traditional ninety-nine (with Our Lady as the hundredth), Salles had thirty, Saint-Victor-de-Cey over thirty, and Lavenne eighty nuns and twenty *domicellae*, presumably novices. Their architectural needs, however, were less lavishly met in the Romanesque period.

The first question that I had to answer was whether the constitution of the Order of Cluny was likely to produce a characteristic architecture. It is commonly admitted that there is a Cistercian architecture and a Jesuit architecture; had the Cluniac monks a government as strong, and needs as characteristic, as the Cistercians and Jesuits? The second question to be considered was whether the level of culture within the Order was high enough and characteristic enough to inspire an artistic movement. The Order was admitted to have left its mark on the history of religion and society: could its influence also be traced in the history of art?

The investigation of both questions led me into a more general study of Cluniac life, de-Longueville, Reuil, Gournay, Cannes, Saint-Sernin-du-Port, Montierneuf, Moissac, Thiers, Souvigny, Sauxillanges, La Voulte, Ris, Mozat, Arles-sur-Tech, Eysses, Figeac, Auch, La Daurade, Baume, Payerne, Romainmôtier, Vaux, and a few English houses.

[1] Marrier, col. 593.

[2] Beaussart, p. 18.

[3] In Central France: Chantenay, Luzy, Semelay, Venizy, Vernelles, Rhèges, Bonnelles, Méricourt. In the Auvergne: Bort, Vernouillet, Mars, *Domus de Sintriaco*, Mainsat, Boisson, Bournoncles, Brenat, Charnat, Lempdes, Guignac, Saint-Marcel. In the Jura: Salins, Frontenay, Clairvaux, Chatelay, Ilay, Saint-Laurent-la-Roche, Chambornay. In the Rhône district: Saint-Romain, Castillon-du-Gard, Saint-Jean-de-Carnas, Selves, Potellières, Saint-Jean-de-Rousigo, Meyranes, Colonzelle, La Garde Paréol, Ancone, Montbrison, Saint-Sauveur-de-Ribaute, Visan, Sainte-Jalle, Condorcet, Saint-André-de-Gap, Saint-Georges-de-Musac, Les Fonts de Rochemaure, Eurre, Barnave, Chosséon, Conzieu, Oyeu, Orpierre, Connaux, Rozières, Vogüé, Notre-Dame-de-Jouffe, Saint-Jean-Lachalm. In Poitou and Saintonge: Concié, Chastellard, Cartalegue, Breuillet, Saint-Médard-des-Prés, Saint-Paul-en-Gâtine, Graves, Saint-Laurent, Bersol, La Foy Mongault, Saint-Genest-d'Ambière, Saint-Laurent-de-Bret, Les Alleuds and the unidentified *Neamia*. In Gascony: Peyrusse Grande. Others of which the numbers are not given by Marrier were probably equally small. As early as 1132 there were enough priories with less than twelve monks for the reformed statutes of Peter the Venerable to make special regulations for them. Marrier, col. 1366, stat. XLII.

the results of which have already been published[1]. The monarchic organization of the Order, in which every dependency was subordinated to the Mother House, and every detail of life and liturgy regulated by the *Consuetudines*, undoubtedly produced in the greatest days of the Order—that is, from the middle of the eleventh century to the middle of the twelfth—uniformity of custom and characteristic architectural needs comparable with those that created a Cistercian art in the Middle Ages and a Jesuit art at the Renaissance. The high place which Cluny took in the civilization, literary, political and religious, of the eleventh and twelfth centuries showed that the Order had attained a level of culture that qualified it to play a great part in the development of the arts.

The third question to be considered was the extent of the Order: was it large enough to play any important part in the civilization and art of its day? My first task was to compile a list from the available sources[2] of all the houses dependent on Cluny before its decline in the thirteenth century; my second to identify these as far as possible, and to plot them on a map. The result showed that while Cluny never—so far as can be proved—had the 2000 dependent houses attributed to it by Ordericus Vitalis, it certainly had some 1450 priories in the early Middle Ages[3]. Just over 1300 of these were in what is now France, or just over the frontiers of Switzerland, Belgium and Baden; it has proved possible to identify all but fifty-six of them. Besides these there were some thirty-five in Lombardy, some forty in England and Scotland, some twenty-four in Spain[4] and Portugal and three or four in other countries. To these must be added the parish churches owned by the Order. These came to it in various ways and for various reasons. Sometimes they were the churches of villages that came into the possession of the Order[5]; sometimes they were given to the Order as a source of revenue like

---

[1] *Monastic Life at Cluny*, 910–1157. Oxford, 1931.

[2] See p. 16. I have not been able to consult a manuscript of the fourteenth century described by M. Jean Virey in *Millénaire*, I, 264. It is necessary to distinguish between lists of dependencies and lists of churches and monasteries *coniunctae* to Cluny, that is, exchanging prayers and obituary rolls. A list of these is given in *Bullarium Cluniacense*, p. 215, and has led astray some distinguished writers—even Professor Kingsley Porter in *Romanesque Sculpture of the Pilgrimage Roads*, I, 175. M. Mâle (*Art. rel. du XIIe siècle*, Pt II, Preface) wrongly ascribes Souillac to the Order; it depended on Aurillac, which was reformed by Odo, but was not in the Order. A further difficulty is that some monasteries of early foundation joined the Order in the late seventeenth century, at the time of the Benedictine reform: and these must, of course, be excluded from a study of the Order in mediaeval times. Dom Beaunier and Dom Besse, in their *La France monastique*, include a certain number of these, as well as a few priories whose attribution is doubtful.

[3] Peter's reforms were accepted by a general chapter of 200 priors and 1212 brethren; Ordericus Vitalis, v, 29.

[4] The churches of San Pere de Casseres, *c.* 1010 and San Martin de Fromista, *c.* 1066, are monuments in the history of Spanish Romanesque architecture, but they were built before the entry of the monasteries into the Order of Cluny. I have, therefore, naturally omitted them.

[5] The possession of the village did not, however, necessarily entail the possession of the church. For example, the village of Lancharre, Saône-et-Loire, was given to Odilo in 1030–1, but the church belonged to a college of canonesses. Dickson, p. 180.

any other form of property. Sometimes there was a wish to develop the property with the help of the local monastic house; in 1074, for example, Moissac was given the church of Saint-Sernin at Cieurac on condition that a village was built near it[1], and about the same time Lézat was given land with a church upon it at Saint-Cristaud-de-Volvestre, on condition that the church was rebuilt of a specified size within sixteen years, with a year's grace if the weather were bad[2]. Certain Latin lists of these parish churches have been published by Marrier, though without identification of the churches named[3]; they are admittedly incomplete, but none the less include over 260 churches, apart from prebends and chantry chapels. To these I have been able to add a considerable number from other sources. I have only included for architectural consideration a certain number of outstanding churches[4]: Saint-Lazare-d'Avallon[5], Semur-en-Brionnais, and Noël-Saint-Martin[6]: and some of the churches of the monastic estates in the neighbourhood of Cluny and in Cluny itself.

The list of Cluniac abbeys and priories published by Marrier[7], which has formed the basis of my researches, is certainly not earlier than the second half of the fourteenth century, and is probably of fifteenth-century date. I have followed its division into provinces, a division instituted by the reformed statues of Hugh V in 1200. The provinces —Lyons, "France", Tarentaise, Dauphiné and Vienne, Poitou and Saintonge, Auvergne, Gascony, and "Germany" (Lorraine and the county of Burgundy)—give a fair idea of the distribution of the houses of the Order[8], chiefly concentrated in Burgundy, Auvergne, Poitou and Saintonge, Provence and Gascony and near Paris: districts which have long been recognized as the great creative centres of the Romanesque style. Similarly, the great abbots of Cluny were natives of Burgundy, Auvergne, Maine, Aquitaine and Provence. In spite of its extension into England, Lombardy, Spain and what is now Switzerland, Cluny was essentially and characteristically French.

I confess that when my list was completed I was surprised at the number of the great Romanesque buildings of France that were included in it. Cluny itself, Charlieu, Paray-le-Monial, Nantua, Souvigny, La Charité, and Vézelay I had known to be

---

[1] Mortet, 1, 232.

[2] *Ibid.*, 1, 178. If the conditions were not kept, a relative of the donors was to have the right to buy the church back for 12 *denarios*.

[3] Cols. 1724, 1757 *et seqq.* See Appendix B. Peter the Venerable, *de Miraculis*, 1, cap. 24, records sixty churches given to Cluny by Guy de Faucigny, but does not give their names.

[4] The well-known church at Aulnay belonged to Saint-Cyprien-de-Poitiers from *c.* 1097 to 1135; it is uncertain whether its building falls into this period, and I have, therefore, omitted it.

[5] Given to Cluny by Hugh I of Burgundy in 1077, and given back to the Bishop of Autun in 1116. Oursel, p. 109.

[6] Dependent on Saint-Martin-des-Champs in 1096. E. Lefèvre-Pontalis, *Arch. rel. dioc. Soissons*, II, 69.

[7] Cols. 1705–52. See Appendix A.

[8] Provided it is remembered that three or four houses in Baden are all that are to be found in Germany as we know it.

Cluniac; but I had not realized that Saint-Gilles[1], Mozat, Menat, Saint-Eutrope-de-Saintes, Saint-Martin-des-Champs and Saint-Julien-le-Pauvre at Paris, Saint-Leu-d'Esserent, Longpont, Saint-Étienne and Saint-Sauveur-de-Nevers, Gassicourt, Airaines, Vizille, Le Moûtier de Thiers, La Voulte-Chilhac, Saint-Révérien, Moissac, Morlaas, Carennac, Saint-Germain-d'Auxerre, Saint-Martial-de-Limoges, Uzerche, Beaulieu, Melle and many of the Romanesque churches of Poitou and Saintonge had been among its dependencies; that such churches as Saint-Lazare-d'Avallon had been among its possessions; and that even great independent abbeys such as Saint-Benigne-de-Dijon and Saint-Denis had had for their builders men who were in close touch with the Cluniac Order, of which they might be called disciples if not members. Obviously, whether I was to find that a definite Cluniac style existed or not, the art of the Order provided a logical way of approach to the study of Romanesque architecture and decoration.

My next and most considerable task was to find out which of all these dependent houses had surviving buildings or sculptures. I found there were over 325 in France, Switzerland, Belgium, Italy and England. I had then to see as many of these as I could, and to get photographs of as many of the rest as was possible; and to compare and classify this material in the hope of obtaining evidence whether it were true to speak of a Cluniac style in art or not.

The results of my investigations are here set forth. Since less than a quarter of the original data survives, they cannot pretend to be conclusive. But they show, I think it is fair to say, that certain ground plans[2] are characteristic of the Order; that a type of architecture commonly associated with Burgundy is found more widely disseminated in Cluniac churches than elsewhere; and that many of the great architectural experiments of the Romanesque period were made under Cluniac auspices.

It is also, I think, possible to show a certain homogeneity in iconography and decoration; but as this is connected rather with the literary sources and the manuscript illumination than with the architectural history of the Order, I have decided to give it separate consideration in another volume[3].

These are, I think, the results that might be expected. Iconographic and decorative schemes reflect the intellectual interests of the Cluniac monks, already partly known to us from the books they read and wrote. Ground plans and a general architectural quality represent a tradition and a standard maintained throughout the Order. Where

[1] Given to Cluny by Gregory VII, c. 1076, and restored by Honorius II, c. 1125. It left the Order later.

[2] I venture to disagree with M. E. Lefèvre-Pontalis, who considers that there is no Cluniac plan. "Essai sur quelques particularités des églises romanes Bénédictines", Millénaire, I, 220. In England the traditional ground plan is followed, but the style of architecture is local; at Castleacre, for example, it is fair to say that outside the plan there is no trace of French influence.

[3] A slight preliminary study of naturalistic decoration in the Order will be found in my Nature in Design, Oxford, 1933, pp. 49–58.

diversity takes the place of uniformity is in the technical solution of architectural problems and in the design of parts of the buildings such as façades and towers, which do not
have to meet the needs of liturgy or custom. Here we find the characteristic style of
the province to which they belong, for here the architect would have a free hand. The
contrast with Jesuit churches is interesting. Jesuit architecture, erected for the needs of
the world outside the cloister, is an architecture of characteristic façades; and Cluniac
architecture, erected for the needs of cloistered monks, is an architecture of characteristic
interiors.

In both instances the work was almost entirely carried out by laymen[1], but both
Orders produced a few men who took a personal part in the work. The romantic idea
that monks were their own architects and builders needs no further disproof[2]; but it is
relevant to enumerate the exceptions in the Cluniac Order who prove the rule[3].

Once more the question has been obscured by inaccurate scholarship. Peter the
Venerable, in a letter to Alberon, Bishop of Liége[4], praises three illustrious men who
came to Cluny from that diocese in the time of Abbot Hugh: Etzelon, a teacher and
orator, Tezelin, a master of the spiritual life, and Alger, a doctor of dogmatic theology.
The first, he says, "multo tempore pro ecclesia ad quam venerat laborans, singulari
scientia, et praedicabili lingua, non solum audientium mores instruxit, sed corporalem
novae ecclesiae fabricam...plus cunctis mortalibus, post reges Hispanos et Anglos,
construxit". On the strength of this text Etzelon is often described as the architect,
or clerk of the works, or *cementarius* of the great abbey church of Cluny[5]. But its
expressions, and especially the comparison with the kings of Spain[6] and England, whose
munificent gifts of money made the building possible, would seem clearly to indicate
that it was by collecting funds and not by planning stonework that Etzelon helped

[1] Lefèvre-Pontalis in *Millénaire*, I, 221 (1910). Enlart, in his *Manuel*, Pt I, vol. I, p. 66, and
Mortet (I, liii) writing in 1911, were the last eminent archaeologists to maintain the thesis of the
monkish builders of Benedictine houses. It is still sometimes put forward in minor works, e.g.
A. Chagny, *Cluny et son Empire*, p. 93, Lyons and Paris, n.d., but later than 1931.

[2] See Swartwout, *The Monastic Craftsman*. When Saint-Remi-de-Reims was rebuilt between
1005 and 1049 "viri architecturae periti" were employed (p. 173; Mortet, I, 40); when Odilo
built the abbey of La Voulte *cementarii* (workmen, not monks) were injured in a fall and were
miraculously cured by him (Swartwout, p. 173; Mortet, I, p. 130); and when Saint-Martin-des-
Champs was enlarged after 1093 lay craftsmen were employed, notably William the master
mason, apparently in charge of the building operations, and his son Robert; and Humbert,
Arnulf and John, carpenters. (Swartwout, pp. 123, 174; *Liber Testamentorum Sancti Martini de
Campis*, p. viii. Publications de la Confédération des Sociétés historiques du Département de Seine
et Oise. Paris, 1905.)

[3] The *Consuetudines* of Saint-Martial-de-Limoges include among the abbey officers a carpenter
to look after the roofs, woodwork, wine-tuns, etc.; the context suggests that he may have been
a monk. Bib. Nat. fonds latin 4720 A; Lasteyrie, Appendix XXI, p. 471.

[4] Marrier, col. 794.   [5] E.g. Pignot, II, 491.

[6] Alfonso VI, who married Saint Hugh's niece, Constance of Chalon.

to build the church. In modern parlance, he was not the architect but the appeal secretary.

Peter the Venerable, moreover, in his reformed statutes of 1132[1], exempts the workshops of the new church and its workmen from the rule of silence that he imposed on the other workshops and workmen of the abbey. In view of the severity of the statutes this suggests that the workmen were here either laymen, or the *conversi* whom Cistercian influence had introduced into the Order[2].

Another Cluniac church to which monastic architects have been ascribed is that of Arles-sur-Tech, consecrated but not finished in 1046[3]. A column of its façade is inscribed[4]: "AMELIVS MAVRELLVS MONACVS CLODESINDVS PRSBR QVI HOC FECERVNT." In this instance proof is impossible; but it is well to remember that in the early Middle Ages *facere* was often used with little precision of meaning, and that the inscription may have no more force than one on a capital in the Cluniac church of Saint-Hilaire-de-Melle: "FACERE ME AIMERICVS ROGAVIT." On the other hand, Amelius Maurell the monk and Clodesinde the priest may have been employed at Arles-sur-Tech to supervise the work. A parallel is to be found in the Cluniac house of Moissac; a document of about 1025 mentions "Odonem studiosum operis fabricae ordinatorem"[5]. In the same way the "restoration" of the grange at Berzé before 1109 under Abbot Hugh, by his three monks Seguinus, Fulcherius, and Petrus Glocens[6], may indicate a similar supervision of work, as may the description of "domini Poncii monachi ejusdem monasterii constructoris", in a deed of gift of about 1080 of the Cluniac monastery of Montierneuf at Poitiers[7].

In some minor decoration this role of supervisor is clearly evident; the mosaic pavement at Ganagobie has the inscription:

"ME PRIOR ET FIERI BERTRANNE JVBES ET HABERI
ET PETRVS VRGEBAT TRVTBERTI MEQVE REGEBAT[8]."

---

[1] Marrier, col. 1353, stat. XIX.   [2] *Ibid.* See stat. XXXIX.   [3] J. Gibrat, p. 26.

[4] de Bonnefoy, *Épigraphie roussillonnaise*, no. 240.

[5] Swartwout, p. 139.

[6] Marrier, col. 496; L'Huillier, p. 523; Pignot, II, 368.

[7] Mortet, I, 255. Another document there cited describes him as "ejusdem monasterii aedificator". The Benedictine abbeys in close connexion with Cluny, but not actually in the Order, afford a few parallels. At Saint-Benoît-sur-Loire about 1026 a monk, Odolricus of Saint-Julien-de-Tours, fell from the scaffolding when painting the vaults of the church of Saint-Pierre (Swartwout, p. 54). Another monk, Gallebertus, "qui cementariis fuerat praefectus", is mentioned as working at the same monastery about 1080 (Mortet, I, 11). The mosaic floor of Saint-Denis, of which fragments are now in the Musée de Cluny, has a figure of a monk, Albericus, described in an inscription as having made the mosaic. Exceptionally, monks worked outside their own order; at Autun the inscription on the frieze of the tomb of Saint-Lazare reads: "Martinus monachus lapidum mirabili arte hoc opus exsculpsit Stephano subpraesule magno." Stephen was Bishop between 1170 and 1189. (Michel, *Histoire de l'Art*, I, 643.)

[8] Mortet, I, 355. Bertran was prior in 1122.

Finally, in 1152 William, Prior of the Cluniac house on the Île d'Aix, orders one of his monks, Pierre de Mougon, to build a parish church in the low town of La Rochelle, as the other church was too far away. The text is here specific: "Ubi Guillelmus prior... coepit aedificare ecclesiam per manum Petri de Mogono, monachi sui, cui hoc opus pro remedio animae suae injunxerat[1]."

Yet against these instances not only the weight of general evidence but certain specifically Cluniac instances of the employment of lay workmen may be adduced. For example, the abaci of the capitals on the left of the porch at Carennac bear the inscription:

> "CIRBERTVS CEMENTARIVS FECIT ISTVM PORTARIVM
> BENEDICTA SIT ANIMA EIVS":

and no monkish workman would be described as *cementarius*.

The whole question is made yet more complicated by our want of knowledge of how a Romanesque plan was drawn up. The latest writer on the subject, Dr Helen Rosenau[2], considers that technical plans in the strict sense of the word did not then exist; but thinks that architects traced rough plans with sticks and tapes on the spot, and perhaps executed rough drawings. This type of plan is that represented in the story of Gunzo, to whom Saint Peter came in a dream to bid him tell Abbot Hugh to build a new Church: "His dictis, ipsi funiculos tendere visus est, ipse longitudinis atque latitudinis metiri quantitatem. Ostendit ei etiam basilicae qualitatem fabricandae, menti ejus et dimensionis et schematis memoriam tenacius haerere praecipiens[3]." Yet any architect who sees the plan of Hugh's basilica, and studies Professor Conant's measurements of its setting out, will be inclined to think that more went to its making than sticks and tapes and a primitive drawing[4].

One art, however, was certainly practised by Cluniac monks in their monasteries; the art of illuminating manuscripts. For them the copying of books to a great extent took the place which agricultural labour occupied in other monastic communities. The beauty of the script and the elaborately decorated initials of such manuscripts of their production as survive show that a high tradition of technical excellence was maintained. Its achievements and influence, however, hardly fall within the realm of architecture; I hope to give them separate consideration. The essential fact here is that an art was practised at a high level of skill within the Cluniac cloister.

If the role of the Cluniac monks as architects is thus diminished, it is none the less difficult to exaggerate the importance of the part played by the abbots of the Order

---

[1] d'Achery, *Spicilegium*, 1723, III, col. 501, quoted Mortet, II, 90.
[2] *Design and Medieval Architecture*, London, 1934.
[3] Marrier, col. 458.
[4] Dr Rosenau (p. 31) sensibly remarks *à propos* of other "miraculous" plans that they represent a lay view that their execution required more than human ability.

as patrons[1]. The first of the great building abbots was Odilo, who was elected in 994 and died in 1049. He restored Payerne and Nantua, enlarged and practically rebuilt Romainmôtier, built the monastic buildings of Saint-Victor at Geneva, built the monasteries of Saint-Flour, La Voulte, Souvigny, Ambierle, Ris, Domène, Charlieu, Sauxillange and San Maiolo at Pavia[2]. At Cluny itself he "marvellously adorned the cloisters with columns and marble brought from the farthermost parts of the province". He is said to have modified the Augustan boast and to have declared: "I found the abbey of wood, I leave it of marble[3]."

It was in the time of his successor, Hugh of Semur, that all the greatest Cluniac churches were built or rebuilt: Moissac, Layrac, Saint-Gilles, Uzerche, Beaulieu, Montierneuf and Saint-Cyprien-de-Poitiers, Saint-Martial-de-Limoges, Saint-Eutrope-de-Saintes, Paray, Marcigny, Vézelay[4], Saint-Martin-des-Champs and La Charité; and at Cluny itself the erection of a great new basilica, that took twenty years to build, was begun in 1088[5]. Suger, abbot of Saint-Denis, said as he was dying, "Domine dilexi decorem domus tuae"; and so might Saint Hugh himself have spoken. Professor Kingsley Porter has wisely said that the one real school of architecture is the construction of a great building; and this tally of great monastic churches testifies that in this sense there was, in the time of Hugh, a Cluniac school of architecture. In these buildings, moreover, we find certain common characteristics of plan and construction, and above all a noble homogeneity of scale. In mere size they were unsurpassed: the abbey church of Cluny was the greatest in Christendom, and Vézelay is the largest Romanesque church left in France. Varied though they may architecturally be, they follow a steady line of development and reach a remarkable level of quality. At Cluny itself the surviving transept never fails to strike the observer with its majestic maturity of style; and similarly the smaller church of Paray-le-Monial—consecrated in 1104[6]—gives an impression not of primitive crudity but of delicacy, accomplishment, and elaboration. To an Englishman accustomed to the standards of Norman architecture Paray and its contemporary, La Charité, come as a surprise; their ambulatories with tall and slender columns, like a chorus of dancers, are something unfamiliar and strange; we have here lyrics written in another form and language than the epic of the North.

[1] The literary sources are not, it must be admitted, strong evidence for the control of the design by the abbot. When Gauzlin, abbot of Fleury from 1005 to 1030, was building a tower to his monastery, the *princeps artificum* asked him "quodnam opus juberet adgrediendum. Tale, inquit, quod omni Gallie sit in exemplo": orders which must have left the clerk of the works a free hand. *Vita Gauzlini*, in Mortet, I, 33.

[2] *Vita Odilonis Jotsaldo*, I, cap. xiii; Migne, *Pat. Lat.* CXLII, cols. 908, 932; Sackur, II, 376; Mortet, I, 128.

[3] *Ibid.*, I, cap. xiii; Migne, *Pat. Lat.* CXLII.

[4] Most of the surviving part is slightly later, but the lost Romanesque choir seems to have been begun in his day.   [5] See Gilo, *Vita Hugonis*.

[6] Lefèvre-Pontalis would set it as late as *c.* 1130 (*Cong. Arch.* LXXX, 1913, p. 53), but this seems a somewhat arbitrary judgment.

With the death of Hugh of Semur in 1109 the Order of Cluny fell upon dissension and decay[1]. Its property and its dependencies both diminished, and not even the heroic efforts of Peter the Venerable, abbot from 1122 to 1157, could bring back its glories. The apse of Saint-Martin-des-Champs at Paris, built between 1130 and 1142, is characteristic of his time. The unnecessary and rather purposeless elaboration of plan, the dryness of style, and the sense that new wine is being forced into old bottles and nascent Gothic constrained to take Romanesque form, all combine to give the impression that the Order of Cluny had passed its prime when this building was planned. Yet even in his day some buildings were erected—for instance the narthex of Charlieu—that were worthy of the old tradition; and even Saint-Martin-des-Champs was remarkable enough to influence Suger's Saint-Denis.

Cluniac influence was not confined to France alone. The Order had dependent priories in Spain, Lombardy, England and in what are now Belgium and Switzerland: and in such of their buildings as were erected before the final decline of the Order after the death of Peter the Venerable similar characteristics to those of the French churches may be found[2]. For Cluny was one of the great unifying forces of the Middle Ages, not only in political organization, in national statesmanship, and in religious thought, but also in the domain of art and architecture.

The Order, that was already seriously diminished in numbers and prestige, came to an end with the Revolution. Its greatest churches—Cluny itself, La Charité, Saint-Martial-de-Limoges—exist either not at all or in fragmentary form. Lesser priories give us an idea of their beauty and dignity, but not of their size: Saint-Étienne-de-Nevers is a smaller version of Saint-Martial-de-Limoges, Paray, a miniature of Cluny, not only much smaller in size, but also simplified to fit the diminished scale.

The almost incredible number of Romanesque churches in France[3] makes a complete study of them the work of a lifetime. It seems to the traveller as if there is more of Romanesque than of Gothic in the ecclesiastical architecture of France, and as if its varieties are more marked and more puzzling to relate one to the other. The great roads run from north to south, and it is along them that he must make his pilgrimages in search

[1] See Evans, p. 37 et seqq.

[2] This influence must be remembered in any affiliation of the Romanesque art of Lombardy and Spain with that of France, and must not be confused or identified with that exercised by the great pilgrimage routes. M. Bédier gives the *Liber Sancti Jacobi* (compiled about 1140, see J. Vielliard, *Le Guide du Pèlerin de Compostelle*, Mâcon, 1938) a Cluniac origin (*Légendes Épiques*, III, 89 et seqq.) but his arguments are hardly conclusive. It is true that the four routes he mentions all include Cluniac houses among their stopping places—the first Saint-Gilles, the second Moissac, the third Vézelay, the fourth Saint-Jean-d'Angely and Saint-Eutrope-de-Saintes (Mâle, *Art religieux du XIIe siècle en France*, p. 291); but in some places where there were important Cluniac houses these are not mentioned. At Toulouse the (then Augustinian) Saint-Sernin and not La Daurade is commended to the attention of the traveller; at Limoges Saint-Léonard and not Saint-Martial is mentioned; and at Poitiers Saint-Hilaire and not Montierneuf.

[3] For an incomplete list see Enlart, *Manuel*, I, 434–54.

of Romanesque. Only gradually does he come to know that the schools of Romanesque architecture must be studied in the other sense, across the breadth of France from east to west. Only thus will he understand the connexion that exists between the architecture of the Auvergne and that of the Deux-Sèvres, and between that of the Forez and of Languedoc. Yet even so the whole subject seems too vast for treatment. Geographical division—even that of the ancient dioceses, which has been the basis of much sound and valuable work in recent years—is unsatisfactory[1] for two reasons: the solution of the architectural problems of any district seems always to lie just beyond its boundary, and the study of any such division cannot take account of monastic filiations which lie beyond its borders. Even the Benedictine architecture of the period seems too large a field, for so much of its building was Benedictine. Yet the monastic churches of the Romanesque period are as worthy of study as the cathedrals of the Gothic age: like them they are the most advanced and most characteristic visible production of their time. Materially and spiritually they were in advance of the cathedrals of their day; up to the middle of the twelfth century it is the abbeys that take the lead. Therefore, I venture to think that it has not been waste of labour to define and to describe the architecture of the Cluniac Order as a logical and integrated province of mediaeval art. I should be ungrateful if I did not record the pleasure I have had in its exploration, not only in the specific architectural beauties of the buildings but also in the great natural beauty of their sites. Remote though we are from early mediaeval monastic builders in time and spirit, we are one with them when we find in the position of monastery after monastery the same obvious appreciation of the beauty of a natural setting that time has changed so little that we too can enjoy it.

[1] M. Bréhier notes, for example, that of the three largest churches in Auvergne two—Souvigny, 84 metres long, and Mozat, originally 60 metres long—are monastic, and the third, Saint-Julien-de-Brioude, is capitular. By contrast Notre-Dame-du-Port at Clermont is only 46·5 metres long. (*Revue Mabillon*, 1923, p. 13.) M. de Lasteyrie observes (Preface to A. de Chalvet de Rochemonteix, *Les églises romanes de la Haute Auvergne*, Paris, 1902) that no one has yet succeeded in indicating the characteristics of the typical Auvergnat Romanesque church; to every criterion there are too many exceptions.

LIST OF PRIORIES

THE HOUSES OF THE ORDER OF CLUNY

THE primary authority for any list of the houses of the Order of Cluny must be the *Catalogus* printed by Marrier[1] (see Appendix A). This is based directly on such MS. *Pouillés* of the late fourteenth and early fifteenth centuries as Bib. Nat. MSS. lat. 17717, drawn up in 1377, 5654 (dated 1428), Moreau 786, nouv. acq. lat. 1502, fol. 168[2] (a copy dated 1615) and nouv. acq. lat. 1916, fol. 86[3]. An abbreviated list is given in B.M. MS. add. 21240, fol. 85, of the middle of the fifteenth century. The houses are enumerated in these MSS. under the Latin versions of their names, which have not always been correctly transcribed.

The particulars of houses that had left the Order before they were compiled must be gathered from many sources, cartularies, visitations and histories; much of the work has already been done by Dom Beaunier, Dom Besse and their collaborators in *Abbayes et Prieurés de l'Ancienne France*[4].

Houses for which no reference is given are taken from Marrier; B. indicates Beaunier and Besse, and V. the Visitations. I should like here to express my indebtedness to M. Léon Kern, Archivist to the Swiss Republic, for his generous help in identifying doubtful names in Marrier's list; and to Mlle Jeanne Vielliard of the Archives Nationales at Paris for help on points of detail. The important work of M. Guy de Valous, *Le monachisme clunisien des origines au XVe siècle*[5], only came into my hands when my list was complete. I have, however, been able to make use of it in revision. I would point out that M. de Valous occasionally gives two modern equivalents for one Latin name, without indicating the duplication. *Val.* stands for a house he includes that I have not found elsewhere: but I have tried in each instance only to give one of his alternatives.

I have kept the division by provinces of the *Catalogus*, and have endeavoured to insert houses not there given in the right division. Saint-Martial-de-Limoges has been included in Poitou and Saintonge, and Beaulieu in Auvergne; both lie on the borders of the Cluniac provinces, whose exact boundaries are nowhere given, and it must be a matter of conjecture as to which province would have appropriated them.

I have not given the *canton* and *arrondissement* for each place, but have in every case

---

[1] Cols. 1705–52.

[2] It formed the basis of the list in the *Pouillé général des Abbayes de France....* Paris, 1626.

[3] On these see Dom A. Wilmart in *Annales de l'Académie de Mâcon*, 3rd series, XXIII, 1922–3, p. 375, Mâcon.

[4] Ligugé and Paris: the first volume appeared in 1905 and the series is still in progress.

[5] *Archives de la France monastique*, vols. XXIX–XLI, 1935–6. Ligugé and Paris.

given the department. Sufficient indications have been given to make it a matter of routine to find the *canton* and *arrondissement*, if required, in the *Dictionnaire des Postes et Télégraphes*.

Houses of which architectural or sculptural remains in Romanesque style survive are printed in capitals; the names of those which have not been identified are given in italics.

PROVINCE OF LYONS

ABBEY AND MOTHER CHURCH
CLUNY (SAINT-PIERRE), Saône-et-Loire[1]

PRIORIES
Ambierle (SAINT-MARTIN), Loire[2]
   DEPENDENCIES
      Boisy (Saint-Martin), Loire. Val.
      Renaison, Loire. B. x, 120
BOURBON-LANCY (SAINT-NAZAIRE ET SAINT-CELSE), Saône-et-Loire[3]
Cercié (Saint-Ennemont), Rhône. Val.
Chandieu (Saint-Pierre), Heyrieux, Isère[4]
CHARLIEU, Loire[5]
   DEPENDENCIES
      Régny (Saint-Martin), Loire
      Saint-Nizier-d'Azergues, Rhône
      THIZY (SAINT-JEAN), Rhône[6]
      Valeins-en-Dombes, Ain. B. x, 135
Charolles (La Madeleine), Saône-et-Loire
Chaveyriat (Saint-Jean-Baptiste), Ain. Pignot, II, 239[7]
Contamine-sur-Arve, Haute-Savoie[8]
   DEPENDENCIES
      Rosay, Savoie (nuns)[9]
      Sillingy, Haute-Savoie[10]
      Thiez, Haute-Savoie

Curciat, Ain. Val.
Divonne, Ain. Val.
Frontenas, Rhône. B. x, 106
GERMAGNY, Saône-et-Loire[11]
GIGNY (SAINT-TAURIN), Jura[12]
   DEPENDENCIES
      P. de Albino, dioc. Grenoble
      Bellevaux-en-Bauges, Le Châtelard, Savoie[13]
      CHAMBORNAY-LÈS-PIN, Haute-Saône
      Champagnat (Mouz), Saône-et-Loire. B. x, 169
      Chatelay, Jura[14]
      CHÂTEL CHEVROUX (SAINT-ÉTIENNE), Saint-Amour, Jura[15]
      Chazelles (Notre-Dame-des-Planches), Jura. B. x, 170
      Clairvaux, Jura
      Clos Saint-Jean, Saint-Jean-d'Étreux, Jura. B. x, 170
      Cuisia, Jura. Gaspard, p. 421
      Dingy-Saint-Clair (Saint-Clair-de-la-Cluse), Haute-Savoie
      DOMSURE, Ain. B. x, 105
      Flacey-en-Bresse, Saône-et-Loire. Gaspard, p. 421
      Ilay, Jura

[1] Founded by William of Aquitaine in 910; dedicated to Saints Peter and Paul.
[2] Confided by Gregory VII to Abbot Hugh in 1076 for reformation. Pignot, II, 243.
[3] Given to Cluny in the eleventh century. Pignot, I, 415.
[4] Given to Cluny in 977. Pignot, I, 415.
[5] Became Cluniac in 938. The church was dedicated in 1094.
[6] Commonly known as Bourg-de-Thizy.
[7] Its Cluniac character was reaffirmed in 1103. Pignot, I, 414.
[8] Given to Cluny in 1083. Bruel, v, 3967.
[9] Founded before 1297. Valous, II, 243.
[10] Given in 1039. Bernard and Bruel, IV, 128. Valous identifies as Sélignat, Ain.
[11] Dickson, p. 155. I have not found other evidence for this priory.
[12] Confided by Gregory VII to Hugh in 1076 for reformation. Pignot, II, 243.
[13] Given in 1078. Gaspard, p. 34.
[14] Valous identifies this as Chatenay, Haute-Saône, II, 251.
[15] Given in the time of Abbot Mayeul. Gaspard, p. 26.

GIGNY, DEPENDENCIES (*cont.*)
    Marboz (Saint-Martin), Ain[1]
    Marnay, Aube
    Maynal, Jura. Gaspard, p. 421
    Montagna-le-Reconduit, Jura. B. x, 173
    Montfort (Notre-Dame), Cuisiat, Ain.[2]
        B. x, 114, 173
    MOUZ or LA MADELEINE, Cuiseaux.
        Gaspard, p. 241
    Oussiat (Saint-Didier), Pont-d'Ain, Ain
    Poitte, Jura. Gaspard, p. 241
    Saint-Hilaire. Gaspard, p. 241
    Saint-Laurent-la-Roche, Jura
    Saint-Nizier-le-Bouchoux (Sanctus Nicetus
        juxta Cortoux), Ain. B. x, 127
    Salins (Château-sur-Salins), Jura
    Treffort (Saint-Pierre), Ain[3]
    Viuz-la-Chiesaz   (Saint-Jean-Baptiste),
        Haute-Savoie. B. ix, 250
Lay (Saint-Symphorien), Saint-Symphorien-de-
    Lay, Loire
Limans, Limas, Rhône. B. x, 111[4]
Losne (Notre-Dame), Saint-Jean-de-l'Osne,
    Côte-d'Or[5]
Lurcy (Saint-Étienne), Ain. B. x, 112[6]
Luzy (Saint-André), Nièvre
Mâcon (Saint-Jean), Saône-et-Loire. V.
Mâcon (Saint-Martin), Saône-et-Loire. V.
MARCIGNY (LA TRINITÉ) Saône-et-Loire
    (nuns)[7]
    DEPENDENCIES
    P. de Acqualia, dioc. Laon
    La Baume-Cornillane (Saint-Étienne),
        Drôme
    P. B. Ioannis de Corello, dioc. Autun
    FONTAINES-D'OZILLAC, Charente

Montausier, Charente
Nevers (Saint-Loup), Nièvre. Val.
Oriol-en-Royans (Saint-Jean), Drôme
SAINT-LOUP-SUR-ABRON, Nièvre
Saint-Nicolas-des-Biefs (ad tres fontes),
    Allier. B. v, 139
VARENNES L'ARCONCE[8] Saône-et-Loire
IN ENGLAND
    P. de Failihigia, dioc. Salisbury
IN SPAIN
    Zamora (San Miguel)
Mesvres, Saône-et-Loire. Pignot, I, 315[9]
Montberthoud (Sainte-Catherine), Ain[10]
MONT-SAINT-JEAN (SAINT-PIERRE), Côte-d'Or
MONT-SAINT-VINCENT, Saône-et-Loire[11]
NANTUA (SAINT-PIERRE), Ain[12]
    DEPENDENCIES
    Ardon, Châtillon-de-Michaille, Ain. B. ix,
        242
    Asserans (Saint-Didier), Ain
    Bohas, Ain.[13] Val.
    Brenod (Notre-Dame), Ain. B. ix, 243
    Ceyzériat, Ain. B. x, 99
    Chêne-en-Semine, Haute-Savoie[14]
    Chindrieux, Savoie. B. ix, 244
    Larenay (Saint-Martin), Dommartin-de-
        Larenay, Ain.[15] B. x, 105
    Louvenne, Jura. B. x, 172[16]
    Montluel (Notre-Dame), Ain[17]
    Mornay, Ain. B. x, 173
    Moûtiers-en-Tarentaise (Saint-Martin).
        Savoie[18]
    Oulx, Hautes-Alpes[19]
    POMMIERS, Loire[20]
    RUMILLY, Haute-Savoie[21]
    Saint-Alban, Ain. B. x, 121

Founded in 974. B. x, 112.   [2] *Mons Firmitatis*, founded in 974.
[3] Given in 974 by Manassés de Coligny. Valous, II, 224.
[4] Given to Cluny before 1046. Valous, II, 220.
[5] Given to Cluny in 976; alienated in 1254.   [6] Given to Cluny in 1149.
[7] The personal foundation of Saint Hugh in 1056. Martène, *Anecdota*, I, 243.
[8] Founded by Abbot Odilo in 1045 and given to Marcigny in 1094. Virey, *Paray-le-Monial et les églises du Brionnais*, p. 83.
[9] Given to Abbot Odilo by Walter, Bishop of Autun, in 995. Pignot, I, 414.
[10] Founded in 936. B. x, 113.   [11] It sometimes appears as dependent on Paray-le-Monial.
[12] Given to Abbot Odilo by Gislebert, Count of Burgundy. Pignot, I, 411.
[13] Its possession was confirmed in 1146.   [14] Valous identifies this as Chanes, Ain.
[15] Held jointly with Saint-Pierre-de-Mâcon in the thirteenth century.
[16] Gaspard, p. 241, ascribes this to Gigny.   [17] Founded in the tenth century. B. x, 114.
[18] Became a dependency of Nantua in the time of Abbot Hugh. Pignot, II, 241.
[19] Valous identifies this as Osselle, Doubs.   [20] Founded in the eleventh century. B. x, 118.
[21] Valous identifies this as Remilleux, Rhône.

NANTUA, DEPENDENCIES (*cont.*)

    Saint-Germain-de-Beynost (*Sanctus Germanus de Vallebona*), Montluel, Ain.[1] B. x, 124

    Saint-Laurent-des-Creux (*de Crues*), Lains, Jura. B. x, 173

    Saint-Martin, Moûtiers, Savoie[2]

    Saint-Martin-du-Fresne, Ain. B. x, 126

    Talissieu (Saint-Christophe), Ain

    Ville-en-Michaille (Saint-Nicolas), Ain

    La Ville-la-Grand, Haute-Savoie. B. ix, 250

    Villette (Saint-Martin), Chalamont, Ain

PARAY-LE-MONIAL (NOTRE-DAME), Saône-et-Loire[3]

POUILLY-LÈS-FEURS (SAINT-DIDIER), Loire

    DEPENDENCY

    Arthun, Loire. Val.

Prin, La Tranclière, Ain. B. x, 119

Sail-sous-Cousan, Loire

Saint-Laurent-lès-Mâcon, Saône-et-Loire.[4]

SAINT-MARCEL-LÈS-CHALON, Saône-et-Loire[5]

    DEPENDENCIES

    Dompierre, Jura

    FLEURY-LA-MONTAGNE, Saône-et-Loire[6]

    P. de Mostranto super Trenam

Pontoux, Saône-et-Loire[7]

Ruffey, Saône-et-Loire

Saint-Martin-en-Bresse, Saône-et-Loire[8]

Saint-Romain, Saône-et-Loire

Saint-Sorlin (*Sanctus Saturninus de Crucheto*), Ain[9]. B. x, 130

Saint-Vérand, Rhône. B. x, 131

Saint-Vivant-de-Vergy, Côte-d'Or[10]

    DEPENDENCY

    Duesme, Côte-d'Or. Val.

SALLES (SAINT-MARTIN), Rhône (nuns)

    DEPENDENCY

    Grelonges, Ain[11]

SEMELAY, Nièvre

TALUYERS (NOTRE-DAME), Rhône[12]

TROUHAUT (SAINT-JEAN), Côte-d'Or[13]

Villeret (Saint-Priest), Roanne, Loire. B. x, 136[14]

DEPENDENCIES OF THE SACRISTY OF CLUNY

    Ajoux (Saint-Loup), Rhône

    P. Daysino

    Saint-Mamert, Rhône

    Saint-Victor-sur-Rhins, Loire[15]

    Villeneuve, Loire

---

[1] Given to Nantua *c.* 930.

[2] United to Nantua in 1116. B. ix, 205.

[3] Given to Abbot Odilo in 999 by Hugh, Count of Chalon and Bishop of Auxerre. Pignot, I, 317.

[4] Given to Cluny in 1039. Pignot, I, 414.

[5] Given to Abbot Mayeul by Geoffrey Grisegonelle, Comte d'Anjou, and his wife and son, in 1050. Pignot, I, 273. The church is early Gothic.

[6] Mentioned as a Cluniac possession by 1119. Valous, II, 219.

[7] Given to Saint-Marcel in 1117 by Étienne de Neublens. Cazet, p. 118.

[8] Given to Cluny by Hugues de Romans, Archbishop of Lyon. Pignot, II, 240.

[9] Reformed by Cluny in 977.

[10] Reformed by Abbot Guillaume of Dijon, who handed it over to Saint Hugh. Pignot, II, 243.

[11] Not dependent until after 1268. Valous, II, 220.

[12] Given in 999. Bernard and Bruel, III, 559. Valous (II, 224) considers it to have been a dependency of Sauxillanges.

[13] Dependent by 1119. Valous, II, 225.

[14] Belonged to Cluny by 1105.

[15] What the *Guide Bleu* of 1927 describes as "les beaux restes d'une église romane" were destroyed by 1934.

PROVINCE OF FRANCE

Abbeville (Saint-Pierre), Somme[1]
DEPENDENCIES
    Abbeville (Saint-Esprit), Somme
    Bethancourt-en-Vaux, Aisne. Val.
    Béthune (Saint-Projet), Pas-de-Calais
    DOULLENS (SAINT-PIERRE), Somme[2]
Annet-sur-Marne (Saint-Martin et Saint-Germain), Seine-et-Marne
AULNAY-LÈZ-BONDY (SAINT-SULPICE), Seine-et-Oise[3]
AUTHEUIL-EN-VALOIS (SAINTE-MARIE), Oise[4]
AUXERRE (SAINT-GERMAIN), Yonne[5] (abbey)
DEPENDENCIES
    Castillon, dioc. Nevers[6]
    Cessy-les-Bois, Nièvre. B. VI, 68
    La Chapelle aux Chats, Chevagnes, Allier. B. VI, 118
    P. de Cutis, dioc. Nevers[6]
    Egry, Loiret. B. VI, 55
    Griselles (Saint-Valentin), Loiret[6]
    Montierhérault (Saint-Gervais), Eury-le-Chatel, Aube. B. VI, 55
    MOÛTIERS, Yonne[7]. B. VI, 100
    Possines (dioc. unknown)[6]
    Saint-Ayrald, dioc. Sens[6]
    Saint-Florentin, Yonne. B. VI, 65
    Saint-Germain-d'Aunay, Orne[6]
    Saint-Germain-de-Mazilles, Isenay, Nièvre. B. VI, 118
    Saint-Léger, dioc. Langres[6]

Saint-Sauveur-en-Puisaye, Yonne. B. VI, 101
Saint-Vérain, Yonne. B. VI, 101
Sommecaise, Yonne. B. VI, 67
Bagneux (Saint-Pierre),[8] Seine
Barly (Saint-Pierre), Abbeville, Somme[9]
Bazenville, Calvados. B. VII, 141
BEAULIEU-EN-ARGONNE, Meuse
Bertrée (Sainte-Marie), Belgium[10]
P. Sancti Odomari de Beurgissant (Bougesaut) in Picardia
Beussent (Saint-Pierre et Saint-Paul), Pas-de-Calais
Boulogne (Saint-Wulmair d'Unicourt), Pas-de-Calais[11] (abbey)
Brou, Eure-et-Loir[12]
LA CHARITÉ (SAINTE MARIE), Nièvre[13]
DEPENDENCIES
    AUBIGNY-SUR-LOIRE (SAINT-AIGNAN), Cher
    Autun (Saint-Simon et Saint-Jude de Saint-Racho, Faubourg Saint-André), Saône-et-Loire
    Beaulieu-le-Petit (Sainte-Marie-Madeleine), Chartres, Eure-et-Loir[14]
    Beaumont-le-Perreux (Notre-Dame), Eure
    Berry (Sainte-Marie), Cher
    Biches (Saint-Victor), Nièvre
    Bonny-sur-Loire (Saint-Pierre et Saint-Paul), Loiret[15]
    BRAISNE-SUR-VESLE (SAINT-REMI), Aisne
    Brassy, Nièvre

---

[1] Given to Cluny by Guy I, Comte de Ponthieu, in 1075. Pignot, II, 274; Bruel, v, 3745. Valous (II, 188) dates the donation to 1100.

[2] Founded early in the twelfth century; the surviving remains date from the very end of the century and are not important.

[3] Given in the time of Hugh. Bernard and Bruel, IV, 237.

[4] Founded before 1119. E. Lefèvre-Pontalis, *Arch. rel. de l'ancien diocèse de Soissons*, II, 3. Valous gave it as dependent on Nanteuil.

[5] An ancient foundation that became Cluniac in 989 and after a relapse again in 1100. Pignot, II, 268.

[6] Brugelès, *Grand Pouillé des Bénéfices de la France*, 1626, II, 568.

[7] Founded in the eighth century to receive Irish pilgrims on their way to Rome, it later became a priory subject to Saint-Germain.   [8] Became Cluniac in 1096.

[9] Given to Cluny by Guy I, Comte de Ponthieu, in 1075. Pignot, III, 274.

[10] Bib. Nat. Moreau 786, fol. 100, gives this as Berthery.

[11] It entered the Order in 1107 by the gift of Eustace of Boulogne (Migne, *Pat. Lat.* CLXIII, col. 226).

[12] A small but ancient abbey which became dependent first on Cluny and then in 1124 on Saint-Père-de-Chartres. Valous, II, 191.

[13] Founded in 1052 or 1056 by Bernard de Chaillent; became Cluniac in 1059. Pignot, II, 247; and see Beaussart, p. 14.   [14] Founded in 1094. Valous, II, 196.

[15] Given to La Charité between 1049 and 1069. Valous, II, 180.

La Charité, dependencies (*cont.*)

Champfrault (Saint-Caprais), Cher. B. v, 65

[Champvoux, Nièvre. B. vi, 116][1]

La Charité (Saint-Nicolas-des-Ponts), Nièvre

Chamigny (Sainte-Marie-Madeleine), Seine-et-Marne. Val.

Châteaurenard (Saint-Nicolas-du-Port), Loiret

Colonges (Notre-Dame), Nièvre

Cosne (Saint-Aignan), Nièvre

Courtenay (Saint-Pierre et Saint-Paul), Loiret

Cravant, Yonne. Val.

La Croix-en-Brie, Seine-et-Marne. B. vi, 58[2]

Dicy (Saint-Sébastien), Charny, Yonne

Le Grand-Souris, Champvoux, Nièvre. Val.

Jailly, Nièvre

Jeuilly (Notre-Dame), Yonne

Joigny (Notre-Dame), Yonne[3]

Lady, Seine-et-Marne. B. vi, 58

Longueville (Sainte-Foy), Seine-Inférieure[4]

  DEPENDENCY

  Croisy-la-Haye, Argueil, Seine-Inférieure. B. vii, 80

  IN ENGLAND

  Newton Longueville, Bucks.[5]

Louroux-Hodemont (Saint-Martin), Allier

Menetou-Ratel (Notre-Dame), Cher

Montambert (Saint-Pierre), Nièvre

Montbéon (Notre-Dame), Saint-Aignan, Yonne. Val.

Montigny-l'Engrain (Saint-Pierre), Aisne

Montmort (Notre-Dame), Marne

Nevers (Saint-Victor), Nièvre

Ouanne (Notre-Dame), Yonne

Ourouer, Cher. Val.

Patinges (Saint-Martin), Cher

Reuil (Saint-Pierre et Saint-Paul), Seine-et-Marne

  DEPENDENCIES

  Dhuisy (Annonciation), Seine-et-Marne. B. i, 330[6]

  La Ferté-sous-Jouarre, Seine-et-Marne. B. i, 330

  Fontaine-Cerise (Notre-Dame), Reuil, Seine-et-Marne. Val.[7]

  Janville, Eure-et-Loir. B. i, 330[8]

  Lizy-sur-Ourcq, Seine-et-Marne. B. i, 330

Rouy (Saint-Germain), Saint-Saulge, Nièvre. B. vi, 119

Saint-Céols, Cher

Saint-Christophe-en-Halatte, Oise[9]

Saint-Cydroine, Yonne

Saint-Fargeau, Seine-et-Marne. B. vi, 66

Saint-Honoré, Nièvre[10]

Saint-Just, Anglure, Marne. B. vi, 160

Saint-Laurent-des-Orgerils, Orléans, Loiret[11]

Saint-Mammès, Seine-et-Marne. B. vi, 66

Saint-Sulpice, Nièvre

Saint-Yon, Seine-et-Oise

Sancoins, Cher

Sens (Notre-Dame-du-Charnier), Yonne

Sézanne (Saint-Julien), Marne[12]

Tours (Saint-Michel-de-la-Guerche), Indre-et-Loire

Valigny (Notre-Dame), Allier

Vanoise (Notre-Dame), La Roche-Millay, Nièvre

Venizy (Saint-Pierre), Yonne

Villacerf (Saint-Sépulchre), Aube

Villiers-sur-Fère (Saint-Quentin), Aisne

IN ENGLAND

Arthington, Yorks.

Bermondsey (Saint Saviour's)[13]

Pontefract (Saint John Baptist's), Yorks.[14]

---

[1] Marrier gives this as a dependency of Souvigny. See below.

[2] Ceded by the priory to the Hospitallers in 1208. Valous, ii, 196.

[3] Given to La Charité in 1080 by Geoffroy, Count of Joigny.

[4] Founded by Walter Gifford, Earl of Buckingham. Pignot, ii, 253.   [5] Guilloreau in *Millénaire*, i, 291.

[6] Founded *c.* 1160 by Simon, Vicomte de Meaux. Valous, ii, 193.

[7] Founded before 1184. Valous, ii, 194.

[8] Valous (ii, 195) gives it as dependent on Saint-Martin-des-Champs.

[9] Founded in 1061 and given to La Charité in 1063. Valous, ii, 204.

[10] Given to La Charité in 1106. Valous, ii, 204.   [11] Given in 1119. Bernard and Bruel, v, 228.

[12] Given to La Charité in 1081 by Hugues Bardolphe, Seigneur de Broyes. Pignot, ii, 244. Valous (ii, 207) gives the date as 1085 and the donor as Étienne Henin, Comte de Champagne.

[13] Founded by Alwin Child in 1088.   [14] A charter given to it by Henry I is dated 1121.

La Charité, dependencies in England (cont.)
    MuchWenlock (Saint Milburga's), Salop[1]
IN PORTUGAL
    Rates (Santa Maria)[2]
IN CONSTANTINOPLE
    Civitot[3]
IN ITALY
    Venice (Santa Croce)[3]
Châteauchinon (Saint-Christophe), Nièvre
Coincy (Saint-Pierre et Saint-Paul), Aisne[4]
    DEPENDENCIES
    Binson-en-Brie (Saint-Pierre), Marne[5]
    La Chaux[6]
    Méricourt-en-Vimeux, Somme. Val.
    Montléan (Notre-Dame), Montmirail, Marne. Lefèvre-Pontalis, I, 15[7]
    Montmirail, Marne
    Notre-Dame-de-la-Fosse, Saint-Guiffort, Marne[8]
    Ronchères (Saint-Germain), Aisne
    Saint-Phal, Aube
    Soissons (Saint-Pierre-à-la-Chaux), Aisne
    Tupigny (Sainte-Croix), Aisne
Colombey-les-deux-Églises (Saint-Jean-Baptiste), Haute-Marne[9]
Conflans (Sainte-Honorine), Seine-et-Oise. Val.
Coudun (Sainte-Marguerite), Oise. Val.
Crépy-en-Valois (Saint-Arnoul), Oise[10]
    DEPENDENCIES
    Chézy-en-Orxois, Oise. Lefèvre-Pontalis, I, 180

Crépy-en-Valois (Sainte-Agathe), Oise
Froncières, Oise
Louvry, Oise. Lefèvre-Pontalis, I, 180
Marestmoutiers (Saint-Pierre), Somme
Vernelles (Notre-Dame), Seine-et-Oise[11]
Dammarie-sur-Saulx, Meuse[12]
Dompierre (Saint-Pierre), Oise[13]
Donzy-le-Pré (Notre-Dame-du-Pré), Nièvre[14]
Élincourt-Sainte-Marguerite (Sainte-Marguerite), Oise[15]
    DEPENDENCY
    Vignemont (Saint-Nicolas), Oise. Val.
Étoutteville, Seine-Inférieure
Gassicourt (Saint-Sulpice), Seine-et-Oise[16]
Gaye (Notre-Dame), Marne[17]
    DEPENDENCIES
    Rhèges (Saint-Sulpice), Aube
    Le Thoult (Notre-Dame or Saint-Nicolas), Marne
    Troyes (Saint-Jacques), Aube
Grandchamp (Notre-Dame), Seine-et-Marne
Lihons-en-Santerre (Saint-Pierre), Somme[18]
    DEPENDENCIES
    Boves (Saint-Aubert), Somme
    Brétigny (Saint-Pierre), Oise
    Davenescourt (Sainte-Marie), Somme[19]
    Fay (Sainte-Marie), Pierpont-en-Laonnais, Aisne
    Méricourt (Sainte-Marie), Somme
    Quierzy (Saint-Martin), Aisne
    P. de Roquemore
    Saint-Aurin[20], Somme

---

[1] Founded by Robert de Lacy in 1090.

[2] Built by Doña Mafalda, wife of the Burgundian Alfonso Henriques, in 1152. See *Diccionario Historico*, Lisboa, 1907, VI, 97.

[3] Both given before 1102. Pignot, II, 254.

[4] Given to Cluny in 1066 by Thibaut III, Comte de Brie, and his family. Pignot, II, 244. The church was dedicated in 1072. Valous, II, 192, gives the date of foundation as 1077.

[5] Given to Coincy in 1077. E. Lefèvre-Pontalis, *Arch. rel. dans l'ancien dioc. de Soissons*, I, 12.

[6] Audry, p. 28.　　　　　　　　　　[7] Founded in 1126; Audry, p. 32.

[8] Valous identifies as La Fosse, Aisne.

[9] Founded *c.* 1100 by the Seigneurs of Vignory. Valous, II, 192.

[10] Given to Cluny in 1074. Bruel, IV, 3493.　　　　[11] Valous identifies as Verneuil, Seine-et-Marne.

[12] Valous (II, 193) identifies as Dammarie, Seine-et-Marne.

[13] Founded in the time of Peter the Venerable. Valous identifies as Dampierre-sous-Brou, Eure-et-Loir, or Dompierre-sur-Authie, Somme.　　　　[14] Founded in 1109. Jullien, p. 195.

[15] Given to Cluny by Guérin, Comte de Rosnay, in 1082. Bernard and Bruel, IV, 807. Valous (II, 192) spells it Alincourt, and dates the donation 1092–5.

[16] Founded about 1074. See E. Lefèvre-Pontalis in *Cong. Arch.* LXXXII, 1919, p. 227.

[17] Given to Cluny in 1079 by Hugh Bishop of Troyes. Valous, II, 194.

[18] Founded before 1119. Valous, II, 197.　　　　[19] Valous (II, 193) makes it dependent on Coincy.

[20] More correctly but less frequently Saint-Taurin.

Longpont (Sainte-Marie), Seine-et-Oise[1]
    dependencies
        Forges (Notre-Dame), Corbeil, Seine-et-Oise
        Milly (Saint-Laurent), Somme. Val.
        Montl'héry (Saint-Laurent), Seine-et-Oise[2]
        Orsay (Saint-Martin), Seine-et-Oise
        Paris (Saint-Julien-le-Pauvre)
        Saint-Arnoult-sur-Touques, Calvados
        Saint-Laurent, Milly-en-Gâtinais, Seine-et-Oise
Lurcy-le-Bourg (Saint-Gervais et Saint-Protais), Nièvre[3]
Maisonnais, Cher. Val.
Mantes, Seine-et-Oise[4]
Margerie-Hancourt (Sainte-Marguerite), Marne[5]
Marmesse (Saint-Martin), Haute-Marne[6]
Montdidier (Sainte-Marie), Somme[7]
Montrot (Saint-Pierre), Haute-Marne
Montvinot, Marne. B. vi, 156
Mortemer (Notre-Dame), Seine-Inférieure
Namèche (Saint-Étienne), Belgium
Nanteuil-le-Haudouin (Notre-Dame et Saint-Babylas), Oise
Nevers (Saint-Étienne), Nièvre[8]
    dependency
        Châteauchinon (Saint-Christophe), Nièvre. Val.
Nevers (Saint-Sauveur), Nièvre[9]
Nogent-le-Rotrou (Saint-Denis), Eure-et-Loir[10]

dependencies
    Céton (Notre-Dame et Saint-Pierre), Orne[11]
    Champrond-en-Gâtine (Saint-Sauveur), Sarthe[12]
    Châteaudun (Saint-Sépulcre), Eure-et-Loir[13]
    Flacey (Saint-Lubin), Eure-et-Loir
    Happonvillers (Saint-Pierre), Eure-et-Loir
    Pontneuf (Saint-Pierre), Beaumont-le-Vicomte, Sarthe
    Saint-Ulphace (Saint-Gilles), Sarthe
Oyes (Saint-Pierre), Marne[14]
Paris (Saint-Martin-des-Champs)[15]
    dependencies
        Acy-en-Multien (Saint-Nicolas), Oise
        Airaines (Notre-Dame), Somme[16]
        Albert. See Encre
        Baillon (Notre-Dame), Seine-et-Oise
        Beaumont-sur-Oise (Saint-Léonard), Seine-et-Oise
        Bonnelles-en-Beauce (Saint-Symphorien), Seine-et-Oise
        Cannes (Saint-Pierre), Seine-et-Marne
        Cappy (Saint-Médard), Somme
        Choisy-en-Brie (Saint-Pierre), Seine-et-Marne[17]
        Crécy-en-Brie (Saint-Martin or Notre-Dame), Seine-et-Marne
        Cressonsacq (Saint-Martin), Oise
        Domont (Notre-Dame), Seine-et-Oise
        Encre (Saint-Gervais et Saint-Protais), Somme (now called Albert)

[1] Given to Cluny by Guy Troussel, Seigneur de Montl'héry, in 1061. Pignot, ii, 273. Abbé Corneaux (*Longpont et ses ruines*, Soissons and Longpont, 1879, p. 4) states that it was Cistercian in 1132.
[2] Given to Longpont by Louis VII in 1154. B. i, 156.
[3] Given to Cluny by Hugues de Lurcy and his wife *c.* 1093. Valous, ii, 198.
[4] Given to Cluny by Simon de Crépy. Pignot, ii, 274. Later a collegiate church.
[5] Given to Cluny by Guérin, Comte de Rosnay, in 1082. Pignot, ii, 244. Valous (ii, 198) dates the donation between 1061 and 1073.
[6] Given to Cluny, *c.* 1070, by Simon, Comte de Bar. Valous, ii, 198.
[7] Formerly a collegiate church; became Cluniac under Peter the Venerable.
[8] Founded by William, Count of Nevers, and given to Cluny in 1097. Pignot, ii, 255; Bruel, v, 3417.
[9] Given to Cluny in 1045 by Hugues II de Champallemant, Bishop of Nevers, with the consent of his canons. Pignot, i, 411. It is now desecrated and used (1932) as a livery stable.
[10] Given to Cluny in 1080. Pignot, ii, 275; Bruel, iv, 3563.
[11] Given to Nogent-le-Rotrou by Gautier Chesnel in 1094; the church was then to be built. Mortet, i, 287.
[12] Founded about 1250. Valous, ii, 191.
[13] The shell of the Gothic chapel exists as part of a factory on the banks of the Loir.
[14] Given to Cluny in 1082. Pignot, ii, 244.
[15] Given to Cluny in 1079 by Philip I of France. Marrier, col. 527; Bruel, iv, 3539; Pignot, ii, 271.
[16] Founded by Count Étienne d'Aumale and his wife Havisse de Mortemer between 1108 and 1119. Marchand, p. 54.   [17] Founded by Bishop Burchard between 1120 and 1134. Valous, ii, 192.

Paris, DEPENDENCIES (*cont.*)

GOURNAY-SUR-MARNE (NOTRE-DAME), Seine-et-Oise

Grosbois (Notre-Dame), Claye-Souilly, Seine-et-Marne

Hienville (Notre-Dame), Eure-et-Loir

L'Isle Adam (Notre-Dame), Seine-et-Oise

LIGNY-SUR-CANCHE (SAINT-VIT ET SAINT-MODESTE), Pas-de-Calais

Marnoue (Saint-Nicolas), Seine-et-Marne[1]

MAROLLES-EN-BRIE (SAINT-ARNOULT), Seine-et-Oise

Mauregard (Saint-Jean-Baptiste), Seine-et-Marne

MOUSSY-LE-NEUF (SAINT-OPPORTUNE), Seine-et-Marne

Pantin, Seine. Val.

Paris (Saint-Denis-de-la-Chartre)[2]

Paris (Saint-Pierre-de-Montmartre)[3]

Pas-en-Artois (Saint-Martin), Pas-de-Calais[4]

Pringy-en-Gâtinais (Notre-Dame), Seine-et-Marne

ROINVILLE-EN-BEAUCE (SAINT-GEORGES ET SAINT-PIERRE), Seine-et-Oise[5]

Sainte-Gemme, Marne[6]

Saint-Samson, Olivet, Loiret. Val.

IN ENGLAND

Barnstaple (Saint Mary Magdalen's), Devon

Exeter (Saint James's), Devon

SAINT CLEAR's, Carmarthen

Les Péniers, Nièvre. Val.

Pierre-Solaire[7] (Notre-Dame), Calvados

Pithiviers (Saint-Pierre-l'Abbaye), Loiret[8]

Pont-aux-Moines (Saint-Jérôme), Loiret[9]

Quessy, Aisne. Val.

Rumilly-le-Comte (Saint-Pierre), Pas-de-Calais[10]

SAINT-CÔME-DU-MONT, Manche

Sainte-Eulalie-d'Orville, Bligny, Aube

SAINT-LEU-D'ESSERENT, Oise[11]

SAINT-OMER (SAINT-BERTIN), Pas-de-Calais[12] (abbey)

SAINT-PIERRE-LE-MOÛTIER, Nièvre[13]

SAINT-RÉVÉRIEN, Nièvre

Saint-Romain, Côte-d'Or. Val.

SAINT-SÉVERIN-EN-CONDROZ, Belgium[14] (originally Saint-Symphorien-du-Bois)

Saint-Victor-de-Cey, Huy, Belgium (nuns)

Sézanne (Saint-Julien), Marne

Tours-sur-Marne (Saint-Pierre), Marne

VALENCIENNES (SAINTE-SAULVE), Nord[15]

Vendœuvre-sur-Barse (Saint-Georges), Aube[13]

VÉZELAY (SAINTE-MARIE-MADELEINE), Yonne[16] (abbey)

DEPENDENCIES

Angios (dioc. Tournai)[17]

Bessy, Yonne. B. VI, 98

La Braye (or Veriols)[17], ? Bray Dunes, Nord

Bulles, Oise[17]

LA CHAPELLE-HUGON, Cher. B. V, 57

Langy (Saint-Pierre), Nièvre. B. VI, 120

Lurcy-sur-Abron, Nièvre. B. VI, 120

---

[1] Founded in 1135. Valous, II, 198.

[2] Given to Cluny in 1133 in exchange for Saint-Pierre-de-Montmartre. Lebeuf-Cocheris, II, 499, Valous identifies it as La Chartre-sur-Loir, Sarthe, I think incorrectly.

[3] See note 2 above. The church was begun in 1137 and is not Cluniac.

[4] Valous (II, 202) gives this as dependent on La Charité.   [5] Founded *c.* 1084. Valous, II, 203.

[6] Given to Saint-Martin-des-Champs in 1096. E. Lefèvre-Pontalis, *Arch. rel. dans l'ancien diocèse de Soissons*, I, 12.

[7] Sometimes written Pierre-Solain. Founded *c.* 1070. In 1350 it was made dependent on Saint-Martin-des-Champs. Valous, II, 202.

[8] Founded and given to Cluny in 1025 by Isambert de Pithiviers and his brother. Pignot, II, 273.

[9] Founded and given to Cluny by King Philip I in 1075. Valous, II, 202.

[10] Given to Cluny in 1105 by Eustace III of Boulogne. Pignot, II, 283.

[11] Given to Cluny in 1080 by Hugues, Comte de Dommartin. Pignot, II, 274.

[12] Became Cluniac in 1100. Pignot, II, 276. According to Guérard (p. xlv) it had left the Order by 1139.

[13] Given *c.* 1070. Bernard and Bruel, IV, 549.

[14] Founded in 1091. *Rev. de l'art chrét.* 1906, LVI, p. 86; Bruel, IV, 3659.

[15] Given to Cluny by Manasses, Bishop of Cambrai, in 1103. Pignot, II, 282; Marrier, col. 535.

[16] Founded by the epic hero Gérard de Roussillon, it came under Cluniac rule in 1026 or 1027 (Sackur, II, 38) and was formally included in the Order by Pascal II in 1103. Pignot, II, 262. It was freed from Cluniac jurisdiction by Pope Alexander III in 1162.   [17] *Pouillé* of 1626.

VÉZELAY, DEPENDENCIES (*cont.*)
P. de Merlo[1]
Mirebeau[1]-en-Poitou, Vienne
Montreuil-sur-Brèche[1], Oise
Moret[1], Seine-et-Marne
Moûtiers-en-Glenon, Sougy, Nièvre. B. VI, 120
Nelles (Saint-Remy)[1], dioc. Sens
Nevers (Saint-Nicolas), Nièvre. B. VI, 115
Oisay, Indre-et-Loire
Pontloup, Moret-sur-Loing, Seine-et-Marne. B. VI, 62
Saint-Germain-l'Esquillier, or de-Moilleron, dioc. Saintes[1]

Saint-Germain-de-Salles, Allier. B. v, 137
Thernay[1]
Tuffet[1] ? Tuffé, Sarthe
Varennes (Saint-Silvestre), Sougy, Nièvre. B. VI, 120
Villemoutiers, Loiret. B. VI, 68
Villeselve, Oise[1]
Vignemont (Saint-Nicolas), Oise
Vitry-le-Chatel (Saint-Thibault), Vitry-en-Perthois, Marne
LE WAST (SAINT-MICHEL), Le Wast, Pas-de-Calais[2]

PROVINCE OF PROVENCE, TARENTAISE, DAUPHINÉ AND VIENNE

Allevard (Saint-Pierre), Isère
DEPENDENCIES
Corvat (Saint-Sébastien), Savoie. Val.
Le Touvet (Saint-Didier), Isère[3]
Allex (Saint-Baudile), Drôme[4]
Arles (Saint-Gervais et Saint-Protais), Bouches-du-Rhône[5]
Artas (Saint-Pierre), Isère
Aubrac, Aveyron. Val.
Aubres (Saint-André), Drôme. V.
Aurel, Drôme. B. IX, 138[6]
Avallon (Saint-Pierre), Isère[7]
Avignon (Saint-Martial), Vaucluse. Lecestre, p. 4
DEPENDENCY
Sorgues, Vaucluse
Barnave (Sainte-Marie), Drôme
Barraux (Saint-Martin), Isère. B. IX, 96[8]
Bathernay, Drôme. V.

Beaumont, Corps, Isère
LE BOURGET DU LAC (SAINT-MAURICE), Savoie[9]
Boze, Ardèche[10]
Caseneuve (Notre-Dame-des-Aumades), Vaucluse
Chosséon (Saint-Jean-Baptiste), Drôme[11]
DEPENDENCY
Combovin, Drôme[12]
CONZIEU, Ain
Die (Saint-Marcel), Drôme[13]
DEPENDENCIES
Beaumont, Drôme
P. de Beluana (? *Beluy, Bouches-du-Rhône*)
Chabeuil (Saint-Andéol), Drôme
La Motte-Chalançon (Saint-Pierre), Drôme
Le Percy, Clelles, Isère
Notre-Dame-de-la-Pierre, Serres, Hautes-Alpes
P. de tribus moeniis

[1] *Pouillé* of 1626.
[2] Founded before 1099. *Bull. Mon.* 1895, p. 222.
[3] Founded 1082. B. IX, 97.
[4] Given in time of Abbot Hugh. Bernard and Bruel, IV, 264.
[5] Given to Abbot Hugh by Rostaing d'Hyères, Archbishop of Aix, and his brother. Pignot, II, 240. Not in Marrier's list.
[6] And see under Marcigny.
[7] Given to Cluny in the time of Abbot Hugh.
[8] Founded 1081.
[9] Given to Cluny in 1024 by Humbert aux Blanches Mains, first hereditary Count of Savoy. Pignot, I, 322.
[10] Destroyed by 1279. Valous, II, 235.
[11] Valous (II, 235) gives it as dependent on Gigors.
[12] Valous identifies it as Cobonne, Drôme.
[13] According to B. IX, 137 this became Cluniac only at the beginning of the thirteenth century.

4

DOMÈNE (SAINT-PIERRE ET SAINT-PAUL), Isère[1]

DEPENDENCIES
Lavars, Isère. B. IX, 140[2]
Saint-Jean-d'Hérans, Isère[3]
Treffort (Saint-Pierre), Isère

Draguignan (Saint-Hermentaire), Var. B. II, 39

Eurre (Saint-Pierre), Drôme

Faillefeu, Bleziers, Basses-Alpes[4]

Faucon (Notre-Dame), Basses-Alpes. Val.

Les-Fonts-de-Rochemaure (Saint-Pierre), Drôme[5]

Fos-sur-Mer (Saint-Gervais et Saint-Protais), Bouches-du-Rhône

GANAGOBIE (NOTRE-DAME ET SAINT-JEAN-BAPTISTE), Basses-Alpes[6]

DEPENDENCIES
Sancti Petri de Albera, dioc. Die
Beaujeu (Notre-Dame et Saint Pierre), Basses-Alpes[7]
Bonnefosse (Saint-Pierre), Basses-Alpes
Costebelle, Basses-Alpes. B. II, 69
Douzard (Saint-Pierre), Hautes-Alpes. Val.
Esparron (Saint-Paul), Hautes-Alpes. B. II, 51
Sancti Petri de Lausardo, dioc. Gap
Lourmarin (Saint-André et Saint-Trophime), Vaucluse. B. II, 15
Mirabeau, Basses-Alpes. B. II, 53
Montfort (Sainte-Madeleine), Basses-Alpes. B. II, 69
Notre-Dame-de-Rorabelle, Malijai, Basses-Alpes. B. II, 53
Peypin, Basses-Alpes. B. II, 69

PEYRUIS (SAINT-PIERRE), Basses-Alpes. B. II, 69
Saint-Auban, Buis-les-Baronnies, Drôme
Saint-Marcellin, Niozelles, Basses-Alpes
Sainte-Marie-de-Bethléem (seu Sanctae Eusemiae de Nogeriis), Noyers-sur-Jabron, Basses-Alpes
Saint-Michel, Basses-Alpes[8]
Saint-Pierre-de-Viziers, Basses-Alpes
Sigonce, Basses-Alpes. B. II, 69

Gap (Saint-André), Hautes-Alpes[9]
DEPENDENCY
Pelleautier (Notre-Dame-de-Belvézer), Hautes-Alpes

Geneva (Saint-Blaise-aux-Liens), Switzerland.[10]

Geneva (Saint-Victor), Switzerland[11]
DEPENDENCIES
Bonneguête (Saint-Blaise), Haute-Savoie
Draillant (Saint-Pierre), Haute-Savoie
Russin, Geneva, Switzerland. B. IX, 348
Sainte-Hélène-du-Lac, Savoie. Val.
Vaulx (Saint-Pierre), Haute-Savoie

Gigors (Saint-Pierre), Drôme

GOUDARGUES (NOTRE-DAME ET SAINT-MICHEL), Gard[12]
DEPENDENCIES
Fons-sur-Lusson (Saint-Étienne), Gard. B. IV, 260
Notre-Dame-d'Arlende, Allègre, Gard. B. IV, 258
Saint-André-de-Roquepertuis, Gard. B. IV, 263
Saint-Jean-de-Suzon, Bouquet, Gard. B. IV, 259

Innimont, Ain[13]

---

[1] Founded in 1027. B. IX, 96.   [2] Founded c. 1075.
[3] Given in 1040. Bernard and Bruel, IV, 151.
[4] Joined the Order of Cluny in 1298. Valous, II, 237.
[5] Valous (II, 240) identifies as Les Fontaines, Ardèche.
[6] Given to Cluny by Jean III, Bishop of Sisteron, at the end of the tenth century. A. d'Agnel, p. 6.
[7] Given to Cluny 1022–3. Valous, II, 234.
[8] Given to Cluny after 967, by Ours, Bishop of Sisteron. Valous, II, 245.
[9] Given to Cluny in 1029. Sackur, II, 82; P. Guillaume, II, 249.
[10] Given to Abbot Odilo by the Empress Adelaide. The monastery was destroyed to make way for the fortifications in 1534. Pignot, I, 323.
[11] Given by Rodolf III, King of the two Burgundies, in 1019. Pignot, I, 415.
[12] Given to Cluny by Raymond de Saint-Gilles in 1065. Bruel, IV, 3404; Roman in Bull. du Com. de l'Art chrétien, Nîmes, 1884, III, 44; Pignot, II, 193. It did not long remain in the Order; Abbot Hugh ceded it to La Chaise-Dieu at the Council of Clermont in 1095. The church probably dates from after this cession and is not within the scope of this book.
[13] Founded c. 1100. Valous, II, 238.

LAGRAND (NOTRE-DAME), Hautes-Alpes [1]
DEPENDENCIES
Les Aymes, Isère. Val.
L'Épine, Hautes-Alpes
Étoile (Saint-Antoine), Hautes-Alpes. B. II, 52 [2]
Eyguians, Hautes-Alpes
Gigors, Drôme [3]
LACHAU, Drôme
Montfroc, Drôme
SAINTE-JALLE, Drôme
DEPENDENCIES
Condorcet (Saint-Pierre), Drôme
Sainte-Lucie, Bésignan, Drôme
P. Sancti Mauri
SERRES (NOTRE-DAME), Hautes-Alpes [4]
LES LÉRINS (SAINT-HONORAT), Alpes-Maritimes [5]
DEPENDENCIES
Albiosc, Basses-Alpes. B. II, 61
Alignosc, Riez, Basses-Alpes. B. II, 61
Angles, Saint-André-les-Alpes, Basses-Alpes. B. II, 194
Antibes, Alpes-Maritimes. B. II, 184
Artignosc, Var. B. II, 61
Bairiols, Alpes-Maritimes. B. II, 189
Baudinard, Var. B. II, 61
Blieux, Basses-Alpes. B. II, 194
BRIANÇONNET, Alpes-Maritimes. B. II, 173
Calliau (Notre-Dame), Fayence, Var. B. II, 38
Clumanc, Basses-Alpes. B. II, 195
Clumane, Les Mées, Basses-Alpes. B. II, 61
Draguignan (Saint-Étienne), Var. B. II, 39
Escragnolles, Alpes-Maritimes. B. II, 184
Esparron-de-Verdon, Basses-Alpes. B. II, 62
Les Ferres, Alpes-Maritimes. B. II, 174
Fourques, Gard. B. II, 89
Fréjus (Saint-Raphael), Var. B. II, 40
Grasse (Saint-Honorat), Alpes-Maritimes. B. II, 184
Ilonse, Alpes-Maritimes. B. II, 189
MARCOUX, Basses-Alpes. B. II, 171

Montagnac, Basses-Alpes. B. II, 63
Moriez, Basses-Alpes. B. II, 195
Mouans, Mouans-Sartoux, Alpes-Maritimes. B. II, 185
Mougins, Alpes-Maritimes. B. II, 185
Mousteiret, Le Brusquet, Basses-Alpes. B. II, 171
MOUSTIERS-SAINTE-MARIE, Basses-Alpes. B. II, 63
La Napoule (Notre-Dame), Alpes-Maritimes. B. II, 41
Notre-Dame-du-Coudouier, Flassans, Var. B. II, 40
Notre-Dame-de-Gratemoine, Séranon, Alpes-Maritimes. B. II, 45
Notre-Dame-des-Clars, Séranon, Alpes-Maritimes. B. II, 45
Pégomas, Alpes-Maritimes. B. II, 185
Puimoisson, Basses-Alpes. B. II, 63
Quinson, Basses-Alpes. B. II, 63
La-Rochette-Chanant, Entraux, Castellane, Basses-Alpes. B. II, 173
La-Roque-Esclapon (Saint-Éloi), Var. B. II, 42
Roquefort, Alpes-Maritimes. B. II, 185
Roquesteron, Alpes-Maritimes. B. II, 174
Roumoulès, Basses-Alpes. B. II, 163
Saint-Antonin, Alpes-Maritimes. B. II, 174
Saint-Barthélemy, Lorgues, Var. B. II, 43
Saint-Dalmas-le-Selvage, Alpes-Maritimes. B. II, 191
Saint-Jean-du-Foux, Peyroules, Basses-Alpes. B. II, 195
Saint-Julien-du-Verdon, Castellane, Basses-Alpes. B. II, 195
Saint-Jurson, Basses-Alpes. B. II, 171
Saint-Mains, Gap, Hautes-Alpes. B. II, 50
Sainte-Marguerite, Carcès, Var. B. II, 38
Saint-Martin-de-Codous, Le Thoronet, Var. B. II, 45
Saint-Pierre-de-Betons, Seillans, Var. B. II, 45

---

[1] According to B. II, 52 this became Cluniac only in 1365. Some of its dependencies, however, appear in Cluniac documents at an earlier date; Bruel (IV, 3541), for example, gives the donation of Serres in 1079. I have therefore included Lagrand and its dependencies.

[2] It appears to have become dependent on Lagrand only in the fifteenth century. Valous, II, 237.

[3] Also given above as directly dependent on Cluny.   [4] See note 1.

[5] Reformed by Abbot Mayeul at the Pope's request, it later entered the Order and remained in it until 1366. It rejoined the Order in the seventeenth century at the time of the Benedictine Reform. At the same time the evidence for its subjection to Cluny is not very satisfactory, and it is possible that the affiliation was little more than nominal. A recent writer, M. H. Moris, considers that it only joined the Order in 1739. I therefore include it under certain reserves.

LES LÉRINS, DEPENDENCIES (*cont.*)
Saint-Pierre-de-Braug, La Verdière, Var.
B. II, 62
Saint-Pierre-de-Figolas, Seillans, Var. B.
II, 45
Sospel, Alpes-Maritimes. B. II, 191
Thiery, Alpes-Maritimes. B. II, 191
Toudon (Saint-Jean), Alpes-Maritimes. B.
II, 174
Toüet-de-Beuil, Alpes-Maritimes. B. II, 191
TOURRETTES-DU-CHÂTEAU, Tourrette-
Levens, Alpes-Maritimes. B. II, 174
Vallauris, Alpes-Maritimes. B. II, 186
Vergons, Basses-Alpes. B. II, 196
Le Villars-du-Var, Alpes-Maritimes. B. II,
192
Villebruque, Valbonne, Alpes-Maritimes.
B. II, 186
Malaucène (Saint-Maurice), Vaucluse[1]
Malemoisson (Notre-Dame), Digne, Basses-
Alpes. B. II, 171
MANTHES (SAINT-PIERRE), Drôme
DEPENDENCIES
Charrière (Saint-Pierre), Châteauneuf-de-
Galaure, Drôme[2]
Loirieu (Saint-Romain), Serre-Nerpol,
Isère. B. IX, 98
Montchatain, Drôme
Peaugres, Ardèche
Saint-Avit, Drôme. B. IX, 41
Mauves, Ardèche. B. IX, 40[3]
Montaubon, Drôme. B. II, 54
MONTSÉGUR (SAINT-AMAND), Drôme. Val.[4]
DEPENDENCY
Montségur (Saint-Jean), Drôme. Val.
NOTRE-DAME-DE-BETHLÉEM, Remoulins, Gard
Orpierre (Saint-Vincent), Hautes-Alpes
Oyeu (Saint-Pierre), Isère
PIOLENC (SAINT-JEAN-BAPTISTE ET SAINT-
PIERRE), Vaucluse
DEPENDENCY
SAINT-ÉTIENNE-DES-SORTS, Gard
Pont-Saint-Esprit (Saint-Sernin-du-Port), Gard[5]

DEPENDENCIES
Ancone, Drôme
P. de Bello-monte
Bollène (Saint-Pierre-de-Senos or de-
Barry), Vaucluse. B. II, 119
BROUZET-LÈS-ALAIS, Gard
Caderousse (Saint-Martin), Vaucluse
Castillon-du-Gard (Saint-Christophe), Gard
Colonzelle (Saint-Pierre), Drôme
CONNAUX, Gard
Entraigues, Vaucluse
La Garde-Paréol, Vaucluse
Méjannes-le-Clap, Gard. B. IV, 262
P. de Meratio
Meyrannes, Gard
MONTBRISON (SAINT-BLAISE), Drôme
Notre-Dame-de-Jouffe, Montmirat, Gard
Potellières (Saint-Pierre), Gard
Rousset, Drôme
Rozières (Sainte-Marie), Joyeuse, Ardèche
RUOMS (SAINT-PIERRE), Ardèche[6]
Saint-André-du-Plan, Mondragon, Vau-
cluse
Saint-Jean-de-Carnas, Servas, Gard
SAINT-JEAN-DE-ROUSIGO[7], Gard
Saint-Jean-de-Vassols, Vaucluse
Saint-Laurent, Vaucluse. Val.
Saint-Pantaléon, Drôme[8]
Saint-Raphael, Vaucluse
Saint-Sauveur-de-Cruzières, Ardèche. Val.
Saint-Sauveur-de-Ribaute, Anduze, Gard
SAINT-TURQUOÎT, Suze-la-Rousse, Drôme
Sarrians (Saint-Pierre), Vaucluse[9]
P. Sancti Ioannis de Silva (? *Selves*, Gard)
Tulette, Drôme
VISAN[10], Drôme
Vogüé (Sainte-Marie), Ardèche
RIBIERS (SAINT-JEAN), Hautes-Alpes
RIBIERS (NOTRE-DAME-DES-FAINS), Hautes-
Alpes
DEPENDENCY
Ribiers (Notre-Dame-du-Serre), Hautes-
Alpes. Val.

---

[1] Given to Abbot Odilo in 1030 by Amadeus I of Savoy-Belley. Sackur, II, 80. Pignot (I, 45) gives the date as 1025.   [2] Became Franciscan in 1456. B. IX, 37.   [3] Belonged to Cluny by 1279.
[4] Given to Cluny 958, ceded to the Chapter of Saint-Paul-Trois-Châteaux 1404. Valous, II, 241.
[5] Labande (*Études d'histoire et d'architecture romane*, p. 20) gives seven dependencies of Pont-Saint-Esprit, but the list does not seem trustworthy.
[6] Valous identifies this as Rioms, Drôme.
[7] Formerly Todouse or Boulas. See *Bull. Mon.* 6th series, VI, 1890, p. 153.
[8] Cluniac by 999. Valous, II, 245.   [9] Became Cluniac *c.* 1031. Pignot, I, 415.
[10] The church was almost wholly rebuilt in the fifteenth century. Valous identifies as Avèze, Gard.

Romette (Saint-Pierre), Hautes-Alpes
DEPENDENCIES
Le Monetier-de-Briançon, Hautes-Alpes. Val.
Saint-Sépulchre-de-la-Beaumette, Oze, Hautes-Alpes. B. II, 54
Veras (Saint-Pierre), Hautes-Alpes. B. II, 54
Rompon, Ardèche
DEPENDENCIES
Francillon, Drôme
Marsanne (Saint-Pierre), Drôme
Ravel (Saint-Blaise), Drôme
La Remeille, Var. Val.
ROSANS (SAINT-ANDRÉ), Hautes-Alpes[1]
Saint-Amand, Ardèche[2]
DEPENDENCY
VILLEPERDRIX, Drôme
Saint-Firmin, Hautes-Alpes[3]
Sainte-Hélène-du-Lac, Savoie
SAINT-GEORGES-DE-MUSAC, Saint-Georges-les-Bains, Ardèche
SAINT-GILLES, Gard[4] (abbey)
DEPENDENCIES
Château-de-Dun (Saint-Gilles), Dun-Doulcon, Meuse. Goiffon, p. 41
Corconne, Gard. B. IV, 219
Fraissinet-de-Lozère, Lozère. B. IV, 65
Montgaillard, Landes. B. III, 26
Moulizan, Saint-Mamert-du-Gard, Gard. B. IV, 263
PREVENCHÈRES, Lozère. B. IV, 65
ROBIAC, Gard. B. IV, 264
Roussillon, Vaucluse. B. II, 29
Saint-Eusèbe, Hautes-Alpes. Goiffon, p. 41
Saint-Geniès-de-Malgoires, Gard. B. IV, 265
Saint-Gilles-de-Lignac, Forcalquier, Basses-Alpes. Goiffon, p. 41

Saint-Gilles-sur-Vie, Vendée. Goiffon, p. 41
Saint-Jean-du-Gard, Gard. B. IV, 145
Saint-Loup-de-Chadent, Le Bleymard, Lozère. B. IV, 65
Saint-Pierre-de-Laugnac, Lédenon, Gard. B. IV, 219
Saint-Sébastien, Montpezat, Gard. B. IV, 219
Sommières, Gard. B. IV, 222
IN HUNGARY
Sirmich[5] (Saint-Gilles). Goiffon, p. 41
IN SPAIN
Barbastro[6]. Goiffon, p. 56
IN CATALONIA
An unnamed house[6]. Goiffon, p. 56
IN ITALY
A house near Milan[6]. Goiffon, p. 56
Saint-Hermentain, Var. Val.[7]
SAINT-MARCEL-LÈS-SAUZET, Drôme[8]
DEPENDENCIES
Aps (Saint-Martin), Ardèche[9]
Antichamp (Saint-Jean), Drôme
Espeluche (Sainte-Marie or Saint-Étienne), Drôme
DEPENDENCY
Le Rosay, Drôme. Val.
Grignan (Saint-André-de-Sarson), Drôme. B. II, 120
Plan-de-Baix (Sainte-Marie), Drôme
Puygiron (Saint-Bonnet), Drôme
Roynac (Saint-Privat), Drôme
Saint-Sébastien-de-Cordiac, Morges, Mens, Isère
Saint-Vincent-de-Barrès, Ardèche. B. IX, 173
Sauzet (Saint-Maurice), Drôme. B. IV, 201[10]
Séderon, Drôme. B. II, 56
Serreméans, Crest, Drôme. B. IX, 141
Suze-la-Rousse, Drôme. B. II, 122

---

[1] The eleventh-century Romanesque parish church survives; it was probably the priory church before the later church (now ruined) was built. The priory was given to Cluny in 988. Sackur, II, 81.

[2] Given to Abbot Mayeul in 958. Bernard and Bruel, II, 146.

[3] Given between 993 and 1048. Bernard and Bruel, III, 296.

[4] Given to Cluny by the family of Saint-Gilles under pressure from Pope Gregory VII, c. 1096. Bruel, IV, 3410; Pignot, II, 203. It did not long remain in the Order, and was out of it before 1226.

[5] Became Cluniac in 1106; founded by King Ladislas of Hungary.

[6] Subject in 1119.

[7] Founded on an estate belonging to the family of Abbot Mayeul in 909, later ceded to Saint-Pons-de-Nice. Valous, II, 244.

[8] Given to Cluny in 985 by Lambert, Count of Valence, and his wife. Sackur, II, 232; Pignot, I, 273. Valous gives the donor as Adhémar, Comte de Valentinois, and the date as 1037.

[9] Valous (II, 234) identifies this as Aups, Var.

[10] Valous identifies this as Sauret, Hérault.

Tain (Notre-Dame), Tain-l'Hermitage, Drôme
TERNAY (SAINT-PIERRE), Isère[1]
Thèze (Notre-Dame), Basses-Alpes
Tornac (Saint-Étienne et Saint-Sauveur), An-
    duze, Gard
    DEPENDENCIES
        Anduze (Saint-Étienne), Gard
        Boisset (Saint-Saturnin), Gard
        Canaules, Canaules-et-Argentières, Gard.
        B. IV, 218
        Colombiers, Boisset, Gard
        Saint-Nazaire-des-Gardies, Gard

P. de Soca
Vabres, Gard
La Touche (Saint-Jean), Drôme. Val.
TRÈVES (SAINT-SEBASTIEN), Gard. Val.
Valbonnais (Saint-Pierre), Isère
Valensole, Basses-Alpes[2]
Valserres, Hautes-Alpes. B. II, 57
Veynes (Notre-Dame), Hautes-Alpes. B. II,
    57
Viuz-Faverges, Faverges, Haute-Savoie[3]. B. IX,
    250
VIZILLE, Isère[4]

PROVINCE OF POITOU AND SAINTONGE

ANAIS (SAINT-PIERRE), Charente-Inférieure[5]
Angoulême (Saint-Cybard), Charente (abbey)
    DEPENDENCIES
        L'Age-Monjau[6], Charente
        BOURG-DES-MAISONS, Dordogne. B. III, 206
        CERCLES, Dordogne. B. III, 207
        CHAMPMILLON, Charente[7]. B. III, 133
        Chassors, Charente. B. III, 298
        CHAVENAT, Charente. B. III, 133
        Dignac, Charente. B. III, 134
        GARAT, Charente. B. III, 208
        GOURVILLE, Charente. B. III, 134
        Jauldes, Charente. B. III, 134
        NERSAC, Charente. B. III, 136
        Palluaud, Charente. B. III, 214
        Saint-Amant-de-Nouère, Charente. B. III,
        137
        SAINT-CYBARDEAU, Charente. B. III, 137
        SONNEVILLE-DE-ROUILLAC[8], Charente. B.
        III, 133
        Tayrac, Lot-et-Garonne. B. III, 121
        Tourriers[6], Charente
        TRÉMOLAT, Dordogne[9]. B. III, 214

Triac, Charente. B. III, 309
Vœuil[6], Charente
Ardin, Deux-Sèvres. B. III, 157
Barbezieux (Notre-Dame), Charente[10]
BERSOL[11] (SAINT-SATURNIN), Gironde
Boisbretaux, Charente. B. III, 296
Breuil-la-Réorte, Charente-Inférieure
BREUILLET (SAINT-VIVIEN), Charente-Infé-
    rieure[12]
Les Brousils (Notre-Dame), Saint-Fulgent,
    Vendée
Cartelègue (Saint-Romain), Gironde
Chastellard (La Madeleine), Charente[13]
Concié, Charente-Inférieure
Cussac, Gironde
Étaules (*Insula in Arverto*) (Notre-Dame),
    Charente-Inférieure. B. III, 299
Graves (Saint-Michel), Charente[14]
Graves (Saint-Nicolas), Charente
ÎLE D'AIX (SAINT-MARTIN), Charente-Infé-
    rieure[15]
    DEPENDENCIES
        Cormes, Charente-Inférieure

---

[1] Given to the "mense conventuelle" of Cluny in 1197. B. IX, 45.
[2] Founded in 990 on land given by Abbot Mayeul. Bernard and Bruel, III, 201; Valous, II, 249.
[3] Some sculptures survive.   [4] Founded at the end of the tenth century. B. IX, 97.
[5] Given to Cluny 1075. Valous, II, 226. Disused and not architecturally interesting.
[6] Nanglard, p. 117.
[7] Given to Saint-Cybard in 1172. Michon, *Statistique monumentale de la Charente*, p. 309.
[8] B. misprints as Bonneville.   [9] The birthplace of Saint-Cybard.
[10] Founded *c.* 1040, given to Cluny *c.* 1050. Valous, II, 226.   [11] Or Berson.
[12] Or less probably Breuillat, Paillé, Charente-Inférieure. See S. Luce in *Bib. de l'École des Chartes*, xx,
1859, p. 237.   [13] Dependent on Cluny by the twelfth century. Valous, II, 226.
[14] Destroyed in 1350. Valous, II, 227.
[15] Given to Cluny by Guillaume IV, Comte de Poitou, *c.* 1107. Pignot, II, 220; Bruel, IV, 2983.

ÎLE D'AIX, DEPENDENCIES (*cont.*)
    Forges (Saint-Laurent), Aigrefeuille, Charente-Inférieure. B. III, 161
    Île de Ré, Charente-Inférieure
    L'Alleu, Charente-Inférieure. Val.
    Saint-Vivant-de-Verneuil, Charente. Val.
    SAINT-VIVIEN-DU-VERGEROUX, Charente-Inférieure[1]
    Salles-lès-Aulnay, Charente-Inférieure
Île de Cordouan, Gironde[2]
Lamboire, Vienne. Val.
Limoges (Saint-Martial), Haute-Vienne[3]. B. v, 219 (abbey)

DEPENDENCIES
    AIXE-SUR-VIENNE, Haute-Vienne[4]
    Alvagnac (Saint-Laurent), Saint-Igest, Aveyron. B. IV, 10
    [Anais, Charente][5]
    Apelle, Tarn
    Arcs, Vienne
    ARNAC-POMPADOUR, Corrèze
    Asprières, Aveyron
    Aubusson, Creuse
    Azac, Charente-Inférieure
    Azérables, Creuse
    Baignes (Saint-Étienne), Baignes Sainte-Radegonde, Charente. B. III, 285[6]
        DEPENDENCIES
        Allas-Champagne, Charente-Inférieure. B. III, 295
        AMBLEVILLE, Charente. B. III, 295
        Archiac, Charente-Inférieure. B. III, 296
        ARTHENAC, Charente-Inférieure. B. III, 296
        Chamouillac, Charente-Inférieure. B. III, 298
        Chantillac, Charente. B. III, 298
        Chevanceaux, Charente-Inférieure. B. III, 298
        CONDÉON (SAINTE-MARIE), Charente. B. III, 299
        MOINGS, Charente-Inférieure. B. III, 303

ORIGNOLLES, Montlieu, Charente-Inférieure. B. III, 303
PASSIRAC, Charente. B. III, 304
SAINT-EUGÈNE, Charente-Inférieure. B. III, 305
SAINT-GERMAIN-DE-LUSIGNAN, Charente-Inférieure. B. III, 306
Saint-Maigrin, Charente-Inférieure. B. III, 307
La Barrède, Dordogne
BELLEGARDE-DU-LOIRET, Loiret. B. v, 218
Benayes, Corrèze
Beuveix, Bellegarde-du-Loiret, Loiret. B. v, 218
La Beyne, Lot
BOUSSAC, Creuse
La Brousse, Creuse
La Brunie, Haute-Vienne
Bussière, Vienne
LES CARS, Haute-Vienne
CELLES-SUR-BELLE (SAINT-CHRISTOPHE-DU-PAS-DE-LA-CELLE), Deux-Sèvres
CHALAIS, Charente
CHAMBON, Cher
Champsevinel, Périgueux, Dordogne. B. III, 207
Chérignac, Creuse
Chezelles, Indre
Cirrat, Haute-Vienne
CLAIRAVAUX, Creuse
Clavières, Creuse
Les Cluzeaux, Dordogne
COUZEIX, Haute-Vienne
La Croix, Charente-Inférieure
La Crouzilhe, Creuse
LE DOUHET, Charente-Inférieure
DUN-SUR-AURON, Cher
Entraygues, Aveyron
Entraygues, Puy-de-Dôme
Excideuil, Dordogne
Eyraud, Dordogne
Felletin, Creuse
Le Fleix, Dordogne
Le Forneu, Gironde

---

[1] Some walls may be Romanesque but there is nothing of architectural interest.

[2] Became Cluniac, *c.* 1090. Pignot, II, 231; Bruel, IV, 3633.

[3] Founded in 832 by Louis le Débonnaire; it became Cluniac under Aimo, abbot from 936 to 42. Sackur, I, 81. It seceded but re-entered the Order in 1063. (Pignot, II, 211.) It had left it before Marrier's *Catalogus* was made.

[4] Its dependencies (when no other reference is given) are taken from C. de Lasteyrie, *Saint-Martial de Limoges*, p. 351, and Map, Pl. VII.   [5] Marrier's list gives this as directly dependent on Cluny. See above.

[6] Given to Cluny in 1097. Bruel, v, 3725.

Limoges (Saint-Martial), DEPENDENCIES (cont.)
Laurens, Hérault
Limoges (Notre-Dame-des-Arènes), Haute-Vienne
Lisse, Lot-et-Garonne
Lussac-les-Églises, Haute-Vienne
Maillol, Dordogne
Manot, Charente
Mansac, Corrèze
Marval, Haute-Vienne
Mauvières, Indre
Montboucher, Creuse
Monteils, Najac, Aveyron. B. IV, 96
Montendre, Charente-Inférieure
Montfaucon, Dordogne
Montlieu, Charente-Inférieure
MONTMORILLON, Vienne
MOUTHIERS, Charente
MOÛTIER-D'AHUN, Creuse
DEPENDENCIES
La Chapelle Saint-Martial, Creuse. B. v, 233
La Chapelle Taillefert, Creuse. B. v, 233
La Cour, Aubusson, Creuse. B. v, 220
Saint-Sulpice-les-Champs, Creuse. B. v, 253
Vidaillat, Creuse. B. v, 258
MOUTON, Charente
Naillat, Creuse
Notre-Dame-de-Beyne, Valence d'Agen, Tarn-et-Garonne. B. IV, 32
La Panouse, Aveyron
Pardailhan, Hérault
Paunat, Dordogne
Peyrat-de-Bellac, Haute-Vienne
Ribagnac, Dordogne[1]
Rieupeyroux, Aveyron
DEPENDENCY
Savignac, Villefranche-de-Rouergue, Aveyron. B. IV, 102
Rosiers, Corrèze
RUFFEC, Indre
Saint-Aubin, Lot-et-Garonne

Sainte-Berthe, Creuse
Saint-Denis-des-Murs, Vienne
Saint-Laurent-sur-Gorre, Haute-Vienne. B. v, 249
Saint-Martin Sainte-Cathérine, Creuse. B. v, 249
Saint-Nazaire, Gironde[2]
Saint-Saturnin, Charente
Sainte-Valerie-de-la-Brosse, Le Ris, Le Dorat, Haute-Vienne. B. v, 220
Sainte-Valière, Nièvre
Saint-Vaury, Creuse
Saint-Victor, Creuse
SAUJON (SAINT-ÉTIENNE), Charente-Inférieure
SAUJON (SAINT-MARTIN)[3], Charente-Inférieure
La Selve, Aveyron. B. IV, 94
Seniac, Corrèze
LA SOUTERRAINE, Creuse[4]
DEPENDENCIES
Angelard (Notre-Dame), Haute-Vienne. B. v, 228
Sagnac, Creuse
SOYANS, Drôme[5]
Tarn, Haute-Vienne
Taussac, Aveyron
TAYAC (SAINT-MARTIN), Dordogne
Terrasson, Dordogne[6]
Vallière, Creuse
VERNEUGHÉOL, Puy-de-Dôme
Veyrines, Dordogne
VIGEOIS, Corrèze
DEPENDENCY
Sainte-Anne-de-la-Faye, Voutezac, Corrèze. B. v, 258
Villards, Charente-Inférieure
Vitaterne, Charente-Inférieure
Vouneuil-sur-Vienne, Haute-Vienne
La Loge Fougereuse (Saint-Gilles), Vendée. Val.[7]
MAILLEZAIS (SAINT-PIERRE), Vendée[8] (abbey)
DEPENDENCIES
Bazoges-en-Pareds, Vendée. B. III, 181
Bréville, Charente. B. III, 290

[1] Dependent jointly on Paunat and Saint-Martial. [2] *Idem.*
[3] Some of its capitals are preserved in the church of Saint-Jean.
[4] The west end of the church belongs to the middle of the twelfth century; the rest is later.
[5] The church shows some traces of Romanesque style but should perhaps be accounted as falling outside the period.
[6] The current *Guide Bleu* reports the existence of ruins; but when I visited Terrasson in 1937 I was informed by the inhabitants that these had recently been pulled down.
[7] United to Saint-Paul-en-Gastine in 1303. Valous, II, 228.
[8] Soon after 989 a dependency of Saint-Cyprien-de-Poitiers; then independent. The church, built 1010, was burnt in 1082 except for four bays. The rest of the monastery was then rebuilt. It is now ruined.

MAILLEZAIS, DEPENDENCIES (*cont.*)
CHAMPDENIERS, Deux-Sèvres. B. III, 258
Chassay-l'Église, Sigournais, Vendée. B. III, 192
CLAUNAY, Vienne. B. III, 260
Denant, Nieul-sur-l'Autise, Vendée. B. III, 160
FONTAINES, Fontenay-le-Comte, Vendée. B. III, 161
Fontenay-le-Comte (Saint-Hilaire), Vendée. B. III, 161
La Forêt-sur-Sèvre, Deux-Sèvres. B. III, 162
LIGUGÉ, Vienne. B. III, 265[1]
Loublande, Deux-Sèvres. B. III, 164
Marans, Charente-Inférieure. B. III, 164
Menomblet, Vendée. B. III, 187
Mervent, Vendée. B. III, 164
Montcoutant, Deux-Sèvres. B. III, 164
MOUZEUIL L'HERMENAULT, Vendée. B. III, 166
Notre-Dame-de-Bourgenet, Saint-Hilaire-de-Talmont, Vendée. B. III, 191
Le Petit Niort (Saint-Étienne)[2], Charente-Inférieure. B. III, 270
PRAHECQ, Deux-Sèvres. B. III, 271
Saint-Hilaire-de-Voust, Vendée. B. III, 166
Saint-Maurice-des-Noues, Vendée. B. III, 166
Saint-Michel-le-Cloucq, Vendée. B. III, 166
Saint-Pierre-le-Vieux, Vendée. B. III, 169
SAINT-REMY-SUR-CREUSE, Vienne. B. III, 274
Saint-Trélody, Gironde. B. III, 106
VAUX (SAINT-ÉTIENNE), Vienne. B. III, 287
Xaintrais, Deux-Sèvres. B. III, 171
Xanton, Vendée. B. III, 171[3]
P. de Manomena
MELLE (SAINT-HILAIRE), Deux-Sèvres
Montbert, Charente-Inférieure[4]
MONTBRON (SAINT-MAURICE), Charente

MORNAC, Charente-Inférieure. B. III, 303[5]
Mougon (Saint-Jean-Baptiste), Deux-Sèvres[6]
MOUTON, Charente[7]
Nercillac (Notre-Dame-de-Montours), Charente. B. III, 303
POITIERS (MONTIERNEUF)[8] (SAINT-JEAN ET SAINT-ANDRÉ), Vienne (abbey)
DEPENDENCIES
ANDILLY, Charente-Inférieure[9]
Artis, Saint-Paul-de-la-Roche, Dordogne. Val.
Aubigné, Deux-Sèvres
BERNAY, Charente-Inférieure[10]
Béruges, Vienne
Boisse, Availles-Limousine, Vienne
Chanteloup, Deux-Sevrès
La Chapelle-Moulière (La Madeleine-de-Moulière), Poitiers, Vienne
Châtellerault, Vienne
Chauvigny (Saint-Étienne), Vienne. B. III, 259
Chauvigny (Saint-Just), Vienne. B. III, 259
Cheneché, Vienne
La Foy-Mongault (Saint-Simon et Saint-Jude), Deux-Sèvres
Île-de-Médoc, Gironde
L'Isle-Jourdain, Vienne. B. III, 265
P. Sancti Nicolai des Issars, dioc. Saintes
LEIGNES, Vienne
Loulay, Charente-Inférieure
MARIGNY, Beauvoir-sur-Niort, Deux-Sèvres. B. III, 266
La Marinière, Vendée
MAZEROLLES, Vienne. B. III, 266
Milly, Maine-et-Loire
MONTREUIL-BONNIN (LA-CHAPELLE-MONTREUIL) (SAINT-EUTROPE), Vienne

---

[1] It became dependent on Maillezais *c.* 1040. A sculptured lion from the original Romanesque church is built into the presbytery wall.

[2] The existing church at Le Petit Niort was a dependency of Savigny and not Cluniac.

[3] To these Dom Beaunier and Dom Besse add Nieul-sur-l'Autise, Vendée (III, 166); but this depended on the bishopric of Maillezais and not on the priory. I owe this information to the kindness of Mlle Jeanne Vielliard.

[4] Valous (II, 229) identifies as Montbert, Loire-Inférieure.

[5] Perhaps a collegiate church. See Bruel, V, 3701.

[6] Given to Cluny in the eleventh century. Pignot, I, 416.

[7] Also given as a dependency of Marcigny. See above.

[8] Founded by William VI of Poitiers and VIII of Aquitaine in 1068. He was the husband of Abbot Hugh's niece, and gave it to Cluny in 1076. The dedication was to the Virgin, Saint John and Saint Andrew. Pignot, II, 221.

[9] Restored drastically; only one original transept remains. Valous identifies this as Andillé, Vienne.

[10] Nothing of interest remains but some Romanesque windows on the exterior.

POITIERS (MONTIERNEUF), DEPENDENCIES (*cont.*)
    Mortemer (Saint-Christophe), Vienne. Val.[1]
    Poitiers (Saint-Nicolas), Vienne
    Poitiers (Saint-Paul), Vienne. B. III, 254
    LE-PUY-NOTRE-DAME (SAINTE-MARIE-DU-PUY)[2], Maine-et-Loire
    SAINT-CYR, Vienne
    Sainte-Flaive-des-Loups, Vendée. B. III, 189
    Saint-Genest-d'Ambière, Vienne
    Saint-Jean-de-Sauves, Vienne
    Saint-Laurent-de-Bret, Deux-Sèvres[3]
    Saint-Sépulchre, Charente-Inférieure
    SAINT-SORNIN, Charente-Inférieure
    Savigny, Vienne[4]
    Vicq (Saint-Sereine), Vienne
    Villefollet (Saint-Hilaire), Deux-Sèvres. B. III, 277
    Vouneuil-sous-Biard, Vienne
    Vouneuil-sur-Vienne, Vienne
Poitiers (Saint-Cyprien), Vienne[5] (abbey)
    DEPENDENCIES
    Aigonnay, Deux-Sèvres. B. III, 255
    Apremont, Palluau, Vendée. B. III, 187
    Bellefonds, Vienne. B. III, 256
    Boismé, Deux-Sèvres. B. III, 158
    BRESSUIRE (SAINT-CYPRIEN), Deux-Sèvres. B. III, 159
    CHÂTEAU LARCHER, Vienne. Redet, p. xxiii
    Chauvigny (Saint-Sépulchre or Saint-Just)[6], Vienne. Redet, p. xxiii
    Marnay, Vienne. B. III, 266
    OULMES, Charente-Inférieure. B. III, 166
    Riez (Notre-Dame), Vendée. B. III, 181
    Saint-Cyr-en-Talmondais, Vendée. B. III, 189

Saint-Hilaire-de-Riez, Vendée. B. III, 191
Saint-Laurent-sur-Sèvre, Vendée. B. III, 166
SAINT-MAURICE, Vienne. B. III, 274
SAVIGNY-SUR-VIENNE, Vienne. Redet, p. xxiii
Villiers-en-Plaine, Deux-Sèvres. B. III, 170
Vitré, Deux-Sèvres. B. III, 277
La Rochelle (Notre-Dame-*de-Congiis*), Charente-Inférieure. B. III, 157
RONSENAC (SAINT-JEAN-BAPTISTE), Charente[7]
    DEPENDENCIES
    D. de Anixa
    Villebois, Charente (nuns)
    Villegats, Charente. Val.
Ruelle (Saint-Médard), Charente. B. III, 157
SAINTES (SAINT-EUTROPE), Charente-Inférieure[8]
    DEPENDENCIES
    LES ALLEUDS (Saint-Eutrope), Deux-Sèvres
    Le Breuil-aux-Moines, Charente-Inférieure
    Campillan (Notre-Dame), Gironde
    Gonzac, Charente. Val.
    GRÉZAC, Charente-Inférieure
    Jarnac (Saint-Albin), Charente[9]
    MÉDIS (SAINT-PIERRE), Charente-Inférieure[10]
    MEUX (SAINT-MARTIN), Charente
    P. de Neamia, dioc. Saintes
    OUZILLY (SAINT-MICHEL), Charroux, Vienne[11]
    RETAUD (SAINT-TROJAN), Charente-Inférieure. B. III, 304
    Roenne, Torsac, Charente[12]
    Saint-André-de-Lidon, Charente-Inférieure. B. III, 305
    Saint-Eutrope-de-la-Lande, Montmoreau, Charente

[1] Given to Montierneuf about 1090. Valous, II, 229.
[2] Given by William of Aquitaine in 1077. The church is Gothic but has a Romanesque tower. Valous identifies as Notre-Dame-du-Pé, Sarthe.
[3] Valous (II, 226) seems to identify this as Bouhet (Saint-Laurent), Charente-Inférieure.
[4] Not to be confounded with the more famous Savigny that was founded as the head of a separate Order that in 1147 was merged in Cîteaux.
[5] Became Cluniac *c.* 1004. Pignot, I, 410.
[6] B. III, 259 gives Saint-Just as a dependency of Montierneuf; see above.
[7] Some sculpture from this church is in the Angoulême Museum.
[8] Founded by the founder of Montierneuf in 1079; it became Cluniac in 1081. Pignot, II, 222. The church, begun at the time of its foundation, was dedicated in 1096.
[9] A very small portion of the church may be Romanesque, but it has been almost entirely rebuilt.
[10] Valous (II, 229) gives it as directly dependent on Cluny.
[11] Valous identifies it as Ozillac, Charente-Inférieure.
[12] Valous identifies it as Rosne, Charente-Inférieure.

---

[1] Given in 1110. Bernard and Bruel, v, 237.
[2] Reformed by disciples of Odilo, it finally left the Order in 1217. Pignot, II, 223.
[3] Brugelès, *Grand Pouillé des bénéfices de France*, 1626, II, 593.
[4] Valous (II, 227) makes this dependent on Île d'Aix.
[5] Only one blocked-up Romanesque window is visible of the original church.
[6] Given to Saint-Jean in 1137. *Bull. Mon.* I, 1843, p. 173.
[7] Brugelès, *Grand Pouillé des bénéfices de France*, 1626, II, p. 593. Possibly Romazières.
[8] Dependent on Cluny and Saint-Jean jointly.
[9] Nothing Romanesque remains but part of the north wall, with arcaded decoration.

Saint-Laurent-de-Belzaguot, Charente. V.
Saint-Médard, La Jarrie, Charente-Inférieure.
    B. III, 166
Saint-Médard-des-Prés, Vendée

Saint-Paul-en-Gâtine, Deux-Sèvres[1]
DEPENDENCY
    Domus de Longa-sagerosa
Villegarde, Charente[2]

PROVINCE OF AUVERGNE

Ajain (Saint-Michel), Creuse. B. v, 219
Ambert, Puy-de-Dôme. Val.
Arronnes (Saint-Léger), Allier. V.
AUGEROLLES (SAINT-GEORGES), Puy-de-Dôme
Aynes, Cantal. Val.
Bachelet, Puy-de-Dôme
BEAULIEU (SAINT-PIERRE), Corrèze[3]
    DEPENDENCIES
        Astaillac (Saint-Étienne), Corrèze. B. v, 220
        BONNEVIOLLE (SAINT-GILLES), Lot. Deloche
        BRIVEZAC, Corrèze. Deloche
        FAVARS, Corrèze. B. v, 299[4]
        Félines (Notre-Dame), Lot. Deloche[5]
        Friat (Sainte-Madeleine), Lot. Deloche
        Girac, Lot. B. IV, 35
        Liourdres, Corrèze. B. v, 237
        Menoire, Corrèze. Deloche
        Saint-Geniès-de-Sarrazac, Corrèze (nuns).
            Deloche
        Sainte-Marie-de-Donnatte, Astaillac, Cor-
            rèze. Deloche
        Tudeils, Corrèze. Deloche
        VAYRAC, Lot. Deloche
        Végennes, Corrèze. Deloche
Belac, Haute-Loire. Val.
Billom (Saint-Loup), Puy-de-Dôme[6]
BORT (NOTRE-DAME), Corrèze[7]
    DEPENDENCIES
        COMPAINS, Puy-de-Dôme. B. IV, 126
        La Mazière-Haute, Eygurande, Corrèze.
            B. v, 233
        MENET, Cantal. B. IV, 132

Le Broc (Saint-Aignan), Puy-de-Dôme. Val.
La Chapelle Antié, Corrèze. B. v, 237
CHAVAROUX, Puy-de-Dôme. Val.
CHÂTELMONTAGNE (NOTRE-DAME), Allier[8]
Clermont (Saint-Allyre), Puy-de-Dôme
    DEPENDENCIES
        Basville, Creuse. B. v, 123
        Chadeleuf, Puy-de-Dôme. B. v, 125
        Clermont (Saint-André)
            DEPENDENCIES
                LE BREUIL-SUR-COUZE, Puy-de-
                    Dôme. B. v, 130
                Cisternes-la-Forêt, Puy-de-Dôme.
                    B. v, 126
                SAINT-JEAN-DE-MERDOGNE, La
                    Roche-Blanche, Puy-de-Dôme. B.
                    VI, 130
        Clermont (Saint-Cassi). B. v, 120
        Clermont (Saint-Ferréol). B. v, 120
        Creuzier-le-Neuf, Allier. B. v, 127
        Gelles, Puy-de-Dôme. B. v, 128
        NEUVILLE, Billom, Puy-de-Dôme. B. v,
            134
        Royat (Saint-Mart), Puy-de-Dôme. B. v,
            136
        Saint-Silvestre, Puy-de-Dôme. B. v, 140
        Savennes, Puy-de-Dôme. B. v, 140
        THURET, Puy-de-Dôme. B. v, 142
        Vichy (Sainte-Croix-du-Moûtier), Allier.
            B. v, 143
Droiturier (Saint-Nicolas), Allier
Grazac (Saint-Pierre), Haute-Loire

---

[1] Given to Cluny in 1018 by William, Duke of Aquitaine. Valous, II, 232.
[2] Given to Cluny by Guillaume IV, Comte de Poitou, *c.* 1107. Pignot, II, 220.
[3] Founded in 855. The donation to Cluny is confirmed by a Bull of Urban II, 1072. Marrier, col. 525.
It ceased to be Cluniac in 1213. Pignot, II, 207.
[4] According to the *Bull. de la Soc. des Lettres, Sciences et Arts de la Corrèze*, VI, 1884, p. 468, Favars was
a vicarage-grange of Beaulieu, not a priory. See also Bernard and Bruel, IV, 602.
[5] Possibly identical with Saint-Marcel-de-Félines, given to Cluny by Aymar, Comte de Valentinois,
and his family in 1037. Pignot, I, 414.
[6] Given to Abbot Odilo, it later seceded. It re-entered the Order in 1094 and was released from it by
Peter the Venerable. Pignot, II, 233.
[7] Founded before 1013. Valous, II, 180.   [8] Founded before 1131. Valous, II, 181.

Gumières (Saint-Barthélemy), Loire[1]
LANGY (SAINT-SULPICE), Allier. B. v, 130[2]
Laveine, Puy-de-Dôme (nuns)[3]
LUBERSAC (SAINT-GERVAIS), Corrèze. Val.
Mailhat (Notre-Dame), Puy-de-Dôme. V.[4]
Manzanes (Notre-Dame), Creuse. Val.
MENAT, Puy-de-Dôme
  DEPENDENCIES
    BELLENAVES, Allier. B. v, 49
    Cellule, Puy-de-Dôme. B. v, 124
    Châteauneuf (Saint-Jean-de-la-Monzie), Saignes, Cantal. B. v, 126
    La Crouzille, Puy-de-Dôme. B. v, 129
    Lapeyrouse, Montaigut, Puy-de-Dôme. B. v, 57
    Lavault-Sainte-Anne, Allier. B. v, 57
    Lunet (Sainte-Madeleine), Aveyron. B. IV, 97
    Marcillat, Menat, Puy-de-Dôme. B. v, 131
    Montluçon (Notre-Dame), Allier. B. v, 58
    Le Quartier, Puy-de-Dôme. B. v, 131
    Saint-Bonnet-de-Chamaraude, Saint-Pont, Allier. B. v, 139
    Saint-Éloy, Montaigut-en-Combraille, Puy-de-Dôme. B. v, 136
    Saint-Priest-des-Champs, Puy-de-Dôme. B. v, 140
    Sussat (Succiacum), Allier. B. v, 141
    Teilhet, Menat, Puy-de-Dôme. B. v, 142
MEYMAC, CORRÈZE[5]
  DEPENDENCIES
    La Daigue (Saint-Léger), Creuse. B. v, 223
    Lestrade (Saint-Clément), Meymac, Corrèze. B. v, 240

Saint-Gilles-les-Forêts, Haute-Vienne. B. v, 248
Saint-Jacques-de-Freytet, Cantal. B. v, 253
Saint-Léger-de-Chastignol, Bonnefond, Corrèze. B. v, 223
Sainte-Madeleine-de-Longeyroux, Corrèze. B. v, 240
Saint-Sulpice-les-Bois, Corrèze. B. v, 253
Mongon, Allier. Val.
Mons (Notre-Dame), Puy-de-Dôme. Val.
Moustier-Ventadour (Saint-Pierre-le-Moustier), Corrèze
MOZAC (SAINT-CAPRAIS ET SAINT-PIERRE), Puy-de-Dôme (abbey)[6]
  DEPENDENCIES
    [BREDONS, Cantal][7]
    P. de Brentauuers
    Châtelguyon (Saint-Maurice), Puy-de-Dôme. B. v, 126
    Clermont (Saint-Bonnet), Puy-de-Dôme
    Graix, Loire
    MARSAT, Puy-de-Dôme (nuns)
    Ménétrol, Puy-de-Dôme. B. VI, 32
    Montpensier (Saint-Benet), Puy-de-Dôme[8]
    Rochefort-Montagne, Puy-de-Dôme
    ROYAT (SAINT-LÉGER), Puy-de-Dôme. B. v, 136[9]
    Saint-Ambroix, Cher
    Saint-Bonnet-sous-Montpensier, Puy-de-Dôme. Val.
    Saint-Georges-de-Mons, Puy-de-Dôme
    SAINT-GERMAIN-DES-FOSSÉS, Allier
    Saint-Hilaire, Saint-Hilaire-Château, Pontarion, Creuse[10]
    Saint-Martin-d'Alloches, Pont-du-Château, Puy-de-Dôme

---

[1] Given to Cluny in 978. B. XI, 107 gives it as dependent on Ris (see below).

[2] Valous identifies this with Langy, Clermont, Puy-de-Dôme.

[3] Became Cluniac under Peter the Venerable.

[4] Valous (II, 183) gives it as dependent on Sauxillanges.

[5] Given to the Cluniac priory of Uzerche by Archambaud de Comborn in 1085, it soon became directly dependent on Cluny.

[6] The abbey was founded at the end of the sixth century and became Cluniac in 1095. In the thirteenth century it seceded from the Order and became dependent on La Chaise-Dieu (Pignot, II, 236; Bruel, v, 3697), but re-entered it later. Valous, II, 184. A capital from it is now in the Victoria and Albert Museum.

[7] Founded in 1050; the church consecrated in 1095. Rochemonteix, p. 68, gives it as a dependency of Moissac.

[8] It appears to have been built while a dependency of Saint-Hilaire-de-la-Croix and lies outside our scope. See *Revue d'Auvergne*, XVIII, 1901, p. 253.

[9] F. Maury (*Royat, Notice descriptive et historique*, p. 33, Clermont Ferrand, 1862) states that it became dependent on Mozat only in 1163. The church is probably earlier, and I have omitted any consideration of it.

[10] Valous (II, 186) identifies with Saint-Hilaire, Haute-Loire.

MOZAC, DEPENDENCIES (*cont.*)

    Saint-Ours, Pontgibaud, Puy-de-Dôme. B. v, 136

    Saint-Pierre-le-Châtel, Puy-de-Dôme
    P. Sancti Viti

    P. Sanae-culturae, prope villam Rionii (*sic:* Riom)

    VOLVIC (SAINT-PROJET), Puy-de-Dôme. B. v, 143

Noirétable (Notre-Dame-de-Pérotine), Loire

PONT-DU-CHÂTEAU (SAINTE-MARTINE), Puy-de-Dôme. V.

RIS (NOTRE-DAME), Puy-de-Dôme [1]

ROSIERS-CÔTES-D'AUREC (SAINT-BLAISE-DE-ROSIERS), Haute-Loire

Saint-Ferréol-des-Côtes, Puy-de-Dôme. V.

Saint-Flour, Cantal [2]

    DEPENDENCIES

    Le Breuil (Saint-André), Puy-de-Dôme. Val. [3]

    Brezons, Cantal. B. v, 276

    Chaudesaigues (Saint-Martin), Cantal. B. v, 278 [4]

    Mentières (Sainte-Madeleine), Cantal. B. v, 282 [5]

    Saint-Étienne-sur-Blesle, Haute-Loire. B. v, 286

    SAINT-HIPPOLYTE, Puy-de-Dôme [6]. B. v, 138

    LES TERNES (SAINT-MARTIN), Cantal. B. v, 280

    Vic-sur-Cère (Saint-Pierre), Cantal. Val.

Saint-Marcel, Puy-de-Dôme. Val.

Saint-Pierre-Colamine, Puy-de-Dôme. Val.

Sanssac-l'Église, Haute-Loire. V.

Sauxillanges (Saint-Pierre et Saint-Paul), Puy-de-Dôme [7]

DEPENDENCIES

    P. de Boisson (*Boisson, Aurillac, Cantal or Boisson, Saint-Cernin-du-Cantal*)

    Bonnac (Saint-Maurice), Cantal

    Bournoncles, Cantal

    Brenat, Issoire, Puy-de-Dôme

    CHALUS, Saint-Germain-Lembron, Puy-de-Dôme. B. v, 125

    Chambezon (Saint-Martin), Haute-Loire. B. v, 277

    Charnat, Lezoux, Puy-de-Dôme

    Châtel, Cleppé, Loire

    CHAUMONT, Puy-de-Dôme

    CHAURIAT (SAINT-JULIEN), Puy-de-Dôme [8]

    Le Claix, Charbonnier, Saint-Germain-Lembron, Puy-de-Dôme. B. v, 126

    P. de Guignac

    LEMPDES, Haute-Loire [9]

    Léotoing (Saint-Vincent), Blesle, Haute-Loire. B. v, 280

    Les Martres-de-Veyre (Saint-Martial), Puy-de-Dôme. B. v, 131

    Montaigut (Saint-Blaise), Puy-de-Dôme

    PLAUZAT-LE-NOIR (SAINT-PIERRE), Puy-de-Dôme. Val.

    Saint-Alyre, Puy-de-Dôme [10]

    Saint-Christophe, Cantal. B. v, 136

    SAINT-ÉTIENNE-SUR-USSON, Puy-de-Dôme. B. v, 136 [11]

    SAINT-GERVAIS, Gannat, Allier [12]

    P. Sancti Marcelli

    Saint-Pardoux, Puy-de-Dôme

    TAUVES (NOTRE-DAME), Puy-de-Dôme [13]

    VERTAIZON (SAINTE-MARCELLE), Puy-de-Dôme. B. v, 142

    Veyre Monton, Puy-de-Dôme. B. v, 142

---

[1] Founded in 952 by Ambard de Thiers, given to Cluny in 994. *Bull. Mon.* XC, 1931, p. 66. I think "Rives, Haute-Loire" given by Valous (II, 184) is another version of the Latin name of Ris.

[2] Given to Cluny in 1025.

[3] Founded *c.* 1210. Valous, II, 183.   [4] Given to Saint-Flour in 1053. Valous, II, 181.

[5] Given to Saint-Flour in 1180. Valous, II, 184.   [6] Dependent jointly on Cluny and Saint-Flour.

[7] Founded in 915 by William of Aquitaine, the founder of Cluny, and given to Cluny by his nephew Acfred in 927. Pignot, I, 43. The dedication was to the Trinity and the Virgin. The monastery was not established until the time of Abbot Aymar (942–65), *ibid.* I, 198.

[8] Founded in 1024 out of three churches given by Étienne IV, Bishop of Clermont, and his canons. Pignot, I, 419.

[9] Valous (II, 183) gives this as dependent on Thiers.

[10] Founded by 1030. Valous, II, 185.

[11] The church has been rebuilt but the tower is ancient.

[12] Much of the church was rebuilt in the thirteenth century but a Romanesque door and the traditional three-apsed plan remain.

[13] Founded in 1078 by Pierre de Chaumettes. Valous, II, 187.

Sauxillanges, DEPENDENCIES (cont.)
    Vézédoux (Saint-Préjet), Auzon, Haute-Loire. B. v, 289
    Viverols (Sainte-Madeleine), Puy-de-Dôme[1]
Singles (Saint-Nazaire), Puy-de-Dôme. Val.
SOUVIGNY (SAINT-MAYEUL), Allier[2]
  DEPENDENCIES
    Beaulieu, Luthenay-Uxeloup, Nièvre. B. vi, 118
    Bessac-le-Monial, Saint-Aubin, Allier. B. v, 68
    BROUT-VERNET (SAINT-MAGERAN-DE-BROUT), Allier
    CHAMPVOUX (SAINT-PIERRE), Nièvre[3]
    CHANTENAY (SAINT-MARTIN), Nièvre
    Chappes (Notre-Dame), Allier
    Chirat-l'Église, Allier[4]
    Cintrat, Chareil-Cintrat, Allier
    COLOMBIER (SAINT-PIERRE), Commentry, Allier[5]
    Cossaye (Saint-Martin), Nièvre. B. vi, 117
    La Ferté-sur-Allier, Allier
    Domus de Flabines
    Jenzat (Saint-Martin), Allier
    Louroux-Bourbonnais, Allier. B. v, 58
    Mainsat (Notre-Dame), Creuse
    MARS (SAINT-JULIEN), Nièvre
    Montempuis, Dornes, Nièvre
    MONTVICQ, Allier. B. v, 58
    Saint-Blaise-de-Gensac, Haute-Loire. Val.
    Domus Sancti Fiacrii
    Souvigny (Saint-Patrocle). Val.
    La Tour, Tauves, Puy-de-Dôme. B. v, 130
    Vaudres, Cher
    Vernouillet, Allier
    Vieure, Allier. B. v, 71

THIERS (LE MOÛTIER) (SAINT-SYMPHORIEN), Puy-de-Dôme (abbey)[6]
  DEPENDENCIES
    COURPIÈRE (SAINT-PIERRE), Puy-de-Dôme[7]
    P. de Ioux (? Joux, Rhône)
    LANDOS, Haute-Loire
    LEZOUX (NOTRE-DAME), Thiers, Puy-de-Dôme. B. v, 131[8]
Treignac, Corrèze. B. v, 256
UZERCHE (SAINT-PIERRE), Corrèze[9]
  DEPENDENCIES
    Agudour, Voutezac, Corrèze. B. v, 258
    Chamberet, Corrèze. B. v, 225
    Chanzac, Perpezac-le-Noir, Corrèze. B. v, 243
    Gartempe, Creuse. B. v, 231
    Gondre (Saint-Paul), Corrèze. B. v, 255
    Magoutière (Sainte-Foy), Corrèze. B. v, 255
    Millevaches, Corrèze. B. v, 240
    Nieuil, Charente. B. iii, 136
    Notre-Dame-de-la-Bessaigne, La Porcherie, Haute-Vienne. B. v, 234
    Sainte-Madeleine-de-Lentilhac, Ussac, Corrèze. B. v, 257
    Saint-Priest-les-Vergnes, Haute-Vienne. B. v, 247
    Saint-Salvadour, Corrèze. B. v, 252
    Saint-Solve, Corrèze. B. v, 252
    SAINT-VIANCE, Corrèze. B. v, 253
    Saint-Ybard, Corrèze. B. v, 254
    Salon, La Tour, Corrèze. B. v, 254
    Veix, Corrèze. B. v, 258
La Voulte-Chilhac (Sainte-Croix), Haute-Loire[10]
  DEPENDENCIES
    Alleyras (Saint-Martin), Haute-Loire
    ALLY (NOTRE-DAME), Haute-Loire. B. v, 275
    Apchat, Puy-de-Dôme. B. v, 121

---

[1] Founded by William, Bishop of Clermont, in 1101. Valous, ii, 188.

[2] Given to Cluny in 921. Pignot, i, 46. H. du Ranquet, in Bull. Mon. LXXIV, 1910, p. 242, gives Saint-Saturnin, Puy-de-Dôme, as one of its priories. I have found no evidence in support of this statement, and so important a church would hardly be likely to be passed over in silence.

[3] B. gives this as a dependency of La Charité. See above.

[4] Valous (ii, 182) identifies this as Chirac, Corrèze.

[5] Given to Souvigny between 1061 and 1071. Valous, ii, 182.

[6] Founded by Guy de Thiers in 1010, it became Cluniac a year later. Pignot, i, 405. The dedication was to Saint-Symphorien.

[7] Founded in 1150; Bréhier in Revue Mabillon, 1923, p. 22. But according to Valous (ii, 182) in 1130.

[8] Desecrated; in 1933 partly a cinema and partly a stable.

[9] Attached to Cluny for reform in 1068. Pignot, ii, 210. The church was consecrated in 1098.

[10] The Abbot Odilo planned its foundation, which was carried out by his nephews later. Pignot, i, 407. The surviving church is of the fifteenth century but retains the door of the older church.

La Voulte-Chilhac, DEPENDENCIES (*cont.*)
 Aubazac (Saint-Projet), Laroquebrou, Cantal. B. v, 276
 Auriac, Courpière, Puy-de-Dôme. B. v, 122
 Bagnols, Puy-de-Dôme. B. v, 122
 Blassac (Notre-Dame), Haute-Loire. B. v, 276
 Céloux (Saint-Roch), Cantal. B. v, 277
 Chaulhac (Saint-Fréjal), Haute-Loire. B. iv, 65
 CHEYLADE, Cantal. B. v, 126
 Lastic (Sainte-Madeleine), Cantal. B. v, 280
 Mazoires (Saint-Saturnin), Puy-de-Dôme. B. v, 132

Mirmande, Saint-Jean-Lachalm, Haute-Loire. Thiollier, p. 151
Morsac, Murat, Cantal. B. v, 282
REILHAC (SAINT-PRIVAT), Langeac, Haute-Loire. B. v, 284
Rochefort, Saint-Poncy, Cantal
Saint-Jean-Lachalm, Haute-Loire
Saint-Paul-le-froid, Lozère[1]
Saint-Vincent *in Vallavia*, Saint-Paulien, Le Puy, Haute-Loire. B. v, 167
Saugues (Saint-Médard), Le Puy, Haute-Loire[2]
Védrines-Saint-Loup, Cantal. B. v, 288
Vèze, Allanche, Cantal. B. v, 143

PROVINCE OF GASCONY

ARLES-SUR-TECH (NOTRE-DAME), Pyrénées-Orientales (abbey)[3]
Astaffort, Lot-et-Garonne[4]
Auch (Saint-Orens), Gers[5]
 DEPENDENCIES
  Montaut (Saint-Michel), Gers[6]
  PEYRUSSE-GRANDE (SAINT-MAMERT), Gers
  SAINT-ORENS-DE-LAVÉDAN, Villelongue, Hautes-Pyrénées
  Saint-Sauvy, Gers. B. iii, 20
  Touget (Saint-Martin), Gers
Camprodon (Saint-Pierre), Catalonia (abbey)[7]
CARENNAC (SAINT-SATURNIN, later SAINT-PIERRE), Lot[8]
 DEPENDENCIES
  Argentat (Saint-Pierre), Corrèze. B. v, 297
  Gourdon, Lot. B. iv, 35

P. de Monte-caluo
Mont-Saint-Jean, Gourdon, Lot
Clunizet, Herault[9]
Courrensan (Notre-Dame), Gers. Val.
Courte (Saint-Pierre), Landes[10]
CUBIÈRES (NOTRE-DAME), Aude[11]
Éauze (Saint-Loubert), Gers
 DEPENDENCY
  Saint-Loubert-d'Escalens, Gabarret, Landes
Eymet, Dordogne
EYSSES (SAINT-GERVAIS ET SAINT-PROTAIS), Lot-et-Garonne (abbey)[12]
FIGEAC (SAINT-SAUVEUR), Lot (abbey)[13]
 DEPENDENCIES
  Anglars (Saint-Martin), Lot. B. iv, 31
  Belmeron (Saint-Eutrope), Lot. B. iv, 31

[1] Valous (ii, 186) gives this as dependent on Sauxillanges.
[2] Valous (ii, 187) identifies this as Salgas, Lozère.
[3] The apse was consecrated in 1046, the church in 1142. Gibrat, p. 30. A further consecration seems to have taken place in 1157.
[4] Dependent on Layrac after 1262. Valous, ii, 208.
[5] Founded in 1009 and given to Cluny *c.* 1068 by Aimeric, Comte de Fezensac et d'Auch. Pignot, ii, 194; Bruel, iv, 3414.
[6] Given to Cluny in 1069 by Bernard de Montaut, Prior of Saint-Orens-d'Auch. Pignot, ii, 194; Migne, *Pat. Lat.* CLIX, col. 961.
[7] Given to Moissac in 1077 (Pignot, ii, 196) but Marrier counts it an independent house.
[8] Given to Cluny in 1045 by Robert, Bishop of Cahors, and his brother. Pignot, i, 416; ii, 207.
[9] Founded in the time of Peter the Venerable.　　　[10] Given to Cluny in 1104. Pignot, ii, 202.
[11] Given to Cluny and Moissac in 1077 by Raymond Pierre, Vicomte de Fenouillède. Pignot, ii, 197.
[12] Given to Cluny in 1088 to be directed by Moissac; later directly dependent on Cluny. Pignot, ii, 207. It is now a prison and I have been unable to see it.
[13] Founded by Pepin of Aquitaine in 820, it became Cluniac in 1074, and remained in the Order until the middle of the seventeenth century. Pignot, ii, 206; Bruel, iv, 3469.

FIGEAC, DEPENDENCIES (cont.)
Camburat (Saint-Saturnin), Lot. B. IV, 32
La Capelle-Cabanac, Lot. B. IV, 35
Cardaillac (Notre-Dame et Saint-Julien), Lot. B. IV, 34
CHARRAS, Charente. B. III, 133
FIGEAC (NOTRE-DAME-DU-PUY), Lot. B. IV, 34
Issepts (Saint-Médard), Lot. B. IV, 35
Peyresse (Notre-Dame), Estaing-d'Aveyron, Aveyron. B. IV, 97
Saint-Blaise-de-Cassagnol, Loupiac, Lot. B. IV, 37
Saint-Julien-d'Empare, Aveyron. Val.
Saint-Martin-de-Peyrissac, Thémines, Lot. B. IV, 41
Salvagnac-Saint-Loup, Aveyron. B. IV, 102
Le Trioulou (Saint-Blaise), Cantal. B. V, 280
Fons, Lot. Lecestre, p. 4
DEPENDENCY
Lalbenque, Cahors, Lot
Laplume (Sainte-Colombe), Lot-et-Garonne[1]
LAYRAC (SAINT-MARTIN), Lot-et-Garonne[2]
DEPENDENCY
Monclar-de-Quercy (Saint-Pierre), Tarn-et-Garonne. Val.
LÉZAT (SAINT-PIERRE), Ariège (abbey)[3]
DEPENDENCIES
Bérat (Saint-Pierre), Haute-Garonne. B. IV, 334
Le Fossat (Saint-André), Ariège. B. IV, 334
Lagrace-Dieu (Magréas), Haute-Garonne. B. IV, 334
Mauzac, Haute-Garonne. B. IV, 334
Montaut, Gers. B. IV, 334
Muret, Haute-Garonne. B. IV, 292

Notre-Dame-de-Grenouillet, Villeneuve-de-Durfort, Ariège. B. IV, 334
Peyrelade (Sainte-Colombe et Saint-Martin), Saverdun, Ariège. B. IV, 334
PEYRISSAS (SAINT-MARTIN), Haute-Garonne. B. III, 48
SAINT-BÉAT, Haute-Garonne. B. III, 48
Saint-Michel-du-Mont-Sabaoth, Cazères, Haute-Garonne. B. IV, 334
Sainte-Suzanne, Ariège. Val.
SAINT-YBARS, Ariège. B. IV, 334
Tarbes (Saint-Licère), Hautes-Pyrénées[4]
Mas-Saint-Antonin (Saint-Antonin-de-Frédélas), Pamiers, Ariège[5]
MEZIN (SAINT-JEAN), Lot-et-Garonne
MOIRAX (NOTRE-DAME), Lot-et-Garonne[6]
MOISSAC, Tarn-et-Garonne (abbey). R.[7]
DEPENDENCIES
[ARLES-SUR-TECH, Pyrénées-Orientales][8]. R.
Les Barthes (Saint-Sulpice), Tarn-et-Garonne. Val.
Belleperche (Saint-Nicholas), Tarn-et-Garonne. R.[9]
Belmontet, La Salvetat, Tarn-et-Garonne. B. IV, 31
Bessens (Notre-Dame), Tarn-et-Garonne. Val.
Boisse. R.
Bondigoux, Haute-Garonne. R.
Bonnecombe, Aveyron. R.
BREDONS, Cantal[10]. R.
Buzet, Haute-Garonne. R.
Caraman, Haute-Garonne. R.
Castelnau-d'Estretefonds, Fronton, Haute-Garonne. B. IV, 316

[1] Valous (II, 211) gives this as dependent on Layrac.
[2] Founded in 1072 by Hunald, Abbot of Moissac. Pignot, II, 195; Bruel, IV, 3385. The church was consecrated in 1096.
[3] In 940 this was governed by a pro-abbot for Odo of Cluny. By the beginning of the eleventh century it had seceded, but by 1073 was once more Cluniac. Pignot, II, 195; Bruel, IV, 3454.
[4] Given between 1056 and 1064 by Heraclius, Bishop of Tarbes. Pignot, II, 195.
[5] Given to Abbot Hugh by Roger, Comte de Foix, and his wife c. 1066. Migne, Pat. Lat. CLIX, col. 940; Pignot, II, 193. The remains of the claustral buildings fall outside the Romanesque period.
[6] Founded in 1049 by Guillaume de Moirax. His son Pierre was its first prior.
[7] The reference R. indicates Rupin, Abbaye de Moissac, p. 181. The abbey was an ancient foundation, destroyed first by the Saracens and then by the Normans. After its restoration it was offered to Hugh of Cluny in 1047. Pignot, II, 189. The abbey was secularized in 1625.
[8] Also given by Marrier as directly dependent on Cluny. See above.
[9] Now destroyed, but some of its sculpture is at Castelsarrasin.
[10] Also given as a dependency of Mozat; see above. It is correctly a dependency of Moissac, to which it was given in 1050. Rochemonteix, p. 68.

MOISSAC, DEPENDENCIES (*cont.*)

CASTELSARRASIN (SAINT-SAUVEUR), Tarn-et-Garonne

Caussade (Notre-Dame), Tarn-et-Garonne. B. IV, 32

CÉNAC, DORDOGNE[1]. R.

CINTEGABELLE, Haute-Garonne. B. IV, 307

Conquêtes (Saint-Romain), Montastruc, Haute-Garonne. R.

Cos (Saint-Saturnin), Tarn-et-Garonne. R.

[Cubières (Notre-Dame), Aude. R.][2]

Cumont (Saint-Cyrin), Tarn-et-Garonne. B. IV, 317

DURAVEL (SAINT-HILARION), Lot. R.

Escatalens (Saint-Julien), Tarn-et-Garonne. R.

[Eymet, Dordogne[3]. R.]

[EYSSES, Lot-et-Garonne][3]

Gandalou (Sainte-Marie), Tarn-et-Garonne. Val.

Gasanpuy, Gers. R.

Gimat (Saint-Cybard), Tarn-et-Garonne. Val.

Glatens (Saint-Martin), Tarn-et-Garonne. Val.

Lagardelle, Haute-Garonne. R.

Lapeyrière, Tarn. R.

Lapeyrouse, Lafrançaise, Tarn-et-Garonne. R.

[LAYRAC, Lot-et-Garonne[3]. R.]

Lectoure (Saint-Geniès), Gers. R.

Lisle, Tarn. B. IV, 14

Majuse (Monclar) (Saint-Pierre), Tarn-et-Garonne. R.

MARCILHAC, Lot. R.

Mas-Grenier, Tarn-et-Garonne. R.

Masquières, Lot-et-Garonne. R.

Massels, Lot-et-Garonne. R.

Meauzac (Saint-Martin), Castelsarrasin, Tarn-et-Garonne. R.

P. de Mirello

Pescadoires, Lot. R.

POMMEVIC (SAINT-DENIS), Tarn-et-Garonne. B. III, 120[4]

RABASTENS (NOTRE-DAME), Tarn[5]

Roqueserrière (Saint-Pierre), Haute-Garonne. B. IV, 293

Saint-Aignan-de-Bragairac (Notre-Dame), Tarn-et-Garonne[6]. Val.

Saint-Jean-de-Cornac, Tarn-et-Garonne. B. IV, 41

Saint-Jean-le-froid, Aveyron. B. IV, 104

Saint-Maffre, Tarn-et-Garonne. R.

Saint-Mary-le-Plain, Cantal. B. V, 138

SAINT-MAURIN, Lot-et-Garonne. B. III, 114

Saint-Nauphary, Tarn-et-Garonne. R.

Saint-Nicolas-de-la-Grave, Tarn-et-Garonne. R.

Saint-Pierre-de-Livron, Caylus, Tarn-et-Garonne. B. IV, 38

Saint-Roch-de-Montbrison, Saint-Michel, Tarn-et-Garonne. B. III, 63

Sainte-Ruffine, Cayrac, Tarn-et-Garonne. B. IV, 33

Saint-Rustice, Haute-Garonne. B. IV, 293

Sallèles (Notre-Dame), Aude. R.

La Salvetat, Caraman, Haute-Garonne. B. IV, 291

P. de sede Leyaco

Sedilhac, Dordogne

Le Ségur, Tarn. R.

SÉRIGNAC (SAINT-GERVAIS), Tarn-et-Garonne. R.

Sermur (Saint-Pierre), Rodez, Aveyron. R.

Sorèze, Aveyron. R.

Toulongergues, Aveyron. B. IV, 101

Toulonjac (Saint-Michel), Aveyron. B. IV, 103

TOULOUSE (SAINTE-MARIE-DE-LA-DAURADE)[7], Haute-Garonne

DEPENDENCIES

Daux (Saint-Barthélemy), Haute-Garonne. B. IV, 292

---

[1] Founded *c.* 1090. See *Cong. Arch.* XC, 1927, p. 243. Asquilin of Moissac is said to have built the church. See Mortet, I, 146.

[2] Jointly with Cluny. Marrier gives it as dependent on Cluny. See above.

[3] Also given by Marrier as directly dependent on Cluny. See above.

[4] The church was dedicated in 1052. See Schapiro in *Art Bulletin*, XI, June 1929, p. 230.

[5] Belonged to Moissac before it was Cluniac: it was the birthplace of Saint-Didier, the founder of the abbey. See *Cong. Arch.* XCII, p. 346.

[6] Ceded to Fontevrault in 1132. Valous, II, 214.

[7] Sculptures in the Musée des Augustins. The priory was given to Cluny for reformation in 1076 by Isarn de Lavaur, Bishop of Toulouse; it entered the Order after some resistance. Pignot, II, 199.

Toulouse, dependencies (*cont.*)

Mondonville (Saint-Pierre), Haute-Garonne. B. iv, 292

Saint-Martin-de-Cormières, Le Vibal, Aveyron. B. iv, 95

Sévérac-l'Église (Notre-Dame), Aveyron. B. iv, 102

Toulouse (Saint-Pierre-des-Cuisines), Haute-Garonne

Vabres, Aveyron. R.

Valuéjols, Cantal. B. v, 288

Virargues (Saint-Jean-Baptiste), Cantal. B. v, 289

Val d'Olette, Pyrénées-Orientales[1]. R.

Villematier (Saint-Pierre), Haute-Garonne. R.

Villeneuve d'Aveyron (Saint-Sépulchre), Aveyron. R.

Toulouse (Saint-Étienne)[2]

Morlaas (Sainte-Foy), Basses-Pyrénées[3]

Mouchan (Saint-Austrégésile), Landes[4]. V.

Rombœuf (Sainte-Catherine), Fourcès, Gers

Sainte-Colombe, Lot-et-Garonne[5]

Monasterium Sanctae Geneverae (in Agennais)[6]

Saint-Lézer-sur-l'Adour, Hautes-Pyrénées[7]

Saint-Loury, Auch, Gers[8]

Saint-Mont (Saint-Jean), Gers[9]

dependency

Riscle, Gers. B. iii, 19

Saint-Pons-de-Thomières, Hérault[10]

dependencies

La Bruguière, Castries, Hérault. B. iv, 250

Caunes (Saint-Pierre), Aude. B. iv, 123[11]

Cessenon, Hérault. B. iv, 249

Escosse, Ariège. B. iv, 327

Lautrec, Tarn. B. iv, 51

La Livinière, Hérault. B. iv, 249

Prémian, Hérault. B. iv, 250

Saint-Étienne-de-Clamous, Malves, Aude. B. iv, 176

Saint-Jaume, Lézignan, Aude. B. iv, 128

Saint-Jean-de-Caps, Mailhac, Aude. B. iv, 128

Saint-Marcel-de-la-Mignarde, Pépieux, Aude. B. iv, 129

Saint-Martin-Lys, Aude

Saint-Paul-de-Massuguiès, Tarn. B. iv, 15

La Salvetat-sur-Agout. Hérault, iv, 250

Terre-Clapier, Tarn. B. iv, 15

Valtoret, Saint-Amans-Valtoret, Tarn. B. iv, 51

in catalonia

Saint-Benoît-de-Bages[12]

Vianne (Notre-Dame), Lot-et-Garonne. B. iii, 147

---

[1] Given to Moissac in 1077. Pignot, ii, 196.

[2] It entered the Order at the same time as La Daurade but did not stay in it very long.

[3] Given to Cluny in 1077 by Centule II, Count of Béarn, brother of Abbot Hunald of Moissac, in expiation of a marriage within the prohibited degrees. Pignot, ii, 197.

[4] Valous (ii, 213) gives it as dependent on Auch.

[5] Given to Cluny between 1031 and 1048. Sackur, ii, 83, note 1; Pignot, i, 416.

[6] Given in 1067. Bernard and Bruel, iv, 520.

[7] Given to Cluny by Bernard I, Comte de Bigorre, and his relative Heraclius, Bishop of Tarbes, in 1064. Bruel, iv, 3402; Pignot, ii, 193.

[8] Became Cluniac in 1087. Pignot, ii, 194.

[9] Given to Cluny in 1062 by Bernard Tumapaller, Comte d'Armagnac. Pignot, ii, 192; Migne, *Pat. Lat.* clix, col. 8.

[10] Sculptures in the Museum of Montpellier, the Louvre, Metropolitan Museum, New York, Museum of Fine Art, Boston and (1937) a Paris dealer. The priory was given to Cluny by Raymond de Saint-Gilles in 1080. Pignot, ii, 204; Bruel, iv, 3009.

[11] Founded before 791, it became dependent on Saint-Pons only after 1182; the existing church is pre-Cluniac.

[12] See Deschamp in *Mélanges...offerts à M. Ferdinand Lot*, p. 162.

PROVINCE OF GERMANY, LORRAINE
AND THE COUNTY OF BURGUNDY[1]

Altkirch (Saint-Morand), Haut-Rhin[2]
DEPENDENCY
Steinach, Haut-Rhin
Bâle (Saint-Alban), Switzerland[3]
DEPENDENCIES
Biesheim (Saint-Jean-Baptiste), Haut-Rhin.
Val.
Enschingen, Haut-Rhin
Bargenbrück, Switzerland[4]
BAUME-LES-MESSIEURS, Jura (abbey)
DEPENDENCIES
Bonnevent, Gy, Haute-Saône
P. de Capella
P. de Coye
Dôle, Jura
JOUHE (SAINT-PIERRE), Jura[5]
Jussanmouthier, Besançon, Doubs[5]
Lantenot, Haute-Saône
LONS-LE-SAULNIER (SAINT-DESIRÉ)[6], Jura
MOUTHEROT, Doubs
Mouthiers-en-Bresse, Saône-et-Loire
Poligny, Jura
Mon. Sancti Eugendi Eticae[5]
SAINT-LOTHAIN, Jura
Mon. Sanctae Mariae Grandifontis[5]
SAINT-RAMBERT-EN-BUGEY, Ain[7]
Salmaise, Côte-d'Or[8]
Bevais (Saint-Pierre), Neufchâtel, Switzerland[9]

Château-sur-Salins (Notre-Dame), Jura
Chaux-lès-Clerval, Doubs
Corcelles, Switzerland[10]
Eberlinsmatt, Haut-Rhin. Val.
Erstein, Bas-Rhin. Val.
Feldbach, Haut-Rhin[11]
Froidefontaine, territoire de Belfort[12]
FRONTENAY (LA MADELEINE), Jura[13]
FROVILLE, Meurthe-et-Moselle[14]
DEPENDENCY
P. de Frouilla-bosco
Grandval, Switzerland. Val.
Hettiswyl (Sainte-Croix), cn. Berne, Switzerland[15]
DEPENDENCY
Luizigen, cn. Berne, Switzerland[16]
Île-Saint-Pierre, lac de Bienne, cn. Berne, Switzerland[17]
Lieudieu, Doubs
MIÈGES (SAINT-GERMAIN), Jura
Morteau (Saint-Pierre et Saint-Paul), Doubs
Mouthier-Hautepierre, Doubs[18]
MÜNCHENWILER (Villars-les-Moines), cn. Berne, Switzerland[19]
PAYERNE, Vaud, Switzerland[20]
DEPENDENCIES
Bassins, Nyon, Vaud, Switzerland. B. IX, 242

---

[1] Valous includes several houses in the dioceses of Paderborn, Cologne, etc., which I omit.
[2] Given in 1105. Bernard and Bruel, v, 194.
[3] Given to Cluny by Burkard von Haselburg, Bishop of Bâle, in 1083. Egger in *Millénaire*, I, 376.
[4] Egger in *Millénaire*, I, 374. Valous (II, 250) gives it as dependent on Hettiswyl.
[5] By 1106. Bernard and Bruel, v, 196.   [6] The crypt is Romanesque.
[7] This is said to have joined the Order in 1138, but the affiliation did not prove effective. B. X, 80. Valous identifies it with Quingey, Doubs.
[8] Salmaise, Saône-et-Loire was dependent on Saint-Bénigne-de-Dijon. See *Bull. de la Soc. nat. des Ants. de France*, 1906, p. 346.
[9] Given to Cluny in 998. Pignot, I, 322.   [10] Founded in 1092. Egger in *Millénaire*, I, 376.
[11] Founded in 1144 by Frederick, Count of Ferrette. Valous, II, 252.
[12] Founded in 1105 by Hermentrude de Montbéliard. Valous, II, 252.
[13] A dependency of Cluny before 1109. B. X, 171.   [14] Given to Cluny in 1091. Bruel, v, 9.
[15] Founded in 1107. Egger, *loc. cit.*   [16] Egger, p. 377.
[17] Given by Guillaume l'Allemand, Count of Burgundy and Mâcon, in 1107. Pignot, II, 241.
[18] Given to Cluny in the time of Abbot Pons. Marrier, p. 577.
[19] Founded by Gerald and Rudolf von Vilar in time of Abbot Hugh. Egger in *Millénaire*, I, 376.
[20] Dedicated to the Virgin, Saints Peter, John and Maurice. Sackur, I, 218. Given to Cluny by the Empress Adelaide soon after 966. Pignot, I, 253.

PAYERNE, DEPENDENCIES (*cont.*)
    Baulmes, Switzerland[1]
    Brussins, Vaud, Switzerland. Egger
    Colmar (Saint-Pierre), Haut-Rhin
    Léaz (Saint-Amand), Ain
    Prévessins, Ain. Egger
Port-sur-Saône, Haute-Saône
RELANGES, Vosges[2]
ROMAINMÔTIER (SAINT-PIERRE ET SAINT-PAUL),
    Switzerland[3]
    DEPENDENCIES
    Brusins, Gilly, Rolle, Switzerland. B. IX, 243
    Corcelles-près-Moûtiers, Neufchâtel, Swit-
    zerland[4]
    Gimel, Switzerland. Val.
    Lay-Damp-Waultier, lac de Saint-Point,
    Doubs
    ROUGEMONT (SAINT-NICOLAS), Switzerland[5]
    Vallorbe, Switzerland
    Villeneuve, Valais, Switzerland. Val.

    Vufflens, Switzerland. Val.
RUEGGISBERG (SAINT-PIERRE ET SAINT-PAUL),
    cn. Berne, Switzerland[6]
    DEPENDENCY
    Rotenbach (Notre-Dame), cn. Berne, Swit-
    zerland. Val.
SAINTE-MARIE-AUX-BOIS, Meurthe-et-Moselle[7]
Sankt Ulrich, Zell, Baden[8]
Salins (Saint-Nicolas), Jura
Sölden, Baden (nuns)[9]
Thicourt, Moselle[10]
Thierenbach (Notre-Dame), Haut-Rhin
Vaucluse, Doubs[11]
VAUX-SUR-POLIGNY (NOTRE-DAME), Jura[12]
    DEPENDENCY
    Montrond, Jura. Val.
Velpach, Bâle (nuns)[13]
Vendœuvre, Meurthe-et-Moselle
Villars-les-Moines. *See* Münchenwiler
Ysteim

PROVINCE OF LOMBARDY[14]

•

P. Sancti Vitalis de Vrsiniaco, alias de Arciniaco.
    See Ursiniaco
Argano (San Paolo)[15], dioc. Bergamo
    DEPENDENCY
    P. Sancti Pauli de Lacu
Bagnaia (San Giovanni), dioc. Vercelli
P. de Burgo de Ultimano, dioc. Vercelli
Calvenzano (Santa Maria)[16], dioc. Milan

Cantù, Como (nuns: abbey)[17]
CAPO DI PONTE (SAN SALVATORE), dioc. Brescia[18]
Castelletto del Cervo (San Pietro), dioc. Vercelli
P. Sanctae Iuliae de Cazago, dioc. Brescia (?Cazzago
    S. Martino)
Cernobbio (Santa Maria), Como
    DEPENDENCY
    BADIA DI VERTEMATE (SAN GIOVANNI)[19]

---

[1] Founded by 1125. Egger, *loc. cit.*
[2] Given to Cluny *c.* 1030. Bruel, IV, 41.
[3] Founded in the middle of the fifth century, it became Cluniac by the gift of Adelaide, Duchess of Burgundy, in 929. Naef, p. 8; Pignot, I, 143.
[4] Charrière, p. 116.
[5] Given in 1093. Bernard and Bruel, V, 23.
[6] Founded by Lütold von Rümlingen in 1070. Egger in *Millénaire*, I, 375.
[7] Later Premonstratensian.
[8] Given to Cluny in 1087. Bruel, IV, 3622.
[9] Founded in 1115 by Gerold von Scherzingen. Valous, II, 257.
[10] Given in 1093. Bernard and Bruel, V, 23. Valous identifies as Thiaucourt, Meurthe-et-Moselle.
[11] Founded by Thibaut, Seigneur de Rougemont. Pignot, II, 241; Bruel, V, 206.
[12] The church should perhaps be accounted Gothic rather than transitional. The priory was given to Cluny *c.* 1030. Pignot, I, 413.
[13] Given in 1144. Bernard and Bruel, V, 445.
[14] Abbot Mayeul reformed Sant' Apollinare in Classe at Ravenna and San Pietro in Ciel d' Oro at Pavia, but these were not included in the Order of Cluny. Monsieur Enlart (in Michel, *Histoire de l'art*, I, 550 and *Revue de l'art chrét.* 1913, p. 1) is inclined to attribute various Italian churches, notably Sant' Antimo near Montalcino in Tuscany, to the Order of Cluny, but there is no evidence whatever for such an attribution.
[15] Founded in 1079. Pignot, II, 290.
[16] This was Cluniac by 1095; alterations were then made to the earlier church. A. Kingsley Porter, *Lombardic Architecture*, II, 225.
[17] Founded 1084. A. Kingsley Porter, II, 82.
[18] Confirmed to Cluny in 1095. A. Kingsley Porter, III, 48.
[19] Founded 1084, consecrated 1095. A. Kingsley Porter, II, 82.

Cremona (San Gabriele)[1]
DEPENDENCY
    Cremona (Sant' Ippolito)
FONTANELLA (SANT' EGIDIO)[2]
P. Sanctorum Nazarii et Celsii de Gercola, dioc.
    Brescia
Lodi (San Marco)[3]
P. Sancti Petri de Magdaniano, dioc. Crema[4]
P. de Othigniaco
Padilorone (Saint-Benoît-sur-le-Po), Mantua
    (abbey)[5]
DEPENDENCY
    San Martino "de Collines", nr. Lucca.
    Pignot, II, 293
Pavia (San Maiol)[6]
Pavia (San Niccolò)
DEPENDENCY
    Piacenza (San Gregorio)
P. Sancti Nicolai de Payona, dioc. Como (?Pagnona)
PONTIDA (SAN GIACOMO), Bergamo[7]

DEPENDENCIES
    SAN COLOMBANO, Vaprio[8] d' Adda
    P. de Gerula
PROVAGLIO D' ISEO (SAN PIETRO IN IAMOSA)[9],
    dioc. Brescia
DEPENDENCY
    Clusane sul Lago, Iseo
Rodigo (San Niccolò)
Rodobbio (San Valeriano), Vercelli[10]
Signa (San Niccolò)
SAN BENEDETTO IN PORTESANA, dioc. Bergamo
P. Sancti Salvatoris de Thigiis, dioc. Brescia
P. de Ulzato
P. de Ursiniaco, seu Arciniaco
DEPENDENCY
    P. Sancti Benedicti de Cousano
Venice, Santa Croce. Pignot, II, 254[11]
P. Sancti Nicolai de Verziano, dioc. Brescia[12]
DEPENDENCY
    P. de Quinsano, dioc. Brescia

PROVINCE OF SPAIN

[Arles-sur-Tech (Notre-Dame), Pyrénées-
    Orientales][13]
Budiño (San Salvador), near Tuy[14]
Burgos (Santa Colomba)[15]
Campomodo (San Jaime)[16]
[Camprodon, San Pere][13]
Carrión de los Condes (San Zoil)[17]

DEPENDENCY
    Fromista (San Martín)[18]
Casseres (San Pere)[19]
DEPENDENCIES
    Sancti Petri de Clarano
    Sancti Pontii de Corbaria
Ciudad Rodrigo (Santa Agata)[20]

[1] Pignot (II, 290) gives the dedication to Saints Gabriel and Raphael. It was founded in 1077.
[2] Begun about 1080, consecrated 1090, badly restored 1910–12. A. Kingsley Porter, II, 422.
[3] Pignot (II, 290) gives the dedication to Saints Mark, Fabian and Sebastian. It was founded in 1068.
[4] See A. Lubin, *Abbatiarum Italiae brevis Notitia*, Rome 1693.
[5] Given to Cluny by the Empress Matilda in 1080. Pignot, II, 293. See A. Kingsley Porter, III, 358.
[6] Founded under Mayeul in 967. Sackur, I, 223. Originally San Salvatore.
[7] Founded in 1087. Pignot, II, 290. The existing edifice is Gothic; fragments of the Romanesque tomb of Sant' Alberto survive.
[8] Professor Kingsley Porter (III, 452) found nothing to show its early history.
[9] Given to Cluny in 1083. The two eastern bays of the north aisle and a fragment of the original apse are Romanesque. A. Kingsley Porter, III, 50.   [10] Founded in 1082. Pignot, II, 290; Bruel, IV, 3591.
[11] Dependent on La Charité before 1102.   [12] See Lubin, *op. cit.*
[13] Given above.   [14] Given to Cluny 1126 by Gómez Núñez and his brother. Valous, II, 263.
[15] Given to Cluny in 1077 by Alfonso of Leon and Castille. Pignot, II, 114.
[16] Given to Cluny by the same in 1077. Pignot, II, 114.
[17] Given to Cluny in 1095 by Teresa, widow of Count Gómez Díaz. Pignot, II, 115. Valous (II, 263) gives the date as 1076.
[18] This did not belong to San Zoil until 1112; the fine church dates from 1066.
[19] Given to Cluny 1079 by Raymond Foulques, Count of Cerdagne. Valous, II, 264.
[20] Given to Cluny by Ferdinand II of Castille between 1157 and 1161. Valous, II, 264.

*Abbatia quae vocatur Corneliana, in Asturia, dioc.
    Oviedo*[1]
Entrapeñas (San Román), León[2]
Gerri, Urgel[3]
JUBIA (SAN MARTÍN), Naron, prov. Coruña[4]
*Sancti Christophori de Layre in Nauarra prope
    Sarragosse*[5]
Najera (Santa Maria)[6]
Ombres, Portugal
Omiliana[6]
Palencia (San Isidoro). Val.[7]
P. Sancti Banduli de Pinal, dioc. Segovia
POMBEIRO (SAN VICENTE), Pantón, prov. Lugo[8]

[Rates (Santa Maria), Portugal][9]
Rodinum[2]
Salamanca (San Vicente)[10]
San Isidro de Dueñas, Pisuerga[11]
San Martino de Nebda[2]
Saragossa (San Adriano)
Domus de Tauro
Villafranca de Valcárcel (Santa Maria de
    Cluny)
Villaverde (San Salvador)[12]
Villaverde Palomar[2]
Vimeiro (Santa Maria), Portugal[13]
[Zamora (San Miguel)][9]

PROVINCE OF ENGLAND AND SCOTLAND

[Arthington, Yorks.][14]
[Barnstaple (Saint Mary Magdalene), Devon][15]
[Bermondsey (Saint Saviour), Middlesex][14]
    DEPENDENCY
    Derby (Saint James)[16]
Church Preen. Guilloreau[17]
Dalmullen, Ayrshire. Guilloreau[18]
Daventry (Saint Augustine). Guilloreau

Dudley, Worcs.[19]
[Exeter (Saint James), Devon][20]
Fail, Ayrshire. Guilloreau[21]
[*Failihigia, dioc. Salisbury (nuns?)*][22]
Kirkby, Yorks.
Lenton (Holy Trinity), Notts.[23]
    DEPENDENCY
    P. de Rupe

[1] Robert and Fita, in *Boletín de la real Academia de historia*, Madrid, xx, 1892, p. 321, give this as Cornellana.   [2] See Yepez, *Cronica general de San Benito*, iv, pp. 198, 201, 319.
[3] Given to Cluny c. 1066. Pignot, ii, 193.
[4] Given to Cluny in 1113 by Pedro, Count of Galicia. Valous, ii, 264.
[5] Conceivably, the well-known church of San Salvador de Leire; if so it only belonged to Cluny for a very short time.   [6] Founded by Garcia of Navarre in 1052.
[7] Given to Cluny in 1073 by Alfonso VI of Leon and Castille.
[8] Given to Cluny in 1117 by Doña Urraca, daughter of Alfonso VI of Leon.
[9] Given above.   [10] Given to Cluny in 1143 by Alfonso VIII.
[11] Given to Cluny in 1072 by Alfonso VI of Leon and Castille. Pignot, ii, 114.
[12] Given to Cluny in 1075 by Iñigo Bermúdez.
[13] Given to Cluny in 1127 by Teresa, Queen of Portugal.   [14] Dependent on La Charité. See above.
[15] Founded by Joel of Totnes c. 1107. Dependent on Saint-Martin-des-Champs, Paris. See above.
[16] Given to Bermondsey by William FitzSweyn in the middle of the twelfth century.
[17] In *Millénaire*, i, 291.
[18] Sometimes spelt Dalmelling. Founded in 1229 as a priory of the Order of Sempringham, it soon lapsed, and its revenues were granted to Paisley and a cell seems to have been refounded there in 1268. (I owe this information to the kindness of Miss M. E. Barbour Simpson.)
[19] Founded by Gervase Paynel in the middle of the twelfth century. Valous (ii, 259) gives it as dependent on Much Wenlock.
[20] Dependent on Saint-Martin-des-Champs, Paris. Founded by the Earl of Devon c. 1148.
[21] A Trinitarian house (Mathurins) was founded here in 1252. By 1459 it had fallen into such ill-repute that the King and Queen complained to the Pope. Its relation with Cluny, if any, remains obscure. (Miss M. E. Barbour Simpson.) Valous (ii, 260) gives it as dependent on Paisley.
[22] Dependent on Marcigny. See above. Possibly Monkton Farleigh, Wilts.
[23] Founded by William Peverel and his family between c. 1105 and c. 1109. Bruel, iv, 3626.

LEWES (SAINT PANCRAS), Sussex[1]
  DEPENDENCIES
    Bromholm, Norfolk[2]
    CASTLEACRE, Norfolk[3]
    Clifford (Saint Mary), Herefordshire[4]
    Mendham
    MONK'S HORTON, Kent[5]
    MONKTON FARLEIGH (SAINT MARY MAGDA-
      LENE), Wilts.[6]
    P. de Reychin
    Prittlewell, Essex[7]
    Stanesgate, Essex[8]
    Treffort
MONK BRETTON, Yorks. Guilloreau
Montacute, Somerset[9]
  DEPENDENCIES
    East Holme or Holne, Dorset[10]
    Kerswell, Devon[11]

Malpas, Cheshire
[MUCH WENLOCK (SAINT MILBURGA), Salop][12]
Newton Longueville, Bucks. Guilloreau[13]
Normansburgh, Norfolk. Guilloreau
Northampton (Saint Andrew's)[14]
Paisley, Scotland (abbey)[15]
  DEPENDENCY
    Crossraguel, Ayrshire (abbey)[16]
[Pontefract (Saint John the Evangelist), Yorks.][17]
Saint Cadix, Cornwall. Guilloreau
[Saint Clear's, Carmarthen][18]
Saint Helen's, Isle of Wight. Guilloreau
SLEVESHOLM, Methwold, Norfolk
THETFORD (SAINT MARY), Suffolk[19]
  DEPENDENCIES
    Little Horkesley, Essex
    Wangford, Suffolk
Witchingham, Norfolk

ASIA MINOR

Civitot, Constantinople[20]
Palmareia *in diocese* of Tiberias[22]

SAINT SAVIOUR ON MOUNT TABOR[21]

[*Note.* Lecestre[23] gives certain additional houses as belonging to the Order, but these only joined it at the time of the Benedictine reforms in the seventeenth century.

BARRAUX, Isère
CHAMALIÈRES, Haute-Loire
SAINTE-ÉNIMIE, Florac
LANGOGNE, Mende, Haute-Loire
MANGLIEU, Puy-de-Dôme

MONASTIER-SAINT-CHAFFRE, Le Puy, Haute-
  Loire
SAINT-ROMAIN-LE-PUY, Saint-Rambert
SÉVÉRAC-LE-CHÂTEAU, Rodez, Aveyron
Their dependencies will be found in B.]

[1] Founded by William de Warenne and his wife Gundrada in 1077. Bruel, I, 3536.
[2] Founded by William de Warenne. Bruel, v, 3748.   [3] Founded by William de Granville in 1113.
[4] Founded by Simon FitzRichard in the reign of Henry I.
[5] Founded by Humphrey de Bohun in 1125.
[6] Founded by Robert de Vere in the reign of Henry II.
[7] Given to Lewes by Robert FitzSweyn in the reign of Henry I. The surviving church is not that of the priory, but the parish church which belonged to the priory.
[8] Founded by Robert FitzBrian before 1121.   [9] Given to Cluny by William de Mortain *c.* 1102.
[10] Founded by Robert de Lincoln.   [11] Founded by Matilda Peverel.
[12] Dependent on La Charité. See above.   [13] Dependent on Sainte-Foy-de-Longueville. See above.
[14] Given to Cluny by Simon de Senlis, Earl of Northampton and Huntingdon, in 1084.
[15] Founded by Walter Fitz-Alan in 1169.   [16] Founded in 1240.
[17] Dependent on La Charité. See above.
[18] Dependent on Saint-Martin-des-Champs, Paris. See above.   [19] Founded by Roger Bigod in 1104.
[20] Pignot, II, 254; given by Alexis Comnenus, dependent on La Charité before 1102. By the time of Peter the Venerable it had lapsed. He claimed it and sent monks from La Charité to ask John Comnenus for its restitution, apparently in vain. *Ibid.* III, 298.
[21] Given to Cluny by Tancred, Prince of Galilee, *c.* 1100. It was destroyed by the Saracens in 1113, but was rebuilt, to be finally destroyed by Saladin in 1187. Enough remains to establish the plan. Pignot, II, 161. Enlart puts its donation to 1130. (And see Migne, *Pat. Lat.* CXXXIX, col. 226; *Monuments des Croisés*, II, 380.)   [22] Given 1170–80. Bernard and Bruel, v, 590.
[23] *Abbayes, prieurés et couvents d'hommes...en* 1768, p. 4.

ARCHITECTURE

Part I

ABBEY AND PRIORY CHURCHES

A. GROUND PLAN

THE FOCUS of Cluniac life was the choir of the monastic church and the altar in its midst; and it followed that this was the centre round which Cluniac churches—like all Benedictine churches—were built. The high altar, indeed, was made the first feature to strike the visitor in most of the great churches of the Order; both at Cluny and Souvigny the west door was entered down a flight of steps, whence the altar could be seen in its aureole of columns, at the end of the long stretch of the nave[1]. In Saint-Eutrope-de-Saintes there is a descent into the nave, and the choir is above a crypt; while in the great church of La Charité and in the priory church of Moirax the floor of the choir slopes towards the nave, as the stage of a theatre slopes towards the auditorium. Similar plans were adopted even in lesser churches: at Salles-en-Beaujolais there are five steps down on entering, and the whole floor slopes downwards towards the altar. At Airaines there are fourteen steps downwards at the entrance, and there are lesser flights at Carennac, Médis, Lozay, Corme-Écluse and Saint-Lazare-d'Avallon. At Jailly the whole church follows a natural rise in the ground, with steps at each bay: at Bourg-de-Thizy and Fontanella there is a sharp rise up to the apse, and at Arnac a steep ramp down to it. Moreover, the colour of the church was concentrated round the high altar: in the frescoes of the apse, as at Cluny and Berzé; in embroidered curtains hung behind it for feasts; in painted sculptures[2] and in its own festal decorations of golden altar frontal, silver ciborium, and jewelled reliquaries, chalices, candlesticks and Gospel

[1] At Saint-Benoît-sur-Loire—Benedictine and not Cluniac, though reformed by Odo—the choir is raised above a crypt. This use was fairly common when the church contained the body of a saint, as Saint-Benoît did that of Saint Benedict; but though it appears in the Cluniac churches of Saint-Germain-d'Auxerre and Saint-Eutrope-de-Saintes, which both held the bodies of their patron saints, it is not characteristically Cluniac.

[2] E.g. at Berzé-la-Ville. At Cluny the sculpture in soft stone was coloured in soft orange-red, ochre, yellowish green and dull blue, but that in hard stone was not. The capitals of Mozat still show distinct traces of red and green colour. At Ternay the capitals of the apse alone show traces of colour.

Books[1]. Here, too, the patterns of the inlaid floors were richest[2]: lions and griffins[3], signs of the zodiac, and figures of men[4] and saints[5].

The second natural need of a Cluniac church was space in the choir for the brethren of the community. The normal minimum was twelve, and many of the small dependent priories did not exceed this number in the course of their history[6]. But at Cluny itself, and in the great abbeys and priories of the Order, the numbers rapidly increased. At Cluny up to 1042 they had not exceeded 70[7]; by 1083 they were about 200[8]; and in 1144 they were as many as 460 monks[9]. At La Charité about 1080 there were 200[10]. Obviously, any ordinary church plan would have to be modified to accommodate such numbers; and a characteristic development of the apse and choir will be found in all the larger churches of the Order. At Paray and La Charité there are bays after the crossing before the apse; at Moirax a domed choir precedes the apse; in nearly all the churches of middle size the apse and crossing are developed to give space for the *chorus psallentium*. But if the main needs of the great Cluniac churches were those of the monks themselves, they yet also served the wants of a lay population of townsfolk and pilgrims, especially at the festival seasons. It is for their use[11] that many Cluniac churches, Cluny, Souvigny, Saint-Martial-de-Limoges, Paray, Payerne, Romainmôtier, Saint-Leu-d'Esserent and others, were furnished with a narthex or galilee before the west door.

These, however, were conveniences rather than liturgical necessities. Cluniac churches

[1] On those at Cluny, see Dr Rose Graham in *Archaeologia*, LXXX, 1930, p. 149 *et seq*. Saint-Martial was hardly less rich: Geoffrey II (1008–19) had a golden *corona* set with precious stones made to hang before the saint's tomb; Odolric (1025–40) ordered a Gospel Book with covers of gold; and Pierre du Barry, d. 1174, gave crosses, chalices, ampulla, book covers, reliquaries and candelabra. When Henry II of England looted it he took 52 marks weight of goldwork and 103 of silver from its treasury. L. Guibert, "L'orfèvrerie à Limoges", in *Soc. arch. et hist. du Limousin*, 1885, p. 45.

[2] The chief Cluniac mosaic that has survived is that at Ganagobie. A further parallel is provided by the mosaic floor found in the church of Saint-Geniès at Thiers. See L. Bréhier, *Les mosaïques mérovingiens de Thiers* (Clermont Ferrand, 1911), p. 6 and Pl. I. Philippe Bouché records: "La portion du sanctuaire [à Cluny] qui s'étend depuis le grand autel jusqu'au chœur avoit il y a vingt ans un mosaïque travaillé en roses, en étoiles, en échiquier, exprimé avec beaucoup de délicatesse."

[3] At San Benedetto di Padilorone, Saint-Bertin, Ganagobie and originally at Moissac. See Bédier, *Légendes Épiques*, IV, 366.   [4] At Ganagobie.

[5] At Cluny according to Saint Bernard (trans. Coulton, *A Medieval Garner*, p. 71) the pavement was inlaid with figures of angels and saints.

[6] Indeed, by the end of the Middle Ages the numbers in many of them had dropped to three or less. See p. 6.

[7] A. Wilmart in *Revue Mabillon*, XI, 1921, p. 117.

[8] Migne, *Pat. Lat.* CXLIX, col. 660.

[9] Marrier, col. 593; the usual maximum for a Benedictine monastery was about seventy monks. Butler, *Benedictine Monachism*, p. 210.

[10] Beaussart, p. 18.

[11] And not primarily for penitents, as Viollet-le-Duc suggests. (*Dict. rais. de l'arch.* I, 259.)

may be said to have been planned from the altars outwards; the rest was but a shell for the ritual centre within. I therefore propose to consider first the ground plans, then the interiors, and finally, as least important and least characteristic, the exterior elevations.

1. CHAPELS WITH TREFOIL APSES

When Berno and his monks came to Cluny in 910 they found a chapel dedicated to Saint Mary and Saint Peter upon the site and included in the gift of William of Aquitaine[1]. The deed of donation further mentions "capellae" so that there may have been more than one chapel on the site[2]. In the eighteenth century the tradition existed[3] that the first church of Cluny was that which still survived as the chapel of Saint Mary

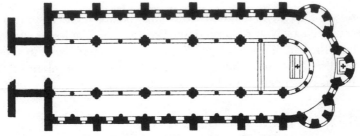

Fig. 2. Saint-Révérien, Nièvre. Plan. Twelfth century.

in the cemetery; it is shown on the late seventeenth-century plan of the abbey buildings (Fig. 13 a)[4], that is now one of the most important documents relating to them, as a small chapel differently oriented from the rest, with a nave of two bays, cut into by a later passage, and ending in a trefoil-shaped apse. I am inclined to think that this may have been the original chapel of the manor, and that its dedication to the Virgin survived when its other patron—Saint Peter—was honoured in the new church dedicated in 927[5]. At all events its size, 45 ft. long, 20 ft. wide and 23 ft. high[6] is rather that of the

[1] Marrier, col. 2. The chapel existed as early as 826, at the time when the land was exchanged between Varin and the Bishop of Mâcon. See J. de Valois in *Millénaire*, I, 190, and Virey in *Millénaire*, II, 249. A confirmation of this speaks of a monastery in honour of Saint Peter and Saint Paul built there and consecrated by Hildebald, Bishop of Mâcon (*Millénaire*, I, 183). This, however, may not be authentic.

[2] So does the Charter of 893 by which Ava cedes Cluny to her brother William "cum omnibus quae ad eam pertinent tam in ecclesiis quam et in capellis". *Millénaire*, I, 185.

[3] D. Martène, *Voyage littéraire de deux Bénédictins*, 1717, Pt I, 223; cf. Virey, *L'Abbaye de Cluny*, p. 15, n. 5. The chapel was destroyed in 1727.

[4] In the Musée Ochier, Cluny; published by M. Jean Virey in *Millénaire*, II, 236.

[5] Mr Clapham, in *Archaeologia*, LXXX, 1930, p. 166, has pointed out that this can hardly be the church of 927, though he is inclined to consider the cemetery chapel as being contemporary with the second church. Its orientation, however, is hardly compatible with this.

[6] According to the *Consuetudines Farfenses*. Albers, p. 137.

chapel of a manor than of the church of a monastery, and its plan is one common in early Christian architecture after the fifth century[1]. The trefoil apse is that of the chapel of Saint-Laurent at Grenoble, and of the lesser chapels of Saint-Honorat in the Île de Lérins that probably date from the eighth century[2].

The type was not a monastic one, and was not perpetuated in Cluniac churches[3]. The one real anomaly is the church of Saint-Maurice[4], which conforms to the usual Cluniac plan in having a small apse to the east in each arm of the transept, but has also a larger apse to north and south. The desire to have the altars oriented to the east must have been the reason why this scheme, architecturally satisfactory, was not followed elsewhere.

2. CHURCHES OF POLYGONAL PLAN

A quite exceptional church, that dated from long before its inclusion in the Order of Cluny, was the church of Notre-Dame-de-la-Daurade at Toulouse. It is said to have been built by the Visigoths on their way to Spain, and was ten-sided, and lit by a circular orifice in the middle. It seems to have had no influence on the plans of other churches in the Order; it was destroyed to make way for another church in 1773.

3. CHURCHES WITH A SINGLE APSE

The first church built by the monks of Cluny for their own use was that in which Berno, their first abbot, was buried[5]. It is, perhaps, this church that was consecrated in 916 or 917. We know little of its aspect, nor can we reconstruct it by comparison with Berno's buildings at Baume, for these were ruined by the Hungarians at the end of the tenth century[6]. Mr Clapham, in reconstructing the plan of the church that followed it, has suggested[7] that the earlier church was left standing to the north of its successor, and that it served as the sacristy. This sacristy is described[8] as being "58 ft. long with a tower in the head" with an adjoining building 45 ft. long, making a total of 103 ft. This, he suggests, is unusual for a sacristy at the time, and probably represents the church where Abbot Berno was buried, which had been divided and turned to subsidiary use. Professor Conant accepts his view of its re-use[9], and has drawn an illuminating parallel

---

[1] For its early history see A. Blanchet, "Les origines antiques du plan tréflé", in *Bull. Mon.* 1909; and O. M. Dalton, *East Christian Architecture*, p. 108.

[2] See *Bull. Arch.* 1893, p. 6. Other examples are the little chapels of Saint Sixtus and Saint Soter at Rome, Saint Martin and Saint Mary of the Capitol at Cologne, and Marignac. (R. de Lasteyrie, *Arch. rel. en France à l'époque romane*, p. 287.) A later example is Sainte-Croix-de-Montmajour, that Rivoira dates to 1016 (*Lombardic Architecture*, II, 34). For Catalonian examples see Puig y Cadafalch, *Premier art roman*, p. 98.

[3] Another trefoil-ended chapel is that projecting from the apse of Saint-Martin-des-Champs at Paris. See Fig. 18.   [4] Near Gençay, Vienne.   [5] Commonly called Cluny I.

[6] Roy, p. 9.   [7] *Archaeologia*, LXXX, 1930, p. 166.   [8] *Consuetudines Farfenses*, I, 138, 164.

[9] Lecture given at the Courtauld Institute of Art, 5 December 1935.

between the description of the sacristy, a tower shown in an early engraving of Cluny, and the surviving chapel of Saint-Laurent at Tournus[1]. This has been ascribed to the middle of the tenth century; but the herring-bone work of the walls would seem to indicate an earlier date, when Gallo-Roman traditions of building yet survived[2]. Its square apse indicates an early date and is hardly ever found in Cluniac buildings of the true Romanesque period[3]. Another church of the type was that of Prayes, which belonged to Cluny by 940. It is now unfortunately destroyed[4].

As the Order grew and developed, such single-apsed churches became characteristic of the smallest priories of the Order. A semicircular apse was universally used. Examples from the Rhône district are Saint-Jean-de-Rousigo[5], which appears to be very early, Tulette[6], and the adjacent chapel of Notre-Dame-du-Roure, Saint-Turquoît, and Notre-Dame-de-Caseneuve[7], and from Italy, San Benedetto in Portesana. Pommevic, a priory church of Moissac dedicated in 1052, follows the same plan. The type is also found, on a rather larger scale, in the Charente district: at Lozay, Saint-Palais-du-Né, Garat, Gourville and Moings; and elsewhere at Lisse, La Chapelle-Hugon, Saint-Mayeul (Veurdre), and Saint-Blaise-de-Genzac[8]. It occurs also in some of the granges and parish churches of the Order, for example at Massy and Blanot[9]. At Bésornay the apse is corbelled out on a cone-shaped base in a fashion that recalls the plan of the chapel of Saint Michael at Cluny itself[10]. The simplicity of this plan was not susceptible of great development. At Pont-du-Château, aisles are combined with a large apse; at Déols also there were aisles and these were continued to form an ambulatory round the

[1] See P. de Truchis, "La Chapelle Saint-Laurent à Tournus", in *Mém. de la Société des Antiquaires de France*, LXV, 1904–5, p. 1; and Dickson, *Les églises romanes de l'ancien diocèse de Chalon*, p. 311.

[2] The recent excavations at Cluny have confirmed the existence of a Gallo-Roman villa on the site.

[3] Cf. the square end of the Moutier-de-Thiers, of tenth-century date. *Cong. Arch.* LXXXVII, 1925, p. 287.

[4] See Virey, *L'Architecture romane dans l'ancien diocèse de Mâcon*, 2nd ed. p. 360. For a similar plan, not so early, cf. the Cluniac church of Vianne, with an aisleless nave, a deep apsidal choir entered through a narrow arch, and a plain square tower. Both arches and vaulting are *en plein centre*.

[5] See Labande, *Études d'hist. et d'arch. rom.* p. 141.

[6] Shallow apse-like niches in the side walls take the place of a transept; the church appears to be fairly late.   [7] See Labande, *Études d'hist. et d'arch. rom.* p. 124.

[8] Sometimes written Jonzac. See Thiollier, *Arch. rel. de l'ancien diocèse du Puy*, p. 142. The apse here is five-sided on the exterior and round within.

[9] And Bey, Colombier, La Frette, Ougy, Péronne, Saint-Martin-des-Champs, Sassangy, Savigny-sur-Seille, all in the department of Saône-et-Loire. It became the standard type of chapel in the castles of the Military Orders in the Holy Land, who carried on certain Benedictine traditions in other fields: e.g. at Safita (Chastel-Blanc), Marqab (Margat), Le Krak-des-Chevaliers, Kerak (Transjordan).

[10] Virey, 2nd ed. p. 93. It probably antedates the abbey church of Cluny.

single apse[1]. A similar plan is followed at Saint-Révérien (Fig. 2), but here the apse is enriched with three shallow radiating apsidal chapels: the result is one of great beauty, and it is probably because it did not successfully meet the liturgical needs of the Order that it was not more widely followed.

4. CHURCHES WITH A TRIPLE APSE

The next Cluniac church we know of was that dedicated at Souvigny in 920 or 921, of which recent excavations have revealed the plan[2]. It had aisles, a transept with an apsidiole to the east in either arm, a choir with an unusual arrangement of three semicircular niches $2\frac{1}{2}$ metres in diameter on either side, and what was almost certainly a semicircular apse. Thus it followed the traditional basilican plan:

Vertice sublimi patet aulae forma triformis[3],

with the addition of a transept and the development of subsidiary apsidioles on either side of the central apse[4].

It is not unlikely that this plan was followed in the church at Cluny dedicated in 927, in the time of Berno's successor Odo[5], but of this church we know nothing but its dedication to the patrons of the abbey, Saint Peter and Saint Paul[6].

We have, however, exact knowledge of the Cluniac church at Romainmôtier (Fig. 3)— the third on the site—which was probably begun at the end of the tenth century and finished early in the eleventh[7]. It had aisles, a transept, and a wide triple apse with almost level apses. The same plan was followed in the daughter house of Rougemont[8]. Variations of this form are typical of Cluniac churches all through the Romanesque period. The plan was well suited to the needs of a monastic church, since transept and choir were merged; and once the problem of vaulting the spacious crossing had been solved, the plan was architecturally satisfying in logic and dignity. With or without aisles and with varying proportions of transept and apsidal chapels, it is that which is

[1] It is possible that a similar plan was followed in the first church of Moissac, dedicated in 1063. The aisles were here very narrow. Anglès, p. 8.

[2] See Deshoulières in *Bull. Mon.* XCII, 1933, p. 480.

[3] Venantius Fortunatus, *Carm.* III, 7.

[4] The change was partly dependent on the rite of Milan, Gaul and Mozarabic Spain, in which the sacramental bread and wine were prepared at separate tables beside the altar. See Puig y Cadafalch, *Premier art roman*, p. 57. On the basilican plan see R. de Lasteyrie, *Arch. rel. en France à l'époque romane*, chaps. III, IV, and VII.

[5] Marrier, col. 32; and see Dr Rose Graham in *Archaeologia*, LXXX, 1930, p. 144.

[6] Bruel, *Recueil*, I, 264, 284.

[7] See Naef, *Guide à l'église de Romainmôtier*, p. 19. He considers that it was certainly finished before 1026.

[8] Of which the plan has been recently discovered by excavation. It is considerably later than Romainmôtier, dating from the years round 1100.

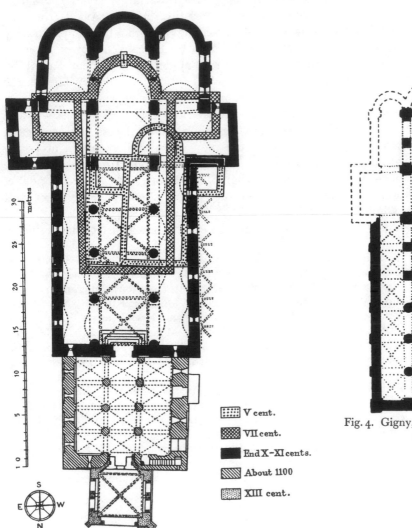

Fig. 3. Romainmôtier, Switzerland. Plan of the
Cluniac church, before 1026.

V cent.

VII cent.

End X–XI cents.

About 1100

XIII cent.

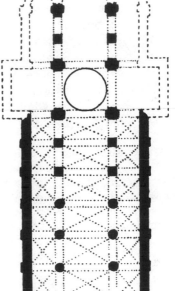

Fig. 4. Gigny, Jura. Plan. Eleventh
century.

EA

most typical of Cluniac priory churches of the middle size[1]. It was followed in the original church of Saint-Martin-des-Champs, dedicated in 1067[2], and in the eleventh-century church at Saint-Leu-d'Esserent[3]. It was used at Moirax a little later (Fig. 5) with the deepening of the central apse made necessary by a larger *chorus psallentium*. At Mezin the apsidioles are also deepened. A remarkably fine example of the type without aisles is the church of Saint-Martin-de-Layrac (Fig. 6) with a broad apse, a deep transept, and a noble simplicity of plan. It was built by Hunald, abbot of Moissac, between 1072 and 1085[4]. The plan recurs in Sainte-Foy-de-Morlaas, near Pau, built between 1078 and 1089 with deep apses and the central apse rather wider[5]. The church at Saint-Séverin-en-Condroz, begun in 1091, follows a similar plan with a characteristically lofty transept and low apses[6]. The church of Charlieu dedicated in 1094 was also of this type, but had a single apsidiole added to the central apse[7]. Baume-les-Messieurs, rebuilt between 1107 and 1139, probably on the plan of an earlier church at Gigny (Fig. 4) also falls into the same category[8]. The crypt of Saint-Lothain shows the same scheme, with the central apse slightly larger than the side ones. At Saint-Hippolyte, a Cluniac parish church, the transept and apses are brought into closer relation, and indeed form a single whole[9].

The plan was modified in various ways. In the church at Moissac, dedicated in

[1] E.g. with aisles: Brancion; Buxy; Capo di Ponte; Carennac; Castleacre; Champvoux; Charlieu (with a single projecting apsidiole); Châtelmontagne (originally); Cosne; La Croix (see Lefèvre-Pontalis, *Arch. rel. dioc. Soissons*, I, 183); Duravel; Gourdon; Iguerande; Jailly; Longpont; Lurcy-le-Bourg; Malay; Mezin; the first church at Monkton Farleigh; Mont-Saint-Vincent (originally); Morlaas; Le Moûtier-de-Thiers; Plauzat; Pommiers; Relanges; Rouy; Saint-Germain-les-Fossés; Saint-Laurent-en-Brionnais; Saint-Pierre-de-Montmartre (see *Bull. Mon.* LXX, vii, 1913, p. 5); Saint-Pierre-le-Moûtier; San Pietro in Ciel d' Oro at Pavia; Saint-Sauveur-de-Nevers (apse now destroyed); Salles-en-Beaujolais (originally); Semelay; Thetford; Vicq; Wenlock.

Without aisles: Bermondsey (dedicated in 1206); Brout; Cénac; Chantenay; Connaux; Corme-Écluse; Domène; Fontenet; Ganagobie; Marolles-en-Brie; cemetery chapel at Menat (now destroyed: plan in *Comm. des Mon. hist.*); Montambert; Montreuil-Bonnin; Mornac; Pouilly-lès-Feurs; Saint-Cydroine (this may originally have had aisles); Saint-Georges-de-Didonne; parish church of Saint-Mayeul at Cluny (original plan: *Bull. Mon.* LXXVI, 1912, p. 44); Ternay; Torsac.

In most of these the central apse projects; in a few—e.g. the chapel at Menat, the parish church at Semur-en-Brionnais, and in the priory church at Torsac—the apses are almost equal in depth.

[2] E. Lefèvre-Pontalis in *Cong. Arch.* LXXXII, 1919, p. 108.

[3] A. Fossard, *Le prieuré de Saint-Leu-d'Esserent*, p. 42.

[4] Aimeri de Peyrac, *Chron.* quoted Mortet, I, 147. Tholin, p. 41, dates it between 1063 and 1102.

[5] Plan in Laplace, *Notice historique... sur Sainte-Foi-de-Morlaas*, Frontispiece. Pau, 1865.

[6] See Schellekens in *Rev. de l'art chrét.* LVI, 1906, p. 88.

[7] Vallery-Radot in *Bull. Mon.* LXXXVIII, 1929, p. 244. He considers it may have been built between 1031 and 1048.

[8] The apse at Gigny has been rebuilt, but Professor Conant has pointed out that the sanctuary resembles that of Mayeul's church at Cluny.   [9] Brune in *Cong. Arch.* 1891.

1063[1], the aisles were continued round the apse as an ambulatory. In certain churches the transept projects so little that they approximate to the classical basilican plan: at Binson,

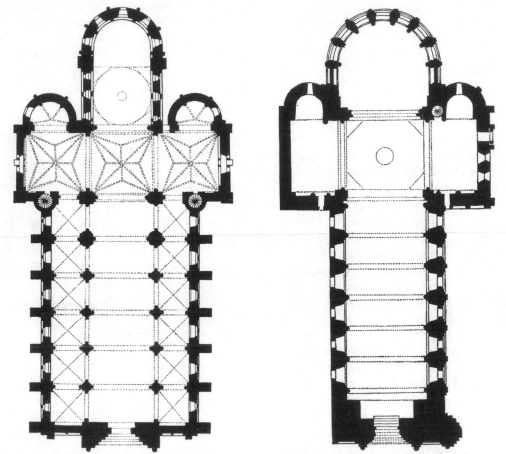

Fig. 5. Moirax, Lot-et-Garonne. Plan. Second half of eleventh century.

Fig. 6. Layrac, Lot-et-Garonne. Plan. Built by Hunald, Abbot of Moissac, between 1072 and 1085.

for example, where the east end probably dates from the end of the eleventh century[2], at Mont-Saint-Vincent[3], at Relanges where the sanctuary is little later[4], and in several

[1] The ground plan was revealed by excavations in 1901–3. See *Cong. Arch.* XCII, 1930, p. 495. For such an ambulatory (without radiating chapels), cf. the eleventh-century Benedictine church of Saint-Saturnin in the Auvergne.

[2] It became a priory of Coincy in 1077: Lefèvre-Pontalis, *Arch. rel. dioc. Soissons*, I, 180.

[3] L. de Contenson in *Bull. Mon.* LXXIV, 1910, p. 286.

[4] The priory was given to Cluny in 1030 and the donation confirmed in 1050. Durand, *Ég. rom. des Vosges*, p. 273.

parish churches belonging to the Order, at Retheuil[1], at Brancion[2] and Semur-en-Brionnais. At Mont-Saint-Vincent the apsidioles, like the apse, are lengthened choir-fashion by a rectangular bay. A few churches show peculiarities in the way that access is given from the subsidiary to the central apse. Some of these are reminiscent of the ambulatory of the second church at Cluny itself[3]. At Romainmôtier they are linked by an arcade[4]; and the same plan was followed in the original apse at Gigny[5], and to link the central apse to the next apsidioles in the fivefold apse at Bourbon-Lancy. At Rosiers-Côtes-d'Aurec there is a narrow arch in the wall between the subsidiary apses and the choir[6], as there is at Meymac. At Pérignac there is a bulge in the central apse to give a curvilinear passage into it round the piers of the crossing[7], comparable with the angular passages at Montbron and Droiturier. At Pouilly-lès-Feurs the transept is entered by a small arch in each aisle. These plans, however, have all a tentative and experimental air, and hardly succeed in forming an independent type.

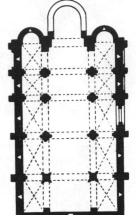

Fig. 7. Saint-Marc-de-Souvigny, Allier. Plan. *c.* 1150.

A few churches, mostly in the Velay, the Forez and Provence, show the local peculiarity of having the apse semicircular within, but polygonal or rectangular without. The exterior is polygonal at Vigeois, Rosiers-Côtes-d'Aurec, Landos, Sérignac, Ganagobie and Saint-Étienne-des-Sorts, and quadrangular at Pommiers-en-Forez. At Alleyras the apse is five-sided within, and is surmounted by a five-sided half dome. These, however, are exceptional local instances; they do not represent an approximation to the earlier angular treatment of the east end at Cluny.

The three-apsed plan with a transept was characteristically a monastic one, since it afforded a considerable space for the choir. Without a transept it was better fitted to meet congregational rather than monastic needs; and thus we find it commonly used for the parish churches owned by the Order. Typical examples are Saint-Marc-de-Souvigny (Fig. 7) and Saint-Lazare-d'Avallon[8]. It was, however, also followed in certain priory churches: at Arles-sur-Tech, of which the apse was consecrated in 1046, in the eleventh-century church of Saint-Germain-les-Fossés, in the destroyed church at Thizy[9], and in the crypt of Lons-le-Saulnier. The plan recurs at Bonneviolle and Saint-Julien-le-

[1] A dependency of Saint-Arnoul-de-Crépy. Lefèvre-Pontalis, I, 219.

[2] Virey in *Bull. Mon.* LXXIII, 1909, p. 276.   [3] See p. 63.

[4] See *Bull. Mon.* LXXVI, 1912, p. 446.   [5] *Loc. cit.* p. 470.

[6] Thiollier, *Art et arch. dans le Dép. de la Loire*, p. 21. Compare the passages from the transept into the apse at Saint-Romain-des-Îles.

[7] Plan in Guérin Boutard, p. 145.

[8] Less important examples are Saint-Point, Beaumont-sur-Grosne and Saint-Julien-de-Sennecey, all in the department of Saône-et-Loire.

[9] Virey, 2nd ed. p. x.

Pauvre at Paris, and in the distant priories of Sant' Egidio di Fontanella in Lombardy, consecrated in 1090[1] and the Cluniac church on Mount Thabor[2]. This had the apse and its flanking apsidioles built into a rectangular wall with a central projection, probably for purposes of defence. In the two rather larger churches that follow the plan—Saint-Sauveur-de-Nevers[3] (Fig. 8) and Saint-Aignan-de-Cosne—the central apse is considerably widened.

5. CHURCHES WITH FIVE OR MORE PARALLEL APSES

The next abbey church at Cluny was built by Mayeul and consecrated in 981[4]. It was not wholly destroyed when the final abbey church was built, but part of it survived as Saint-Pierre-le-Vieux[5]. An account written in 1623[6] describes "*La chapelle de Saint-Pierre-le-Vieil* au bout du grand dortoir vers l'église, quarronnée, voûtée, couvert de tuiles creuses, ayant plusieurs jours, la plupart sans vitres, a 40 pieds de long et de large, y compris les deux collatéraux 52 pieds. . . . Le cloître du côté de soir en partie occupé par un grand corps de logis dit *la chambrerie* composé de quelques agencements dans les masures et tours de l'ancienne église de Saint-Pierre. . . a de long 56 pieds sur 37 de large."[7] Saint-Pierre-le-Vieux is indicated on the late seventeenth-century plan of the abbey buildings

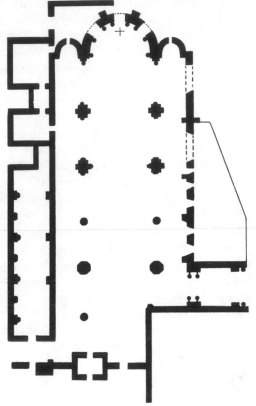

Fig. 8. Saint-Sauveur-de-Nevers, Nièvre. Plan. End of eleventh century.

[1] Kingsley Porter, *Lombard Architecture*, ii, 422.

[2] Enlart, *Monuments des Croisés*, ii, 380. It became Cluniac in 1130 and was razed to its foundations by Saladin in 1187.

[3] Now desecrated and partly ruined. In 1931 it was used as a livery stable.

[4] Marrier, cols. 560, 1619, 1635; *Millénaire*, ii, 231. Commonly called Cluny II.

[5] It is possible that such a partial survival may also account for a chapel with a very similar ground plan, that of Saint-Pierre-du-Sépulchre, that existed to the north of the abbey church of Saint-Martial-de-Limoges. (C. de Lasteyrie, Pl. II.) It was built in the tenth century (*ibid.* p. 321) and probably formed part of the pre-Cluniac abbey church. The same may be true of the chapel of Notre-Dame-des-Infirmes at Saint-Bertin, built between 1095 and 1123, but probably on older foundations.   [6] J. Virey in *Millénaire*, ii, 236.

[7] Professor Conant suggests (fig. 13 *b*) that these were adaptations of the narthex.

now in the Musée Ochier at Cluny[1]. It there appears as a small building, almost square, but for the rounded apse to the east.

The reconstruction of this church has been one of the intellectual exercises beloved of archaeologists. The first really serious attempt was that of Schlosser[2], who devised a plan with a square-ended apse broken by a central apsidiole. This was followed by Dehio and Bezold[3], who produced a flat-ended plan based on analogies with the church of Saint Peter of Hirschau, which, though it followed the customs of Cluny, was not included in the Order. Professor Mettler[4] then related Cluny with the semicircular apses of Saint Aurelius, Hirschau, rather than with the square-ended plan of Saint Peter's. Monsieur Vallery-Radot followed with the suggestion[5] that the second church at Cluny resembled Charlieu and Anzy-le-Duc.

The next important reconstruction was made by Mr Clapham[6], who ingeniously combined the indications afforded by the plan of Saint-Pierre-le-Vieux with the description of the abbey church given in the *Consuetudines*[7] written for the abbey of Farfa at a time when Mayeul's church was still the *ecclesia major* of the abbey. His plan gives an aisled church of five bays, preceded by a narthex of four. The transept has a semicircular niche in the east side of either arm, to hold the subsidiary altars of Saint Philip and Saint James and Saint John the Evangelist and Saint James; the apse has an ambulatory and three radiating chapels, to hold the three altars, which, the *Consuetudines* tell us, were behind the high altar. In the planning of the apse with angular chapels Mr Clapham followed that of the nearly contemporary abbey of Tournus; the apse of Tournus, however, is of extremely uncertain date[8].

Finally, Professor Kenneth Conant has been able to excavate enough of the apse of Mayeul's church to determine the shape of its eastern end, a shape natural enough in its main lines—a series of parallel apses—but so unusual in its details as not to be arrived at by any process of pure reasoning (Fig. 9).

---

[1] Published by M. Virey, *Millénaire*, ii, 231. Mabillon in 1682 found only the apse of the chapel surviving, and even this was destroyed in 1727.

[2] *Die abendländische Klosteranlage des früheren Mittelalters*, 1889, p. 51.

[3] *Die kirchliche Baukunst des Abendlandes*, i, 1892, p. 273.

[4] "Die zweite Kirche in Cluni und die Kirchen in Hirsau nach den 'Gewohnheiten' des XI. Jahrhunderts" in *Zeitschrift für Geschichte der Architektur*, iii, 1910, p. 273; and iv, 1911, p. 1 (Heidelberg).   [5] In *Bull. Mon.* 1929, p. 243.   [6] *Archaeologia*, lxxx, 1930, Fig. 2, p. 167.

[7] Mortet, *Recueil de Textes*, i, p. 133. The presence of a transept is in no way surprising. A type of early basilica found in North Africa, Syria and England has no aisles, but has a small square chamber on either side of the apse. This type is represented by the two pre-Cluniac churches at Romainmôtier (Fig. 6) dating from the fifth and seventh centuries, and the Cluniac church of Relanges (see Enlart, *Monuments des Croisés*, i, 48). When the use of aisles was revived, the tradition of these side chambers was perpetuated by a transept.

[8] See Gall, "Die Abteikirche Sankt Philibert in Tournus", in *Cicerone*, 1912, p. 624; and J. Baum, *Romanesque Architecture in France*, n.d. (*c.* 1932), p. xxii; Virey in *Bull. Mon.* vol. lxvii, 1903, p. 515; and *Cong. Arch.* vol. xci, 1929 (Dijon), p. 368.

Professor Conant's researches have revealed a triple apse, the central apsidiole considerably wider than those on either side, and a transept with a secondary apsidiole on either side, parallel to the rest. Such a plan is an ordinary and logical development of

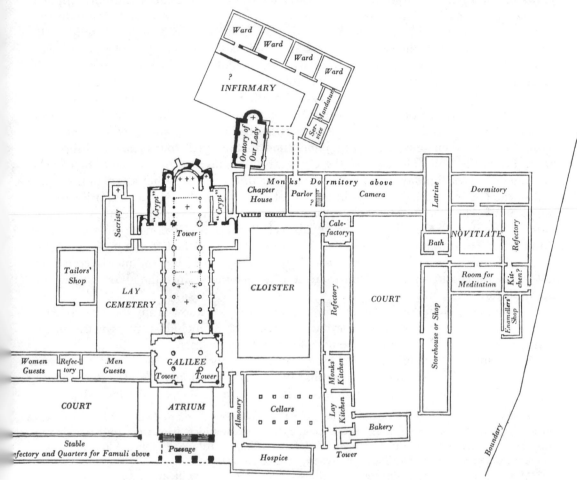

Fig. 9. Cluny, Saône-et-Loire. Reconstruction plan of the second church and monastic buildings at Cluny, begun about 955 and dedicated in 981. By Professor K. J. Conant. *Not definitive (Conant 1965: 183)*

the traditional triple apse: it is, indeed, what is known as the "Benedictine plan"[1]. But its appearance at Cluny is remarkable under several aspects. First, it is much the earliest example of such a plan. The church was consecrated in 981 and was probably

[1] "Le caractère essentiel d'un plan bénédictin consiste dans la longueur du chevet, flanqué de profondes absidioles qui s'ouvrent sur les croisillons et qui communiquent avec le chœur par une ou plusieurs arcades." E. Lefèvre-Pontalis in *Bull. Mon.* LXXVI, 1912, p. 440.

begun nearly fifty years earlier[1]: and the other monastic churches that follow the plan are later than this in date, and are historically dependent upon it[2]. Secondly, the apse is not circular on the exterior, but is treated with buttresses in an angular fashion that shows the architectural traditions of the early flat-ended Burgundian churches applied to another scheme. Thirdly, it has an ambulatory in the choir, but a square ambulatory[3]: and the high altar within this was not divided from the apse by a high and solid wall, but by a division that allowed the central apse and its subsidiary apsidioles[4] to appear as a noble setting to the high altar. Not only was the high altar (here dedicated to Saint Peter and Saint Paul, the patrons of the abbey) thus given a new beauty and a new importance, but fit places were also provided for other altars[5]. The chapel of Saint Mary and Saint John was in the middle of the apse, behind the high altar, with that of Saint Paul on the north and Saint Peter on the south. In the south transept was the altar of Saint John the Evangelist and Saint James, and in the north that of Saint Philip and Saint James the Less. The altar of the Cross, at which laymen might make their communion on Easter Sunday, was the principal altar in the nave. Other altars in the nave and in the chapels were dedicated in honour of Saint John the Baptist, Saint Bartholomew, Saint Thomas, Saint Stephen, Saint Martin, Saint Gregory, Saint Augustine, Saint Columban, Saint Taurin, Saint Marcel (bishop of Chalon-sur-Saône), Saint Philibert of Tournus and Saint Agatha. The altar of Saint Benedict was in the sacristy. Even with this increase, the *Consuetudines* written about 1083 bid the monk remember not to kneel too long in prayer, but to make way for others, since the altars are few for the multitude of monks[6].

To provide a choir large enough for the brethren we know from the *Consuetudines* that its enclosure was prolonged beyond the transept to include a part of the nave, leaving only the western bays of the nave for the use of laymen.

The scheme of Mayeul's abbey church was only applicable to the larger priories of the Order, and then usually on a scale that precluded an ambulatory. It is found with few modifications in the priory church of Saint-Nazaire-de-Bourbon-Lancy, which was

[1] Professor Conant pointed out to me in 1933 that as Abbot Aymard (who died in 953) was buried behind the matutinal altar, in the usual place for a founder, it was not unreasonable to suppose that Mayeul began the building while he was still Aymard's coadjutor, not long after 950. Mayeul himself was buried at Souvigny, where he died in 994.

[2] Many of the monastic churches that follow the scheme were built under Cluniac influence. The excavations at Charlieu suggest that it was followed there in the early tenth century. William of Volpiano who went from Cluny to Saint-Benigne-de-Dijon in 990, and rebuilt this before 1018, also influenced the building of Bernay (begun 1013), Mont-Saint-Michel and Cerisy-la-Forêt. The Cluniac origin of the "Benedictine" scheme was pointed out by Dehio and Bezold.

[3] Its existence is proved by the discovery of the pier at the angle. It is possible that there was such an ambulatory at Bernay.

[4] These must have been the "cryptae" mentioned in the *Consuetudines Farfenses*.

[5] On these see Dr Rose Graham in *Archaeologia*, LXXX, 1930, p. 147.

[6] Quoted, *Archaeologia*, LXXX, 1930, p. 153.

built between 1030 and the middle of the eleventh century[1], and probably of all surviving monuments gives the best idea of its greater prototype. The plan is followed without an ambulatory in the priory church of Payerne (Fig. 10), of which the east end probably dates from the second half of the eleventh century, and in the other Swiss house of Rueggisberg that is probably of the third quarter of the twelfth century; at Castleacre, begun in 1089, the year after Mayeul's church at Cluny was pulled down; at Thetford, built between 1107 and 1114[2]; and in the church at Ruffec pulled down soon after 1160[3]. A later instance of the same scheme is Saint-Marcel-lès-Sauzet, probably dating from the second half of the twelfth century. At Longueville a plan of 1752[4] shows the four secondary apses as rounded in the interior and flat outside[5].

Even the five apses of Cluny were not the final achievement. The scheme was further developed at La Charité (Fig. 11). The nave had double aisles, and the original apse, dedicated in 1107[6], had three apses of diminishing depth on either side of the central apse. Only the exterior two still exist[7], for even this splendid edifice was not allowed to continue unchanged, but was altered soon after it was finished in order to emulate more closely the mother church of Cluny as rebuilt by Abbot Hugh.[7]

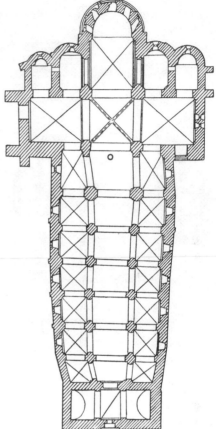

Fig. 10. Payerne, Switzerland. Plan. Second half of the eleventh century.

---

[1] See Perrault Dabot. [2] Both now ruined.

[3] Hubert and Barge in *Bull. Mon.* LXXXVIII, 1929, p. 205.

[4] *Bull. Mon.* VIII, 1893, p. 305.

[5] Instances of fivefold apses in Benedictine churches outside the Order of Cluny are not uncommon: e.g. Méobecq, Chezal-Benoît, Saint-Amant-de-Boixe, La Sauve. See Lefèvre-Pontalis in *Bull. Mon.* LXXVI, 1912, p. 464. None the less de Truchis describes the scheme with apses of diminishing depth as "essentiellement l'œuvre de Cluny". *Bull. Mon.* LXXX, 1929, p. 35.

[6] It was probably finished considerably earlier; Bishop Geoffrey of Auxerre was buried in it in 1076. Pertz, *Mon. Germ. hist. script.* XXVI, 1882, p. 49.

[7] Benedictine churches with seven apses are: Châteaumeillant, Cher; Saint-Sever, Landes; Saint Albans, Herts.; and Saint Mary's, York.

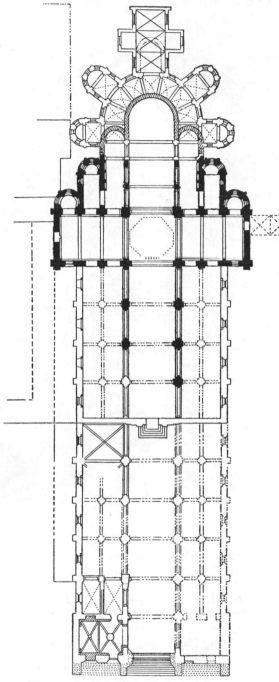

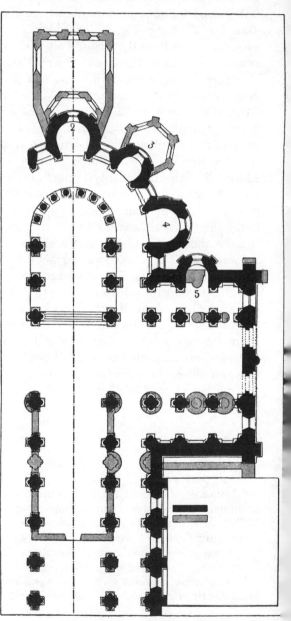

Fig. 11. La Charité-sur-Loire, Nièvre. Plan.
Consecrated 1107; the apse modified in the
middle of the twelfth century.
After Beaussart.

Fig. 12. Saint-Martial-de-Limoges, Haute-Vienne.
Reconstruction plan. Consecrated 1095.
After C. de Lasteyrie.

6. CHURCHES WITH RADIATING CHAPELS TO THE APSE

The "Benedictine" plan with parallel apses is characteristic of the earlier phase of the architectural history of the Order; the scheme with semicircular chapels radiating round the apse is characteristic of the later. Yet it is found in the crypt of Uzerche, begun in 1030, and presumably was followed in the church above; and it was followed by Abbot Hugh in his rebuilding of Saint-Martial-de-Limoges after its cession to the Order in 1062[1]. Though this was destroyed between 1792 and 1797, its disposition is definitely known from a plan made in 1784[2] (Fig. 12), which shows five radiating chapels round the apse, the central and terminal ones slightly larger than those intervening.

The earliest great example of an apse with semicircular radiating chapels was that of the basilica of Saint-Martin at Tours, which had five such chapels, the central one slightly larger than the rest[3]. The date of this is not absolutely certain, but it probably belongs to the late tenth century[4]. As at Saint-Martin the apse at Limoges was deepened to provide a noble setting for the high altar; and the plan was enriched by the transept being widened and given aisles, to provide a greater space for all the choir of monks. At the same time the plan provided a fit setting for a larger number of altars than could well be accommodated in a simple basilican plan. This fact was recognized by the adoption of the Limoges plan, yet further enriched, for the third and last abbey church of Cluny, begun in 1088[5] (Fig. 13 *a* and *b*). The list of its altars is given on the old plan and shows how history increased their number. For among them are included the patron

---

[1] On the dates of the pre-Cluniac buildings at Limoges see Mortet, I, 59; it is not unlikely that the earlier church also had radiating chapels and served as a model to the daughter house at Uzerche. Hugh's church was dedicated by Pope Urban II on the last day of the year 1095; but though its dedication is thus almost contemporary with that of Cluny, there can be little doubt that Hugh began to rebuild it before he started on Cluny. The nave, which had originally eleven bays, was again destroyed by fire in 1167, but the apse does not seem to have been seriously damaged. (C. de Lasteyrie, p. 295.) The rebuilding of the nave was begun in 1182 and finished early in the thirteenth century. The east end was modified in 1449. Nothing now remains.

[2] By the Abbé Legros; reproduced in C. de Lasteyrie, Pl. II.

[3] Now destroyed, but its plan is known from excavations. See R. de Lasteyrie, *Arch. rel. en France à l'époque romane*, p. 185; and in *Mém. de l'Acad. des Inscriptions et Belles Lettres*, XXXIV, Pt I, p. 1.

[4] Monsieur R. de Lasteyrie set it in the beginning of the tenth century, but it seems much more likely that it was built soon after a fire in 994. Rivoira (*Lombardic Architecture*, II, 108) was inclined to assign it to the reconstruction of the east end by Hervé de Busançais, dedicated in 1014 and 1020. Confirmatory evidence for the early date of such radiating chapels is provided by the apse of the Cathedral of Clermont consecrated in 946, of which the plan was revealed by excavation in 1909. See V. H. du Ranquet in *Cong. Arch.* LXXXVI, 1924, p. 9.

[5] Marrier, col. 457. According to Gilon, *Vita Sancti Hugonis*, it took twenty years for completion; Marrier, col. 458. An inscription formerly in the sacristy ascribed twenty-five years to the task. Mabillon, *Itinerarium Burgundicum*, II, 19–24. On the point see Oursel, *L'art roman en Bourgogne*, 61 *et seqq.*, and Conant in *Speculum*, V, 1930, p. 77 *et seqq.*

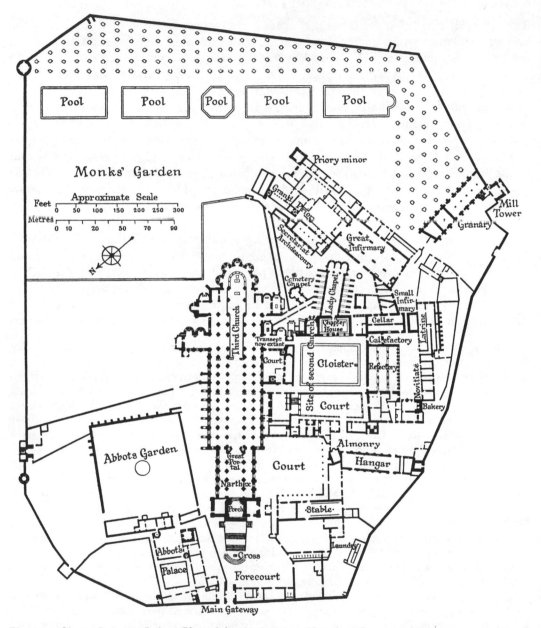

Fig. 13 *a*. Cluny, Saône-et-Loire. Plan of the third Abbey Church and monastic buildings reconstructed from the records, the site and a late seventeenth-century plan in the Musée Ochier, Cluny. By Professor K. J. Conant.

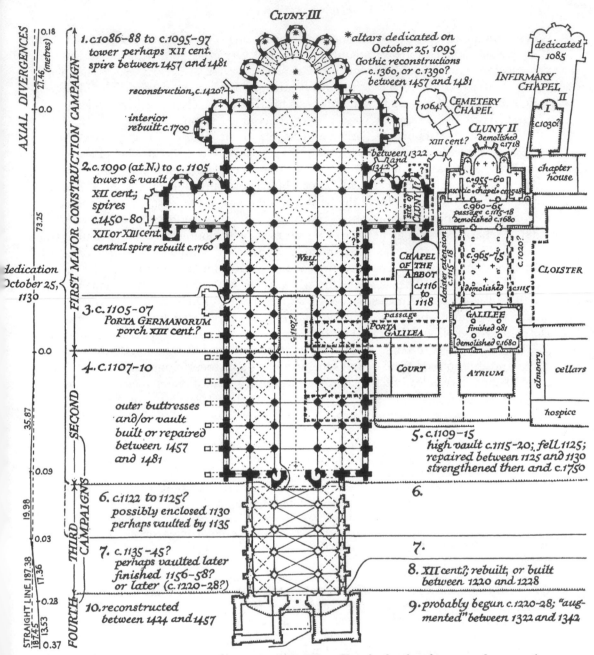

CLUNY III

1. c.1086–88 to c.1095–97
tower perhaps XII cent.
spire between 1457 and 1481

reconstruction, c.1420?

interior
rebuilt c.1700

2. c.1090 (at N.) to c.1105
towers & vault
XII cent.;
spires
c.1450–80
XII or XIII cent.
central spire rebuilt c.1760

3. c.1105–07
PORTA GERMANORUM
porch XIII cent.?

4. c.1107–10

outer buttresses
and/or vault
built or repaired
between 1457
and 1481

6. c.1122 to 1125?
possibly enclosed 1130
perhaps vaulted by 1135

7. c.1135–45?
perhaps vaulted later
finished 1156–58?
or later (c.1220–28?)

10. reconstructed
between 1424 and 1457

*altars dedicated on
October 25, 1095
Gothic reconstructions
c.1360, or c.1390?
between 1457 and 1481

CEMETERY
CHAPEL
1064?

between 1322
and 1342

WELL
X

CHAPEL
OF THE
ABBOT
c.1116
to
1118

c.1107?

passage
PORTA
GALILEA

COURT

5. c.1109–15
high vault c.1115–20; fell 1125;
repaired between 1125 and 1130
strengthened then and c.1750

6.

7.

8. XII cent.?; rebuilt, or built
between 1220 and 1228

9. probably begun c.1220–28; "aug-
mented" between 1322 and 1342

INFIRMARY
CHAPEL
I II
dedicated
1085
c.1030?

CLUNY II
demolished
c.1718
XIII cent.?

chapter
house

c.955–60
ascetic chapel c.1518

c.960–65
passage c.1115–18
demolished c.1680

cloister extension
c.1115–18

c.965–75

demolished c.1115

CLOISTER

c.1020?

GALILEE
finished 981
demolished c.1680

ATRIUM

almonry

cellars

hospice

AXIAL DIVERGENCES

0.18
27.46 (metres)
0.0

73.25

dedication
October 25,
1130

0.0

35.87

0.09

19.98

0.03

STRAIGHT LINE 187.38
187.45
17.36
13.53

0.28

0.37

FIRST MAJOR CONSTRUCTION CAMPAIGN

SECOND

THIRD
CAMPAIGNS

FOURTH

Fig. 13b. Cluny, Saône-et-Loire. Plan of the third Abbey Church, showing the stages of construction.
By Professor K. J. Conant. Not definitive (Conant 1965: 193)

saints of many of the dependent houses: Saint Nazarius and Saint Celsius of Bourbon-Lancy, Saint Vincent of Mont-Saint-Vincent and Orpierre, Saint Andrew of Montier-neuf, Rosans and Gap, Saint Martin of Ambierle, Layrac and Paris, Saint Nicholas of Salins, Poitiers, Graves, Châteaurenard, Rodigo, and Signa, Saint Agatha of Crépy-en-Valois and Ciudad Rodrigo, Saint Mary Magdalen of Vézelay and Bermondsey, Saint Orens of Auch, Saint Denis of Nogent-le-Rotrou, Saint Eutrope of Saintes, Saint Martial of Limoges, Saint Stephen of Tornac and Nevers, Saint Taurin of Gigny, Saint Marcel of Saint-Marcel-lès-Chalon and Saint-Marcel-de-Die and Saint-Marcel-lès-Sauzet; as well as the monastic saints Saint Benedict (patron of Padilorone) and Saint Anthony; Saint James the saint of Spain and Saint Thomas of Canterbury the saint of England, whose kings had helped to build the basilica; and altars of the Rosary and of the sainted abbots of the Order, of whom one, Saint-Mayeul, was patron of Souvigny.

Hugh's basilica had a great nave of eleven bays, with double aisles[1] and double tran-septs; the rounded apse was surrounded by a rounded ambulatory with five apsidal chapels radiating from it. The nave was 260 ft. long inside[2]; from the door to the apse was just over 415 ft. The width of the whole nave was about 118 ft. When Mabillon saw it, still complete after nearly 600 years, he wrote: "Quam si centies videris toties ejus majestatem obstupesces." Its high altar was consecrated by Urban II in 1095; the complete whole was dedicated by Innocent II in 1131. It endured almost unchanged until the very end of the eighteenth century[3]. Its piecemeal destruction began on 16 July 1798, and did not end until 1811. One arm of one transept alone remains to give the scale of the lost whole; but the seventeenth-century plan already referred to, recently checked by the excavations undertaken by the Medieval Academy of America, under Professor Conant, establishes its ground plan beyond dispute. This was, as befitted the

[1] This characteristic is early found in the crypt of the Cluniac church of Saint-Germain-d'Auxerre, probably built between 999–1039. It was probably there employed for structural reasons. Double aisles are no new thing in a basilica; they adorn Justinian's at Bethlehem, and may have figured in its Constantinian predecessor. Saint Peter's and Saint Paul's at Rome had both double aisles. Saint-Benigne-de-Dijon and Pisa had them before Cluny.

[2] According to Professor Conant's measurements when a narthex was added in 1220 it became the longest church in Christendom; he then reckons the exterior measurement at about 616 ft. at the ground line. It has since been challenged only by the new Saint Peter's which measures 675 ft.

[3] When the Société française d'Archéologie visited Cluny in 1850, they were received by M. Ochier, who as a child had seen the abbey church still almost perfect. He spoke of "ces gloires passées dont j'ai pu encore dans mon enfance être témoin". *Cong. Arch.* XVII, 1851 (Auxerre, Cluny, Clermont), p. 112. It is one of the ironies of archaeological history that if any of the members asked his impressions of it, none seems to have written them down or published them. One of the former monks of the abbey, Dom Louis, was living as late as 1837 (*Millénaire*, II, 116), but again, no one thought his memories worthy of preservation. The only document we have is the manuscript of Philippe Bouché (Bib. Nat. nouv. acq. français 4336) written between November 1793 and May 1798.

Mother Church of a great Order, the highest development of the basilican plan with radiating chapels round the apse[1].

The dependent houses of the Order generally followed this plan with radiating chapels on a less stupendous scale. A considerable number have three chapels radiating from the apse and an apsidal chapel in each arm of the transept. An early instance is Saint-Étienne-de-Nevers (Fig. 14)[2]. The church was given to Cluny in a ruined state in 1068[3] and was rebuilt by 1097, when it is described in a charter of confirmation. It has a nave of six bays, with aisles, a transept with an apse to the east in either arm, and an apse with an ambulatory and three radiating semicircular apsidal chapels of equal size[4]. The same number of radiating chapels is to be found in other Cluniac churches built in the time of Abbot Hugh: Paray-le-Monial[5] (Fig. 15), Montierneuf-de-Poitiers[6], Beaulieu[7], Souvigny[8], Chambon (Fig. 16) and (though the dates are less certain) Dun-sur-Auron, Arnac (with a pentagonal apse and semicircular apsidioles), Saint-Saveur-de-Figeac and Saint-Hilaire-de-Melle. The scheme survives in the second church at Monkton Farleigh, which dates from the end of the twelfth century. At Saint-Eutrope-de-Saintes the choir was exceptionally long, and the radiating chapels were all clustered right at the eastern end: but the plan was essentially the same[9].

After the completion of Hugh's basilica at Cluny, however, fewer churches were built

[1] It should be noted, however, that Saint-Léonard, Haute-Vienne (not Cluniac), has seven chapels. See *Archives de la Commission des Monuments historiques*, IV, Pl. 18.

[2] I do not include Saint-Sernin-de-Toulouse in the Cluniac Order; but it is worth noting that it follows the same plan as Saint-Martial, with aisled transept. It came under Cluniac rule for a short time in 1083; and, like Cluny and Saint-Martial, was dedicated by Urban II, early in 1096.

[3] See Bruel, *Chartes*, IV, 258; Deshoulières, *Au début de l'art roman*, p. 119; H. du Ranquet, in *Rev. d'Auvergne*, XXXVI, 102.

[4] Almost exactly the same plan was followed in William the Conqueror's church at Battle Abbey, consecrated in 1094. See *The Times*, Monday, 16 Sept. 1929, p. 9. A similar plan, with apsidal chapels in the transepts and three radiating apsidal chapels in the apse, was followed in the eleventh century at Saint Augustine's, Canterbury. See J. Bilson in *Bull. Mon.* LXIX, 1905, p. 29. It should be noted that an ambulatory with radiating chapels is not found in Normandy before the twelfth century. Jumièges had an ambulatory in the eleventh century, but not radiating chapels. (*Bull. Mon.* LXXVII, 1928, p. 108.) Even in the twelfth century they are rare. Saint-Lucien-de-Beauvais was finished in 1109 and the Trinité of Fécamp consecrated in 1106. Some seem to be influenced by Cluniac models: the plan of the Cathedral of Thérouanne (consecrated in 1133) recalls Saint-Martin-des-Champs, and that of Saint-Omer-de-Lillers, of about the same date, is an imitation on a smaller scale of La Charité. See Reinhardt in *Bull. Mon.* LXXXVIII, 1929, p. 269.

[5] Since it is so much smaller than Cluny it has a choir bay before the apse. See Oursel, p. 77.

[6] Built between 1075 and 1096.

[7] With an ambulatory. On its date, see Lefèvre-Pontalis in *Bull. Mon.* LXXIX, 1920, p. 58.

[8] Before it was rebuilt. The original apse was probably finished in 1095, when the tomb of Mayeul was moved there.

[9] See Dangibeaud in *Bull. Mon.* LXXI, 1907, p. 13.

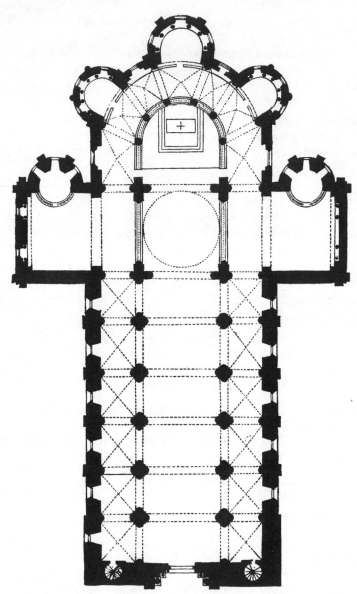

Fig. 14. Saint-Étienne-de-Nevers, Nièvre. Plan. Consecrated, 1097.

with three radiating apsidal chapels. Whenever possible, in emulation of the Mother Church, there were five. One of these imitations was the church of Saint-Gilles, which was included in the Order of Cluny from about 1076 until 1226. Its ruined choir, dating from the early twelfth century, has five radiating chapels, the three central ones rather

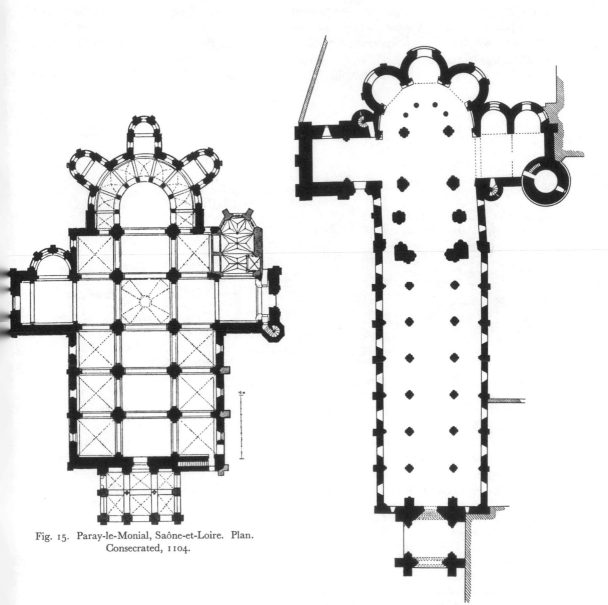

Fig. 15. Paray-le-Monial, Saône-et-Loire. Plan.
Consecrated, 1104.

Fig. 16. Chambon, Creuse. Restored plan. *c.* 1100.

larger than the others[1]. At Saint-Leu-d'Esserent there was no transept, but five shallow radiating chapels[2]. At Uzerche[3] there were also originally five chapels. The influence of Hugh's basilica at Cluny is, however, best seen at La Charité (Fig. 11) and Lewes (Fig. 17). Both of these had been originally built, like Mayeul's abbey church at Cluny, with a series of parallel apses[4]; and towards the middle of the twelfth century both were altered to have five radiating chapels like those of Cluny[5]. Châtel-montagne too, that

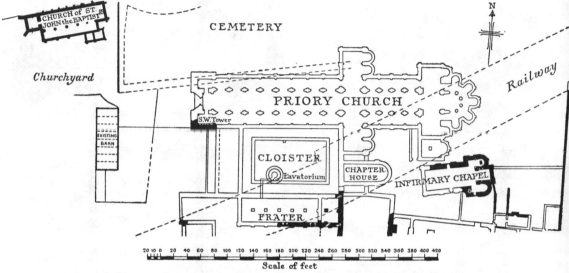

Fig. 17. Saint Pancras, Lewes, Sussex. Plan, after W. H. Godfrey.

originally had three parallel apses, had its east end rebuilt at the end of the twelfth century, with an ambulatory and four radiating chapels. Similarly, when the choir of Saint-Martin-des-Champs was rebuilt under Abbot Hugh I, between 1130 and 1142, it too had five radiating chapels, though the plan was yet further elaborated. The chapels were themselves linked by an aisle round the ambulatory, and the central one, much larger than the others, was itself formed of three shallow apses[6] (Fig. 18).

[1] See *Archives de la Commission des Monuments historiques*, v, Pl. 22.
[2] See Woillez, p. 23.
[3] The plan at Uzerche may be earlier; it is also followed in the crypt, which seems to be considerably earlier than the twelfth-century apse above it.   [4] See p. 63.
[5] W. St J. Hope, in *Arch. Journ.* XLI, 1884, p. 13, suggests that at Lewes this modification belongs to the church dedicated in 1131. The scheme of Cluny was adapted to a smaller church: there was only one apsidiole in the lesser transept, only four columns between the sanctuary and the ambulatory, the transepts were divided by only two bays, and there was a single aisle.
[6] It is comparable with the cemetery chapel at Cluny: Fig. 13 *b*. The churches with three radiating chapels sometimes show a special development of the central one. The apse at Souvigny

In lesser churches, without an ambulatory, the radiating chapels were reduced to niche-like proportions. At Vigeois the five niches are alternately semicircular and polygonal[1]; at Montbron all are extremely shallow and the central one is slightly larger than the others; there is a narrow passage on each side from the transepts into the apse. At Saint-Étienne-des-Sorts[2], a little priory on the bank of the Rhône, the plan of the great basilica is reproduced on the scale of a small chapel. The small transept has its two apsidal chapels; half-way down the nave two projecting side chapels take the place of a second transept[3]; and the apse has five niches to take the place of the radiating chapels. There is no room for aisles or ambulatory; it is a *reductio ad absurdum* of a great scheme.

In the Auvergne the plan with radiating chapels was modified by local custom. The important Cluniac churches of Mozat, Menat[4], and Châtelmontagne (as rebuilt at the end of the twelfth century) have four radiating chapels. It has been suggested that this plan is peculiar to churches dedicated to the Virgin, in which the high altar, and not that of the central apsidal chapel, would be dedicated to her; but the evidence hardly supports this view[5].

The double transept of Hugh's basilica at Cluny could only be imitated in churches of considerable size. It reappears at Saint-Benoît-sur-Loire, which, though independent of Cluny, was, as the resting place of Saint Benedict's shrine, naturally in friendly relations with the Burgundian abbey; it was originally a feature at Souvigny[6] and it reappears at the Cluniac priory of Saint Pancras at Lewes (Fig. 17). This became a model for Canterbury Cathedral[7], and so passed the scheme on to Lincoln, Worcester, Salisbury and Beverley.

Where such a duplication of the transept was impossible, a single transept was sometimes modelled on the second transept at Cluny and given two apsidioles. An instance

(*c.* 1095) seems to have had two semicircular chapels, with a central square one; and a similar arrangement was evident in the altar niches of the Cluniac church of Saint-Pierre-à-la-Chaux at Soissons. (E. Lefèvre-Pontalis in *Cong. Arch.* LXXVIII, 1911, p. 140.)

[1] There seems originally to have been an ambulatory, but it has disappeared. (*Bull. Mon.* VI, 1890, p. iii.) Cf. Arnac (consecrated in 1147) and Mailhat. At Mailhat, according to Auvergnat use, the radiating chapels are built in the thickness of the wall and do not show outside. R. de Lasteyrie, *Arch. rel. en France à l'époque romane*, p. 300; and *Archives de la Commission des Monuments historiques*, IV, Pl. 17.

[2] The church has been a good deal restored, but the plan is authentic. The apse is pentagonal outside.

[3] The nave has been rebuilt but probably follows the earlier plan.

[4] The plan of both is preserved, though the apses have both been altered. See Luzy in *Cong. Arch.* LXXX, 1913, p. 124; Bréhier in *Revue Mabillon*, 1923, p. 21; and Abbé Crégut in *Bull. hist. d'Auvergne*, 1911, p. 208.

[5] Châtelmontagne was dedicated to Our Lady, but Mozat was dedicated to Saint Caprais and Saint Peter.   [6] See Deshoulières (Petite monographie), p. 26.

[7] See Prior, *Eight Chapters*, p. 41.

is the priory church of Chambon in the Creuse (Fig. 16); another—a church outside the Order but strongly influenced by Cluny—is Reading Abbey[1]. Similarly few churches could have double aisles; but La Charité had them, in a great nave of eleven bays[2], and the nave of Souvigny was altered, in the first half of the twelfth century, to follow the plan of the Mother Church[3].

7. CHURCHES WITH FLAT EASTERN EXTREMITIES

When the Order of Cluny was in its prime, it outrivalled and did not emulate the Order of Cîteaux; but after the troubled reign of Pons de Melgueil, Peter the Venerable availed himself of Cistercian experience in his reforms. His new statutes of 1132 show Cistercian influence; and Hugh V's statutes of 1200[4] renounce the characteristic autocracy of the abbot of Cluny in favour of constitutional government on Cistercian lines.

A similar, if lesser, wave of Cistercian influence is evident in certain Cluniac churches that, for the most part, date from this age of transition. Instead of the semicircular apse or apses characteristic of nearly all the other churches of the Order[5], they are built with the flat east end that is characteristic of Cistercian churches. At Lewes the infirmary chapel compromises, with a square end flanked by an apse at either side[6]. An exceptional early instance of a flat end is the little church of Pont-aux-Moines, built between 1075 and 1080[7]. Another early example of a square end is at Autheuil-en-Valois[8], of which the church dates from about 1130; one of the middle of the century is Saint-Christophe-en-Halatte, near Senlis; a later one is at Ruffec, a dependency of Limoges, built between 1160 and 1184 to replace an apse with two apsidioles on either side[9]. Other dependencies of Limoges with "chevets plats" are Moûtier-d'Ahun[10], built in the second half of the twelfth century, and La Souterraine, begun late in that century and finished in 1220[11]. Other late examples are Gassicourt[12],

---

[1] Dedicated in 1164. Hurry, *History of Reading Abbey*, p. 4.

[2] Almost entirely destroyed in the fire of 1559.

[3] The second aisles at Ripoll are probably a later addition (though so far rebuilt that it is difficult to judge of this) and were perhaps also inspired by Cluny. On the connexions between Ripoll and Cluny, see Puig y Cadafalch, p. 86; and Deshoulières in *Bull. Mon.* LXXXIV, 1925, p. 296.

[4] Migne, *Pat. Lat.* CCIX, cols. 882–98.

[5] The exceptions are very early, such as the first church at Cluny (presumably) and the Moûtier-de-Thiers, of which the apse dates from before 1000. See *Cong. Arch.* LXXXVIII, 1925, p. 287. It was given to Cluny in 1011.

[6] Cf. the plan of the Mozarabic churches of Spain, e.g. San Quierze de Pedret.

[7] E. Jarry in *Bull. de la Soc. arch. et hist. de l'Orléanais*, XIV, Orléans, 1907, p. 579.

[8] A dependency of Nanteuil. See E. Lefèvre-Pontalis, *Arch. rel. dioc. Soissons*, II, 3.

[9] See Hubert and Barge in *Bull. Mon.* LXXXVIII, 1929.

[10] See Deshoulières in *Cong. Arch.* LXXXIV, 1923, p. 132.

[11] C. de Lasteyrie, *Saint-Martial*, p. 378. It has a Perigourdin dome at the crossing.

[12] Dating from the time of Saint-Louis.

Saint-Marcel-lès-Chalon and Saint Milburga of Wenlock[1]; and the list is completed by the minor churches of Jauldes[2], Le Breuil-sur-Couze, Sonneville, Saint-Jean-Lachalm[3], Thetford, Trémolat, Champlieu, Saint-Julien-de-Sennecey, Saint-Martin-du-Tartre, Sassangy, Saint-Remy-sur-Creuse, the little transitional chapel of Notre-Dame-de-Bethléem[4] and other small churches. Even at Carennac the original apse was replaced by a flat chevet in the thirteenth century[5]. The very existence of such Cistercian forms within the Order is proof that its traditions were beginning to decay by the latter half of the twelfth century.

8. GALILEES

The *Customs* of Cluny, written for the Abbey of Farfa between 1030 and 1048[6], describe the church as having a *galilea*[7] or narthex 65 ft. long, with two towers in its façade[8]; and under the towers an *atrium* where the lay folk stand, so as not to impede the procession. The narthex or galilee, which is found as early as the end of the fifth century in the monastic church of Qalaat Seman in North Syria, was developed in Italy into such *atria* as that of the old Saint Peter's and Sant' Ambrogio in Milan; and was transferred from smaller monastic churches in Rome, such as Santa Saba, to Benedictine churches in other lands. The galilee of the second abbey church of Cluny, consecrated in 981, seems to have been one of the earliest of its type in France. The nearest analogy to it in place and time is undoubtedly the narthex of the Benedictine abbey of Tournus, which fairly certainly dates from the end of the tenth century[9]: it may once have been a basilica[10]. It has aisles and is of three bays, rather narrower than the nave which it precedes. Mr Clapham restores the galilee at Cluny by analogy with it, but as having four bays. It would seem that the tower porch added to Saint-Martial-de-Limoges between 979 and 991[11] must

---

[1] See Cranage, *The Home of the Monk*, p. 109, for plan. The church was rebuilt in the thirteenth century.

[2] See Guérin Boutard, p. 154.

[3] See Thiollier, *Arch. rom. dioc. du Puy*, p. 151.   [4] Near Remoulins, Gard.

[5] See E. Lefèvre-Pontalis in *Cong. Arch.* LXXXIV, 1923, p. 420.

[6] Ed. Albers, p. 137.

[7] So called because the celebrant, entering it in front of the procession of monks on Sunday, the Feast of the Resurrection, symbolized Our Lord going before His disciples into Galilee. (A. Hamilton Thompson, *English Monasteries*, p. 51.) Rupert of Deutz, *de divinis officiis*, V, 3 (Migne, *Pat. Lat.* CLXX), says: "Locus ille, quo processionem suprema statione terminamus, recte a nobis Galilaea nuncupatur." The name at Cluny was later transferred to a door in the nave: "La porte appelée la Galilée qui communique sur le droit de l'église au cloître entre le sixième et septième rang...." Philippe Bouché.

[8] The towers survived as part of the monastic buildings until the seventeenth or eighteenth century. See *Millénaire*, II, 240.

[9] Puig y Cadafalch, pp. 107 and 112, dates it in the first half of the eleventh century.

[10] See Oursel, p. 45.

[11] See Deshoulières, *Au début de l'art roman*, p. 50.

have been of the same kind. The Moûtier-de-Thiers had a narthex as wide as the church, with the traditional two towers, early in the eleventh century[1]. A plain porch, not much later, exists at Ris. At Mozat, again, there is a narthex open on three sides under the west tower, that is probably not later than 1000[2]; at Tremolat and Bredons[3] there are fortified porches of the end of the eleventh century, and at Meymac a porch under the tower. The narthex of Paray-le-Monial (Fig. 15) dates from the time of Abbot Hugh, and is earlier than the church it precedes; it is another tower porch, aisled, of two bays only. These in no wise correspond with those of the nave, nor is its axis true to that of the church, nor does its door open on to the middle of the nave. It may have been destined to give place to further bays of the nave (which is hardly long enough in relation to the apse) and Saint Hugh's death in 1109 may alone have prevented its supersession.[4] The narthex recently excavated at Souvigny[5], probably of much the same date, was like-wise as wide as the nave and was in three bays. Only the southern side wall, with tall engaged columns set against a pilaster and supporting an arcade, remains to show its style. That at Romainmôtier (Fig. 3) is also of the eleventh century; it is planned as a minor nave with aisles and four bays. At Moissac the tower porch of about 1125 is of two storeys[6], but is not planned as a nave.

In the twelfth century a galilee, either aisled and nave-like or smaller and porch-like, had become a general feature of Cluniac churches of the larger sort[7]. At Payerne a bay of the tenth-century church was left as a narthex[8].

The finest example of the nave-like type is the great narthex of Vézelay (Fig. 19), begun about 1120 and dedicated in 1132; it is the same width as the nave, and its four piers follow the same general plan as those of the great church[9]. It would seem that the second galilee of Saint-Martial-de-Limoges, built after 1167, and the lost narthex of Saint-Eutrope-de-Saintes were of the same type.[10] The great narthex of the third abbey church of Cluny (Fig. 13 b) was certainly of this sort. Though it lacked the second aisle

[1] It had aisles but was only of one bay. See *Cong. Arch.* LXXXVII, 1925, p. 287.

[2] See Bréhier in *Revue Mabillon*, 1923, p. 10.

[3] See Rochemonteix, p. 68. The priory was a dependency of Moissac.

[4] See Oursel, p. 65. The narthex was burnt by the Protestants in 1562, and was then strengthened by being filled in with masonry. The architect Millet removed this about 1860 and reconstructed the narthex. The sculpture of the doorway is ancient; the rest he had to renew. *Ibid.* p. 71.

[5] See Deshoulières in *Bull. Mon.* LXXXIII, 1924, p. 160.

[6] See Aubert in *Congrès archéologique*, XCII, 1929, p. 501. Toulouse.

[7] The existence of a narthex at La Charité is still uncertain. The two western bays of the nave, wider and later than the rest, and probably added when the choir was modified in the twelfth century, may perhaps occupy the site of an earlier galilee. See Beaussart, pp. 107, 141.

[8] The windows were added in 1834.

[9] The Abbé Despinez identifies it with the Pilgrim's Church, dedicated to Saint John the Baptist, mentioned by Hugh of Poitiers, p. 40.

[10] The Moûtier-de-Thiers had a narthex, but its plan is not known.

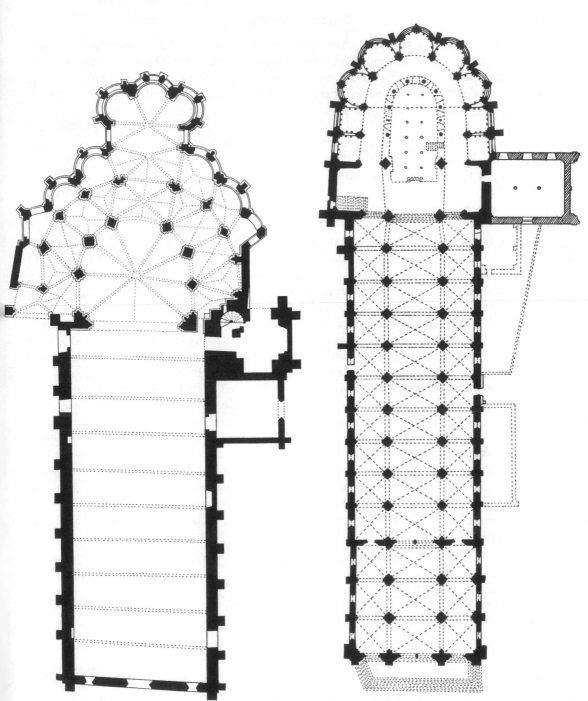

Fig. 18. Saint-Martin-des-Champs, Paris. Plan. The
Choir rebuilt 1130-42.

Fig. 19. Vézelay, Yonne. Plan of the Church of
the Madeleine. The Church, 1089-1120;
the Narthex, 1120-32; the choir
thirteenth century.

of the nave, and was that much the narrower, it was planned as a continuation, with similar piers and general proportions. It is commonly said to have been added by Roland de Hainault in 1220, but the surviving pictures of it represent it as Romanesque in style and closely resembling the nave.[1] Professor Conant, who has investigated its remains, is of opinion that it was begun as soon as the nave was completed; and that its construction was far advanced by the middle of the century. Like that at Maillezais it followed the earlier type in having towers; but these were not over the narthex but projected beyond it. These towers seem to have been erected under Roland de Hainault, probably at the time when the vaulting of the narthex was finished. The tradition of the galilee continued into Gothic times; that at Saint-Leu-d'Esserent is transitional, and one was built at the Cluniac priory of Rougemont in Switzerland in the thirteenth century.

Many Romanesque churches, that did not boast a galilee, had porches of wood that have since disappeared; the corbels for such a porch are still visible on the façade of Saint-Étienne-de-Nevers. These in their turn influenced stone constructions, that hardly merit the name of narthex or galilee and are yet of considerable size. Twelfth-century Cluniac porches of the kind, not remarkable in plan, are those at Mont-Saint-Vincent, which has no aisles but is square and as broad as the nave, Moûtiers-en-Puisaye[2] and Saint-Leu-d'Esserent; and others existed at Sainte-Foy-de-Morlaas, Semelay and Saint-Marcel-lès-Sauzet, but are now destroyed. At Charlieu the exquisitely sculptured porch narthex is entered at the side. It was probably built between 1140 and the death of Peter the Venerable. Such porches influenced the beautiful sculptured portals of the type of Beaulieu and Carennac, which are so deep set as to be almost porches.

None of the plans here described can be considered the characteristic creation of the Order of Cluny, unless it be that of Abbot Hugh's basilica, which is rather a logical development on a scale not hitherto attempted than a new creation. But the survey here attempted does show a remarkable consistency of adherence to certain types of plan, as remarkable as the Cistercian adherence to plans of another kind. It also shows, it is fair to say, an exceptionally high development of those plans to meet the liturgical needs of the Order of Cluny. An equally high architectural development will be found in the planning of the interiors.

[1] Bouché says that nave and narthex were "dans le même goût à peu de chose près". He says its piers had fluted pilasters on three sides and a projecting engaged column towards the aisle, all set against a pier with double-stepped angles.

[2] It to some extent follows a local type; cf. Boesse, Préfontaines, Girolles and Gaubertin, Loiret and Mondreville, Seine-et-Marne.

B. INTERIORS

A. THE NAVE

1. WITHOUT AISLES

The naves of Cluniac churches built without aisles are necessarily of great simplicity; for the Romanesque is a logical type of architecture, and there is little in the necessities of a buttressed wall and a flat roof or a barrel vault to form a basis for an architectural scheme. Yet even within these limits interiors of an austere and simple dignity were achieved.

Plainest of all are the churches that were intended to have a flat roof: Ternay, Bellegarde-du-Loiret, Saint-Cydroine, and a few others; their walls are for the most part unbroken except by a few plain windows, set rather high.

The use of a barrel vault brought about a slight enrichment, since the *arcs-doubleaux* or cross arches which strengthened it had to rest upon half columns or pilasters against the walls. A fine simple example is Vianne (Fig. 20), that depends upon boldly sculptured capitals for its effect. One of the earliest datable barrel-vaulted aisleless churches is Layrac, built between 1072 and 1085[1]. The springing of the vaults is stressed by a cornice, and the cross arches are multiplied and set close together, so that their supports frame an arcade of comparatively narrow arches. Plain deep windows framed in a simple arched moulding are set between the lofty half columns. A somewhat similar scheme is used at Mouthiers (Fig. 21), but here the windows are framed by an arcade that springs from half columns with sculptured capitals, resting on a trefoil base shared by the half columns of the vaulting system. The effect is rich and curiously happy; it is strange that it was not more widely imitated.

At Marcigny[2] the cross arches rested on plain pilasters. More often, however, the supports of the cross arches were themselves linked by an arcade; a typical example, probably of the second half of the eleventh century, is Breuillet; the cross arches there rest on half columns which are joined by a simple semicircular arcade in the wall, framing the plain windows. At Rosiers-Côtes-d'Aurec[3], dating from the end of the century, and at Arnac a little later, the scheme is enriched by the half columns being set against pilasters. At Champagne-Mouton, though the vaulting is still a rounded barrel vault, these arcades are pointed, the half columns are set much closer together, and there is only one window on each side.

The adoption of the *berceau brisé* or cross vault brought no essential change into this scheme; indeed, it was so early adopted in Cluniac churches[4] that it is impossible to

---

[1] See p. 58.   [2] Thiollier, *Art roman à Charlieu*, p. 70.   [3] *Ibid.*

[4] E.g. at Saint-Hippolyte, a parish church of Cluny. The *berceau brisé* or cross vault lessens the lateral pressure on the nave walls by making the pressure more vertical. Thus it is less apt to force them outwards.

consider it as a mark of later date than a barrel vault; in many instances their use must have been contemporaneous. The church of Montbron is an example of the use of a pointed vault with an exceedingly simple wall treatment. The scheme at La Chapelle-Hugon and Retaud is equally simple, though at Retaud the windows are framed by half columns with sculptured capitals. The nave of Charras shows an elaboration in the setting of the alternate half columns against a pilaster, and the corresponding enriching of the cross arch; but the walls remain perfectly plain, hardly broken even by windows. In the slightly later church of Montreuil-Bonnin all the supporting half columns are thus elaborated, and the string course is broken to follow the line of the plain round-headed window in each bay. At Gourville the supports are elaborated as half piers, the half column being set against a pilaster with a second pilaster behind it. At Corme-Écluse the wall scheme is like that at Breuillet, with the addition of a simple moulding over the arcade and over the window. Other instances of simple arcading occur at places as far apart as Médis and Ganagobie.

The other developments in vaulting an aisleless nave created their own simple schemes of decoration. The characteristic Périgourdin system of a succession of domes on pendentives needed no enrichment, but its arches could rest either on an angular pier, as at Tremolat[1] and Bourg-de-Maisons, or on a half column and pilaster, as at Champmillon (Fig. 22)[2].

2. WITH AISLES

A considerable number of early Cluniac churches, of the aisled basilican plan, were originally roofed with a flat wooden ceiling. The early eleventh-century church at Baume-les-Messieurs probably had such a roof before it was vaulted in the thirteenth century; and so had Froville (certainly earlier than 1080)[3], Salmaise[4], Saint-Désiré-de-Lons-le-Saulnier, Ternay, Acy-en-Multien, and Capo di Ponte. Saint-Nazaire-de-Bourbon-Lancy (Fig. 24), dating from the middle of the eleventh century, was never vaulted; neither was Binson[5] nor Gassicourt[6]. The story of the fire in the Madeleine of Vézelay on the eve of her feast, 21 July 1120, when the roof was burnt and fell on the

[1] See *Cong. Arch.* LXXX, 1927 (Périgueux) where it is suggested that the domes replaced a barrel vault.

[2] Cf. Gourville. It seems likely that the domes were added when it was given to Saint-Cybard-d'Angoulême in 1172. Moissac may have had such a cupola roof originally.

[3] Sant' Egidio di Fontanella, in Italy, is not vaulted, but the long engaged columns on the nave walls seem to have been intended to take the cross arches of a vault.

[4] See de Truchis in *Bull. Soc. des Ants. de France*, 1906, p. 346.

[5] Which became a priory of Coincy in 1077.

[6] Deshoulières, *Au début de l'art roman*, p. 112. The choir and apse are later. It may originally have had a barrel vault, but the domes are of twelfth-century date.

assembled pilgrims[1], suggests that up to that date it had had a wooden roof, perhaps of barrel form; and the same may be true of other churches that, like Vézelay, now have Romanesque stone vaults. The churches with wooden roofs are remarkable for the simple form of the piers of the nave. At Bourbon-Lancy (Fig. 24) the pillars are square, and have imposts with mouldings on the sides[2]. At Gigny (Fig. 27), at Baume (Fig. 25) and Lons-le-Saulnier the piers are successively square, round and hexagonal; at Saint-Séverin-en-Condroz square piers alternate with round, octagonal and quadrilobed columns[3] (Fig. 23). At Carennac and Froville a square or cruciform[4] pier is set between two columns[5]; at Gassicourt (Fig. 26) they are cylindrical columns with sculptured capitals.

Vaulting, however, is found at a very early date. The early Middle Ages had inherited the tradition of supporting a nave by narrower and less lofty aisles from classical antiquity, though the channels by which the tradition reached them are complex and uncertain in their course[6]. By the very beginning of the eleventh century such buildings as the chapel above the narthex of Saint-Philibert-de-Tournus, certainly earlier than 1008[7], were built with a barrel-vaulted nave of which the thrust is taken by the "voûtes en quart de cercle" of the aisles: vaults that find an ancient parallel in the Arènes of Nîmes.

This plan is early found in the churches of the Order of Cluny. The nave of Ris, a Cluniac priory in the Puy-de-Dôme, is probably one of the earliest; it was founded in 952, given to Cluny in 994, and was fairly certainly built in the time of Abbot Odilo[8]. Here the problem was dealt with by men who feared to venture overmuch; the lofty nave is exceedingly narrow—2·85 metres—and is linked to the aisles by what are really arches in the walls, since the openings are small and the arches rest on massive cruciform piers[9] without capitals; the arches are received on imposts with shallow mouldings. The aisles are almost as broad as the nave—2·15 metres—and are roofed by half-barrel vaults. This system of a barrel-vaulted nave buttressed by aisles with half-barrel vaults was one that remained in use during the early and mature periods of Romanesque architecture; it was both logical and strong. A good example of the eleventh century is Saint-Germain-les-Fossés. Saint-Béat (Fig. 28) is of a far more developed type than Ris, but maintains the tradition of massive piers. At Bredons the piers are more elegant;

---

[1] The figure of 1120 killed is almost certainly a dittograph of the date.

[2] At Bourbon-Lancy there is no impost towards the nave.

[3] The nave is not vaulted, though the aisles are groin vaulted.

[4] At Saint-Julien-de-Sennecey all the piers are cruciform. Dickson, p. 255.

[5] This alternation is a very ancient tradition; the alternate use of round and rectangular piers is found as early as Minoan times. Evans, *Palace of Minos*, II, 567.

[6] See H. and E. du Ranquet in *Bull. Mon.* XC, 1931, p. 48.

[7] *Cong. Arch.* vol. XC, 1928, pp. 419, 422.

[8] See du Ranquet, *loc. cit.* p. 66. The transept, choir and apse are of the twelfth century.

[9] Cf. the cruciform piers of the nave of Uzerche.

but there perhaps too much was sacrificed to grace, for the nave vaults have fallen. A similar scheme is used with happy effect for the ambulatory (and probably for the nave) of Saint-Eutrope-de-Saintes (Fig. 31) and for the aisles of Uzerche (consecrated in 1098), Duravel, Saint-Marcel-lès-Sauzet, Ronsenac (with square piers with half columns on three sides but not towards the aisle, where it is strengthened by cross arches), Courpière (c. 1150), Brancion (a Cluniac parish church) and Granson (a Swiss priory of Souvigny). So wide a distribution proves that this system of vaulting cannot be considered characteristic of a single province.

In Châtelmontagne, an Auvergnat church of the Order, the half-barrel vault is modified by strengthening cross walls resting on arches (Fig. 30): a compromise between the barrel and half-barrel systems. At Saint-Étienne-de-Nevers the half-barrel vaults are in the triforium, and the aisle beneath is cross vaulted.

An interesting early Cluniac church, Champvoux in the Nièvre, once much larger than it is now, has a vaulting system of another kind. The choir and its aisles have each a simple barrel vault, unbroken even by cross arches[1] (Fig. 35). This form, strengthened by cross arches, is found in a considerable number of Cluniac churches, mostly in Central France. At Romainmôtier[2] the barrel vault is taken to the wall, and the thrust is partly borne by a double arcade on the wall, cutting up into the curve of the barrel vault. This disposition is exceptional; normally the solution for barrel vaults is extremely simple (Fig. 29). At Sagnac[3], Maillezais, and Saint-Marc-de-Souvigny, the nave has a barrel vault, and the aisles a cross vault; but normally they both have the same system, generally cross vaults[4]. An early example with narrow nave and aisles and extremely massive piers was Saint-Victor, now unhappily destroyed[5]; in general proportions it must have been comparable with Ris, but the vault used was a *berceau brisé*. At Carennac, Bellenaves, Colombier and Saint-Hilaire-de-Melle, the *berceau brisé* or cross vault is also used. In the relation in height between the three vaults a great variety is possible: sections of the not distant churches of Mezin and Moirax sufficiently illustrate this (Figs. 33, 34). This use of triple vaults, all strengthened by cross arches, naturally led to an elaboration of the piers supporting them. At Colombier

[1] M. Lefèvre-Pontalis considered that Mozat originally had no cross arches. See *Bull. Mon.* LXXX, 1921, p. 77. At Pouilly-lès-Feurs the nave of four bays has only one cross arch, between the second and third bays.

[2] In the part not reconstructed after the roof fell at the end of the thirteenth century; i.e. the aisles and three bays before the choir.

[3] See J. de Cessac, in *Mém. de la Soc. des Sciences naturelles et archéologiques de la Creuse*, 2nd series, II, 1888, p. 9. Sagnac was a dependency of La Souterraine which depended on Saint-Martial-de-Limoges.

[4] In Poitou and the south-west the barrel vault is used well into the twelfth century, e.g. Champdeniers, Ronsenac.

[5] A full description by M. Tholin, originally published in the *Revue du Lyonnais*, 3rd series, IX, 1870, p. 132, is reprinted in Virey, 2nd ed., p. 99, n. 2. Tayac similarly has notably narrow aisles.

the piers have to east and west half columns with sculptured half capitals to take the arches of the nave. On the inner side are half columns which rise to take the cross arches of the nave; and opposite are pilasters to take the cross arches of the aisles[1]. In the great church of Saint-Martial-de-Limoges there was a similar scheme[2]. At Buxy the nave vault rises from pillars, resting on consoles that form part of the capital of the pier. At Saint-Révérien there is a similar scheme, with half columns and separate half capitals, alternating with single columns (Fig. 32). At Saint-Hilaire-de-Melle (Fig. 36) these disparate elements are fused into a single complex cruciform pier, with engaged columns to take the arches of the nave and the cross arches of the aisles. At Semelay a moulding

Fig. 33. Mezin, Lot-et-Garonne.
Section of the Nave. First half
of twelfth century.

Fig. 34. Moirax, Lot-et-Garonne.
Section of the Nave. Second half
of eleventh century.

runs round the pier and serves as abacus to the half capitals of the arches (Fig. 37). The solution of the problem attempted in Hugh's basilica at Cluny (Fig. 38 a and b) erred on the side of boldness[3]. The nave was covered by a cross vault on cross arches rising to a height of over 98 ft. above the floor; the inner aisles had barrel vaults nearly 60 ft. high, and the outer aisles similar vaults 39 ft. high[4]. Auvrai's rather unsatisfactory engraving of Lallemand's drawing (Fig. 38a) and Bouché's description give indications of the solution used here: the face of the pier towards the nave had a fluted pilaster with a capital on the same level as those which took the arches, on which stood two stages of columns that rose to take the cross arches of the vault. The pier took the cross arches of the aisles

[1] The scheme is obscured on some piers which have been strengthened later.

[2] C. de Lasteyrie, p. 299.

[3] In 1125, according to Ordericus Vitalis (*Hist. eccles.* ed. Le Prévost, IV, 426): "ingens basilicae navis, quae nuper edita fuerat, corruit; sed protegente Deo, neminem laesit." The interpretation of this passage has been disputed; Ordericus Vitalis is the only authority for the catastrophe, and probably exaggerates a minor fall. (He is not very trustworthy in Cluniac affairs.) The work done in Peter the Venerable's time was probably the repair of part of the nave vault. See *Radulphi vita Petri Venerabilis* in Migne, *Pat. Lat.* LXXXIX, col. 20. The roof was strengthened by flying buttresses after 1145.

[4] Bouché says the aisles had "bonnets carrés", presumably groin vaults.

and the nave arcade on engaged columns, that likewise had sculptured capitals. The eighteenth-century Philippe Bouché described the nave as having "three orders"; and indeed this characteristically Burgundian arrangement seems ultimately to have been derived from a Roman tradition. In such a derivation there is nothing surprising; for not only was Burgundy rich in surviving Roman buildings, but also Roman architectural treatises were known at Cluny: the Catalogue of its library includes a text of Vitruvius[1].

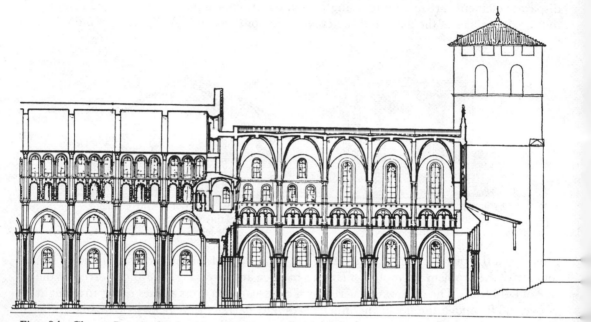

Fig. 38 *b*. Cluny. Longitudinal section of the western bays of the Nave and the Narthex, showing the Chapel of St Michael above the Great Portal. Reconstruction by Professor K. J. Conant.

This system of engaged columns or pilasters in stages is as characteristic of the second style of Cluniac architecture as a vast length of unbroken shaft is of the first. At Saint-Séverin-en-Condroz (Fig. 23) its influence begins to be felt; there is a clear marking of stages, but the recessing is almost imperceptible[2]. At Moirax and Vézelay[3], again, there is little variation in the planes of the stages (Fig. 39); it is as if one of the immensely long shafts of the early tradition had been broken first by the abacus of the capital and then by the string course, though actually at Vézelay the upper stage is set back enough to take the pilasters that receive the bay arcade. At Cluny the two upper stages seem

[1] Delisle, *Inventaire des MSS. de la Bibliothèque Nationale, Fonds de Cluni*, 188, Appendix, pp. 337 *et seqq.* No. 30.

[2] Note the twin colonnettes inserted into the second stage of the pilaster.

[3] Built by Saint Hugh's nephew, Renaud de Semur.

to have been slightly recessed, probably much as the upper stage is recessed at Avallon[1] (Fig. 40). At Paray the delicate gradation of the three stages, in each of which the form of the column is modified, preludes a Gothic treatment[2].

The commonest and most satisfactory solution for vaulting the aisles was neither the half-barrel nor the barrel vault, but a groin vault. This is found surprisingly early. The church of Gigny (Fig. 27) is in its massive and rude simplicity of unquestionably early date; but its aisles have contemporary low-pitched groin vaults to take part of the thrust of the high barrel vault of the nave, borne on short flat pilasters ending in consoles. Another early instance is the church of Saint-Séverin-en-Condroz, begun in 1091. The groin vaults of the aisles are separated by heavy cross arches pitched lower than the vaults. Both the groins and the cross arches rest on double pilasters set against the walls; the piers are alternately round or quadrilobed and square. Something the same plan is followed in the Cluniac church of Saint-Maurice (Fig. 41); the cross arches of the nave rest on half columns, but all the others on pilasters. At Varennes-l'Arconce, also dating from the end of the eleventh century, the next step is made; the groin vaults of the aisles rest on pilasters, and the arches and cross arches of the nave on half columns. Very soon, however, a composite pier was planned with half columns on all four sides to take all these thrusts. At Champdeniers[3] (Fig. 42) the half columns are set back to back, giving a characteristic pier of quadrilobar section; at Montierneuf-de-Poitiers this is enriched by lesser engaged columns in the angles. Generally, however, the half columns are set against a pier. This varies in form. At Saint-Étienne-de-Nevers, Le Moûtier-de-Thiers (Fig. 43), Saint-Marc-de-Souvigny, Lurcy-le-Bourg, Saint-Pierre-le-Moûtier (Fig. 45), Marcilhac, Iguerande and Sagnac it is quadrangular; at Moirax (Fig. 44) the pier is itself a column; at La Charité[4] and Vézelay (Fig. 54), where the aisle vaults are probably earlier[5] than the nave vault that replaces an earlier roof, the pier is cruciform, and the groins spring from the angle of the moulding. On the nave side there is no capital, but the abacus moulding is continued round the pier and a second half column rests on it. This is broken by the string course and then continues into a sculptured capital bearing the cross arch of the nave vault. These cross arches are emphasized by the alternating blocks of brown and white local stone[6], giving a particoloured decoration of which the model is to be sought in such Arab buildings as the Mosque of

[1] It should be noted how closely the bay plan of Avallon follows that of Vézelay, with everything transformed from the round-headed to the pointed arch-form.

[2] For a detailed comparison between Cluny and Paray, see Oursel, p. 79.

[3] The same plan is used at Saint-Hilaire-de-Melle, though here the aisles are cross vaulted.

[4] On the fragmentary evidence for the aisles at La Charité, see Beaussart, pp. 117, 127. The destruction of the northern aisle was aided by the cession of its western bays to the town to form the parish church of Sainte-Croix.

[5] The Abbé Despiney (p. 38), however, draws attention to blocked-up windows above the side doors of the great portal which seem intended to light the aisles but come above the present vault. Did they perhaps light the "combles"?

[6] In the parts reconstructed by Viollet-le-Duc, paint is used instead of the brown stone.

Cordova[1]; the oriental effect is heightened by the use of tie-rods. At Paray-le-Monial the pier is likewise cruciform, with half columns on the three outer faces: on the nave side is a fluted pilaster, on which rests another, which in turn receives a half column to take the cross arches. A simplified form of the same scheme is followed at Mont-Saint-Vincent, and was used in the church at Charlieu now destroyed[2].

At Longpont the pier is cruciform, with four engaged columns, and four colonnettes at the corners[3]. At Mozat the pier is quadrangular (Fig. 47), but there is no half column towards the nave. This suggests that originally the nave may have had a wooden roof; the present vault is a Gothic rib vault on consoles. Exactly the same plan is followed at Pont-du-Château (Fig. 48). At Souvigny the original aisle—high, narrow and barrel vaulted—had piers of cruciform section with short half columns east and west, for the arches of the nave, and longer ones north and south, for the cross arches of the vaults. But when a second aisle, broad and low, was added in emulation of Cluny, it had to have unusually massive piers (Fig. 46) to take the place of the former exterior wall; and these were planned as hexagonal, with the groins springing from a kind of console at the angles[4]. At Castleacre the piers are almost equally complex; the square, central core has great half columns, spirally decorated in the English manner, to east and west, flanked by two recessed columns on either side, very lofty double columns to take the nave vault, flanked by similar recessed members, and short double columns to take the aisle vaults.

While unceasing experiment was thus perfecting the vaulting of the aisles, the builders were not yet content with the solutions found for the problem of vaulting the nave. At Mont-Saint-Vincent (Fig. 49) the nave is divided into two bays by cross arches; and each of these bays is vaulted by a transverse barrel vault with its axis running across the nave. The aisles have the usual groin vaults. This experimental solution[5] did not oust the barrel and cross vault from common use. It was succeeded by a much bolder experiment, the application of a groin vault to a nave. The earliest instance is in the nave of Vézelay (Fig. 39), revaulted after the fire of 1120[6]. Generally speaking the groin-vaulted aisle bays were square[7], but here a new plan had to be adopted and a

---

[1] Dating from 961–7. See Mâle, *Art et artistes du moyen âge*, pp. 33 *et seqq.*

[2] See Virey, 2nd ed. p. 143.

[3] The vault is of the early twelfth century and Burgundian in type. See *Bull. Mon.* LXI, 1896, p. 115.

[4] At Prittlewell, Essex (an English Cluniac priory) there are round pillars supporting a square abacus, to which there were originally brackets as at Saint Anne's, Lewes and Telscombe. See Coulton, *Art and the Reformation*, p. 156.

[5] Also found in the aisles of the narthex and in the nave at Tournus. It has been suggested (Dickson, p. 20) that the vaults at Mont-Saint-Vincent were not envisaged by the architect when the church was first planned, but were finally built in emulation of Tournus.

[6] The four bays nearest the choir lost their Romanesque vault when the Gothic choir was built between 1170 and 1190. Viollet-le-Duc remade the Romanesque vault for three of them, leaving only that nearest the choir in its Gothic state. Despiney, p. 64.

[7] E.g. at Vézelay, Donzy-le-Pré, Mozat, Thiers, Pont-du-Château and Moirax. The scheme is also found in such Cluniac parish churches as Toulon-sur-Arroux.

wide oblong vault achieved over a span of some 14 metres. Viollet-le-Duc, when he was restoring this vault, noted its tentative and inexperienced technique; the vault was extraordinarily thick, badly set out, and built of unsuitable stone[1]. This vault, indeed, was from the beginning strengthened with concealed iron rods[2]. But it was an important step towards the final solution by the invention of the rib vault[3]: a change of great economic importance, since it only necessitated a light centring in wood instead of the heavy centring required for a groin or barrel vault[4]. This vault appears in the four western bays of the nave of Vézelay and in the upper storey of the last bay of its narthex. Its appearance in the nave heralds the transition to another style, for its use breaks up the homogeneity of the Romanesque scheme. What seemed an integral and almost living form, in which, as in a body, stresses were hidden, was transformed into an articulated skeleton of visible stresses. Gothic architecture is thus within sight even in the first half of the twelfth century; and already the majestic unity of the earlier style is broken[5].

The rib vault is most easily set out on a square plan: but curiously enough it was used in the twelfth century almost entirely for oblong bays. An exception is the church of Notre-Dame-d'Airaines, which became a priory of Saint-Martin-des-Champs a little before 1119 and was built soon afterwards[6]. Here the aisles, low built to buttress the nave walls, are vaulted with groin vaults in oblong bays and the nave is narrow enough to have highly domed quadripartite vaults with heavy ribs likewise in almost square bays (Fig. 50). The scheme is here still experimental; the western bay has curious subsidiary ribs; but already the scheme has been devised by which the ribs are borne by half capitals inclined outwards on either side of the capital of the cross arch: the scheme which is to be a fundamental characteristic of the early Gothic vault. The vaulting scheme is almost Gothic, but the windows are still round headed. Much the same scheme is followed at Acy-en-Multien, with square bays and ribs of rectangular section in the rib vaulting added about 1140[7]. At Marolles-en-Brie (Fig. 52), which is not earlier than

[1] Oursel, p. 118. The construction in the narthex he found notably better.

[2] The same expedient was used in the first four bays of the Cluniac church of San Pietro in Ciel d' Oro at Pavia, dedicated by Innocent II in 1132. Here the piers have diagonal shafts. The idea is essentially Eastern.

[3] M. Oursel (p. 107) traces the rib vault back to a Roman tradition, and considers that its earliest medieval use was for crypts, e.g. Saint-Andoche at Autun. Mr Bilson dates that at Durham as early as 1093.   [4] See A. K. Porter, *Construction of Lombard and Gothic Vaults*, p. 2.

[5] M. Oursel considers the rib vault, while Burgundian, to be un-Cluniac. He considers that it originated at Saint-Martin-d'Autun, and is found in priories such as Anzy-le-Duc, Bragny-en-Charollais and Saint-Martin-d'Avallon, that were in relation with it. He points out the relations between Vézelay and Saint-Martin, and concludes that its adoption at Vézelay had a political significance. *Op. cit.* pp. 99–121. His view has been severely criticised by J. Vallery-Radot in *Bull. Mon.* 1929, p. 259. See also Schapiro in *Art Bulletin*, XI, 1929, p. 225.

[6] See Enlart in *Bull. Mon.* LX, 1895, p. 208. He considered the vaults here to be the earliest ogival vaults in the region. M. Aubert dates the vaulting to *c.* 1130–35, *Cong. Arch.*, XCIX, 1936, p. 460.

[7] The nave originally had a wooden roof. See Lefèvre-Pontalis, *Arch. rel. dioc. Soissons*, I, 86.

1125, a rather similar plan is used but in oblong bays and with a less tentative air[1]. Further progress is evident at Nantua (Fig. 55) in the enriched moulding of the rib and the use of a sculptured key stone; but here it is evident that the masons have had difficulty in setting it out and there are signs of dangerous deformation in spite of the later addition of flying buttresses. At Longpont (Fig. 51) the vaulting follows a similar scheme but is definitely more accomplished. Here there is only a single capital for the cross arch, and the ribs run from curious squinch-like projections on either side of it.

It was not long before the rib vault was applied to the aisles. About 1150 a desire was felt to widen the nave arches, thus turning the aisle bays into oblongs; and these were best vaulted by rib vaults. An early example[2] is the great church of Beaulieu, of which the nave has a barrel vault and the aisles sexpartite rib vaults (Fig. 53). A similar plan is followed in a Cluniac church as far distant as Saint-Côme-du-Mont, near the English Channel; it has quadripartite vaults. With the interior of Saint-Marcel-lès-Chalon (Fig. 57) a yet completer whole is achieved, and we have almost crossed the frontier that divides Romanesque from Gothic[3]. If we proceed to Saint-Sauveur-de-Castelsarrasin, with piers formed of half columns set against a core with three right angles between each, true Gothic has been attained.

It has been shown that the piers of an aisled church cannot be studied apart from the vaulting system they support; their formal evolution depends upon the functions they perform. But their decorative enrichments are not so prescribed, and another process of evolution can here be studied. The earliest churches have cushion capitals or cornices to their piers, but as soon as the art of sculpture was revived in France—and it was revived earlier than is sometimes supposed—Cluniac churches were adorned with sculptured[4] capitals and half capitals. Their decoration is better considered under the heads of ornament and iconography. Their proportions vary considerably, especially in the depth of the capital from the abacus to the shaft; but this proportion is partly governed by structural requirements, and where these do not enter it remains fairly constant. What may fairly be called a Burgundian proportion, represented, for example, by the capitals of Vézelay, is widely distributed at the beginning of the twelfth century; but narrower types, as in some of the engaged capitals at Saint-Eutrope, and a squarer form, as at Saujon, are also represented. The one constant feature is the importance of the abacus, generally moulded at a sharp angle.

The development of the base of the column is more obvious[5]. In the churches with simple piers, such as Baume and Gigny, and in those with more pilasters than columns

[1] See *Bull. Mon.* LXI, 1896, p. 118.

[2] See E. Lefèvre-Pontalis, *À quelle école faut-il rattacher l'église de Beaulieu, Corrèze*, p. 6.

[3] It is worth noting that the groin vault was used contemporaneously with the rib vault, e.g. at Domont, *c.* 1155.

[4] Where they are not sculptured—e.g. at Saint-Étienne-de-Nevers and Breuillet—they were fairly certainly decorated with painted ornament.

[5] On Cluniac column bases see Viollet-le-Duc, *Dictionnaire raisonnée de l'architecture*, II, 128.

in their composition, for instance Saint-Maurice, there are no base mouldings. At the next stage, for instance at Colombier and Champdeniers, a simple torus is employed. This is quickly multiplied into the classic double torus divided by a scotia, for instance at Le-Moûtier-de-Thiers, Marcilhac and Donzy-le-Pré. This remains the normal base moulding[1]; but as the pier is developed as an integral whole, it comes to be used all round the pier, which is set on a low pedestal of varying form. At Moirax (Fig. 58) it is extremely simple; at Saint-Eutrope-de-Saintes (Fig. 59) the complex pier is set upon a circular base.

Less often a base of this kind is further elaborated. At Mouchan the double form is treated as a cable moulding; at Saint-Étienne-de-Nevers some turned colonnettes have it multiplied (Fig. 62); at Mouthiers (Fig. 21) it is sevenfold. There is rich foliate decoration[2] at Vézelay, La Charité[3], Avallon and Paray-le-Monial. At Saint-Révérien (Fig. 60) a whole frieze of rosettes appears; at Charlieu a reed and bead moulding and a plait (Fig. 61).

The other common development is the addition of angle-spurs to the base. At Montbron, Fontanella and Champmillon they are very simple; at Saint-Pierre-le-Moûtier (Fig. 45) the engaged columns on the nave side rest on high bases with wide and shallow griffes like a reversed capital, a type found in the late eleventh-century work at La Charité[4]; at Saint-Marcel-lès-Sauzet the spurs are more fully developed (Fig. 63). At Sail-sous-Cousan and Rosiers-Côtes-d'Aurec the whole is more richly ornamented; besides spurs, the bases have a triple torus, of which the central mouldings are decorated with cable, bead and nailhead ornament. From such decoration it was but a step to the sculptured ornament of the bases at Cénac, Beaulieu, Bonneviolle and Vézelay (Fig. 54).

The west wall of the nave is generally thought of as the back of the façade rather than as a part of the church meriting an independent treatment. Exceptionally (as at Cluny and Semur-en-Brionnais) its architectural design was centred on a tribune that forms part of a chapel of Saint Michael beyond. The west wall of Saint-Étienne-de-Toulouse, that is almost the only Romanesque part that survives, has an arcade enclosing windows framed by columns with richly sculptured capitals[5]. Occasionally, in the Auvergne, the western wall has a small tribune, generally of three arches; a typical example is at Mozat. At Castleacre (Fig. 64) the English liking for arcaded decoration finds expression on the west wall; there are two tiers of interlaced arcading, and a row of simple arcading between. The treatment of the upper part has been lost through the insertion of a great Gothic window.

The aisle walls of Cluniac churches were usually left plain, and at the most (like the walls of churches of the aisleless type) decorated with a more or less structural arcade

[1] E.g. Saint-Lazare-d'Avallon, crypt of Saint-Eutrope, Moissac. See Deshoulières in *Bull. Mon.* LXXV, 1911, p. 77.

[2] Viollet-le-Duc considered this form of ornament characteristic of Cluniac style.

[3] In the twelfth-century work.

[4] See Beaussart, p. 149. A somewhat similar form occurs at Saint-Aignan-de-Cosne. In the interior of the transept certain capitals are formed of such bases re-used. *Ibid.* p. 188.

[5] See *Cong. Arch.* XCII, 1929, p. 69. Its disposition suggests that the nave was not vaulted.

beneath the windows: Souvigny is a good example (Fig. 65), with the supports of the arcade alternately columnar and rectangular. At Montierneuf the windows are larger and more richly decorated than usual, and the arcade is set low beneath them. At Marcilhac, on the other hand, the arcade is set high enough to frame the windows. At Saint-Hilaire-de-Melle the walls are strengthened by pilasters between the windows of trefoil section; the two side half columns take the arch of the windows, and the central one, ending in a conical finial, is there simply to support the wall.

Most churches of the type described had windows in the aisles; some were further lighted by clerestory windows set high above the arches of the nave. These were ordinarily small, plain, deep and round headed, as at Vézelay, Nantua and Notre-Dame-d'Airaines. At Cluny itself they were in the upper tier of a double false triforium. One bay of it still exists in the northern bay of the surviving transept (Fig. 68). The clerestory itself is set within an arcade adorned with billet moulding, resting on twin engaged columns; the arcade below is set within fluted pilasters, and is enriched with a characteristic scalloped ornament. Mabillon speaks of the church as being "commoda, sonora" but says[1] "fenestrae omnes angustae, adeoque basilica tota subobscura"; and indeed the long nave must have been dark, when the size of its windows, numerous though they were, is compared with its height. Doubly welcome must have been the golden candle-light of festival seasons, when the great hanging *coronae* and the standing triangular sconces and the seven-branched candlestick before the altar were all lit[2]. Paray likewise has a double triforium; the lower arcade is blind, the upper fenestrated. At Semur-en-Brionnais (Fig. 67), Saint Hugh's own home, the triforium follows a similar scheme; it appears to be a true triforium, but is in fact only a decorative buttress, since the piers that divide the bays of the nave are not pierced to provide a passage way. The arcade of the triforium originally opened into the "combles" of the aisles; they were walled-up later. It ends to the west with a "tribune" such as must once have existed at Cluny itself[3] (Fig. 38 b). At La Charité there is another false triforium in the surviving western bays of the nave (Fig. 69) that is a mere decorative application to the wall. It was surmounted by a second arcade of groups of three round arches of which the centre one was a window and the others blind. The four last bays have a false triforium of different kind (Fig. 70) which belongs to a construction of the late twelfth century which was also surmounted by a triple arcade[4]. At Châtelmontagne, however, a practical use of arcaded triforium of the kind is found (Fig. 71); there it serves to give light to the lofty aisle beyond.

[1] Ann. ord. Sancti Benedicti V, quoted Virey, in *Millénaire*, II, 233.
[2] See *Cons. Mon.* I, 43–5; Herrgot, 258, cap. LXIV.
[3] Such a tribune, later rebuilt, formed part of the church of Ganagobie.
[4] See Beaussart, Pl. 30; they are certainly earlier than 1202. For a tentative reconstruction of the nave, see *ibid.* p. 141. It was burnt in 1559, and the four eastern bays were reconstructed after 1695. For a parallel between the triforium at La Charité and Santa Maria la Blanca at Toledo, see Mâle, *Arts et artistes du moyen âge*, p. 50.

At Saint-Séverin-en-Condroz the square pillars of the nave are surmounted by pairs of spirally turned colonnettes with cubical capitals and a string course above. They seem to be purely decorative, and may be the prototypes of the curious little arcades at Beaulieu (Fig. 53)[1]. These form a true triforium, but so small as to form a very un-important part of the scheme, though it helps to take the thrust of the nave on its half-barrel vaults. At Nogent-le-Rotrou it is not much more important; three little arcaded windows open in the middle of each bay of the nave and two in each bay of the ambulatory. Like those at Beaulieu they are not enclosed in an arcade, and seem modelled on such false tribunes as are found in the Forez, for example at Champdieu.

Another early Cluniac church, however, only second in importance to the Mother Church, had a triforium, and inspired a certain number of imitations. Saint-Martial-de-Limoges (Fig. 73) had a triforium in the eleven bays of the nave and in the first two bays of the choir[2], and exactly the same plan is followed at Saint-Étienne-de-Nevers, built about 1080, though here the triforium has a row of plain windows above it. At Saint-Étienne everything is round arched: the vault, the arches of the nave and the triforium[3], the arcade and the windows; nowhere are the possibilities of the *arc en plein cintre* more fully exploited, or with less superfluous buttressing. In a later example of the same scheme, Saint-Sauveur-de-Figeac[4] (Fig. 72), the pointed arch is employed everywhere save for the arches of the nave. At Maillezais the scheme has become completely Gothic.

The full development of the triforium is not found in Cluniac churches until late in the transitional period between Romanesque and Gothic: at Saint-Anatoile-de-Salins, with four arcades of doubled columns to the bay, at Domont and Doullens and at Saint-Leu-d'Esserent, which may be claimed as one of the earliest examples of the true Gothic triforium. It is, indeed, in the Cluniac houses in England rather than in the Cluniac houses of France that the Romanesque triforium is fully developed: witness the nave of Castleacre, consecrated by 1148, with a triforium arch as wide as that of the nave, surmounted by a rich triple arcade with a window in the middle (Fig. 74). Such emphasis on the triforium is hardly found as early in the Cluniac churches of France, and represents the influence of English taste on the French tradition of Cluniac architecture[5].

---

[1] Lefèvre-Pontalis sets the church in the second quarter of the twelfth century: there is no documentary evidence.

[2] The triforium passage had a "voûte en quart de cercle"; the whole vaulting scheme (with a triforium) was indeed a development of the simple scheme in which a central barrel vault is supported by half-barrel vaults in the aisles. One of the most recent writers (Deshoulières, *Au début de l'art roman*, p. 49) considered that Saint-Martial was finished by 1080.

[3] The aisles are cross vaulted; the triforium has a half-barrel vault.

[4] Note the vaulting: the nave has oblong groin vaults, the aisles sexpartite rib vaults. The older tribunes in the transept closely resemble Limoges; see R. Rey, *La sculpture romane languedocienne* (Toulouse and Paris, 1936), p. 14.

[5] The tradition continues into the mature Gothic period; see the fine triforium at Much Wenlock.

In thus studying the development of the aisled type of Cluniac church, it has become evident that the vaulting system is an essential characteristic and the arch-form an accidental one[1]. It is truc that a sequence can be formed for the great churches; Saint-Étienne-de-Nevers, like Saint-Martial-de-Limoges, uses a round arch throughout, for vaults, arches, doors, windows and arcade; at the next stage at Cluny the structural

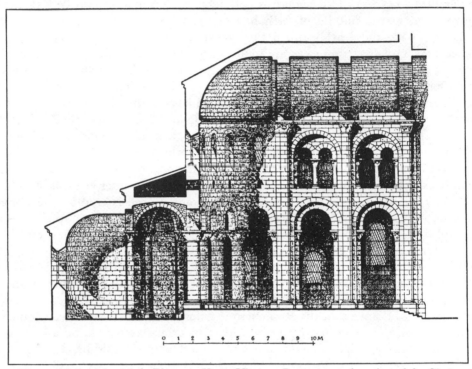

Fig. 73. Saint-Martial-de-Limoges, Haute-Vienne. Reconstructed section of the Choir. Consecrated, 1095. After C. de Lasteyrie.

arches of the nave and of the vaulting were pointed[2], and the doors, windows, and internal arcades were round. At Paray and Saint-Lazare-d'Avallon the windows and arcades are still round headed. At La Charité the ogival line is as universal (except for the

[1] It is hardly necessary to point out that the pointed arch is used much earlier in the East, and notably in Syria, than in the West. Captain Cresswell finds it used earliest at Qasr-el-Wardan in 561. See his letter in *The Times*, 16 Jan. 1931. See also J. Baltrusaitis, *Le problème de l'ogive et l'Arménie* (Paris, 1936).

[2] The vault as rebuilt in 1125 was a *berceau brisé* of pointed section. Professor Conant has drawn attention to the interesting relation that exists between the pointed arches used in the Benedictine abbey of Monte Cassino (finished in 1087) and those used at Cluny (begun in 1088). It is perhaps worth mentioning that pointed arches are first found in England at Durham, *c.* 1130.

windows) as is the round line at Nevers. But the short time that is covered by this sequence—Saint-Étienne-de-Nevers was finished about 1097, and La Charité consecrated in 1106—shows that the change of arch form is not the crucial change in a development that takes place over a much longer period; and the continued use of round-headed forms with more advanced vaulting systems shows that the twelfth-century mason did not see in the creation of the pointed arch so great a step forward as some later historians of architecture have done. On the other hand, its wide use in the Cluniac Order served to distribute it in areas normally outside the sphere of Burgundian influence; it is used, for example, in the Cluniac priory churches of Ganagobie in the Basses-Alpes and of Le Wast in the Pas-de-Calais (built in the last years of the eleventh century) and appears in an apsidal window of Saint-Wulmer-de-Boulogne built in 1090[1].

B. THE TRANSEPT

The transepts of the smaller Cluniac churches are usually even plainer than the nave. Except for an undecorated window or windows set high, they generally offer few features of interest. At the most, as at Pommiers and Layrac, the wall arcades of the aisles are continued round them. It is only in and near Auvergne that their northern and southern walls are commonly decorated with an arcade, whether blind, as at Saint-Étienne-de-Nevers, Lurcy-le-Bourg[2], and Pérignac, or fenestrated as at Courpière[3] (Fig. 75). Their vaulting is generally a simple barrel or cross vault, until at the very end of the Romanesque period they are given rib vaults[4].

In the larger churches of the Order, however, they took a fresh development. At Cluny itself one arm of one of the transepts yet survives (Fig. 80); ennobled by the tremendous height of the vaulting piers, it is further adorned with two stories of arcading on the south wall. The restored section by Professor Kenneth Conant gives an idea of the grandiose scheme of the crossing (Fig. 78). Yet, even here, the decorative scheme of the nave only appears on the bay nearest to it (Fig. 81) and no two bays of the arm are alike. The same was true of the original transept of Souvigny[5].

At Paray-le-Monial, however, the transept is treated as part of the choir; and though the northern and southern extremities have only two stories of simple arcading, the side walls are as richly decorated as those of the choir. At La Charité the eleventh-century transept is elaborated nave fashion (Fig. 76); the three-tiered scheme of the

---

[1] Enlart, *Monument des Croisés*, 1, 67. Le Wast was built by Ida, mother of Godfrey de Bouillon, and he suggests that its use may here have been subject to Eastern influences from Palestine.

[2] An arcade with alternate pilasters and half columns.

[3] A dependency of Le Moûtier-de-Thiers, founded in 1150 and built then.

[4] E.g. at Noël-Saint-Martin.

[5] The upper floor of the south transept still exists above the present ceiling. On the south side the windows are framed in colonnettes, which are linked in the centre by a single abacus with a fluted pilaster between them.

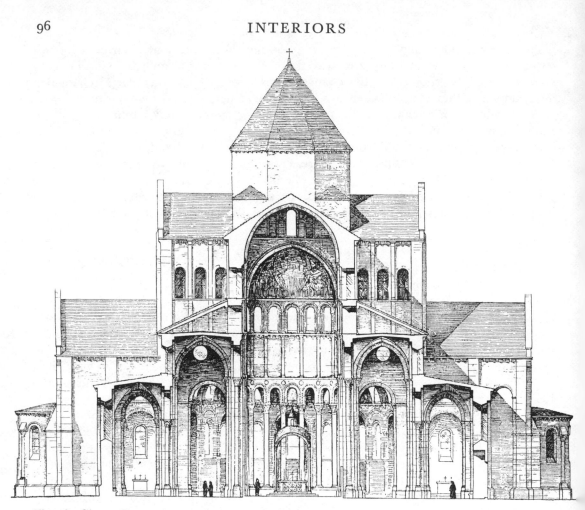

Fig. 78. Cluny. Restored section of Abbot Hugh's Basilica, taken between the Transepts, looking east.
By Professor Kenneth Conant.

side walls is rich and elegant, and the windows to north and south are larger and better proportioned, and are framed in a tall round-headed arcade[1]. At Saint-Martial-de-Limoges the transept was aisled, and had triforia like those of the nave; a similar disposition may still be studied in Saint-Sernin-de-Toulouse.

[1] The east side has a similar arcade to frame the eleventh-century apsidioles. A smaller windowed arcade was added above, when the choir was altered in the twelfth century. See Beaussart, p. 147.

C. THE CROSSING

If the transept is an unimportant part of the Cluniac scheme, the treatment of the crossing is generally bold and characteristic. From very early times it was the custom to surmount it by an octagonal cupola; the plan of the tower that masks this outside varies, but the scheme of the cupola itself is remarkably constant[1]. A cupola on squinches occurs at Romainmôtier and Champvoux, both of the early eleventh century, and at Saint-Étienne-de-Nevers, indubitably not later than 1097[2]. A classical instance of such a cupola on squinches is that of the surviving transept of Cluny (Fig. 77); and the type is followed in many Cluniac churches up and down France[3]. Occasionally the type is elaborated. At Montbron a double corbel is set above the squinch (Fig. 80); at Uzerche it rests on corbels; at Courpière (Fig. 83) a corbel is set below the squinch. At La Charité the squinch is double[4], and a sculptured man's head is set in the niche of the lesser squinch[5]; at Saint-Marcel-lès-Sauzet (Fig. 84) the squinch is likewise double, and the lesser one is filled with sculptures of the Evangelistic symbols, one to each corner[6]. At Saint-Sauveur-de-Castelsarrasin, a late and almost Gothic church, the octagonal cupola rests on a triple squinch. At Saint-Germain-les-Fossés a triangular block forms the base to the arch of the squinch (Fig. 82)[7]. At Compains the squinch (Fig. 81) is of unusual form; its arch rests on a base more or less triangular, but with a re-entrant angle on the long side; and this rests on a bracket[8]. At Nantua, which has a rib-vaulted nave, the same system is boldly applied to the lofty cupola; it rests on shallow squinches, and half-way up the drum are sculptured consoles from which spring the ribs (Fig. 85). At Prahecq (Fig. 86) this experimental treatment is courageously carried to its logical conclusion: four ribs spring from the angles, and suffice to support a lofty ovoid dome.

[1] It is not, of course, present everywhere; Brout is an example of a fine church without it; Champagne-Mouton of a plain one.

[2] According to Sr Puig i Cadafalch (*Premier art roman*, p. 88), such a cupola is found as early as between 1020 and 1040 at Sant Vincens de Cardona.

[3] Saint-Marcel-de-Cluny, Gourdon, Torsac, Connaux, Saint-Cydroine, Iguerande, Pouilly-lès-Feurs, Moûtier-d'Ahun, Maillezais (parish church), Saint-Germain-les-Fossés, Saint-Gengoux, Vaux (cupola now lost), Genzac, Mailhat, Paray-le-Monial, Varennes-l'Arconce, Layrac, Rosiers-Côtes-d'Aurec, Ternay, Saint-Sornin, Lozay, La Chapelle-Hugon, Corme-Écluse, Saint-Hilaire-de-Melle, Sagnac, Jailly, Rouy, Chantenay, Saint-Étienne-de-Nevers, Mont-Saint-Vincent, Blanot, Salles, Pouilly-lès-Feurs, Saint-Genis-d'Hiersac, Passirac, Champvoux. At Saint-Hippolyte the cupola has an oculus to the east; at Châtelmontagne a narrow opening to the west.

[4] As in the priory churches at Montambert and Saint-Cydroine, at Pont-du-Château the squinch is double, but plain.

[5] As in the single squinch at Sagnac. Sculptured ornament also occurs at Connaux.

[6] The arches of the cupola, including an arcade opening on the nave, follow the local use.

[7] The type is Auvergnat: an early example is at Néris, Allier, *c.* 1070.

[8] A simpler bracket squinch is used at Bourg-de-Thizy.

A four-ribbed dome with a circular key is also used at Meymac and Bellenaves, but it is less well planned. At Montreuil-Bonnin, a rib vault of eight ribs is used[1]; it may be rather later than the rest of the church. At Mouchan (Fig. 87) another system is used with impressive effect; instead of ribs there are wide flat *arcs doubleaux* that intersect to support a low-pitched vault. A similar scheme with narrower ribs is used at Relanges, where there is a vaulted room over it before the belfry. At Saint-Sornin (Fig. 88) there is another exceptional scheme; the cupola is on plain squinches as usual, but is supported by eight column-like ribs rising from consoles to a circular key. The alternative to squinches, pendentives, are much less common in Cluniac churches since they are more appropriate to a dome than an octagonal cupola. The rare examples are in Western France, at Courçon, Moings, Champmillon, Saint-Maurice (where the pendentive is adorned with sculpture), La Souterraine, Sérignac, Arthenac and Talmont[2].

This use of a cupola at the crossing naturally necessitated heavy piers to support it. They are normally based on the same system as that used for the nave; exceptionally, at Saint-Marcel-lès-Sauzet, they do not have the engaged columns which form part of the nave piers. At Montreuil-Bonnin the columns are doubled, and at Corme-Écluse, though it is an aisleless church of comparatively simple type, the piers at the crossing are complex, and rise in stages to the squinch. In many churches, such as Nantua, the effect of height given by these piers is most impressive; but with the tentative adoption of rib vaults they become more and more massive. A striking example of this tendency is Noël-Saint-Martin.

Various expedients were also adopted to give strength across the nave at this point. The most characteristic is the Auvergnat arch, which appears not only at Saint-Étienne-de-Nevers, Plauzat, and Courpière (Fig. 83), but also as far from Auvergne as Saint-Marcel-lès-Sauzet (Fig. 84). At Montbron another expedient is adopted: a low arch leads aisle-fashion into the transept, and above it the pier of the crossing is joined to the side wall. A similar device was used at Villeneuve, Aveyron.

D. THE CHOIR AND APSES

1. WITHOUT AMBULATORY

With few exceptions[3], the churches of the Order of Cluny ended to the east in one or more semicircular apses, vaulted in half domes[4]. The interior treatment of this apse shows a steady course of development. Many of the eleventh-century apses have been rebuilt; one of a primitive type survives at Saint-Séverin-en-Condroz. It is much lower

[1] And in the later church of Saint-Marcel-lès-Chalon.
[2] Taluyers near Lyons also has pendentives, but these look as if they may be a later modification.
[3] See p. 76.
[4] At Alleyras the half dome is five-sided, a local type, following the angular plan of the apse (see p. 60).

than the oblong choir; above it the wall is pierced by a trefoil window. The apse itself is lit by three round windows[1]. In Central France the apse is normally framed in an arch that cuts it off from the choir or crossing. The apse is often lit by three windows[2] and they are commonly framed in an arcade and often have colonnettes by their jambs. At Lezoux, Saint-Germain-les-Fossés and Payerne the arcade rests on twin columns with good effect. At Saint-Lazare-d'Avallon the scheme is a little extended: the apse is framed by an arch resting on fluted pilasters; the four windows are divided by twin columns; and between the windows and the pilasters an arcade of two arches forms a rudimentary choir.

There is often a plain rectangular choir before the apse[3], but usually the framing arch marks a clear division between the two. At Airaines and Le Wast the choir is formed by walls filling the arcades of the easternmost bay of the nave. The church of Semur-en-Brionnais (Fig. 89), of the middle of the twelfth century, is an example of a church mature in its ornamentation which yet still has the three elements of crossing, choir and apse conceived of as separate entities: it is far more developed in decoration than in plan.

The churches of the early and middle eleventh century show a remarkable austerity of treatment. At Champvoux (Fig. 90) the apse is of extreme simplicity; the choir is treated as a lesser nave, and the apse is framed in an unmoulded round arch spanning this. The treatment at Bourbon-Lancy (Fig. 91) is equally simple but more majestic in scale. In parts of Central France the scheme was modified by the adoption of an arcade of Auvergnat type round the apse, with smaller blind arches between the window arcades. At Riom-ès-Montagne, Claunay, Semelay and Rouy (Fig. 92) all the arcades are rounded; at Courpière the lesser arcades have the characteristic Auvergnat triangular head. In the Lyonnais, Taluyers and Rosiers-Côtes-d'Aurec have three arcades resting on twin columns, while Ternay (Fig. 95) has triple columns, the centre a fluted pilaster. In the Limousin, arcading of this type was developed by transforming the windows into niches, with or without lights; Vigeois (Fig. 94) is a typical example of a simple niched arcade on a large scale; Sagnac has an arcade of seven graduated arches which dates from the earliest years of the twelfth century[4], and Arnac-Pompadour (Fig. 93) has a smaller and more elaborate one, completed by a rib vault from consoles. The substitution of such a vault

[1] Cf. the early church of Ris, with three windows and an oculus.

[2] E.g. Mont-Saint-Vincent (Fig. 49), Mouthiers, Charente (Fig. 21), Saint-Marcel-lès-Sauzet (Fig. 84), Montbron, Saint-Séverin-en-Condroz, Varennes-l'Arconce, Semelay, Bonneviolle, Lempdes, Saint-Blaise-de-Genzac, Bellenaves, La Chapelle-Hugon, Pommevic, Binson. One window at Sainte-Colombe-en-Brulhois, Vicq; four at Saint-Lazare-d'Avallon; five at Menat, Montreuil-Bonnin, Meymac, Payerne; none at Saint-Genis-d'Hiersac.

[3] E.g. Semelay, Droiturier, Iguerande, Riom-ès-Montagne, Saint-Cydroine, Alleyras, Cénac, Sainte-Colombe-en-Brulhois, Vicq, Lisse, Pouilly-lès-Feurs. Saint-Allyre-de-Clermont (destroyed) had a choir in two bays 15½ metres long. Bréhier in *Revue Mabillon*, XIII, 1923, p. 21.

[4] See *Bull. Mon.* LXXXIX, 1930, p. 549.

for the traditional half dome marks the decline of true Romanesque; interesting early examples are Meymac[1] and Marolles-en-Brie with heavy ribs of rectangular section[2].

In Western France the tendency was rather to fuse the apse and choir, but it only gradually made itself felt. At Champdolent and Vaux-sur-Mer (Fig. 97) the apse remains extremely plain, but is lengthened by a barrel-vaulted bay; and the same scheme is used at Talmont and Saint-Maurice with the addition of an arcade to frame the three windows of the apse. At Peyrusse-Grande the arcade runs right round the choir and apse, and the windows are set above it; at Mornac (Fig. 98) the apse is arcaded and the choir is decorated with an arcade on consoles. The further development of this scheme occurs at Mezin and Mouchan. At Mezin (Fig. 102) the half dome of the apse and the barrel vault of the choir are united in a single whole, unbroken even by a cross arch; the walls have an arcade, and a line of arcaded windows above it; and the result is one of great dignity and accomplishment. At Mouchan the general scheme is the same, but the windows are not arcaded; in compensation the wall arcade is more richly decorated (Fig 96). In the fine choir of Cénac, probably dating from early in the twelfth century[3] (Fig. 101), the elongated half dome is strengthened by a heavy rib, but the integrity of the design is not affected[4]; the five windows are under the arcade, of which the engaged columns are cut by a string course to link them with the abaci of the capitals of the columns that frame the windows.

A unique development of this scheme was made at Moirax. The choir is there treated as a second "crossing", with a great dome, open to the sky at the centre, resting on squinches, and followed by the elongated half dome of the apse (Fig. 103). The result shows that the effect of an apsidal east end need not depend upon an ambulatory to give it dignity and impressiveness.

2. WITH AMBULATORY

An ambulatory of quadrangular plan formed part of the plan of Mayeul's abbey church at Cluny; and semicircular ambulatories are found in Cluniac churches of the middle of the eleventh century[5]. At Saint-Martial-de-Limoges (Fig. 73) the whole choir was a little raised, while the ambulatory went round it on the level of the nave; the arches were surmounted by an arcade and a clerestory of seven windows. Much the same plan is followed at Saint-Étienne-de-Nevers, consecrated in 1097, that closely follows Saint-Martial in its main lines; there is a small arcade above the rather stunted arcade of the ambulatory, and three windows, framed in colonnettes above, held together by a string

[1] See *Archives de la Commission des Monuments historiques*, IV, 52. Here the two flanking apsidioles are polygonal.   [2] Good later examples occur at Compains and Tauves.

[3] See Banchereau in *Cong. Arch.* XC, 1927, p. 243, and Mortet, I, 146.

[4] Cf. the four ribs of the half dome at Meymac, R. Fage in *Bull. Mon.* LXXXIII, 1924, p. 69.

[5] On early ambulatories, see L. Bréhier, *L'Art en France des invasions barbares à l'époque romane*, p. 140. Paris, n.d. (1930).

course. At Beaulieu the apsidal arcade is divided into pairs like that of the triforium, and there are four windows curving into the half dome. The plan of Saint-Étienne is reproduced in little in the church at Volvic (Fig. 100); here there is no arcade immediately above the arches, but the three windows are framed in an Auvergnat arcade with lesser arches between them[1]. At Saint-Hilaire-de-Melle the whole is reduced to a small scale with only four columns.

Of the great apse at Cluny nothing remains but its splendid capitals[2]. The recent publication[3] of a sketch of the apse made just as its demolition was begun has, however, made it easier to reconstruct it from the known data[4] (Fig. 105). Its dominating feature was the extraordinary height and slenderness of the columns[5] of the ambulatory, that stood like tall tapers round the high altar. That these were as impressive to their contemporaries as their image is to us is proved by the description of them by Hildebert du Mans[6]: if it were possible, he says, for those who dwell in heaven to take pleasure in a house made by hands, the ambulatory at Cluny would be a place where angels walked[7]. At Paray-le-Monial (Fig. 107) the columns are as slender but less lofty[8]. At Cluny the space between the eleven windows of the apse and the string course above the arches of the ambulatory was broken by fluted pilasters, as it is by a more closely set arcade at La Charité (Fig. 108). The windows were in line with those of the choir, but the traditional division between the apse and choir in height and decoration seems to have been maintained. At Paray and La Charité, however, another step toward unity was taken in the continuous treatment of apse and choir: they are more richly decorated instances on a large scale of that conception of choir and apse as one whole which we have already noted in Western France. The remains of the choir at Saint-Eutrope-de-Saintes, which has short colonnettes above the continuous frieze-like capital on the inner side to take the choir vault, suggests a similar unity of scheme. In most of the churches that emulated the great basilicas of the Order in having an ambulatory, the vault springs directly from above the arches, with no intervening space of wall to take arcading or windows. Uzerche is a simple example (Fig. 111) and Saint-Révérien a far more beautiful one (Fig. 109), doubtless inspired by La Charité but unpretentious in its imitation of the lower storey of the choir[9]. Dun-sur-Auron (Fig. 113) is exceptional in having the

[1] Mozat had an ambulatory originally, but its plan is uncertain. See *Cong. Arch.* Moulins, Nevers, p. 92.

[2] In the Musée Ochier at Cluny.

[3] By M. Marcel Aubert, in *Bull. Mon.* XCIV, 1935, p. 375.

[4] For a reconstruction made before this sketch was known see K. J. Conant in *Speculum*, VII, 1932, p. 23.

[5] Recut from antique shafts; cf. the re-use of material from the destroyed Roman city of Aventicum at Payerne. See Conant in *Speculum*, V, 1930, p. 278.

[6] *Vita Sancti Hugonis*, c. VI, Marrier, col. 432.   [7] *Deambulatorium angelorum*.

[8] Paray also followed Cluny in having the ambulatory narrower than the aisle of the choir.

[9] Here, as at Saint-Étienne-de-Nevers, the drums of the columns of the ambulatory are turned. They are almost the only large ones known. See *Cong. Arch.* LXXX, 1913, p. 346.

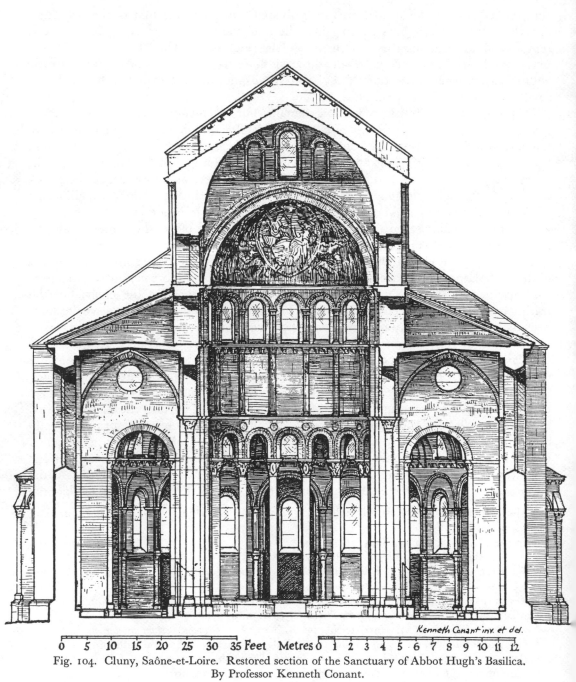

0 5 10 15 20 25 30 35 Feet Metres 0 1 2 3 4 5 6 7 8 9 10 11 12

Kenneth Conant inv. et del.

Fig. 104. Cluny, Saône-et-Loire. Restored section of the Sanctuary of Abbot Hugh's Basilica.
By Professor Kenneth Conant.

quadrilobed piers, often used for the nave in Eastern France[1], used for the ambulatory, with happy effect, since their composite capitals receive the cross arches of the ambulatory and choir vaults as well as the ambulatory arcade.

In most of the surviving instances the treatment of the walls of the apse within the ambulatory and its radiating chapels is comparatively simple. The drawing of the ambulatory at Cluny made from behind the high altar (Fig. 105) before its destruction shows an arcaded wall not unlike that at Paray-le-Monial (Fig. 112); because of the great height the pilasters were treated in two stages.

At Paray (Fig. 112) there is a row of small clerestory windows as well as a row of lower ones, with colonnettes at their jambs and a rich billet moulding as an arcade round them. At Uzerche there is a plain long window with an oculus above between the chapels. Elsewhere, however, the proportions are not so lofty as to admit a double range of windows. At La Charité (Fig. 114) this is compensated for by the rich fluted pilasters that support the cross arches of the vault, which are planned on the same principle as the nave piers of Cluny and Paray with lesser columns above them to take the actual cross arch. The windows of the circuit are framed in pilasters of equal richness, and those of the radiating chapels by simpler colonnettes[2]. At Saint-Révérien the windows are plain, but at the beginning of the apse a single bay on either side has two decorated windows one above the other[3].

The problem of vaulting the ambulatory was met by as many solutions as was the cognate problem of the vaulting of the aisles. The simplest and earliest type is the trapezoidal bays of groin vaulting used at Saint-Étienne-de-Nevers[4]. At Paray-le-Monial and Saint-Révérien (Fig. 110) there are multipartite groined vaults; at Saint-Eutrope-de-Saintes half-barrel vaults. The vaulting of the ambulatory at La Charité, probably dating from about 1130, with its cross arches out of centre with the arch of the vault, has an experimental quality about it[5]. Not less experimental is the vaulting of the contemporary double ambulatory at Saint-Martin-des-Champs[6] (Fig. 115). Unequal vaulting spaces are avoided by doubling the number of the outer supports,

[1] E.g. at Champdeniers.
[2] For a detailed description, see Beaussart, p. 224.
[3] Now blind but probably originally glazed.
[4] Cf. the ambulatory of Saint-Sernin-de-Toulouse. A. Rhein in *Bull. Mon.* LXXXII, 1923, p. 254.
[5] Dr Upham Pope tells me that it is paralleled in the East, for example at Isfahan in the Masjid-i-Jami about 1088. The parallel might be dismissed as pure coincidence; but Eudes Harpin, who became prior of La Charité in 1107, had gone, as Vicomte de Bourges, to Jerusalem, had fought the infidel and had been taken as prisoner to Bagdad, whence he was ransomed by Alexis Comnenus (Pignot, II, 338). Thus he may well have seen such constructions in Bagdad, where the same people were building as at Isfahan. Unfortunately, the pilgrimages of Cluniac monks to the East seem only to be recorded if they died on the way; thus we know that Roger, abbot of Figeac, and Richard, abbot of Saint-Cybard, so died, but we do not know who returned. See Ebersolt, *Orient et Occident*, p. 76.
[6] See E. Lefèvre-Pontalis in *Bib. de l'École des Chartes*, XLVII, 1886, p. 345.

giving alternate triangles and rectangles of groin vaulting[1]. A real advance is seen in the application of a rib vault to the large apse with an ambulatory (Fig. 116); choir and apse are treated as one, and all vaulted by a single system of eight ribs, sustaining gore-shaped cells with rounded sections that fall away from the centre of the vault almost as sharply as a half dome would. The piers used are of exceeding complex and irregular section in order to take the vaulting ribs of apse and ambulatory[2]. The next step is made about 1155 in the Cluniac apse at Domont (Fig. 117) with a blind triforium interposed between the arches and the windows[3]. The modulation of the scheme into true early Gothic in the choir of Saint-Leu-d'Esserent recaptures in another form the slender and lofty grace of the apse of Cluny[4]. In one detail it shows a new and interesting emphasis on orientation: the altars of the radiating chapels are no longer in the natural centre, according to Romanesque usage, but follow Noyon and Senlis in being strictly oriented and therefore set to one side[5].

E. CRYPTS

A crypt is not a normal part of a Cluniac church[6]; when it is found, it may usually be assumed that it was built to receive relics of especial importance of the patron saint of the church. In spite of Cluny's wealth of relics Saint Hugh's basilica had no crypt; and neither had the other eleventh- and twelfth-century churches of the Order, unless they were unusually rich in relics or held the body of a saint[7]: as at Saint-Lothain (Jura), Saint-Germain-d'Auxerre, Saint-Eutrope-de-Saintes, Coincy and Duravel, which owned the bodies of Saints Piamon, Agathon and Hilarion. Mozat, which had as many relics as Cluny and was a true centre of pilgrimage, had a crypt under its presbytery: a square room with niches on either side the altar and an ambulatory round it with four apsidal chapels[8]. The type, with or without apsidioles, is the classic one; for in a crypt an

---

[1] Cf. the single ambulatory of Uzerche, which is probably earlier.

[2] Illustrated by E. Lefèvre-Pontalis, *Cong. Arch.* LXXXII, 1919, p. 114.

[3] The great height is here made possible by the use of flying buttresses of primitive form, perhaps the earliest instance of their use.

[4] Cf. the Gothic choir of Vézelay, begun in 1170 and finished in 1201, which resembles it, but is a little loftier in proportion. Both have the traditional five radiating chapels.

[5] Viollet-le-Duc, *Dictionnaire raisonnée de l'architecture*, II, 461 *et seqq*. Saint-Denis followed the earlier use.

[6] The *cryptae* of the *Consuetudines Farfenses* were not crypts in an architectural sense, but chapels for private meditation.

[7] The Cluniac examples are Mozat, Saint-Eutrope-de-Saintes, Saint-Lothain, Saint-Gilles, Coincy, Duravel, Champdeniers and Île d'Aix: too widely scattered to be explained on any provincial basis. Uzerche has a crypt of about 1030, but this may have been built to solve the problem of an irregular site. The crypt at Vézelay dates from long before its inclusion in the Order; Royat and Saint-Germain-d'Auxerre are also pre-Cluniac.

[8] See Bréhier in *Revue Mabillon*, XIII, 1923, p. 10.

ambulatory is not a decorative luxury but an architectural necessity to bear the weight of the superstructure.

The chief problem to be met was that of the vault. Above the saint's tomb at Saint-Germain is a plain barrel vault; at Champdeniers (Fig. 118) cross arches joined the columns lengthways and across, and groin vaults were thrown across the bays thus formed. The chief experiment, however, was made at Saint-Eutrope-de-Saintes[1]. Here the piers of the crypt lie under the piers of the choir[2], and for the first time the oblong rib vault is applied to the wide central quasi-nave of the crypt (Fig. 120). The vault is supported by wide, low, unmoulded circular ribs; the ambulatory is (like that above) rather narrow; its vaults are pitched to the same height as those of the central part and are supported on similar cross arches rising on the inner side from the same height, but on the outer side received on columns standing higher than the piers. These are formed of a cruciform pier, with engaged columns on the ends of the arms and smaller columns in the angles, rather like the nave piers of Longpont; the apse itself is supported by heavy flat *arcs doubleaux*[3]. The church of Saint-Eutrope was consecrated in 1096[4] and the crypt cannot be later than this date. After more than eight hundred years it still successfully bears the weight of the choir above, and stands as a lasting testimony to the skill of the masons of the eleventh century.

F. CHAPELS OF THE ARCHANGELS

Not only did the church itself and its crypt have altars, but so also did the towers that rose above the nave. At Cluny the Tour-de-l'Horloge held a chapel of Saint Gabriel and Saint Raphael below the belfry; and a chapel of Saint Michael was set above the portal[5], in the thickness of the wall, with a miniature apse giving on to the nave by a corbelled-out tribune. Bouché tells us that it was lit by windows on every side: on the west by a niche window giving into the narthex; on the east by five narrow windows set between fluted pilasters framed above and below by a string course, giving on to the nave; and to the south and north by larger windows opening on to the outer air. It was vaulted in three bays of groin vaulting.

At Souvigny the northern tower of the façade held a chapel dedicated to Saint Michael; at Payerne the Tour-Saint-Michel has a vaulted niche high up inside it for

---

[1] The visitor to Saint-Eutrope must remember that the nave has been destroyed, and only the crossing and choir left.

[2] R. de Lasteyrie dates this crypt to the second quarter of the ninth century. *Arch. rel.* 1929, p. 157.

[3] Cf. the vault of the room over the porch at Moissac (Fig. 122).

[4] See Besnard in *Cong. Arch.* LXXIX, 1912, p. 195.

[5] Cf. the plan of the Carolingian church of Saint Gall, which shows two tower chapels dedicated to the two Archangels, Michael and Gabriel. Another early chapel of Saint Michael was at Saint-Maur-de-Glanfeuil: see C. de la Croix, *Fouilles archéologiques de l'Abbaye de Saint-Maur-de-Glanfeuil*, Paris, 1899. One such chapel is in the tower of Saint-Benoît-sur-Loire.

his altar, on a floor now lost[1]. At Romainmôtier his chapel is in the upper floor of the narthex (Fig. 123) and at Vézelay it is reduced to a niche in the first floor of the galilee, visible from below. At Semur-en-Brionnais the tribune at the west end (Fig. 66) probably represents another such chapel[2], modelled on that at Cluny itself. There was a kind of tribune at the west end of Layrac, before it was restored[3], that was probably the vestige of a chapel of Saint Michael; and similar tribunes once formed part of the porches at Châtelmontagne, Mont-Saint-Vincent and Mozat.

The chapel of Saint Gabriel at Cluny[4] remains remote in its eyrie, at the head of eighty-one steps, on the last floor but one of the Tour-de-l'Horloge. In it the visitor even of to-day enters into the time of the ascetic Bernard, silent and given to melancholy meditation, who used it as his oratory in the time of Peter the Venerable. The chapel is small and oblong, with a groin vault and a small semicircular apse adorned with a triple arcade resting on half columns with sculptured capitals. Round its straight walls runs a bench of stone. The walls are whitewashed; on them are painted the consecration crosses and an inscription recording the dedication to the Archangels Michael and Gabriel. The capitals are finely sculptured[5], and the whole, despite its recondite position and its small size, is conceived with the same finish as the great abbey that lay beneath it.

G. GALILEES

The galilee in which the lay folk gathered and the processions were marshalled was, in the great churches of the Order, conceived as a part of the nave. At Cluny, indeed, *navis minor* became its official appellation.

The surviving Cluniac galilees of this type are few. We know little of that of the second church at Cluny; and though it is tempting to suppose that it resembled that at Saint-Philibert-de-Tournus, we have no positive proof[6]. At Souvigny the outer wall of the narthex to the south alone survives; it has lofty wall arcades resting on engaged columns. At Romainmôtier there is still a narthex on two floors, preceded by a later porch. It is simple in construction. The exterior has a lombard cornice and pilaster strips; the ground floor has four aisled bays, quadrangular piers with engaged half

---

[1] See J. Vallery Radot in *Bull. Mon.* LXXXVIII, 1929, p. 461.

[2] The later tribune at Ganagobie may take the place of such a chapel.

[3] Tholin, p. 47.

[4] See Kenneth Conant, "La Chapelle Saint-Gabriel à Cluny" in *Bull. Mon.* LXXXVII, 1928, p. 55.

[5] Since it was dedicated, in a finished form, by a bishop who died in 1115 it provides a valuable *terminus ad quem* for the date of Hugh's church at Cluny. It is an integral part of the greater transept, so the choir must by then have been finished; and the likeness of its sculptures to those of the rest of the church confirms their early date.

[6] Professor Conant considers that it was probably a double narthex in the Byzantine manner, part for clergy and part for laymen.

columns on two sides, and a groin vault on cross arches. The upper floor (Fig. 123) is loftier and more elegant in proportion; it has circular columns with sculptured capitals, and a similar vault to that below. It was originally completed by two low square towers.

The galilee at Romainmôtier probably dates from about 1100[1], but is definitely primitive in style for that date. For by then, in Burgundy at any rate, nave and galilee alike were enormously enriched. The surviving narthex at Vézelay, dedicated in 1132, has piers like those of the nave, and shelters a series of sculptured portals of the utmost beauty (Fig. 124).

Already, however, the narthex was often conceived of less as part of the nave than as a porch[2]. At Mozat the early galilee[3] under the west tower is open on three sides; at Bredons the porch, dating from the end of the eleventh century[4], is fortified. At Paray-le-Monial the galilee built in the time of Saint Hugh is thought of as a porch, with its sides an open arcade. It is of two bays, divided into nave and aisles, with groin vaults. Its massive piers are so richly decorated that they are not alike even in section[5]. The room above it is similarly aisled and with cruciform piers without capitals. This porch narthex becomes the classical type for the twelfth century: typical early examples are those at Chambon, Mont-Saint-Vincent, and Châtelmontagne[6] (Fig. 127). At Moûtiers-en-Puisaye (Fig. 128) the porch type is strongly influenced by cloister construction[7]. At Moissac the extraordinarily rich side portal leads to a galilee before the church (Fig. 121). The curious massive rectangular ribs of its vault are repeated with greater skill in the vault of the chamber above[8] (Fig. 122). The narthex at Charlieu (Fig. 208) is another example of the porch type, unique in having an entrance to the side; simple in plan, it is incredibly rich in decoration. Above it is a room beautified by the sculptured framing of its great window, originally unglazed (Fig. 129). It probably dates from about 1140[9]. One of the last great Cluniac narthex porches is that at Saint-Leu-d'Esserent (Fig. 126). Here Romanesque is modulating into Gothic: and in the arcaded windows on either

[1] The porch that precedes it is nearly a century later.

[2] It should be noted, too, that the idea of a porch exercised some influence on the planning of such portals as those of Beaulieu and Carennac, that are considerably recessed.

[3] Bréhier, in *Revue Mabillon*, XIII, 1923, p. 10, sets it before 1000. Cf. the galilee porch of the end of the eleventh century at Saint-Benoît-sur-Loire. If so it is pre-Cluniac, as Mozat did not enter the Order until 1095.

[4] The church was rebuilt in 1074 and consecrated in 1095. Rochemonteix, p. 68.

[5] They have been reconstructed, but follow the original design.

[6] Châtelmontagne also has a spacious porch to the south.

[7] The filling of the arcades is later.

[8] On their construction see A. K. Porter, *Construction of Lombard and Gothic Vaults*, p. 12.

[9] This was at one time dated just before the death of Peter the Venerable in 1156; but at that time the priory was in such financial difficulties that he attempted to sell or mortgage it to Cluses: obviously so expensive an undertaking as the porch cannot date from so late a period in his life. Virey (*Les Églises romanes de l'ancien diocèse de Mâcon*), 2nd ed. p. 133, also puts it in the first half of the twelfth century.

side of the central door, the influence of the cloister plan is manifest[1]. Above is a gallery, with transverse rib vaulting of an acutely pointed form. Its Gothic successor at Binson, cruelly mutilated in the Great War, is on a smaller scale, but perpetuates the tradition of the Cluniac narthex porch.

These porches with rooms over show the narthex yet further incorporated into the abbey buildings. Just as at Cluny itself the towers of the narthex were used as muniment rooms, so at Saint-Leu-d'Esserent and Charlieu—and probably at Moissac, Paray-le-Monial[2] and Romainmôtier—was the room over the porch used for the storage of documents. In other instances the analogy is rather with the inner side of the narthex at Cluny, for at Vézelay, Châtelmontagne, Mont-Saint-Vincent and Mozat there is a "tribune" which serves as a chapel opening into the church.

H. ALTARS

The high altar at Cluny was consecrated in November 1095 by Urban II, the first monk of the abbey to attain the Papal throne. Its marble slab yet survives (Fig. 130), decorated with a cusped border sculptured with foliage. Such cusped ornament is of great antiquity in Syria, and is found on rectangular altars in the Hauran as early as the fifth century[3]. M. Paul Deschamps has shown[4] that the French altar slabs with this type of border ornament are to be found grouped in the departments of the Hérault and the Pyrénées-Orientales, and sporadically in the cathedrals of Rodez and Gerona, at Saint-Sernin-de-Toulouse and at Cluny[5].

The earliest of these is that at Capestang in the Hérault, dating from the time of Charles the Simple, that is to say, from the closing years of the ninth or early in the tenth century; the latest may well be those at Cluny, consecrated in November 1095, and at Saint-Sernin consecrated in May 1096, likewise by Urban II. An eighteenth-century traveller[6] compared the Cluny example with one in the church of Saint-Pierre-le-Vieux: but the evidence is hardly sufficient to justify an assertion that the altar slab of Mayeul's church was of the same type.

[1] Cf. the earlier "narthex" at Moutiers-en-Puisaye: but it is just possible that this once formed part of a cloister.

[2] The room has a window into the church, but it is above eye level.

[3] I owe this information to the kindness of Mr George Horsfield. He tells me that two semi-circular altar stones with similar ornament are in the Corinth Museum. A fragment of a rectangular stone is on the path to S. Paolo alle Tre Fontane near Rome.

[4] "Tables d'autel de Marbre exécutées dans le Midi de la France au Xe et au XIe siècle", in *Mélanges d'histoire du moyen âge offerts à M. Ferdinand Lot...*, p. 137, Paris, 1925; and "L'autel roman de Saint-Sernin-de-Toulouse..." in *Bulletin archéologique*, 1925.

[5] I omit the two he mentions at Damascus, as these probably belong to the earlier Syrian group.

[6] *Voyages liturgiques de France...par le Sieur de Moléon*, p. 148, Paris, 1718, cited by Deschamps, "Tables d'autel", p. 157.

M. Deschamps concludes that they are made of Pyrenaean marble; it is interesting that among the quarries he enumerates two were on Cluniac estates at Arles-sur-Tech and Saint-Béat, and a third, which he is inclined to consider the true source, at another Cluniac centre, Saint-Pons-de-Thomières. It is actually within this monastery that he is inclined to place the workshop from which they all emerged[1].

The Cluny altar slab was probably originally set, like two at San Colombano and a late twelfth-century altar surviving at Paray-le-Monial[2], with pilasters at the corners and a sculptured slab in front. An altar at Notre-Dame-d'Airaines (Fig. 131) is similarly constructed, but with three colonnettes to support it and plain stonework between.

I. LECTERN

The liturgical furnishings of the Cluniac churches do not for the most part fall within the domain of architecture. An exception may perhaps be made in favour of the lectern at Much Wenlock[3], of which the desk part was discovered buried in the priory grounds some years ago. It was of stone, architecturally treated; the desk block has a moulded edge and sides that are adorned with sculpture of scrolled foliage. The stone appears to be local.

[1] M. Deschamps is inclined to follow Rohault de Fleury in thinking the lobes were indications of how the sacred elements should be placed upon the altar. On this I would not express an opinion without further knowledge of Syrian usage. M. Rey considers that the marble is from Saint-Béat. *Sculpture romane languedocienne*, p. 24.

[2] Illustrated in Viollet-le-Duc, *Dictionnaire raisonnée de l'architecture*, II, 55, Fig. 23.

[3] My thanks are due to Mrs Ward, the present owner of Much Wenlock Priory, for drawing my attention to this unusual object.

C. EXTERIORS

The liturgical problems of the Romanesque monastic church were to provide fit sites for the altars, adequate space for the choir, and a resonant setting for the almost ceaseless chanting; its architectural problems were the lighting and vaulting of the nave and aisles, and the discovery of a right cadence for the apse. All its purpose and significance lay within the building, and its exterior was but the casing of the shrine within.

Consequently, it is idle to expect the same majesty of ornament on the outside of a Benedictine church as is found within. Mabillon himself was disappointed with the first sight of the exterior of the abbey church of Cluny: "Primus coenobii aspectus non omnino representat animo conceptam loci majestatem, nec quisquam facile in animum induxerit, sub vili tegularum concavarum operimento tantae dignitatis basilicam residere[1]." Such rich Romanesque façades as Notre-Dame-la-Grande at Poitiers or the cathedral of Angoulême were primarily evolved for cathedral and city churches that served the outside world rather than a cloistered community; it was only late in the Romanesque period that the triforium arcadings of the nave were applied to the exterior of such monastic churches as La Charité, and that the priories of South-Western France came, by analogy with the local churches, to have richly sculptured façades.

The exception to this rule is the portal that links the monastic community within the abbey with Christendom without. From early times this was adorned with architectural enrichments and, as the art was reborn, with sculpture; but the finest Cluniac portals, such as those of Vézelay and of Hugh's basilica at Cluny itself, were destined to be protected and enclosed by a narthex, and do in fact form part of the interior decoration of the church. It is when a recess takes the place of the narthex, as at Carennac and Beaulieu, that such portals, while still protected, seem indeed to form part of the exterior of the church. The fantastically rich carving of the porch at Charlieu, that dates from the last years of Cluniac greatness, serves to show the decline of this principle, and marks another stage in the relation between sculpture and architecture.

A. THE APSE

1. WITHOUT RADIATING CHAPELS

Since the high altar was the true centre of the church, the apse that contained it was an important feature of the exterior. It held the altar as a reliquary holds a relic, and like a reliquary it was ornamental. It was the first part of the exterior of the church to receive any architectural enrichment; and styles of ornament evolved for apsidal use gradually extended to other parts of the exterior.

[1] "Voyage en Bourgogne", in *Œuvres Posthumes*, II, 1724, p. 19.

We have no knowledge of the exterior treatment of Mayeul's church at Cluny; its ground plan suggests a series of massive angular buttresses. The earliest apses are, generally speaking, the plainest. The triple apse of Champvoux (Fig. 132) is absolutely devoid of ornament; the single apse of Saint-Cydroine was once equally plain[1]. An equal simplicity is evident in the rather low-pitched apses of parish churches in the neighbourhood of Cluny, such as Blanot, Colombier, La Frette, Massy, Taizé and Bergesserin, that belonged to the Order and for the most part date from the middle of the eleventh century at latest. Another rather later plain apse is that of the priory of Augerolles in the Puy-de-Dôme, which is five-sided. It has no buttresses; its only adornment is a billet course that frames and links the windows.

In the next stage the apse is strengthened by pilaster buttresses[2]. In eastern districts these pilaster strips followed Lombard tradition and were linked by an arcade forming a kind of cornice. A fine early example is the apse of Saint-Lothain in the Jura (Fig. 133). At Saint-Séverin-en-Condroz (Fig. 236) the decoration is applied to all three apses; it is noteworthy for the height of the choir in comparison with the apses. Such "Lombard" decoration is also to be found in the region near Cluny, for example at Vaux, Mazille, Laizé and Germagny, but the tendency is to cut down the number of arcades and to widen their span: an example of this is the church of Bey, belonging to Saint-Marcel-lès-Chalon[3]. At Coudun the pilasters are stepped and the arcade is enriched with sculpture. At Arnac the arcade is reduced to a single arch spanning the space between the pilasters. Alternatively at Malay there is an arcade and no pilaster strips. At Payerne (Fig. 138), as on the narthex of Romainmôtier, the pilaster changes half-way up into an engaged column[4]. Here the central apse is thus enriched, and the subsidiary apsidioles are left plain. At Semur-en-Brionnais (Fig. 139) there is an oddly composite plan; a cornice arcade recalls the earlier Lombard style, and the pilaster buttresses are enriched with capitals.

Outside the eastern area pilaster buttresses were commonly used without any arcade. A very early and simple example is at Lieu-Dieu, in the Doubs, where all three apses are thus treated. At Saint-Hippolyte (Fig. 224) only the central apse has pilaster buttresses[5]. At Relanges the central apse has rather narrow pilaster buttresses, oddly supplemented by secondary ornamental pilaster strips rising from the centre of the arch over the windows. In Saint Hugh's chapel at Berzé-la-Ville (Fig. 166) an arcade is used on the lower part of the apse, with simple pilaster strips above. Here the whole is completed by a cornice on modillions: and such a cornice becomes increasingly important in the development of the scheme, especially in Auvergne. Typical examples are

[1] Two heavy buttresses were added later.

[2] Mr Clapham considers that their earliest appearance may be at San Pietro Civate, Como, early in the eleventh century.   [3] See Dickson, p. 80.

[4] The same scheme is followed the other side of France at Mezin, but with a billet cornice and modillions instead of a Lombard arcade.

[5] At Figeac the central apse has modillions and the subsidiary apses have not.

Brout, Courpière[1], Mars and Lempdes, but the scheme is found as far north as Binson[2] and Bellegarde-du-Loiret, and as far west as Layrac and Corme-Écluse. The *modillons à copeaux* that French Romanesque architecture derived from the East[3] are found at Brout Lezoux and Saint-Marc-de-Souvigny; cornices of the Western type, with a metope-like decoration in sculpture, at Retaud, Saintes and Ruffec; an Auvergnat inlay of different coloured stones at Mozat; a crenellated cornice at Saint-Martin-des-Champs at Paris; a "berrichon" cornice with spherical segments between the modillions, at Marolles-en-Brie; and an egg-and-dart-like form, with an indented part between the modillions, at Vézelay. The simple modillion cornice, sculptured or plain, occurs in all districts. The cornice, indeed, is one of the architectural features of the churches of the Order that follow local usage and contemporary fashion; all that can be said is that the Burgundian modillion cornice is found very widely distributed in the Order[4]. Occasionally the cornice is set well below the line of the roof, leaving a frieze-like space above it: examples are Pommevic and Mouchan[5]. At Charras the whole is massive and simple as a fortress: it may probably represent a rather later modification of the original apse to meet the needs of more troubled times. At Layrac a very simple system of pilaster buttresses and modillion cornice is lightened by a perfectly plain arcade of which the head reaches half-way between the low windows and the cornice.

The culminating scheme of stepped pilaster buttresses is La Charité (Fig. 140). Here radiating chapels were added later in imitation of Cluny[6]; but though the modification was successfully assimilated into the interior scheme, it remains irrelevant to the exterior, which is essentially that of a church with parallel apses. Outside (as inside) transept, choir and apse are of one plan. A polylobed arcade resting on columns (on the transept) and on decorated pilasters (on the apse) runs right round; below it comes the long line of round-headed windows. Transept and apse alike are supported by stepped pilaster buttresses. In its original form, completed by two subsidiary apses on either side of the central apse, the effect must have been magnificent.

In Western France the arcade had another development; it was less in relation with the windows than with the cornice. At Mouthiers (Fig. 134) there still seems to be a faint reminiscence of the Lombard plan; the central apse has a double arcade in each bay, rising from a pilaster strip that makes a background for the column buttress.

---

[1] Enriched by a billet moulding beneath the cornice. An example near Cluny is Saint-Point, on all three apses.

[2] With sloped tops to the buttresses and a billet cornice. It was sadly damaged in the Great War.

[3] See Mâle, *Art et artistes du moyen âge*, pp. 30, 55 *et seq.*

[4] For a classification of Romanesque cornices, see Deshoulières, in *Bull. Mon.* LXXIX, 1920, p. 27.

[5] It is possible that this represents a change in the level of the roof; but it seems to be so far a local peculiarity as to make it likely that it is an original feature. Cf. the apse at Saint-Lizier, with an angular base and a semicircular top.

[6] They imitate those at Cluny in having engaged column buttresses with capitals, a modillion cornice and plain round-headed windows.

An alternative form of such buttresses was to shape them as engaged columns; and this usage was widespread in the Order of Cluny, doubtless because it was that followed in Abbot Hugh's great church at Cluny itself. In early examples, as at Lezoux and Fontanella, the columns have no capitals and end cone-wise below the cornice; but capitals were soon added, and the scheme thus given a new decorative importance. This development is characteristic of Western France, and of the mature Romanesque period. The central apse of Cénac (Fig. 136) affords an excellent example, with rather slender columns giving great apparent length, and small foliate capitals that take their place among the modillions of the cornice. The columns are cut by a string course running from the abaci of the capitals of the window arches[1]. A parallel instance is the apse of Moirax (Fig. 137) which is alike in essentials but more happily proportioned. Here the windows have no frame but a course of billet moulding that cuts the columns about two-thirds of the way up. At Moings the column is set against a wide pilaster[2] and thus a similar moulding is given a new variety of plane. At Varaize (Fig. 141) the column is unbroken, but is duplicated.

In Central France the column buttresses were developed into an arcade. At Meymac the three polygonal apses have a column buttress at each angle, linked to the next by a single plain arch over each window. At Champdolent the cornice between the column buttresses is arcaded and rests on elaborate consoles. At Vaux this arcade is developed into a little colonnade resting on an ornamental frieze.

Finally, the two types of arcade were combined to form one of the beautiful and characteristic features of West French architecture of the mature Romanesque period. At Saint-Maurice (Fig. 142) the windows are themselves framed by column buttresses and a decorated arch, and above is an arcade resting on a moulding that cuts the long column buttresses of the apse. The arcade is continued round the apses that (exceptionally) terminate the transept to north and south. At Talmont the apse (Fig. 143), romantically and dangerously set on the edge of the cliff, has a similar scheme yet further enriched: a moulding below the window cuts both sets of column buttresses, the arcading is closer set, and the cornice more elaborate. At Retaud (Fig. 144) the scheme is finally elaborated. The base of the whole polygonal apse is conceived as a moulded column base; the course below the window is yet more richly carved, the arches over the windows are pointed, and the upper arcade in the side bays rests on coupled colonnettes and has a triple moulding on the architrave and a frieze above. This represents the culminating point in the decoration of apses without radiating chapels as it may be studied in the architecture of the Order of Cluny.

[1] The pilaster buttresses of the subsidiary apses are similarly cut. Instead of a true cornice there is a course of billet moulding borne by figure modillions on the central apse, and without modillions on the others. The whole (including the cornice) is closely paralleled at the Cluniac priory of Bonneviolle in the Lot. Cf. also Bersol in the Gironde.

[2] As on the otherwise plain apse at Saint-Cyr.

2. WITH RADIATING CHAPELS

The use of radiating chapels round the apse not only created fresh possibilities of interior treatment but also greatly enriched the exterior. With these as buttresses, the choir and central apse could be bolder and loftier; and with these to provide a broad and varied base the whole composition of the east end passed beyond structural needs into artistic creation. "C'est sans doute le plus beau crescendo architectural qui existe", says M. Male[1]; "théorème au dedans, l'église...s'achève en ode au dehors."

There is no worthy picture surviving of the grouped apses of Saint-Martial-de-Limoges; we must remain uncertain of its details. But its lesser derivative, Saint-Étienne-de-Nevers (Fig. 145), though unhappily modified on the southern half, may serve to give us some idea of the scheme. Here the lofty central apse follows local usage in having an arcade between the cornice and the windows; it has heavy stepped pilaster buttresses with a blind arcade on little colonnettes between[2]. The ambulatory walls are plain but for a simple cornice; the absidioles have alternately pilaster buttresses and engaged columns cut by a line of billet moulding that frames the windows. The want of relation between their windows and the ambulatory windows that come between suggests that the scheme has been designed from the interior, with the exterior design as a secondary consideration. Châtelmontagne (Fig. 146) follows the general scheme of Saint-Étienne, but has no arcade round the choir and a simplified moulding round the windows. Volvic is not unlike in plan, though on a much smaller scale; its central apsidiole, that forms a chapel for the relics of Saint-Priest, is enriched with a cornice resting on *modillons à copeaux* and with an Auvergnat stone inlay above the string course. Beaulieu likewise resembles Châtelmontagne in its general proportions, though enriched by absidioles in the transept; these have pilaster buttresses, while those round the apse have engaged-column buttresses. The scheme, however, is hardly yet completely integrated.

It did not, indeed, receive its authoritative form until the great apse of Hugh's abbey church at Cluny was planned in 1088. Certain rather inadequate drawings of it[3], and one of the transept absidioles that still exist, make it possible to reconstitute it with reasonable security (Fig. 147). Here the whole was dominated by the line of the lofty transept, considerably higher than the central apse. This apse had a line of windows, probably arcaded; then came the great semicircle of the ambulatory, heightened in

---

[1] *L'Art allemand et l'Art français au moyen âge*, 1917, p. 102.

[2] A similar scheme is used on the central apse of Saint-Aignan-de-Cosne, and greatly enriched at La Charité. A. Philippe ("L'architecture religieuse au XIe et XIIe siècle dans l'ancien diocèse d'Auxerre", in *Bull. Mon.* 1904, p. 76) states that the usage is not found on the other bank of the Loire, or in the dioceses of Mâcon, Autun, Chalon or Langres.

[3] See e.g. a lithograph of 1823 reproduced in Conant, "Five old prints of the Abbey Church of Cluny", *Speculum*, III, 1928, p. 403. Another by Lallemand seems greatly to exaggerate the depth of the chapel buttresses, while their form is inconsistent with that of the buttresses of the surviving absidiole.

effect by its buttresses, and then (much lower) the five radiating apsidal chapels of which the line was continued by the absidioles of the transept. Their detail may fairly be taken from the surviving examples (Fig. 148). One has plain windows, engaged-column buttresses with capitals up to the spring of the window arch, and a cornice with rather small modillions. The second apsidiole that survives shows a similar cornice and similar buttresses, but enriched by a billet moulding over the window and round the absidioles at the level of the capital of the buttress. The east end of Paray-le-Monial remains (Fig. 149) to give us an idea in miniature of that of its great prototype: the same lofty transept and choir, the same windowed apse (with the windows beautifully framed in a decorated arcade resting on fluted pilasters), the same quasi-Lombard arcading below the cornice, the same great ambulatory and the same radiating chapels with the same buttresses and billet moulding: all minished and stinted and yet composing a splendid architectural whole[1].

Yet if Paray is a lesser imitation of Cluny, the other great churches of the Order were not content merely to imitate. Saint-Hilaire-de-Melle depends upon line and proportion alone for the elegance of its eastern end. The choir apse is level with the transept; below it comes the sweeping line of the ambulatory, and below this again the radiating chapels. There is no ornament except for bracket modillions used for every cornice, and for engaged column buttresses on the absidioles.

At Montbron, on the other hand, while there are five chapels in imitation of Cluny, the upper apse, the chapels and the absidioles of the transept are all arcaded, with an arcade resting on engaged columns with capitals[2]. At Vigeois (Fig. 150) a similar arcading is applied to the central polygonal apse and to the apsidioles of the transept; the two secondary chapels have pilaster buttresses up to the tops of the windows. The apses of the churches with radiating chapels in Western France follow local usage and are richly arcaded. A noble example—now unhappily incomplete—is that of Saint-Eutrope-de-Saintes (Fig. 152)[3]. This has the engaged-column buttresses of the choir linked by a sculptured arcade. The windows, themselves arcaded, are surmounted by a small ornamental oculus. A sculptured moulding links their abaci, and cuts across the buttresses. A string course below the windows likewise cuts them, and below this come the decorated windows of the crypt. The surviving absidiole has similar buttresses similarly broken; below the cornice is a small arcade resting on a sculptured plinth. Here the general scheme is quite different from that at Cluny; there is no gradual culmination to the main apse, no "crescendo architectural", but a ground plan followed out at an almost uniform height and depending on sculptural enrichment for its effect. Similarly at Dun-sur-Auron (Fig. 153) the whole remains low; the ambulatory rises little above the chapels, and these are linked by an arcaded cornice and to some extent obscured by their elaborate buttresses of a half column set against a pilaster and flanked by another on either side.

[1] See *Archives de la Commission des Monuments historiques*, IV, Pl. 57.   [2] *Ibid.*
[3] The buttress is a later addition.

The final expression of the Cluniac Romanesque scheme may be taken to be the apse of Saint-Martin-des-Champs at Paris, built between 1130 and 1140. This follows the tradition of Cluny itself in having the central apse of simple design and set lower than the main roof line. A fresh balance is given to the design by the prolongation of the central absidiole; and a simpler line to the apse as a whole by a continuous cornice corbelled our squinch-wise over the re-entrant angles of the chapels (Fig. 151). The windows of the central chapel follow the Cluniac tradition in having billet moulding above; the buttresses are alternately simple pilasters and rather ungraceful column buttresses rising from rectangular bases without capitals but with cone endings. The subsequent Cluniac apses—such as Domont and Saint-Leu-d'Esserent—have renounced the Romanesque outline, and with their range of flying buttresses are close precursors of true Gothic. Vézelay itself has a purely Gothic apse; but, if later buttresses are discounted, its clustering chapels, lofty choir and round-headed windows show a remarkable survival of the Cluniac Romanesque tradition into the thirteenth century.

B. THE TRANSEPT

It has been said that the transepts of Cluniac buildings tended to be simple in their interior aspects; they were no less simple on the exterior. Perfectly plain transepts with plain buttresses exist, for example, at Relanges, Jailly, Semelay, Mézin and Nantua; and transepts with no more ornament than a simple cornice at Beaulieu, Thuret, Vigeois, Uzerche, Saint-Eugène, Varennes-l'Arconce and Rouy. At Romainmôtier, however, as at Saint-Séverin-en-Condroz and Sant' Egidio di Fontanella, the transept has a Lombard arcade and pilaster strips.

At Cluny itself the transepts gained new importance from their height, but their decoration was confined to a simple modillion cornice and to pilaster strips running between the windows (Fig. 154). The same plan is followed at Paray-le-Monial (Fig. 157) for both choir and the eastern side of the transept; the north and south ends are broken only by their windows (and the string course that runs beneath them) and the sculptured doors leading into the church, and the western side has only a single pilaster buttress.

In Central France, however, local tradition gave the transept a greater importance. At Saint-Étienne-de-Nevers (Fig. 155) its three upper windows are framed by an Auvergnat arcade, with alternate round and pointed heads to the arches, and the base line of the pedimental gable is broken by an oculus. At Courpière (Fig. 158) it has a double arcade resting on an engaged column with a handsome capital. At Chauriat (Fig. 156) the whole is even more characteristically Auvergnat. The lower windows are set in a double arcade, the upper in another of five arches; and above this the whole gable is filled with an inlay of coloured stone.

At La Charité the transept was for the first time considered as a part of the choir in its interior planning; and this view of it had an equal influence on its exterior design (Fig. 140) which in its fenestration and in its richly sculptured arcading follows with little modification the design of the apse. Nothing to equal this elaboration can be found elsewhere, except in the few churches of Western France—for example Talmont— which for practical reasons have their main entrance in the northern or southern wall of the transept, and therefore have it endowed with the dignity of a façade and adorned with sculptured arcading.

C. THE FLANKS OF THE CHURCH

1. WITHOUT BUTTRESSES

The side walls of any building have their structure dictated by the stresses within: the exterior is the corollary of the interior. If a church is not vaulted, but ceiled, it may have perfectly plain outer walls, but if it is vaulted, these walls must usually be strengthened by some form of buttress in places that correspond with the bays of the nave and with other points of stress.

The entirely plain exteriors of Cluniac churches are therefore nearly always those of churches that have, or were originally intended to have, wooden roofs. Typical examples are the churches of Saint-Cydroine (Fig. 233), Bourg-de-Thizy, Chavenat, and Saint-Martin-du-Tartre, which have never received a vault. Another is the church at Noël-Saint-Martin (Fig. 159), also an aisleless church, built soon after it was acquired by Saint-Martin-des-Champs in 1096[1]. Further examples are common among the small aisleless churches of the south and south-west, such as Saint-Turquoît[2] (Fig. 190).

The exterior of Montreuil-Bonnin is equally plain, with nothing to break the expanse of dressed stone but the plain round-headed windows and the simple modillions of the cornice of the transept. This is an aisleless church, and is vaulted: but the half columns that support the cross arches of the vault are set against a pilaster that in fact forms an interior buttress. A similar plan is more simply followed in the little Cluniac church at Taizé, which has no aisles but has a cross vault[3]. At Malay, a grange of Cluny[4], though it is vaulted—the nave with a cross vault and the aisle with groin vaults—the side walls are plain. Probably they were originally intended for a wooden roof, and proved massive enough to take the vault.

2. WITH RECTANGULAR BUTTRESSES

We know little of the exterior of Mayeul's abbey church at Cluny. Its apse was but- tressed, and we may safely assume from its known size that the aisle walls were buttressed likewise. That its exterior was of extreme simplicity is probable on every ground;

[1] Here it has later been found necessary to add buttresses to the façade.

[2] By analogy with vaulted churches, ceiled churches also sometimes have their walls broken by pilaster buttresses. E.g. Mazille, a doyenne of Cluny from c. 1055, and Péronne.

[3] See Virey, 2nd ed. p. 431.   [4] *Ibid.* p. 331.

local usage[1], the ground plan, and Prévost's drawing of the tower have enabled Professor Conant to produce a sketch reconstruction (Fig. 219). A similar scheme is followed at Mont-Saint-Vincent. It is slightly more developed at Mozat: here the nave buttresses are less heavy, and the aisle buttresses are broken by a string course beneath the windows. At Baume (Fig. 165) the nave is not buttressed, but the aisles have heavier buttresses in two stages. At Bourbon-Lancy (Fig. 160), built between 1030 and 1050[2], and at Gassicourt, since they were never vaulted, these buttresses are slighter.

The normal tendency was to lengthen these buttresses, whether by continuing them by an angular termination of some length, as at Semelay, or by prolonging them pilaster-wise. This course was followed at Saint-Martial-de-Limoges. Other examples are Bernay, Saint-Félix, Vigeois, Rouy (where they are in three stages), Bourg-de-Maisons, Varennes-l'Arconce, Uzerche and Pont-du-Château. At Paray-le-Monial such pilaster buttresses are used for the walls of both nave and aisles.

In certain churches of the mature Romanesque period the rectangular buttresses are prolonged as far as the cornice. Father Martellange's drawing of Abbot Hugh's basilica at Cluny (Fig. 161), when compared with the surviving transept (Fig. 154) and with the transept of Paray-le-Monial (Fig. 157), suggests that this was the scheme originally employed for the nave walls before they had to be strengthened with flying buttresses.

At Saint-Marc-de-Souvigny this pilaster-like prolongation is made after an angular stage, a form that does not seem to have been structurally very successful. In Western France they are more usually, and more successfully, in one straight line, as at Breuillet, Fontenet and Saint-Béat. At Saint-Béat, Moirax and Iguerande the aisles (vaulted with half-barrel vaults) are pitched so that their roof is continuous with that of the nave. At La Souterraine, a larger and later aisled church (Fig. 162), rectangular pilaster buttresses are used for both nave and aisle walls, with happy architectural effect. In the early twelfth century Cluniac churches of Cotte and Mazille the side walls have pilaster buttresses and a cornice, while the apse is treated with pilaster strips and a Lombard arcade. At two churches that have little else in common the aisle buttresses are elaborated into an arcade. At Saint-Étienne-de-Nevers the nave itself has simple rectangular buttresses with sloped tops; the aisles have the triforium windows linked by a moulding; the aisle windows framed in a heavy plain arcade of which the supports form pilaster buttresses. At Layrac, which is aisleless, a similar scheme is adapted to meet different needs: the whole is in one stage, and the very long plain pilaster buttresses are linked by an arcade below the cornice.

In certain churches of the Dordogne, such as Tremolat (Fig. 163) and Tayac, the pilaster buttresses are slightly recessed; the reason is structural, but the practice serves to give a little relief to a whole that is of great severity and fortress-like. On the aisle walls at Saint-Séverin-en-Condroz shallow pilaster strips are linked by equally shallow

[1] E.g. at Chapaize, about 1030.
[2] M. de Truchis suggests (*Mém. de la Societé Éduenne*, xxxiv, 1906, p. 293) that the exterior buttresses at Bourbon-Lancy are a later addition.

relieving arches. Exceptionally at Saint-Hilaire-de-Melle, the pilaster buttress of the nave follows a form not unusual in those of the apses of the region, and is formed as twin engaged columns closely framing the decorated windows.

3. WITH PILASTER STRIPS AND LOMBARD ARCADES

The use of pilaster strips and arcades is found as early as the ninth century[1] on the apses of churches, but even in Italy it is not found on their lateral walls much before the middle of the eleventh century[2]. By about 1050 it was in use in the churches of the Order of Cluny that lie in Switzerland on the road to Italy and on the eastern borders of France.

Payerne, defaced as it is[3] (Fig. 164), is yet an outstanding example. At Romainmôtier (Fig. 167) such pilaster strips are used both for the nave—divided by only two arcatures— and for the narthex, where they turn into engaged columns for the upper part, and are more widely spaced. Pilaster strips and a Lombard arcade appear again on the exterior of the nave of Saint-Séverin-en-Condroz, probably begun in 1091, on the north wall of the church of Vaux, not far from Cluny, and on the chapel of Berzé-la-Ville (Fig. 166), built by Saint Hugh before his death in 1109. His work has a slightly alien air in the Mâconnais, and it is easy to recognize other than local influences in it. Pilaster strips and multiple arcades are, indeed, rarely used on the nave walls of Cluniac churches. On the south side of the church of Saint-Martin-des-Champs, Saône-et-Loire[4], the scheme is simplified so that there are only two arcades between each pilaster strip; and normally such ornamentation is confined to the apse and tower.

4. WITH FLYING BUTTRESSES

The increasing boldness, and occasional rashness, of the design of Romanesque nave vaults brought about a change in buttress design at the end of the period. At Cluny itself part of the nave roof collapsed in 1125[5], and in the subsequent reconstruction (probably completed by 1135) a great range of flying buttresses was added along the nave. They are clearly shown in Father Martellange's drawing (Fig. 161). Professor Conant has pointed out that this was the first range of such buttresses to be built in France, or indeed in Europe. They were followed about 1155 by the flying buttresses of Domont, that are probably as early as any now existing. With the flying buttresses of Saint-Leu-d'Esserent the system has attained its full Gothic beauty.

Elsewhere modifications like those at Cluny were carried out at a later date. In the thirteenth century the original simple pilaster buttresses of the nave of Vézelay had to

[1] At San Pietro d' Agliate, c. 875.
[2] See Puig y Cadafalch, *Le premier art roman*, p. 53. Ripoll (1038) is perhaps the earliest.
[3] Its restoration by the efforts of the Société des Amis de l'Abbaye de Payerne proceeds apace.
[4] Given to Cluny in 948. See Dickson, p. 273.
[5] See p. 85.

be strengthened with flying buttresses, that in the nineteenth century were reconstructed by Viollet-le-Duc; the same course had to be followed at Nantua and about the same time Gigny was strengthened by a range of solid wall buttresses like those shown in Martellange's drawing of the narthex at Cluny.

D. THE FAÇADE

No great Cluniac church survives with an imposing façade. Those of Cluny, La Charité, Saint-Martial-de-Limoges and Saint-Eutrope-de-Saintes have disappeared; Souvigny was modified later; Paray, Vézelay and Mozat have their façades masked by a narthex. Even the churches that have splendid sculptured porches and portals, such as Saint-Gilles, Beaulieu, Moissac, Carennac, and Charlieu, do not have them integrated into complete or remarkable façades. Excluding such portals, it may be said that the façade was by its very nature not an important part of a monastic church, dedicated to introspection within and not to connexion with the world without.

1. WITHOUT A NARTHEX

What is probably the earliest surviving façade is also the plainest. Saint-Nazaire-de-Bourbon-Lancy (Fig. 168) has no ornament whatever; it is only broken by a plain round-headed window and a relieving arch over the doorway[1]. Such a scheme, usually with a more richly decorated door and window and the addition of string courses, is familiar in Cluniac churches as far apart as San Colombano di Vaprio d'Adda in Lombardy, Montbron in the Charente (Fig. 177), Lozay in the Lower Charente, Oulmes in the Vendée (Fig. 178), Pont-aux-Moines in the Loiret[2], Bourg-de-Maisons in the Dordogne, Ouzilly in the Vienne, Ternay in the Isère, and Uzerche in the Corrèze. Even an important church like Saint-Étienne-de-Nevers (Fig. 169) adds no more than an Auvergnat arcade above the window; but this originally had a wooden porch, for which the corbels remain, and was dignified, narthex fashion, with two lateral towers of which the upper stories have now disappeared.

At Saint-Séverin-en-Condroz the nave section has two superimposed relieving arches in the gable, and there is a similar one (framing a small window) in each aisle section. At Aubigny the portal is set on a projecting rectangle; at Airaines in the department of the Somme (Fig. 170) a slight projection enclosing both door and window gives relief to the whole. So elementary a scheme could not satisfy indefinitely, and it was not long before it was modified. At Saint-Palais there is a tall arcade on the second stage (Fig. 171) and at Varennes-l'Arconce a system of pilasters and quasi-Lombard arcades[3] (Fig. 172). At Saint-Pons-de-Thomières[4] the great round-headed portal has an arcade of five arches

[1] Later.   [2] Built between 1075 and 1080; see Jarry, p. 579.
[3] M. Oursel (p. 139) considers that classical influence is evident in this scheme.
[4] See Sahuc, p. 22.

above, surmounted by two windows, with an oculus in the pediment; at Arles-sur-Tech
a similar pedimental scheme is achieved entirely with windows. At Elincourt-Sainte-
Marguerite the portal is surmounted by three windows, linked by a moulding, by two
similar ones above, and finally by an oculus[1]. Pouilly-lès-Feurs is exceptional in having
a "giant" triple arcade as the sole adornment of its façade; the high central arcade
frames both door and window; beyond it come pilaster buttresses, and other less lofty
arcades correspond to the aisles. The engaged columns of the arcades are remarkable
in being facetted: presumably the local granitic stone did not lend itself to the more
usual system of fluting.

   At Sainte-Jalle two little niches appear on either side of the door and at Coudun a single
large one; at Layrac, Saint-Cybardeaux, Marcigny and Fontenet (Fig. 199) a blind
arcade; at Meymac (Fig. 174) and Bellegarde du Loiret (Fig. 175) this arcade is more
important and the window above is triple. At Bellenaves (Fig. 173) the central door is
yet more important, and the window forms part of an arcade across the face of the
church. This scheme of a triple arch is the basis of the most splendid of all surviving
Cluniac façades: that at Saint-Gilles (Fig. 179). Here the three doors are linked by a frieze
continuous with that of their lintels, supported by columns between the door arches; the
main lines are simple enough, but the elaboration of the sculpture is unique in
Romanesque France. The plan of the upper stage (if it were ever built) is unknown. In
Western France a simpler form of this three-arched scheme became classic, and received
much sculptural enrichment. Typical examples are Talmont (Fig. 176) and Corme-Écluse
(Fig. 182): both conform to a well-known local type. At Moings[2] and Le Douhet (Fig.
180) the upper arcade is made window fashion, with colonnettes to frame the blind spaces;
at Fontaines this has become an arcade on twin columns (Fig. 183). At Pérignac (Fig.
184), where the portal has been modified, a row of pointed arcading on a kind of double
window jamb is set below a loftier round-headed one simulating double windows, that is
broken by a larger real window in the centre. The niches of the arcades and the space
above are enriched with figure sculpture. With this may fittingly be compared the one
Cluniac Romanesque façade that survives in England: Castleacre (Fig. 182). Its
sculpture is less rich but its architectural ornament is richer than the French examples; it
may serve to show how much the style of Cluniac architecture in England was influenced
by local tradition.

   In the next stage of development the lower storey of the front was enriched with
engaged-column buttresses. Retaud is an example; it seems not to have had an arcade
above. At Blasimont and at Chalais (Fig. 186) the engaged columns are double; on the
latter church the sculpture is very rich, and there was originally an arcade above. At
Saint-Hilaire-de-Melle the façade is divided by two strongly marked cornices below the
second or window stage; the twin columns are treated as three superimposed orders
between these. The pediment is balanced, Poitevin fashion, by a little columned pinnacle

[1] See Woillez, Appendix, Pl. II, 1–11.
[2] The door here is large and has no subsidiary arches.

on either side. Esnandes (Fig. 187), which has also lost its upper stage, is a later example of the type, with the columns of the subsidiary arches in two stages. At Breuillet (Fig. 185) the portal is surmounted by a blind arcade and the twin engaged columns make their appearance on the third stage. At Maillezais parish church (Fig. 192), the columns are in two stages, the second springing from the abacus level of the ground floor of the façade; there is no arcade above, but a graceful pedimental composition with a tall window in the centre and a blind window arch and an oculus on either side.

The culmination of this scheme was to continue the engaged column on the upper stage of the façade. Champmillon (Fig. 193) is a comparatively simple example; Saint-Savinien is later and more elegant.

A small group of façades have as the essential of their scheme an oculus over the portal[1]. Plainest of all is Saint-Turquoît (Fig. 190); the next stage is reached at Vienne. At Salles, instead of this cornice, the "Lombard" arcade of the gable is repeated across the façade, and is supported by the richly ornamented pilasters that frame the door (Fig. 191). At Gassicourt (Fig. 188) the oculus and the door are not so close as nearly to touch each other[2].

Exceptionally the whole façade was treated as the base of a western tower. Moirax is a fine example (Fig. 189), with its central section projecting and its upper stage filled by a pointed relieving arch for the tower above. A similar arch occurs at La Souterraine[3] (Fig. 194) but at the base of the tower little pinnacle turrets crown the façade which has become no more than the base of the tower.

2. WITH A NARTHEX

The great galilees of the Cluniac Order nearly all terminated in two massive square towers, that completely dominated the façade. An exception is the early narthex at Romainmôtier[4], which is simply gabled, with a line of Lombard arcading running straight across the front; its lower part has been modified by the addition of a later porch. The description of Mayeul's church at Cluny in the *Consuetudines*, however, includes a galilee, "et duae turres sint in ipsius galileae fronte constitutae": so we may reasonably assume that it was the narthex of this church which established the type. The narthex at Paray-le-Monial (Fig. 195) that is earlier than the church, is probably modelled on this original narthex at Cluny. In general scheme it appears to be of the eleventh century, and the southern tower is of this date, with two tiers of double windows and a single window below. The top of the northern tower was rebuilt early in the twelfth century[5]. All the interest is centred in the towers, and the façade is no more than

[1] The oculus at Gigny and Nantua appear to be later.

[2] The type with a cornice goes on into Gothic times; e.g. Mézin (Lot-et-Garonne) and Bersol (Gironde).   [3] Cf. the closely similar church of Le Dorat.

[4] Payerne seems to have had towers, but all this part was rebuilt in the fifteenth century.

[5] M. Oursel (p. 65) suggests that it may have fallen on the earlier church.

a gable wall that joins them. At Vézelay (Fig. 1, frontispiece), probably dating from fairly late in the first half of the twelfth century, the scheme must originally have been much the same. But the use of sculpture to enrich the triple portal, of a line of arcading over it, and of more numerous and more richly decorated windows in the towers, must have transformed the scheme into one of real architectural beauty and dignity[1]. A rather later version of the same scheme, with a twin arcade to take the place of the side portals, exists at Saint-Leu-d'Esserent (Fig. 196); the repetition of the windows of the lower stage of the towers across the front (as may originally have happened at Vézelay) gives it a real façade quality. At Cluny itself the termination of the narthex built by Abbot Roland in 1220 followed the earlier tradition in having two towers, but instead of being linked to form a façade they projected beyond it.

In England the towers of Castleacre are perfectly integrated into the façade (Fig. 182). Their rich arcaded decoration forms a part of the scheme of the front, but is continued on the other sides. The fourth storey is unfortunately lost.

The lesser porch narthexes had comparatively simple façades like that of a church. That at Charlieu (Fig. 208) shows a single window in a sculptured frame over the richly sculptured portal, which, like that of the church at Cluny and that at Salles, has a line of Lombard arcading horizontally above it. The façade at Châtelmontagne (Fig. 127) is more ambitious, though the use of the local volcanic stone has precluded any elaborate decoration. The triple entrance is simply framed in stone, and above this another triple arcade, rising to the pediment, frames the windows. The angle of the pediments has a double arcade in the Auvergnat manner. At Saint-Martial-de-Limoges the eleventh-century porch was partly rebuilt after 1167 and was still unfinished in 1217. It was the base of a tower[2]. The stage above was lit by three round-headed windows; then a transition was made by Limousin gables with buttresses between to an eight-sided stage, with an octagonal drum with tall windows surmounted by an eight-sided spire.

E. THE PORTAL

So soon as the art of sculpture revived in Burgundy in the eleventh century, it became the custom to adorn the portals of Cluniac churches with figured or decorative capitals and mouldings. The iconography of such sculptures must receive separate consideration, but there are certain marked architectural types of decorated portals that should be mentioned here.

The basic principle of a Romanesque portal of the late eleventh century was a rect-

---

[1] It was subsequently modified by the insertion of a great Gothic window enriched with figure sculpture and by a Gothic top to the southern tower (Tour-Saint-Michel). It is uncertain if the northern tower were ever completed.

[2] See Bib. Nat. MS. lat. 11907 (a drawing made in 1726) and Rostand in *Bull. Mon.* LXXXIII, 1924, p. 172.

angular door with a round-headed relieving arch resting on columns[1]. The door at the
end of the north aisle at Souvigny and the door at Pouilly-lès-Feurs are simple examples;
both have the tympanum recessed to form a second relieving arch. From this it was
natural to proceed to a multiplication of the angular mouldings formed by these arches.
The early portal at Charlieu[2] (Fig. 197) is a good plain example of this; the archivolt
is triple and the sculptured tympanum is slightly recessed, but the sculpture is confined
to this, the lintel and the capitals of the columns—one a side—on which the main arch
rests. Much the same plan is followed at Marcigny[3] (Fig. 198), where the scheme is
integrated into that of an arcaded façade. The door is here more deeply recessed. At
Saint-Révérien the deep return is filled by sculptured angels. At Menet (Cantal) there
are two columns each side, and the arrises are correspondingly multiplied; at Saint-
Georges-de-Didonne this scheme is transferred to a pointed arch. At Bellenaves (Fig.
173) such an arch rests on pilasters without capitals: the sculptured ornament is concentrated on the tympanum and lintel. At Moings there are four columns each side and
a plain fourfold arch. Its development depended, however, on the splaying of the jambs
to form a decorative frame, and on the use of sculptured enrichments on the archivolt.
In Western France the angular line of the arris was maintained and their sculptured
enrichments kept on one plane. Characteristic examples with a double arris are
Champagne-Mouton and Mouthiers (Charente), Saint-Béat and Corme-Écluse (Fig.
182); with a triple, Lozay, Esnandes (Fig. 187), Talmont (Fig. 176), Fontaines (Fig. 183),
Saint-Maurice and Château-Larcher (Fig. 200); with a fourfold arris, Breuillet, le
Douhet (Fig. 180), Saint-Savinien, Maillezais (Fig. 192) and Chambon, and with a
fivefold, Fontenet (Fig. 199) and Chalais (Fig. 186). At Médis the four arrises show
a gradual transition; the outer two are in a vertical plane, and the inner two progressively bevelled. In Central France[4], however, the tendency was to adopt a more
plastic treatment and to soften the angles of the arrises. This system, which was followed
on the portal of Cluny itself, appears in a simple form at Oulmes (Fig. 178); at Donzy-
le-Pré, Carennac, Saint-Marcel-lès-Sauzet, and Moissac it frames sculptured tympana,
of great beauty and richness; and at Morlaas it is modified to include sculptured figures;
but its most characteristic development is as an archivolt with a great multiplicity of
mouldings, so complex that it eventually loses any direct relation with the pillars that
appear to support it. In the Nièvre, at Jailly and Cosne, Lurcy-le-Bourg (Fig. 201)
and Rouy (Fig. 202), in the Dordogne at Cercles and further east at Vizille and
Sainte-Jalle, the old sharp lines are kept, only slightly modified by sculptured ornament.
At Layrac, Lézat, Moirax, Lisle and Marsat, there are heavy torus mouldings that

[1] A central column is unusual; it occurs in the door of Saint-Marc-de-Souvigny, but is otherwise
only found on the great sculptured portals such as Vézelay, Beaulieu and Moissac.

[2] Within the porch; probably dating from the completion of the church in 1094.

[3] The tympanum and lintel plain. The façade dates from the time of Abbot Hugh.

[4] Castleacre combines the two systems with a flat arris for the outer and inner mouldings and
four sculptured mouldings of torus section between.

coincide with the capitals and serve to mark the architectural unity of the whole[1], and at Bagneux, Binson and Saint-Leu (Fig. 196) the force of these is only slightly modified by the interposition of foliate or zigzag mouldings; but in such portals from Central France as Le-Breuil-sur-Couze (Fig. 203), Mailhat and Bredons (Fig. 204), and further south in the transitional portal of Rabastens, with nine torus mouldings and four colonnettes, complete confusion has been reached. Alternatively, as at Semur-en-Brionnais (Fig. 205) and the west door at Paray-le-Monial (Fig. 207) and Bellegarde-du-Loiret (Fig. 175), the columns were sculptured to match the moulding, producing an effect of rather restless splendour[2].

This procedure was probably influenced by that of the great door at Cluny (Fig. 206) of which the columns, though not of the same design as the mouldings of the archivolt, were richly carved. This seems to have been designed from the beginning as part of a narthex rather than as part of a façade, though some time elapsed between its construction (c. 1115) and the completion of the narthex before it in 1220. It was set after the fashion of an Arab "arraba"[3] with a line of arcading above it, joined to it by a frieze of sculptured roundels. Such a scheme, with the sides of the moulding prolonged to fall upon pilasters, or right to the ground, recurs at Salles-en-Beaujolais (Fig. 192), Paray-le-Monial (Fig. 207) and Charlieu (Fig. 208); from their dignity and richness we can gain some idea of the splendour of their far greater prototype, that is now known to us only by its fragments.

The portal of the narthex at Charlieu is probably some thirty years later than that at Paray, and dates from the third decade of the twelfth century. In it, as in the contemporary triple portal at Saint-Lazare-d'Avallon (Fig. 209), a break-up of the traditional scheme is marked by the over-enrichment of the columns and the ornamental emphasis on other parts of the jamb. At Saint-Lazare some columns are twisted, and others not only twisted but plaited as well. Here, too, as at Morlaas, tall sculptured figures begin to take their place alongside the columns. The portal of the chapter house of Saint-Étienne at Toulouse marks the next step[4]: it had statues of six apostles on either side instead of columns, and while purely Romanesque in style, finds its analogy in the *portail royal* of Chartres.

A detail of the great door at Cluny—the cusp-like relief of its inner moulding that recurs on the arcade of the triforium[5]—recurs on other churches of the Order, in churches as distant from each other as Landos in the Velay (Fig. 210), Gassicourt, north of Paris

[1] Cf. Saint-Gilles, where the torus mouldings are marked although the lintel and the subsidiary capitals are fused into a sculptured frieze.

[2] Cf. the Gothic portal at Bersol, Gironde. At Airaines and Tauves with greater logic the capitals were omitted, and the archivolt becomes a continuous moulding round the portal.

[3] See Mâle, *Art et artistes du moyen âge*, p. 46. He considers Cluny to be the only specimen in France.

[4] Its sculptures are preserved in the Musée des Augustins at Toulouse and have lately been set up in order as they were on the portal. See *Bulletin des Musées de France*, I, No. 6, June 1929, p. 133.

[5] Such blind cusping may perhaps owe something to the decorative use of the Lombard arcade.

(Fig. 188) and Pérignac and Montbron in the Charente (Fig. 177). At La Souterraine (Fig. 194) the cusped mouldings are double. At Celles-sur-Belle the late Romanesque portal has it fourfold, enriched with a torus moulding with animal heads[1] at the points:

Fig. 206. Cluny. Reconstruction sketch by Professor Conant of the façade of Abbot Hugh's church at Cluny later masked by the narthex.

the effect is startlingly barbaric. The lesser door at Semur-en-Brionnais (Fig. 211) has the moulding in a different form, with elegant palmate finials, to fill the tympanum.

Such lobed cusping was used not only as a moulding in relief, but also to outline an arch. Such a use is found, as well as two courses of relief, at Montbron[2]. This characteristic is widely disseminated in the Order, from Meymac and La Souterraine (Fig. 194),

[1] Cf. the zigzag moulding round the arch at Le-Breuil-sur-Couze (Fig. 203).
[2] Cf. the cusped arches of the triforium at La Charité. On Arab analogies see Mâle, *Art et artistes du moyen âge*, pp. 32 *et seqq*; and "Les influences arabes dans l'art roman", in *Revue des Deux Mondes*, 15 Nov. 1923, p. 335.

Lubersac and Vigeois (Fig. 212) in the Limousin to Le Wast (Fig. 213) in the north, Colombier (Fig. 214) in the centre, Ganagobie (Fig. 218) in the south-east, Saint-Ybars (Fig. 215) in Gascony to Tayac (Fig. 216) in the Dordogne and Condéon in the Charente[1] (Fig. 217). There are local variations. At Colombier, Saint-Ybars, Montbron and Condéon the cusps are sharply pointed; in the Limousin and at Tayac they are clove ended[2] (with sculptured ornament at Vigeois and Lubersac); at Le Wast[3] they are graduated and complex; at Ganagobie and Bretigny they are in reverse, with rounded projections and clove-ended divisions: but all are unusual and characteristic. There can be no question of the Oriental origin of the form, and M. Émile Mâle, in some delightful pages[4], has linked together many of these polylobed arches as being on the pilgrimage routes that led from France to Spain[5].

F. WINDOWS

The Romanesque windows of the churches of the Order of Cluny show a completely normal progression from simplicity to ornament. The earliest, as at Romainmôtier (Fig. 167) and Bourbon-Lancy (Fig. 160), are perfectly plain; on the apsidioles at Cluny itself (Fig. 148) and at Paray (Fig. 149) they were either plain or simply crowned by a moulding. The next stage was to frame the window in an ornamental head supported by a column on either side. Examples may be found everywhere: at Montbron (Fig. 177), Charlieu, Moirax (Fig. 137), Saint-Eutrope-de-Saintes (Fig. 152) and Cénac (Fig. 136). In the apses of Retaud (Fig. 144) and Talmont (Fig. 143) the columns are present but the head is plain; instead, the window is framed by a great arcade. At Bellegarde-du-Loiret, Saint-Savinien and Maillezais the central window of the façade has a double frame, with two columns on either side; at Airaines (Fig. 170) the window has no columns but a continuous moulding. At San Colombano *oculi* with sculptured cross mullions exceptionally appear below the three moulded windows of the apse.

A similar series is to be found on the interior face. The nave windows are often plain;

---

[1] Cf. also the polylobed edges to the jambs at Beaulieu and Moissac, and the derived curved mouldings that frame their *trumeaux*.

[2] A type of finial derived from Spain; see for example the bishop's door of the Cathedral of Zamora.   [3] See Enlart in *Gazette des Beaux Arts*, 1927, p. 1.

[4] *Art et artistes du moyen âge*, chap. III; and see *Art religieux du XIIe siècle en France*, p. 291.

[5] See on these Bedier, *Légendes épiques*, III, 89 *et seqq.*; Fita and Vinson, p. 28; G. G. King, *Way of St James*, I, 77; Vielliard, *Le Livre de Saint-Jacques*, 1938. I repeat that it is easy to exaggerate the Cluniac character of the "Way of St James". The four great routes all include Cluniac houses among their stopping places—the first Saint-Gilles, the second Moissac, the third Vézelay, the fourth Saint-Jean-d'Angely and Saint-Eutrope-de-Saintes; but in some places where there were important Cluniac houses these are not mentioned. At Toulouse the (then Augustinian) Saint-Sernin and not La Daurade is commended to the traveller's attention; at Limoges Saint-Léonard not Saint-Martial, and at Portiers Saint-Hilaire and not Montierneuf. Mr A. W. Clapham, in his last book (*Romanesque Architecture in Western Europe*, 1936), is inclined to deprecate the emphasis laid on the pilgrimage route.

windows with a colonnette on either side and a plain archivolt appear everywhere—in the ambulatory at Paray-le-Monial (Fig. 107) and La Charité (Fig. 108); in the choir at Moirax (Fig. 99) and Vaux-sur-Mer (Fig. 97); in the apse at Cénac (Fig. 101), Retaud and Mezin (Fig. 102); in the transept at Cluny (Fig. 80) and La Charité (Fig. 76); in the aisles at Souvigny (Fig. 46) and Blasimont[1].

G. ROOFS

The passage of some seven hundred years has naturally destroyed practically all the original roofs of Cluniac churches[2]. At Cluny itself and in the neighbourhood[3] they followed local custom and were of "laves" resting directly on the vault without the interposition of any elaborate timberwork. At Moirax in 1910 there was discovered under the tiles of the choir a stone roof, a truncated cone, covered with scales with their rounded sides uppermost[4], like that of some pinnacle spires in Poitou and Saintonge. At Marolles the apsidiole has a stone roof of rectangular slabs, resting directly on a stone cornice. In the Auvergne, then as now, the ancient churches were probably roofed with curved tiles. In sum, what little evidence there is goes all to show that Cluniac churches followed local custom in their roofing systems.

H. TOWERS

A bell tower is not one of the legacies that Romanesque architecture received from classical Rome, but appears to have been the creation of the architects of the fifth-century churches of North Syria[5]. It arose, like many Romanesque developments, out of liturgical needs.

In early churches its place was often to the side of the church; at Froville, of which the eleventh-century belfry is probably earlier than its donation to Cluny in 1091, it occupies this position. The normal position of the tower in the Order was that found in France as early as the church of Germigny-les-Prés, that is, over the crossing, or, if there is no transept, over the choir[6]. This disposition was followed (so far as we can

[1] The exceptionally rich treatment of the large window of the room above the galilee at Charlieu dates from the time when it was an arch giving on to the open air.

[2] On the whole question, see E. Lefèvre-Pontalis, *L'architecture religieuse en France à l'époque romane*, 1929, pp. 340, 341; Deneux, *L'évolution des charpentes du XIe au XVIIIe siècle*, Paris, 1927.

[3] E.g. at Varennes-l'Arconce, Mazille, Bourg-de-Thizy (Virey, 2nd ed. p. 99), Berzé-la-Ville.

[4] See *Revue de l'Art chrét.* LX, 1910, p. 279.

[5] E.g. Qasr-el-Banat, on the road from Antioch to Aleppo. These early towers are for the most part square, but there is a parallel Ravennate type (hardly found in France) of circular plan. E. Lefèvre-Pontalis, *L'Architecture religieuse en France à l'époque romane*, chap. XII, considers that they are found in France as early as the fifth century.

[6] E.g. Brancion and La Chapelle-sous-Dun, Laizé, Massy, Taizé. This was probably the scheme followed in the early church at Cluny, if we accept Professor Conant's theory of its likeness to the chapel of Saint-Laurent near Tournus.

tell) in Mayeul's church at Cluny. There are a few exceptions to this general rule. At Baume-les-Messieurs a plain square tower was built to the side of the church in the twelfth century, presumably because the crossing had not been built to bear one. At Bersol the tower occupies a similar position. At Noël-Saint-Martin (a parish church) the massive square tower is likewise to the side. At Marcigny (Fig. 223) the tower is above the façade; at Morlaas at the west end; at Mazille it is on the south transept. These are the chief exceptions to the general rule[1].

In the larger churches, however, this central tower was not the only one. Saint-Martial-de-Limoges had a *clocher porche* over the nave, and this disposition was imitated in the related priories of Chambon, Meymac (Fig. 174), La Souterraine (Fig. 194) and Uzerche[2] (Fig. 229), and in a different form in the *clocher porches* of Mont-Saint-Vincent and Moissac. The churches preceded by galilees, such as Paray-le-Monial, both Mayeul's and Hugh's churches at Cluny, Vézelay, and Maillezais, had two towers as part of their façade, and this disposition was also followed at La Charité[3], Saint-Étienne-de-Nevers[4], Marcilhac, Castleacre and in the Cluniac church on Mount Tabor. Further, the greater abbeys had towers at the transept. At Cluny itself the eastern transept had the "Clocher des Lampes" over the crossing, and the second or great transept the great square "Clocher du Chœur" over the crossing, with the octagonal "Clocher de l'Eau Bénite" (Fig. 234) over the northern arm, and the twin "Clocher des Bisans" over the southern. A simpler form of this disposition was used at Saint-Gilles, which had two towers over its single transept; at Vézelay (Fig. 231) and Saint-Leu-d'Esserent they were set in the western angles of the transept and at Saint-Martin-des-Champs (Fig. 232) to the south of the choir.

The abbeys and priories of the Order of Cluny were outside the power of lay feudalism, and could build and fortify towers as they would[5]. Consequently, many of the priories, especially in the south-west, had their towers fortified by the fourteenth century: Saint-Pons-de-Thomières, Charras, Uzerche, Moissac, Tayac and Tremolat remain as witness to the practice[6]. A classic instance is the church of Saint-Hippolyte not far from Cluny (Fig. 224), that by 1319 had its early twelfth-century tower extended laterally on either

---

[1] It seems likely that Uzerche was intended to have a central tower, whether it was ever built or not; and the Moûtier-de-Thiers is now so incomplete that the position of its tower was probably originally more central than now appears. The central tower (if there were one) at Vézelay must have gone when the choir was rebuilt.

[2] This was completed by a stone *flèche*, destroyed by lightning in 1622.

[3] Where the existence of a narthex is uncertain. One tower survives; the second, if it was ever finished, had disappeared by 1505. Beaussart, p. 94.

[4] These, and the central tower, were pulled down in 1792.

[5] Cf. the case of the Augustinian canons of Saint-Lazare-d'Autun, whom in 1178 Hugh III, Duke of Burgundy, permitted to alter their church provided that no tower or fortification be built that "non ad formam ecclesie, sed ad usum propugnandi pertineat evidenter". Quoted Mortet, II, 133.

[6] See R. Rey, *Les vieilles églises fortifiées du midi de la France*, Paris, 1925.

side to form a great oblong keep[1]. Once at least such protection was turned against the
Order, for Geoffroy de Vigeois recounts how in 1171 the tower of the church of La
Souterraine (Fig. 194) was held by the burgesses of the place against the officers of the
abbey of Saint-Martial, who were exacting a heavier *taille* than usual[2].

1. SQUARE TOWERS

A square tower was the normal early type, and is found in most of the earlier churches
of the Order. An engraving of 1640 shows the tower of Mayeul's abbey church at
Cluny, then still surviving as the church of Saint-Pierre-le-Vieux. Professor Conant has
noted its resemblance to the tower of Chapaize[3] that probably dates from the first quarter
of the eleventh century. He has been able to produce a sketch restoration (Fig. 219),
showing a square tower, lofty yet massive, divided into marked stages, with two windows
in the topmost storey and three below.

Lofty towers of this type are found in Cluniac churches only in the area of the
Mâconnais, Charollais and Beaujolais; they date, indeed, from a time when the influence
of the Order was almost confined to that area[4]. A fine example, built soon after 995,
existed at Mesvres until it fell down on Christmas day 1836[5]. It was notably lofty, with
windows in the three upper stages. On the lowest of these there was a single plain
window, above this a double window, and in the topmost a larger triple window framed
in a relieving arch. Several of the granges and parish churches of the Order of Cluny
in the neighbourhood of the Mother Abbey have a tower of this type as their chief
architectural feature, though it may be on a smaller scale than at Chapaize or Mesvres;
examples are Laizé, with two stages of wide-arched lombard arcades between the
pilaster quoins and a twin window above; Bergesserin, which has pilaster strips on its
lowest stage, an arcade on the next, and an arcade and two windows on the third[6];
Domange, with a lombard arcade and pilaster strips on the lower storey, and two
windows above; Blanot (Fig. 222), with two stages of arcade with a string course and
cornice added; Massy (Fig. 221), with two sets of windows, one framed in a simple arch
and the other with double columns[7]; Chazelles, Taluyers, Mazille, with two windows
in two stories, and Pommiers, of which the lower stages have been refaced but which

---

[1] See Virey, 2nd ed. p. 382.   [2] Quoted Mortet, II, 120.

[3] See J. Virey, "L'église de Chapaize", in *Annales de l'Académie de Mâcon*, 3rd series, XXVII,
1930–1. It depended on the Benedictine abbey of Saint-Pierre-de-Chalon.

[4] A possible exception is that at Sainte-Jalle, but this is lower and plainer than the Burgundian
type.

[5] See P. de Truchis in *Bull. Mon.* LXXX, 1921, p. 21.

[6] The fourth storey is later.

[7] Other towers of the same sort, not particularly remarkable, are to be found at Sassangy,
a dependency of Paray (Dickson, p. 292) with a lombard arcade on the lower stage, Saint-Julien-
de-Sennecey (*ibid.* p. 255), Saint-Martin-du-Tartre (*ibid.* p. 269), Saint-Martin-des-Champs (*ibid.*
p. 273), and Saint-Mayeul at Cluny, all in the department of Saône-et-Loire.

still shows similar windows separated by twin columns above. The tower at Thizy resembles that of Blanot, with a single plain window below the string course; that at Taizé is of the same sort, with a crude lombard arcade below the cornice. The tower at Marcigny (Fig. 223), which is presumably that mentioned in the early *Life* of Saint Hugh[1], is of this slender type, with twin windows divided by a single colonnette[2].

The normal late eleventh-century tower, however, was broader and squatter. Saint-Nazaire-de-Bourbon-Lancy is a perfectly plain example (Fig. 160); Romainmôtier is of similar proportions, and is decorated with lombard arcades and pilaster strips. Similar decoration appears on the lower stage at Oulmes in the Vendée (Fig. 178) and at Saint-Hippolyte (Fig. 224), which like Massy has its lower windows plain and its upper divided by twin columns. At Lozay and Relanges[3] the lombard arcading is replaced by a wider arcade on twin columns; at Corme-Écluse (Fig. 182) this becomes a close-set arcade on single columns like that across the front of the church. Similarly at Prahecq the engaged columns recall those used on the façades of the province; while the exceptionally squat and massive tower at Moûtier-d'Ahun (Fig. 225) has pilaster buttresses. The almost equally massive tower at Saint-Sulpice has a double blind arcade on each face; its upper stage is wanting. At Lozay there is a blind arcade of three arches. It is difficult to classify these low broad central towers, for their type depends on the size of the church as well as on their date. Two churches in the Cantal, Menet and Bort, have simple double windows primitive in type if not in time, and the triple one of the same sort at Plauzat in the Puy-de-Dôme is hardly more advanced. There is more elegance in the two grouped windows at Noël-Saint-Martin (Fig. 159) or the three at Gassicourt (Fig. 188) and Mezin, and the series is continued by three at Rosiers-Côtes-d'Aurec, with two beneath, four at Salles (Fig. 226) balanced by a single one beneath, and the four at Châtelmontagne (Fig. 146) divided by engaged columns and repeated as an arcade on the lower stage. At Ternay the four upper windows are in two groups, divided like the bays of a cloister by a fluted pilaster. On the central square tower over the western transept at Cluny there seem to have been two stages of four windows each.

In the next type, chiefly found in the Nièvre and Bourbonnais, the windows seem to be influenced by the triforium scheme that sets twin windows, divided by columns, beneath a framing arch. At Rouy the unit is doubled and a tall arcade is set beneath. At Varennes-l'Arconce (Fig. 220) the triforium scheme appears above an ordinary double window. At Mont-Saint-Jean and Souvigny (Fig. 227) there are two stages of it, in the latter instance with an arcade below; in the great Tour-Sainte-Croix at La Charité (Fig. 230) the same scheme is repeated with every detail enriched by cusping

[1] "Erexit ergo ibi (Marcigny) basilicam parvam, sed bene compositam, firmisque membris et capite suo atque optimo turrito conspicuam." *Life*, by the monk Hugh, Marrier, col. 455.

[2] Cf. the similarly proportioned tower far south of it at Sorgues, a priory church which it is not easy to date. Saint-Étienne-des-Sorts, in the same district, has one of the same type with a single larger window.

[3] Where there is a vaulted room between the belfry and the crossing.

and sculpture[1]. Castleacre must once have been, in its English fashion, hardly less rich; but here richness was achieved not by cusping and sculpture but by a multiplicity of simple and interlaced arcading.

In Eastern France another type was provided in the famous tower of Saint-Martial-de-Limoges, which has now completely vanished[2]. A drawing of it[3] shows a triple portal on the ground floor; on the next floor, which is set back a little, this is surmounted by three niches. Above this the next stage, likewise set back, has a window. The centre of the stage above is occupied by a gable; the angles are sloped to make a transition to an octagonal lantern above. The upper floors of this provided a model for the central tower at Saint-Germain-d'Auxerre (Fig. 228) and in a late example with pointed arches at Uzerche (Fig. 229). These were all destined to be completed by a little eight-sided stone spire.

The twin towers of Cluniac narthexes, and of church façades that imitate them, have already been considered. The tower in the angle of the transept at Vézelay (Fig. 231) is of the type with two stories with two windows in each: it is handsome but not unusual. A similar plan was probably followed at Saint-Martin-des-Champs (Fig. 232), but here the upper stage, if it ever existed, has now disappeared.

Few of these Romanesque towers retain even the form of their original roofs. The Burgundian ones seem originally to have had pyramidal roofs less steep than those that now cap them; Gassicourt and Noël-Saint-Martin followed local usage and were roofed gable-wise. The tower at La Charité originally had an octagonal stone spire, with a pinnacle at each corner where the angle was set back.

2. OCTAGONAL TOWERS

Many of the larger churches of the Order had an octagonal tower at the crossing[4], while Hugh's basilica at Cluny had octagonal towers over the transept. Gigny still shows the base of such a tower, with the lowest stage framed by pilaster strips and a lombard arcade, and further adorned with two blind arches on each face, outlined by a plain double arris. At Saint-Cydroine (Fig. 233) there are three such arches, with a single arris, on each face; the upper stage has a triple arcade on colonnettes to correspond, of which the two outer arches enclose small window apertures. At Thuret there is a similar arcade below; the upper stage has been rebuilt. Saint-Marcel-lès-Sauzet has a blind arcade on the lower storey, while the upper originally had twin windows. The next stage is reached at Paray, of which the lower storey[5] has a double arcade on each face,

[1] M. Mâle compares it with Arab examples, *Art et artistes du moyen âge*, p. 42.

[2] See R. Fage, "Le clocher Limousin à l'époque romane", in *Bull. Mon.* LXXI, 1907, p. 263. He points out that such towers are represented on the lateral sculptures of the porches at Moissac and Beaulieu.

[3] R. de Lasteyrie, *L'architecture religieuse en France à l'époque romane*, 1929, fig. 767.

[4] Chiefly in Central France: but a more northerly example may be found at Acy-en-Multien. Saint-Étienne-de-Nevers had one originally.

[5] The upper storey is of nineteenth-century construction.

with twin columns in the centre. The story told by Rainaud of Semur of his uncle Saint Hugh[1], who miraculously healed a novice who had been hit by a beam that fell from the tower at the crossing of Paray, seems to prove that this arcade is earlier than Saint Hugh's death in 1109. This may well be, for a similar arcade with twin columns, lightened by a window in the middle, appears on the corresponding stage of the surviving tower of Saint Hugh's church at Cluny (Fig. 234). The cornice and quoins of this show lombard arcades and pilaster strips surviving as purely decorative forms; the pilaster strips are treated as fluted pilasters. The upper storey has a twin window in the centre, divided by a single column but framed in double columns or pilasters; the ornamented heads of the windows are continued as an arcade[2]. At Nantua (Fig. 235) the double columns again appear, this time on the upper storey[3], with a line of single windows below; and their use survives as late as the tower at Castel-Sarrasin, that has arcades thus divided on two stories, the lower blind and the upper fenestrated. At Torsac the tower is shorter; a tall double arcade on each face masks a single window behind it.

The next stage in the development of octagonal, as of square, towers consists in the use of a triforium-like unit of a double window enclosed by an arch. An early example is that of Saint-Séverin-en-Condroz (Fig. 236), built soon after its foundation in 1091. Here the window unit appears below a line of the lombard arcade that ornaments all the exterior of the church. At Menat it is set below a line of single windows, and follows Auvergnat use in having angular heads to the arches; at Jailly, the heads are round, as is normally the case. The great lantern over the crossing at La Charité has two windows of this type to every side, so set as to form a continuous arcade. The whole is enriched with sculpture. At Semur-en-Brionnais (Fig. 139) there is only one to each side, but it is set portal-wise in a splayed arch with multiple mouldings, with a lower storey decorated with a blind arcade with fluted pilasters. Finally, in the parish church of Saint-Marcel at Cluny (Fig. 239), the tower built by Abbot Hugh III in 1159 has two stories of such windows, with a plain blind arch below[4]. The graceful spire was added late in the thirteenth century. Another example near Cluny, probably even later, is that of Saint-Gengoux, which has a plain base, a simple arch on the middle storey, and a triforium window above. Each angle is marked by a torus moulding, set on the two lower stages against a pilaster, so that the effect, emphasized by a curved string course, is of an octagon with the sides recessed. Heads of men and animals are carved on either side of the windows in the middle storey.

A small and scattered group of towers should also be mentioned, that are built as irregular octagons, that is as square towers with the angles cut off. The most easterly

---

[1] *Acta Sanctorum*, April, III, p. 652; see Oursel, p. 77.

[2] The roof was originally less steeply pitched than it is now.

[3] The section above its cornice has been added later.

[4] Transitional octagonal lanterns occur at Mouthiers, Charente (Fig. 134) (with cusped arches); Beaulieu, Corrèze and Marsat, Puy-de-Dôme (in two stages).

example is Colombier in the Allier; the next is Saint-Eugène, with an arcade on the angle, and the most westerly is Retaud in the Charente-Inférieure (Fig. 144). With them may be connected the unusual tower at Moings which is square with rounded corners; its arcade superposed upon the windows recalls the treatment used at Torsac.

3. WALL BELFRIES

A *clocher-arcade* or *clocher-mur*[1] is to be found in a few Cluniac churches in Central and Southern France. Landos (Fig. 238) is an example from the Velay; Remoulins, Notre-Dame-de-Bethléem and Caderousse (Fig. 239) from the Rhône valley; and Saint-Béat and Montaut from the south-west. Moirax has a belfry of a cognate type, made of two piers of masonry with a little wooden roof. While such belfries sometimes are, and usually look, Romanesque, there is little doubt that they are often later than they appear.

[1] See R. Fage, "Les Clochers-Murs", in *Bull. Mon.* LXXX, 1921, p. 165 *et seqq.*

Part II

MONASTIC BUILDINGS

Quadratam speciem structura domestica praefert
　　Atria bis binis inclyta porticibus.
Quae tribus inclusae domibus, quas corporis usus
　　Postulat, et quarta quae domus est Domini,
Discursum monachis, vitam dant, et stationem,
　　Qua velut in caulis contineantur oves.
Quarum prima domus servat potumque cibumque,
　　Ex quibus hos reficit juncta secunda domus.
Tertia membra fovet lassata labore diurno;
　　Quarta Dei laudes assidue resonat[1].

So a mediaeval poet described the monastic buildings of a Benedictine abbey, and his description can be almost universally applied. The origin of the plan is still uncertain; it would seem that the cloister is not derived from the Roman atrium, but from the angular walled structures of the East that provide shelter and enclosure whether for soldiers or travellers or monks. Compare a Syrian Khan[2] with a cloister, and the likeness is at once apparent. That cloisters did not take their origin from the exigences of the Rule is proved by the fact that Egyptian coenobites planned their monasteries corridor-fashion, without them. Yet cloisters are found in Syria as early as the fourth century, and by the end of the fifth century the monastery of Qalaat Seman in North Syria[3] already had its quadrangular cloister, fitting, Benedictine-fashion, into the angle of a cruciform church. A parallel to this development from a walled enclosure may be found in England, where the seventh-century monastery of Abingdon had a circular or oval cloister, evidently derived from an enclosure formed by a mud wall[4].

The first church of Benedict at Aniane[5] was a humble thatched building, but in 782 he began to build, by command of Charlemagne and by the help of the rich men of his

---

[1] Verses once ascribed to Marbode of Rennes, now to Geoffroi de Vendôme, 1093–1132. Quoted Mortet, I, 285.

[2] For instance, one lying off the Antioch-Alexandretta road on the way to Bagréas.

[3] The eminent Bollandist Dom P. Peeters tells me that the Rule followed here is not known.

[4] *Chron. mon. de Abendonia*, ed. Stevenson, II, 272. It had twelve *habitacula* and twelve *capellae* round the enclosure, a church and refectory in the middle, and a parlour by the gate.

[5] On this see Dr Rose Graham, *English Ecclesiastical Studies*, p. 11.

court, a splendid church with quadrangular cloisters annexed adorned with pillars of marble[1], that provided a tradition for subsequent Benedictine builders to follow[2].

Since Cluny was founded as an ordinary Benedictine monastery, there was no reason for it to break away from a tradition based upon the practical necessities of the Benedictine Rule. We know little or nothing of its earliest monastic buildings[3]; they may well have been modifications and adaptations of the farm buildings already existing on the site. It has been suggested[4] that Mayeul's monastic buildings were only of wood; at all events his successor Odilo is said to have modified the Augustan boast and to have declared: "I found an abbey built of wood, I leave an abbey built of marble." His biographer Jotsaldus says that the whole fabric within and without (except for the church that Mayeul had already rebuilt) was renewed and beautified by him: "ubi etiam in novissimis suis claustrum construxit columnis marmoreis, ex ultimis partibus illius provinciae, ac per rapidissimos Durantiae Rhodanique cursus non sine magno labore advectis, mirabiliter decoratum." A monk who accompanied Peter Damian thither in 1063 speaks of the monastic buildings being all of stone, and lauds the beauty of the cloister and the paintings in the great refectory[5].

This monastery of stone, built by Odilo, is that which is described in the *Consuetudines Farfenses* written between 1030 and 1048 when it was a-building. Just as archaeologists have tried to reconstruct Mayeul's church from the descriptions there given, so have they endeavoured to reconstitute the plan of the monastic buildings[6]. An ingenious attempt by Mr A. W. Clapham[7] has now been considerably modified by Professor Conant[8]; the result is probably as near as we shall get to the truth with the existing data (Fig. 9). The most striking feature is the way in which the angle of the transept projects into the cloister of which the eastern walk starts from the eastern corner of the end wall of the transept; this unusual disposition is repeated in the abbey of Hirschau, that in most essentials[9] follows the early plan of Cluny. The succession of buildings round the cloister is made certain by the description in the *Consuetudines* and by the route there

---

[1] Migne, *Pat. Lat.* CIII, cols. 360, 363–5.

[2] The exception is the Carolingian abbey of Centula, that Saint Angelbert had built with a triangular cloister in honour of the Trinity. Mortet, I, 285, n. 1.

[3] Can they be represented by the "logis de l'Abbé Ode" in the 1623 description of the abbey? (*Millénaire*, II, 244.) These are described as "faisant un demi carré avec les chambres et salles, tous couverts de tuiles creuses, à d'un côté 75 pieds de longueur et de l'autre 60 pieds sur 30 pieds de largeur". Or were these built by Ode II (de la Perrière) in the fifteenth century?

[4] Dr Rose Graham in *Archaeologia*, LXXX, 1930, p. 146. That monastic buildings were often of wood is proved by the Life of Saint Eugenius (Mabillon, *Acta Sanctorum*, I, 588): "omne illud monasterium...ex lignis fabricatum antiquitus." Quoted Schlosser, p. 1, n. 1.

[5] *Pat. Lat.* CXLI, col. 908, quoted R. Graham, *loc. cit.*

[6] See, for instance, J. Schlosser, *Die abendländische Klosteranlage des früheren Mittelalters*, Vienna, 1889, fig. 2.

[7] *Archaeologia*, LXXX, 1930, p. 166.

[8] *Liturgical Arts*, June 1935, p. 4.　　　　[9] But not in the planning of the apse.

prescribed for the claustral prior's visits of inspection. The cloister itself was only 75 ft. square. On the eastern side lay the chapter house, the inner parlour and the novices' chamber, with the great dorter lit by ninety-seven tall glass windows and the reredorter above them. The chapter house had four windows to the east, three to the north, and twelve *balcones* or arcades each with two columns to the cloister on the west[1].

The southern walk included the "calefactorium", a chamber 25 ft. square, and the great refectory, 25 ft. high and 90 ft. long, with eight windows on each side, with the monks' and lay kitchens, each 35 ft. by 25 ft., beyond. A lesser court to the south of this seems to have served the novices' quarters—a miniature cloister of its own—with a bath house and quarters for workmen. The remaining western walk of the main cloister contained the cellar and almonry.

To the side of the narthex of the church was a "palatium", the guest house, with accommodation for forty men and thirty women and a central refectory. A court to the west seems to have divided it from a long range of stables, with quarters for grooms above. Alongside this, on the other side of the church, there was a hospice for poor pilgrims. Somewhere east of the great cloister lay the six-roomed infirmary and its chapel of Saint Mary.

With the great increase in the number of monks under Abbot Hugh these buildings became insufficient and were once more remodelled. The cloister was built by his successor Pons de Melgueil. The whole lay-out was shifted farther north, the apse of Mayeul's church being retained as the chapel of Saint-Pierre-le-Vieux in the northern end of the east walk of the cloister. A plan of the monastic buildings at Cluny made in the seventeenth century (Fig. 13) and now in the local museum, combined with the description of them made in 1623[2], gives information of many of these buildings and of those constructed later in the Middle Ages. Louis Prévost's view of the abbey, made between 1668 and 1672, also in the Musée Ochier[3], also gives a somewhat sketchy idea of their appearance. Of all the early constructions nothing remains to show the simple and dignified style of their architecture but one building, now called the *écuries de Saint-Hugues* and used as a theatre (Fig. 257). The retention of some earlier buildings and the addition of later ones makes it difficult to consider the plan as a whole; instead its Romanesque parts will be considered singly.

Time has made a comparative study of the plans of the many houses of the Order of which the monastic buildings were erected between 1050 and 1170 a practical impossibility. Every age has seen some of them modified or destroyed. Fire, for example, ravaged La Charité in 1204 and 1559; the English destroyed the monastic buildings at Mouchan about 1368, and at Airaines in 1422; war destroyed much at Moûtier-d'Ahun in 1489, in 1591, and again at the end of the seventeenth century. Apart from such

---

[1] Mr Clapham justly compares them with those still existing at Charlieu. See Fig. 241.

[2] See J. Virey in *Millénaire*, II, 231, a paper indispensable for the study of the buildings at Cluny. The description was first published in Penjon, p. 109.

[3] Reproduced in Bruel, *Cluni*, Pl. III.

accidents, monastic buildings were more seriously affected by changing standards and conditions of life than were the churches in which the same changeless ritual continued to be performed. Even in the twelfth century the primitive Benedictine scheme was modified at Cluny by the construction of an abbot's chapel, dedicated in 1118 by Guy, Archbishop of Vienne, afterwards Pope Calixtus II. It is uncertain at what date a separate lodging for the abbot was instituted; the plan of that at Souvigny, drawn up in 1769, suggests that it was a good deal later than the prior's chapel adjoining it[1]; the 1623 description of Cluny gives no information. But, apart from such innovations, increase of size and changing standards led to much rebuilding.

The early monastic buildings are better studied in England than in France, since the Dissolution of the monasteries did not always destroy all and prevented later rebuilding. The plan of much of Lewes is visible (Fig. 17) and more Romanesque work remains intact at Wenlock than anywhere in France but Ganagobie. At Castleacre the whole plan of the cloister can be followed—church to the north, chapter house and dorter (with a vault beneath) in the eastern walk, warming house and refectory in the southern, and cellarer's quarters and the prior's lodging in the western walk with the infirmary to the east of the dorter, all according to the traditional plan.

But in France, rebuilding began early. We know nothing of the buildings at La Charité begun in 1052; nothing is left that is earlier than the end of the thirteenth century. The cloisters of Saint-Pons were reconstructed in 1171; those of Le Bourget-du-Lac, Vézelay, and Moissac reconstructed, and those of Saint-Leu and Arles-sur-Tech built, in the thirteenth century. At Cluny the whole precinct of the abbey was enclosed by a wall about 1180, and between 1257 and 1457 fresh accommodation had to be built for the abbey stores and for its administrative officers. The façade known as that of the Palace of Pope Gelasius remains as testimony to the work of Bertrand de Colombiers, abbot from 1295 to 1308. At Carennac and Souvigny the monastic buildings were rebuilt early in the fourteenth century and again in the middle of the fifteenth. At Saint-Étienne-de-Nevers the cloister was rebuilt in 1328 and the priory in the fifteenth century. With the fifteenth century such rebuilding became general, whether for ancient houses like Baume and Charlieu, lesser priories like Montreuil-Bonnin, or granges like Blanot.[2] Moreover, the abbatiate at Cluny and certain of the greater priorships (such as that of Souvigny) passed to titular holders who were not members of the Order. They built their own abodes: at Cluny the palace of Jean de Bourbon, abbot from 1456 to 1485, was soon balanced by the palace of Jacques d'Amboise, abbot from 1485 to 1510.

The sixteenth century brought yet more serious changes. After 1518 Cluny itself was ruled by commendatory abbots appointed by the king, who took no real part in the life of the Order. In 1538 the monks of Vézelay were secularized; thirty years later the Protestants ravaged the abbey, and they went to live in the town. The monastery of

[1] Cf. the "Château de la reine Berthe" at Payerne, which is the remains of the prior's house.
[2] The fifteenth-century cloister from Froville is now in the Metropolitan Museum, New York.

Payerne was suppressed in 1536, and its monastic buildings destroyed in 1640. The monastic buildings of Cénac were razed by the Huguenots in 1589. At Taluyers and La Charité there was much rebuilding in the first half of the sixteenth century; yet in 1587 there were only eighteen monks left at the latter. The plates of the *Monasticon Gallicanum* show how general was this rebuilding of the living quarters of the great Benedictine abbeys from the middle of the fifteenth century onwards[1]. In the late seventeenth and eighteenth centuries, while numbers were greatly decreased, the larger houses of the reformed order of Cluny enjoyed a modest prosperity, and the work of demolition was completed by the partial destruction of the monastic buildings at Moissac in 1767, by the rebuilding of such houses as Paray-le-Monial and Souvigny, and the complete reconstruction of the monks' quarters at Cluny by Dom Dathoze in the middle of the eighteenth century, even before the Revolution brought the final destruction[2].

It is, therefore, only by assembling scattered fragments from many places that we can get an idea of the appearance of the Cluniac monastic buildings of the Romanesque period.

1. CLOISTERS

It has already been said that the normal place for the Benedictine cloister was to the south of the church; but occasionally the site made another disposition advisable. At Beaulieu, Moissac and Thiers it was for this reason set to the north of the church: but these are exceptional. We know nothing of Odilo's cloister but that it had marble columns and was accounted beautiful; and that it was divided from the chapter house by twelve *balcones* or bays each with two columns. This detail enables us[3] to compare it with the remaining part of the early cloister at Charlieu (Fig. 240), which includes a similar arcade resting on twin columns, with multiple torus mouldings on their bases and sculptured capitals, rising from a plain stone plinth[4]. The character of the bases and capitals points to a date in the middle of the eleventh century, that is to say little later than the time of Odilo who built the cloister at Cluny. A similar date can be predicated for two[5] similar *balcones* at Payerne (Fig. 254); these, like those at Cluny, gave into the chapter house. The sheltering cloister has disappeared.

Hugh did not build a new cloister at Cluny, though the construction of his new abbey church eventually necessitated the destruction of the old; but many cloisters in other

[1] Only in England did it not take place, but there the mediaeval buildings were most often ruined and destroyed at the Dissolution.

[2] "Final" is an exaggeration. When I visited Montreuil-Bonnin I found the fine late mediaeval tracery of the prior's chamber freshly torn out to go to a Paris dealer, and various Cluniac sculptures have recently gone to America.

[3] The analogy was first indicated by Mr Clapham.

[4] Thiollier, *Art roman à Charlieu*, p. 46.

[5] Three more exist in a restored state as windows.

Cluniac houses dated from this time, and some of these still survive in part. His contemporary, Abbot Ansquilinus of Moissac, built a famous cloister at Moissac; and the capitals of this—perhaps the best known of all Romanesque sculpture—survive in a splendid cloister rebuilt in the thirteenth century[1] (Fig. 242). The columns are alternately single and double, with a united capital for the double ones: the effect must have been even more beautiful when they were surmounted by a plain round-headed arch better proportioned to their abaci[2].

A rather similar disposition on a higher plinth, with capitals less rich and of a more Burgundian form, is to be found in the charming fragment of the cloister that remains at the Cluniac nunnery at Salles-en-Beaujolais (Fig. 241). This must belong to the early years of the twelfth century. To this type must have belonged the cloister of the Daurade at Toulouse[3]. Most of its capitals—which are all that survive[4]—are for double columns[5] such as were used in the other Cluniac cloister at Toulouse, that of Saint-Étienne[6]; the capitals of the two columns are here more definitely united than at Moissac or Salles. Their varied and fantastic themes recall what Saint Bernard tells us of Pons de Melgueil's cloister at Cluny[7].

The plan of Cluny in the Musée Ochier (Fig. 13 a) shows Pons de Melgueil's cloister as oblong, with the longer sides to east and west. The 1623 description of the abbey[8] describes it as 170 ft. by 135 ft., with walks 17 ft. wide. It was "à simples petits piliers, sans aucun pilier bouttant", and had a wooden roof covered with tiles. The same oblong shape was imitated at Lewes, and probably originally at Wenlock, where the cloister seems to have had single pillars.

All the cloisters hitherto considered, with continuous arcades, were intended to have wooden roofs. At the corners the arcade was broken by a massive pier on which the timber work could rest. When the general progress in vaulting caused it to be applied

---

[1] In 1865 the members of the Congrès Archéologique visited a "terre de démolition" at Moissac where the lesser cloister of the abbey was still visible. It had twin columns, plainish capitals and pointed arches, and must have been contemporary with the reconstruction of the great cloister and with the cloister at Arles-sur-Tech, built by Abbot Raimond Desbach between 1261 and 1303, which it seems closely to have resembled. See *Cong. Arch.* xxxii, 1865, p. 147.

[2] Cf. the beautiful cloister of Saint-Lizier, Ariège, which has the same alternation of single and coupled columns, and a similar disposition of capital and base, but has never been rebuilt.

[3] I.e. the Cluniac cloister of about 1100. Fragments of the sixth-century cloister survive at Montégut Ségla, Haute-Garonne. See R. Rey, *La sculpture romane languedocienne* (Toulouse and Paris, 1936), p. 36.

[4] In the Musée des Augustins at Toulouse.

[5] Cf. the twin capital under one abacus, now re-used in the War Memorial, that survives from the cloister of the Moûtier-de-Thiers. *Cong. Arch.* lxxxvii, 1925, p. 322.

[6] See lithograph of its ruins by Delor, 1842.

[7] *Apologia*, written to William of Saint-Thierry about 1125. Translation by G. G. Coulton, in *A Medieval Garner*, 1910, p. 72.

[8] *Millénaire*, ii, 236.

to cloisters, these piers were multiplied and developed. An early instance is Carennac (Fig. 243) where the arcade is divided into bays of two arches by tall fluted pilasters. The columns are double, and while their capitals are not more fused than at Salles, the columns are joined midway by a curved band between them. I have not found this feature elsewhere. The pier that here divides the bays has on the inner side towards the cloister walk a pilaster with a capital to take the cross arch of the vault. At Ganagobie (Fig. 244) there is a similar system of bays, each containing four narrow arcades. The central support in each bay is a lesser pier with a column at each angle; between it and the great pier double columns are used. The cross arches of the barrel vault rise from a bracket on the great piers and are received on a bracket higher up on the wall opposite[1]. The cloister of Le Bourget-du-Lac—with two trilobed arches to the bay, resting on twin colonnettes—is of the very end of the twelfth century and falls into the Gothic period[2].

The cloister at Cluny, according to the description of 1623, had a *lavoir* under a roofed shelter 22 ft. square in the middle of the southern walk[3], to be used by the monks on the way to the refectory. At Wenlock the octagonal lavatory still survives in the south-west corner of the cloister (Fig. 250). The basin has sculptured panels and cornice. It was later sheltered by an elegant superstructure resting on slender twin colonnettes, comparable with those found in such Cistercian houses as Poblet in Catalonia. The *lavoir* at Moissac was in the north-west corner; only ruined fragments remain. The circular lavatory at Lewes was in the same place; the foundations alone remain, but a considerable fragment of the arcaded basin is in the museum. Other Cluniac houses, such as Payerne and Baume, still have picturesque washing fountains, but these are all post-mediaeval in date.

2. CHAPTER HOUSES

The chapter house off Odilo's cloister at Cluny is described in the *Consuetudines Farfenses* as being 45 ft. long and 44 ft. wide, with four windows to the east, three to the north, and an arcade to the cloister on the west[4]. It appears certain that it was the first building in the cloister on leaving the church. The building at Payerne, now called *Vendo*, includes an eleventh-century chapter house that was probably built upon its model. The arcades to the cloister in part remain[4], and the plan of a long rectangle with two columns down the centre lengthwise is preserved; but it was burnt and revaulted in the fifteenth century and has lost its Romanesque appearance. The next chapter house at Cluny built in the time of Hugh or his successor was in the centre of the eastern cloister

[1] The visitor should be warned against the cloister at Vézelay, which is the work of Viollet-le-Duc. The Romanesque cloister there was rebuilt in the thirteenth century, and Viollet-le-Duc, finding the earlier foundations, beneath the ruins of the Gothic cloister, that had fallen in the eighteenth century, set upon them a fancy construction of his own.

[2] The Gothic cloister of Saint-Leu-d'Esserent has bays of two arches on single columns, with an oculus in the spandrel.

[3] Cf. that of the Cistercian cloister of Poblet in Catalonia.

[4] See above, p. 139.

walk, for the apse of the former abbey church was left as the church of Saint-Pierre-le-Vieux, and was the first building in that walk. The plan (Fig. 13 *a*) shows this chapter house as a great room some 80 ft. long and 45 ft. broad, with four columns down its longer axis, a door in the centre with two arcades on either side, and a door opposite into the Church of Saint Mary of the Infirmary. Nothing remains to show what it was like.

The chapter houses of the Order generally followed that at Cluny in being of oblong shape. According to Benedictine custom they were set next the church in the eastern walk of the cloister. That at Marcilhac is as early as any that survives in France (Fig. 246). It is oblong, without pillars, with a single entrance framed by twin columns. The next stage is to be found at Beaulieu (Fig. 245), with a groin vault resting on two piers. Its entrance to the cloister has bays on either side with two arcades on double columns, framed triforium-fashion by a moulded arch resting on a slender colonnette. The later chapter house at Vézelay, dating from about 1170, is similarly divided lengthwise by two columns with fine foliate capitals, from which spring elegant quadripartite rib vaults. Towards the cloister (Fig. 247) it imitates Cluny in having two arcades on either side of the door. The same disposition is followed in the contemporary room at Auxerre[1]; here too the vaults spring from finely sculptured capitals. At Souvigny[2] the late twelfth-century chapter house is similar in style, but has its vaults springing from a central pier of grouped colonnettes. The chapter house at Moissac, now divided into three chapels, is not earlier than the thirteenth century. The ogival vault rests on pilasters and brackets with little ornament.

Three English monasteries curiously follow the Mother House in an imitation of Saint-Pierre-le-Vieux in their chapter houses[3]. At Monkton Farleigh (as at Cluny) the actual apse of the earlier church seems to have been retained; at Lewes and at Castleacre[4] it was built *de novo* of the same apsidal form. At Wenlock it lacks the apse. The two of these that survive in a ruined state are remarkable for the rich arcading applied to their walls. At Castleacre the chapter house, dating from the first quarter of the twelfth century, was some 52 ft. long and 23 ft. wide; it had, as usual, a round-headed unglazed window on either side of the central door. Its walls are decorated with three tiers of arcading[5]: first a low arcade of plain round-headed arches, then a tall arcade of intersecting arches more closely set, and above this a third arcade of round-headed arches with carved capitals. At Wenlock the chapter house, probably of *c.* 1140, has a similar entrance (Fig. 248). It was vaulted with three bays of oblong quadripartite vaulting. This has a yet more complicated scheme of arcading (Fig. 251) rising from dado height.

---

[1] See Tillet in *Cong. Arch.* LXXIV, 1907, p. 627. It is now built into the hospice.

[2] See Deshoulières, *Souvigny*, p. 75.

[3] Cf. an apsidal chapel to the east of the cloister at Moissac. Taylor and Nodier, *Voyages pittoresques et romantiques dans l'ancienne France*, vol. I, Pt. II, Languedoc, Pl. 70 A.

[4] Probably built in the first quarter of the twelfth century.

[5] Now much damaged.

From a composite triple column springs both a simple round-headed arcade and an intersecting arcade richly moulded. From its intersections springs another; and from the intersections of this yet another. The effect is one of barbaric richness: every element is architectural, yet each is unstructurally used.

3. REFECTORIES

The classic site for a Benedictine refectory was in the south walk of the cloister and this seems generally to have been adopted in the Order of Cluny[1]. The *Consuetudines Farfenses* describe the refectory in Mayeul's buildings as being 90 ft. long and 25 ft. wide; the walls were 23 ft. high, and the glass-filled windows, of which there were eight on either side, were 5 ft. high and 3 ft. broad. The monk who accompanied Peter Damian to Cluny in 1063 says that it was large enough to seat all the monks, and had paintings on the walls[2].

The *Chronicum Cluniacense*[3] describes the refectory built in the time of Abbot Hugh as "longitudinis circiter xxxviij et latitudinis xxiiij passuum"; if for xxxviij we read lxxxviij we get a measurement closely approximating to that of the earlier building. The description of 1623[4] describes it as having two rows of pillars, and being 112 ft. long and 67 ft. wide. The plan in the Musée Ochier shows it of this size and proportion; it looks as if an aisle, and perhaps a bay, had been added later[5]. The *Chronicum* tells us that it had six tables down its length, "tam in medio quam a dextris et sinistris", that is two rows of three tables counting lengthwise. There were also a high table on a dais, a table for the grand prior on the right and another for the claustral prior on the left. It was decorated with wall paintings of founders and benefactors, and of a great figure of Christ with a Judgment scene.

This refectory was given to the abbey in the time of Saint Hugh by one Roger, whom Dr Rose Graham identifies[6] with Roger de Montgomery, Earl of Shrewsbury and founder of the Cluniac house at Wenlock, who died in 1093. Unfortunately, the refectory at Wenlock itself was rebuilt in the thirteenth century, so that we cannot compare the two. Indeed, so far as I know, the only Cluniac refectory of the Romanesque period which survives[7] is that at Ganagobie. This has an entrance from the cloister (Fig. 249); the plain door has a double arcade on either side, like that of a chapter house. The interior has a rib vault in two bays; this, like the wall arches, rises from a group of colonnettes with sculptured capitals. The whole is notably rich and well finished (Fig. 252).

[1] At Moissac, where the cloister is exceptionally to the north of the church, it was in the north walk. See Taylor and Nodier, *loc. cit.*

[2] Migne, *Pat. Lat.* cxlv, cols. 873–4; quoted R. Graham, *Archaeologia*, lxxx, 1930, p. 146.

[3] Marrier, col. 1639.   [4] *Millénaire*, ii, 237.

[5] That at Lewes seems to have been even longer.   [6] *Archaeologia*, lxxx, 1930, p. 155.

[7] There is a wall with round-headed windows at Vézelay, and one window with a sculptured moulding at Prittlewell. The refectories at Moissac and Wenlock were rebuilt in the thirteenth century.

4. INFIRMARIES AND INFIRMARY CHAPELS

Such primitive monasteries as Qalaat Seman had a chapel—there to the north-east of the great church—for use as a mortuary chapel; and the tradition was continued in the Benedictine Order by the provision of a special chapel for the sick[1]. Traditionally it was near the infirmary, but removed from the main church[2]. The deed of gift of Saint-Étienne-de-Nevers to Cluny mentions such a chapel as one of the essentials of a monastery; the donor states: "I have built the cloister and the offices, large enough to suffice for the monks who are to come to dwell therein, and a chapel for the sick[3]."

At Cluny the chapel seems always to have been known as that of Saint Mary; it is described under that name in the *Consuetudines Farfenses*, and the description of the infirmary succeeds it, though no specific connexion is there made between the two. The chapel was rededicated, presumably after an enlargement, in 1085 by Odo de Lagery, who had been grand prior of Cluny before he became Cardinal Bishop of Ostia in 1085[4]. It was hither that Abbot Hugh was borne to die in 1109[5].

The *Consuetudines* drawn up by the monk Bernard in the time of Abbot Hugh[6] describe it as having three apses, the central one dedicated primarily to the Virgin and the Archangel Michael, that on the right to Saint Stephen and Saint Clement, and that on the left to Saint John the Baptist. Each had many subsidiary dedications[7]. It appears on the seventeenth-century plan, which shows it as having a long aisleless nave, lit on either side by eight windows, with three round apsidioles in a straight line at the east end. Two piers by the apse suggest that it originally had aisles. It is not oriented to the true east, but a little to the east-south-east, which throws it out of line with Mayeul's abbey church and its conventual buildings[8] and with the great church and new buildings that replaced it. Such an orientation strongly suggests that it was built before these. If so, it must have dated from the time of Odo or Aymard or the early years of Mayeul[9]. In the plan it has a cloister on either side of the nave. These were probably added after its original construction, to provide accommodation for the invalids in the infirmary: they are not mentioned by Bernard. They may perhaps date from the rededication in

[1] E.g. in the Carolingian monastery of Saint-Riquier, where it was dedicated to the Virgin.

[2] See Isidore of Seville, *Etymologiae*, ed. Holsten, I, 188.

[3] Pignot, II, 256.

[4] Herrgott, ed. Bernard, *Consuetudines Cluniacenses*, p. 262.

[5] Marrier, col. 436. It must be distinguished from the Chapel of the Virgin dedicated in 1118 (Marrier, col. 564). This was pulled down and reconstructed at the Renaissance, whereas Notre-Dame-de-l'Infirmerie survived into the seventeenth century.

[6] Herrgott, *loc. cit.* The account of 1623 (Virey, *op. cit.* p. 249) describes it as vaulted and as having "deux chapelles au clef des collatéraux". It was 125 ft. long and 40 ft. wide.

[7] See Dr Rose Graham in *Archaeologia*, LXXX, 1930, pl. 154.

[8] Their orientation is definitely known from that of Saint-Pierre-le-Vieux.

[9] M. Virey is inclined to attribute it to the time of Odilo. *Millénaire*, II, 243, n. 5.

1085. It is tempting to suppose that when they were built, as the nave was thus strongly buttressed, the original aisles were thrown into the nave[1].

If this hypothesis is correct, its plan is perfectly consistent with an early date. The engraving after Prévost's drawing[2] shows it with a tower towards its eastern end, of two stories with windows in the upper storey.

Whatever the original date and intention of Saint Mary of the Infirmary, it served as a model for infirmary chapels in other houses of the Order[3]. At Menat an old plan[4] shows an aisleless nave, a small transept, and three apsidioles; Notre-Dame-des-Avents at Souvigny, that also served as a hospital chapel, had aisles but was otherwise of the same plan[5]. This was oriented with the priory church; it was destroyed to make way for its sacristy about 1770. The infirmary chapel at Lewes[6] likewise had a small transept; it had no aisles and a square east end flanked by semicircular apsidioles. At Saint-Bertin and Moissac[7], however, it was an aisleless chapel with a single apse, differently oriented from the abbey church, while at Wenlock it is set in the angle of the lesser cloister formed on the eastern side of the dorter range by the infirmary buildings and other dependencies.

At Cluny itself the infirmary seems always to have had several chambers. The *Consuetudines Farfenses* describe its early form as being of six cells, four each with eight beds in cubicles, the fifth a smaller room where the sick brethren were to have their feet washed on Saturdays, and to be bled; and the sixth a little pantry where the servants were to wash up. The seventeenth-century plan shows a lesser infirmary, a congeries of irregular rooms surviving from some earlier buildings, and a great infirmary of vast size—the 1623 description says 165 ft. by 78 ft.—that appears to be later than the twelfth century.

The plan of the infirmaries in the English houses of Castleacre, Wenlock and Lewes can still be traced. At Lewes alone it was aisled. At Castleacre there are two infirmary halls, one Norman and one a little later. The first has three doors, a dais (presumably for the infirmarian) and the remains of what appears to be a wall pulpit; the second, divided from it by a screen, may have been a flat-ended infirmary chapel.

5. DORTERS

Of all monastic buildings the monks' dorters were most liable to change; nearly all were rebuilt between the thirteenth and the eighteenth centuries. Yet had a dorter in one of the great houses survived intact it might have served to give us a true idea of the scale of early mediaeval life, and such a room as that in the Cistercian house of Poblet in

---

[1] See Mortet, I, 302.   [2] Bruel, *Cluni*, Pl. II.

[3] When Prosper Mérimée visited the Moûtier-de-Thiers in 1838 he noted the remains of a second church which has now disappeared. *Cong. Arch.* LXXXVII, 1925, p. 322.

[4] A copy is in the archives of the Commission des Monuments historiques.

[5] Plan by Evezard made in 1769, reproduced in Deshoulières, *Souvigny*, p. 73. See also Vallery Radot, *Églises romanes*, p. 86.   [6] Which was not oriented with the priory church.

[7] Chapelle-de-tous-les-Saints; see Taylor and Nodier, *op. cit.* Pl. 70 A.

Catalonia, if we furnish and populate it in the light of the *Consuetudines*, is still most impressive. The dormitory at Cluny early in the eleventh century[1] was 160 ft. long and 30 ft. wide, with 97 windows in it, each as tall as a man with his arms stretched up as far as they would go, and 2½ ft. wide. The walls were 23 ft. high. At the end of the dorter away from the church there was the *latrina* or reredorter, 70 ft. long and 23 ft. wide, with forty-five conveniences with wooden seats, and a little window in the wall directly above each, as well as a higher range of seventeen larger windows. The drainage seems to have been by a conduit running into the Grosne[2].

This dorter occupied the classic position for such a room, on the first floor of the eastern range of buildings in the cloister. When the conventual buildings were rebuilt, its successor was set above the great chapter house and over the cellars beyond. According to the 1623 description, its reredorter was 105 ft. long and 48 ft. wide. The disposition of the dorter had been altered by the time that the description was made. It had no "night stair" to the abbey. Peter the Venerable[3] tells the story of brother Alger, who dreamed that he heard the bell sound for nocturns and hurried from the further dorter in which he slept down to the lesser cloister[4] and so through the great cloister to the church. The bell no longer sounded, the lamps were not lit as they should have been, and the church doors that should have stood open were shut fast: for it was a dream sent by the Devil to wake him at the wrong hour. Similarly at Maillezais the stairs led from the dorter[5] to the cloister and there was no direct communication with the church. At Payerne, however, the late fifteenth-century dorter over the chapter house has a door and a stairway into the church.

In England, Castleacre still has its dorter, nine bays long, on the first floor above a vaulted undercroft that may have served as a day room. The windows are set high, their sills being 5 ft. from the floor, above a plain blind arcade. There are considerable remains of the reredorter behind, showing a similar plan to that followed at Cluny. At Wenlock the dorter range forms part of the present dwelling house. Alterations to this in 1936 revealed eleven of its windows, each framed by a moulding resting on sculptured capitals. The floor below is windowless, and must have served as a cellar. At Monk's Horton only the walls, with plain stepped buttresses, are of the twelfth century, as the windows were replaced in the fourteenth.

[1] *Consuetudines Farfenses*; Mortet, I, 134.

[2] The later reredorter at Lewes (which lay away from the dorter and was connected with it by a bridge) was 158 ft. long and contained sixty-six seats. See A. Hamilton Thompson, *English Monasteries*, p. 85.

[3] de Mirac. I, 17; Marrier, col. 1274.

[4] I.e. that south of the refectory.

[5] Rebuilt or greatly modified in the late thirteenth or early fourteenth century.

6. OTHER CONVENTUAL BUILDINGS

The general disposition of Mayeul's buildings has already been indicated[1] and little remains to be said. There is little material, except for the seventeenth-century plan and description, for reconstructing Abbot Hugh's buildings further, and Prévost's view chiefly serves to show how much subsequent rebuilding had taken place. Apart from the actual conventual buildings already described, they were for the most part[2] intended for domestic use: warming rooms, kitchens, cellars, rooms for the administrative officers, quarters for guests and their servants, workrooms and innumerable storerooms. The granaries and mills at Cluny were begun by Abbot Yves I (1257–75) and finished by Yves II (1275–89)[3].

Interesting as the early buildings would have been from the historical point of view, they were probably architecturally unpretentious enough. The cloister, chapter house and refectory apart, there is no evidence for any but the plainest and most utilitarian of edifices.

The possible exception is the guest house, where less austerity was natural. This is confirmed by the remains of the west cloister walk at Ruffec[4], now used as barns and stables. It dates from the second half of the twelfth century. The lower floor was probably always used for storage. The first floor is occupied by one great room, lit by five pairs of twin windows, and heated from a great fireplace with sculptured capitals. All the windows give on to the side away from the cloister; and this fact, together with the presence of the fireplace, shows that the room must have been a guest hall. Similarly, the parlour at Castleacre has a sculptured doorway and an ornamented frieze within.

At Payerne (Fig. 253), Charlieu (Fig. 258) and Salles walls survive that, though modified later, show traces of their early construction and fenestration; the general impression is one of austerity and plainness. This is confirmed by the extreme exterior simplicity of the buildings at Ganagobie. The western range of buildings at Monkton Farleigh, which include a hall 20 ft. long, is quite plain except for the necessary pilaster buttresses and two lancet windows. It is only from such scanty remains, and from the rather more complete whole at Wenlock[5], that we can judge of the general appearance of the Romanesque domestic buildings of the Order.

[1] See pp. 63 and 136.

[2] Except of course the sacristy. The *Consuetudines Farfenses* described it as 58 ft. long with a tower; and this has been identified with the earlier church (see p. 54). The customs prescribed that the sacred wafers should be baked there; ovens for the purpose can be seen at Castleacre and Thetford.

[3] To these the Tour Fabry was added by Abbot Hugues Fabry (1347–69) and the Tour des Fèves by Abbot Eudes de la Perrière (1424–57).

[4] See *Bull. Mon.* LXXXVIII, 1929, p. 235.

[5] Dr Cranage suggests that a large vaulted chamber of the early thirteenth century that there forms part of the church may be a library: this, however, is a later development of the Cluniac scheme. *The Home of the Monk*, p. 4.

7. GATEWAYS

Abbot Hugh's basilica at Cluny was approached through a great double archway built by him or his successor. Its two arches are all that now survive (Fig. 255), but up to the beginning of the nineteenth century these were crowned by an open arcade of ten decorated round arches, in a scheme exactly like that of the inner face of the Porte-Saint-André at Autun, a Roman building dating from A.D. 69 (Fig. 256). Obviously, this ancient arch provided the model: it is one of the few definite instances of the imitation of a classical Roman building in the Romanesque period. The priory of Le Wast had a rather similar gateway, with three great arches and a building above[1].

The walls round the abbey property were begun in 1179, and were originally fortified with fifteen towers. Two of these remain—the Porte-Saint-Odilon and the Porte-Saint-Mayeul—but neither has any architectural pretensions.

8. *LANTERNES DES MORTS*

Since the surviving *Lanternes des Morts* in France are all in Western France[2], it is tempting to think of them as being characteristic of that district; but there is literary evidence to prove that they were built in the cemeteries of Cluniac priories even in Burgundy. Peter the Venerable[3] tells that in 1135-6 a boy had a vision of a more than earthly light in the cemetery at Charlieu; and in telling the story he describes the *Lanterne des Morts* in the cemetery and its purpose. "Obtinet medium coemeterii locum structura quedam lapidea, habens in summitate sui quantitatem unius lampadis capacem, que ob reverentiam fidelium ibi quiescentium totis noctibus fulgore suo locum illum sacratum illustrat. Sunt et gradus per quos illuc ascenditur, supraque spatium duobus vel tribus ad standum vel sedendum hominibus sufficiens...." One such Cluniac *Lanterne des Morts* yet survives at Château-Larcher (Fig. 257) in testimony to the accuracy of Peter's description. The fitful light that it used to cast, "ob reverentiam fidelium ibi quiescentium", may serve as a symbol for that which these enquiries have thrown upon the visible remains of Cluniac monasticism.

[1] C. Enlart, *Monuments religieux de l'architecture romane...dans la région picarde* (Amiens and Paris, 1895), p. 212.

[2] In Limousin, Poitou and Saintonge. See Viollet-le-Duc, *Dictionnaire raisonnée*, VI, 154; Enlart, *Manuel*, I, 917; R. de Lasteyrie, *Architecture religieuse...romane*, p. 720.

[3] de Mirac. II, xxvii; Marrier, cols. 1327-8.

CONCLUSION

"Cluniacensis congregatio, divino charismate cœteris imbuta plenius, ut alter sol enitet in terris, adeo ut his nunc temporibus ipsi potius conveniat quod a Domino dictum est: Vos estis lux mundi."

Letter of Pope Urban II to Abbot Hugh of Cluny, 1098 (Marrier, col. 250).

THIS brief survey of Cluniac architecture has been confined to the buildings that actually belonged to the Order. Its influence naturally extended over a much wider field. In the early years of the abbey, before the idea of an Order was developed, many great monasteries were reformed and occasionally colonized from it, without ever being formally subjected to it. Odo thus reformed Saint-Géraud-d'Aurillac, Saint-Austremoine-de-Clermont, Saint-Pierre-le-Vif-de-Sens, Saint-Martin-de-Tulle, Saint-Sauveur-de-Sarlat, Saint-Sore-de-Genouillac, Saint-Benoît-de-Fleury and Saint-Julien-de-Tours, as well as San Pietro in Ciel d' Oro at Pavia and various Roman monasteries including San Paolo fuori le Mure[1]. Mayeul reformed Marmoutiers, Saint-Maur-les-Fossés, and Saint-Benigne-de-Dijon in France, and Sant' Apollinare in Classe at Ravenna and San Salvatore at Pavia in Italy[2]. With Odilo the conception of a Cluniac Order emerges, and with it the codification of the customs of Cluny into *Consuetudines* for its daughter houses to follow. With this institution Cluniac influence became exercised in other spheres, for monasteries that were not in the Order might decide to follow its code of customs. Thus the earliest surviving *Consuetudines* are those drawn up for the monastery of Farfa, that was never in the Order. Under his successor Hugh, the Order was completely systematized and greatly increased. Certain great houses, like that of Saint-Sernin at Toulouse when it was a-building, were subjected to it for a time[3] but soon regained their independence. Others followed its Rule but never accepted subjection: such were La Cava in Italy[4], Battle in England, Sahagun, San Salvador de Ogna, San Juan de la Peña, San Salvador de Leyre and Santa Maria de Yrache in Spain[5], and Hirschau and its imitators in Germany. Under the next great abbot, Peter the Venerable, the material influence of Cluny was diminished; though Reading and Faversham followed its customs without entering the Order, the future lay with the rival Cistercians.

The individual monks of the Cluniac houses might also be agents in spreading its influence in other fields. Each was familiar with the Mother House, since each, however remote the monastery of his adoption, came to Cluny to make his profession; and some of the greatest of these, especially in the earlier years of the Order, passed from its

---

[1] Evans, *Monastic Life at Cluny*, p. 10. I omit the houses he reformed that entered the Order later.
[2] *Ibid*. p. 16. He also reformed once more Saint-Pierre-le-Vif and San Pietro in Ciel d' Oro.
[3] Pignot, II, 200.   [4] *Ibid*. p. 290.   [5] *Ibid*. p. 115.

monasteries to rule Benedictine houses outside its dominion. So about 1008 the Prior of Cluny, Vivian by name, became Abbot of Saint-Denis[1]; so William of Volpiano, who was a monk at Cluny before 990, passed thence to Saint-Bcnigne-dc-Dijon and ended by reforming and rebuilding the great monasteries of Northern France, in which the plan of Mayeul's church is imitated[2]. So Gregory, brought up from childhood at Cluny, left it about 1057 to become Abbot of Saint-Sever and later Bishop of Lescar[3]; so Henry of Blois began his career as a monk of Cluny and ended it as Bishop of Winchester; and so in England priors of Bermondsey were appointed by Henry II abbots of the Great Benedictine houses of Saint-Ouen at Rouen (1157), Evesham (1160), Abingdon (1176), Faversham (1178) and Glastonbury (1189)[4]. Certain abbeys, again, traditionally maintained a close friendship with Cluny; at Ripoll the builder-Abbot Oliva was a friend of Saint Hugh of Cluny; at Le Monastier-Saint-Chaffre it was on the advice of Saint Hugh that Abbot William began his buildings in 1074[5]; at Fleury (Saint-Benoît-sur-Loire) it would be reasonable to look for Cluniac influence. Finally, though it is doubtful whether Pope Gregory VII was ever a monk of Cluny as Radulphus Glaber declares[6], it is certain that Odo de Lagery passed his youth as a monk of Cluny and acted as grand prior of the abbey before he wore the tiara as Urban II, and that Pascal II was equally a child of the abbey. One came to Cluny in 1095 to dedicate the high altar in Hugh's new abbey church, and the other for Christmas in 1106 when it was half built.

"Great art, that has power to stamp an epoch and influence a cycle of centuries, would seem to concentrate to a definite nucleus of space as distinctly as it does to a point of time, and the one is as limited as the other[7]." Such a centre was Cluny, and to trace all the lines of influence that radiate from it would involve an investigation of almost impracticable complexity and size. But if the nucleus of this influence within the Order itself has been made precise and definite, something has been achieved which can form the basis of further specific investigation in the case of any church which seems to show Cluniac influence. For example, Payerne seems to have served as a model for the cathedral of Lausanne; Vézelay for Avila[8] and for the vault of Maria Laach[9]; Saint-

---

[1] Sackur, II, 32.

[2] At Bernay, begun in 1013, and in the construction of his disciple Hildebert at Mont-Saint-Michel. Bernay was copied at its priory of Eye in Suffolk. *Bull. Mon.* LXXVI, 1912, p. 470.

[3] Pignot, II, 342.   [4] See Dr R. Graham in *Brit. Archaeol. Assoc. Journal*, N.S. XXXII, 1926, p. 165.

[5] See F. Lacroix, "L'Abbaye de Saint-Chaffre-du-Monastier et ses rapports avec Cluny", in *Annales de l'Académie de Mâcon*, 2nd series, x, Mâcon, 1892, p. 8. The two abbeys were not formally connected until 1667.

[6] Hist. lib. v, cap. 1. See L. M. Smith, "Cluny and Gregory VII", in *English Historical Review*, XXVI, 1911, p. 30.   [7] E. S. Prior, *A History of Gothic Art in England*, p. 6.

[8] See Lambert in *Bull. Mon.* LXXXIII, 1924, p. 263: the likeness, however, is not exact, and there is much Burgundian influence in the architecture of Avila that is easily explicable for political reasons.

[9] The likeness is mentioned by M. Aubert (*Cong. Arch.* LXXXV, 1922 (Rhénanie), p. 124); but he incorrectly includes Maria Laach in the Order of Cluny.

Martin-des-Champs to have had some influence on Saint-Denis[1]; and the Cluniac churches of Western France on the Crusading architecture in the Holy Land[2]. Such Spanish churches as San Pedro at Avila and San Martin de Fromista[3] show clear Burgundian influence, which is probably due not merely in general to the Burgundian Crusades there but also more particularly to the close connexion between the leaders of the Crusades and the Order of Cluny[4]. Hugh himself twice went to Spain in connexion with the substitution of the Roman for the Mozarabic rite; and Peter the Venerable travelled there, and had the Koran translated while he was at Toledo in order that he might refute it[5].

The relation between Saint-Martial-de-Limoges, Saint-Étienne-de-Nevers, Sainte-Foy-de-Conques, Saint-Sernin-de-Toulouse and Sant' Iago de Compostela has often been pointed out. Here, too, whether the relation is primarily due to the Spanish Crusades or not, the exact measure of Cluniac influence has to be investigated, since Saint-Martial and Saint-Étienne were Cluniac and Saint-Sernin was rebuilt at the time that Bishop Isarn of Toulouse was vainly endeavouring to bring it into the Order. The list of such influences might well be extended; their investigation is one of the tasks that await the rising generation of mediaevalists.

As the Order passed the culminating point of its material glory, its influences passed into more general and less personal channels, and became less a specific influence than a part of the tradition of Western civilization. In the Benedictine churches of the Order of Cluny, we may see the foundations of the structure of the Gothic cathedrals being slowly laid. The extraordinarily rapid development of Gothic architecture, between Saint-Germer-de-Fly, built between 1160 and 1180, and Amiens, begun in 1220, would be miraculous, were it not that it is the crescendo of an architectural movement that begins in the early eleventh century. Problems of plan and of vaulting had been progressively solved in the century before 1160; even the pointed arch had been in use in France for nearly a century when Saint-Germer-de-Fly was finished; and the line between Romanesque and Gothic is hard to draw. In Saint-Révérien, with its ambulatory and untransepted nave, we have the forerunner of the plan of Bourges; in Saint-Martin-des-Champs we have the prototype of its double ambulatory, and in the Burgundian system of engaged columns in stages the origin of its incredibly bold system of piers. Once the architectural needs of an age were comprehended, the constructional

---

[1] And its squinch-like exterior arches reappear in the thirteenth-century Gothic of Saint-Étienne-de-Caen and Coutances Cathedral.

[2] M. Enlart cites Beaulieu, La Souterraine, Moirax and Saint-Maurin, as well as certain Burgundian influences such as are commonly found in the Order. *Les Monuments des Croisés*, I, 30.

[3] Built in 1066, it did not become Cluniac until 1112.

[4] For example the body of Abbot Hugh's relative, Thibault de Semur, Comte de Chalon-sur-Saône, who died on crusade at Tolosa in 1063, was brought back for burial at Paray-le-Monial. Petit, *Les croisades Bourguignonnes*, p. 260.

[5] Pignot, III, 536.

basis of a style found, and the human spirit at work upon its problems, miracles of artistic creation could be performed in a few decades.

In the twentieth century we visit the Romanesque churches of France very much as Pausanias in the second century visited the ancient temples of Greece. We share in the religious tradition that created them, but are yet far removed in time and spirit; we are versed in learning other than that of the monastery, and find expression for our thoughts and feelings in other arts. It is hard for us to enter into the spirit of the Romanesque period: we have little instinctive sympathy with an age that, capable of immense feats of constructive reasoning in certain spheres, could unquestioningly accept the authority of tradition in other departments of life. Consequently, there is to the modern mind a quality in Romanesque architecture that at first sight is at once impressive and repellent. Its churches are filled with a religious spirit that is alien to us: in them we dimly realize the unquestioning strength, the fantastic ecstasy and the ascetic ferocity of mediaeval religion. They are manifestations of a life corporate yet self-contained, deep yet narrowly limited, in every essence strongly characterized and in every essence hard of comprehension. Yet in the churches of the Cluniac Order these qualities of a virtue more primitive than ours are irradiated by an entirely human love of beauty, dignity and splendour, in which we still share. In virtue of that community of feeling we may perchance still gain spiritual access to the life of cloisters that Time has long since violated.

APPENDIX A

Key to

Catalogus Abbatiarum, Prioratuum, et Decanatuum, mediate et immediate Abbatiae, seu Monasterio Cluniacensi subditorum. . . .

Marrier, Bibliotheca Cluniacensis, cols. 1705–52.

(The numbers of monks given are also taken from this, and give the number in the fifteenth century, when the membership of the Order was considerably diminished. Where he gives two figures, that recorded as the earlier is here given.)

PROVINCE OF LYONS

1. Abbatia Cluniacensis — Cluny, Saône-et-Loire (5 officers and 260 monks)
2. Prioratus Sanctae Trinitatis Marciniaci — Marcigny, Saône-et-Loire (prior, 12 monks and 99 nuns)

3. P. de Cariloco — Charlieu, Loire (prior and 31 monks)
4. P. de Gigniaco — Gigny, Jura (prior and 31 monks)
5. Decanatus de Paredo — Paray-le-Monial, Saône-et-Loire (prior and 25 monks)

6. [Prioratus] Montis Sancti Vincentii — Mont-Saint-Vincent, Saône-et-Loire
7. P. Nantuaci — Nantua, Ain (25 monks)
8. P. Sancti Marcelli — Saint-Marcel-lès-Chalon, Saône-et-Loire (25 monks)

9. Decanatus Sancti Viventii de Vergeio — Saint-Vivant-de-Vergy, Côte-d'Or (28 monks)
10. P. de Amberta — Ambierle, Loire (20 monks)
11. P. de Salis — Salles, Rhône (prior, 2 monks and 30 nuns)
12. P. de Magobrio — Mesvres, Saône-et-Loire (prior and 6 monks)
13. P. de Saltu subtus Cosanum — Sail-sous-Cousan, Loire (prior and 2 monks)
14. P. B. Mariae Magdalenae de Cadrelis — Charolles, Saône-et-Loire (prior and 2 monks)
15. P. de Lusiaco — Luzy, Nièvre (prior and 1 monk)
16. [P. de] Semelaio — Semelay, Nièvre (prior and 1 monk)
17. Decanatus Montis Bertrandi — Montberthoud, Ain (decanus and 2 monks)
18. P. Sancti Petri Montis Sancti Joannis — Mont-Saint-Jean (Le Glanod), Côte-d'Or (prior and 3 monks)

19. P. de Talues — Taluyers, Rhône (prior and 3 monks)
20. Decanatus de Poilliaco — Pouilly-lès-Feurs, Loire (decanus and 2 monks)
21. P. Sancti Ioannis de Truando (Truaudo) — Trouhaut-le-Grand, Côte-d'Or (prior and 2 monks)

22. P. Sanctorum Nazarii et Celsii prope Castrum de Borbonio Lancy — Bourbon-Lancy, Saône-et-Loire (prior and 5 monks)
23. P. de Cha[m]diaco — Chandieu, Heyrieux, Isère (prior, 2 monks and vicar)

24. P. B. Mariae de Laudona	Dioc. Besançon: ? Les Landons, Jura (prior, 3 monks and vicar)
25. P. Sancti Romani	Saint-Romain, Saône-et-Loire (prior, 1 monk and vicar)
26. P. de Contamina	Contamine-sur-Arve, Haute-Savoie (prior and 11 monks)

Dependent on Contamine-sur-Arve

27. P. de Silnigiaco	Sillingy, Haute-Savoie
28. P. de Tiés	Thiez, Haute-Savoie
29. P. de Rosaco	Rosay, Savoie (prior, 3 monks and 12 nuns)

Dependent on Gigny

30. P. Castri Salinensis	Château-sur-Salins, Jura (prior and 7 monks)
31. P. de Bella-valle	Bellevaux-en-Bauges, Le Châtelard, Savoie
32. P. de Clara-valle	Clairvaux, Jura (prior and 1 monk)
33. P. de Marbosio	Marboz, Ain
34. P. de Clausa Sancti Bertrandi (Bernardi)	Saint-Clair-de-la-Cluse, Dingy-Saint-Clair, Haute-Savoie
35. P. de Albino	Not identified; dioc. Grenoble
36. P. de Castro Chiurel	Châtel-Chevroux, Saint-Amour, Jura
37. P. Doucieul	Oussiat, Ain (prior, 2 monks and priest)
38. P. de Tresfort	Treffort, Ain
39. P. Doncieure	? See no. 37
40. P. de Chatenay	Chatelay, Jura (prior and 1 monk)
41. P. d'Ilay	Ilay, Jura (prior and 1 monk)
42. P. Sancti Laurentii de Rupe	Saint-Laurent-la-Roche, Jura (prior and 1 monk)
43. P. de Chambournay	Chambornay-lès-Pin, Haute-Saône (prior and 1 monk)
44. P. de Marnay	Marnay, Aube
45. P. Pontis Indis	Oussiat, Pont-d'Ain, Ain (see no. 37)

Dependent on Nantua

46. P. de Pomeriis	Pommiers, Loire (prior and 12 monks)
47. P. de Villeta	Villette, Chalamont, Ain
48. P. de Traffortio	See no. 38
49. P. Montis-Lupelli	Montluel, Ain
50. P. Villae, in Michalia	Ville-en-Michaille, Ain
51. P. de Quercu	Chêne-en-Semine, Haute-Savoie
52. P. de Asserento	Asserans, Ain
53. P. de Remeliaco	Rumilly, Haute-Savoie
54. P. de Talusiaco, alias de Talissun	Talissieu, Ain
55. P. de Ocellis	Oulx, Hautes-Alpes
56. P. Sancti Martini in Tarentesia	Saint-Martin, Moûtiers, Savoie

Dependent on Charlieu

57. P. Sancti Ioannis Thisiaci	Thizy, Rhône (prior and 5 monks)
58. P. Sancti Nizecii	Saint-Nizier-d'Azergues, Rhône (prior and 4 monks)
59. P. Sancti Martini de Rigniaco	Régny, Loire (prior and 5 monks)

Dependent on Marcigny

60. P. Sancti Michaelis de Burgo de Zemora, in Hispania	Zamora, Spain (prior and 2 monks)
61. P. de Balma Corneliana	La Baume-Cornillane, Drôme
62. P. de Aqualia	Not identified; dioc. Laon
63. P. B. Ioannis de Corello	Not identified; dioc. Autun
64. P. de Montosis...prope Cogniacum (seu Montonis)	Montausier, Charente
65. P. de Fontanis	Fontaines-d'Ozillac, Charente
66. P. Sancti Lupi	Saint-Loup-sur-Abron, Nièvre
67. P. de Failihigia	Dioc. Salisbury; Monkton Farleigh?
68. P. Sancti Ioannis de Oreolis	Oriol-en-Royans, Drôme

Dependent on Saint-Marcel-lès-Chalon

69. P. de Mostranto super Trenam	Not identified (prior and 2 monks)
70. P. de Ruffeio	Ruffey, Saône-et-Loire (2 monks)
71. P. de Donna-petra	Dompierre, Jura
72. P. de Floriaco	Fleury-la-Montagne, Saône-et-Loire (2 monks)
73. P. de Pontouz	Pontoux, Saône-et-Loire

Dependent on Sacristy of Cluny

74. Domus de Villa-nova	Villeneuve, Loire (2 monks)
75. D. Sancti Victoris	Saint-Victor-sur-Rhins, Loire (2 monks)
76. D. de Alto-iugo	Ajoux, Rhône (2 monks)
77. D. Sancti Mammerti	Saint-Mamert, Rhône
78. P. Daysino	Not identified (prior and 1 monk)
79. P. Montis Sancti Vincentij	See no. 6 (prior and 2 monks)

PROVINCE OF FRANCE

80. Abbatia Belli-loci in Argonia	Beaulieu-en-Argonne, Meuse (20 monks)
81. P. B. Mariae de Charitate ad Ligerim	La Charité-sur-Loire, Nièvre (80 monks in 1343)
82. P. Sancti Martini de Campis	Saint-Martin-des-Champs, Paris (60 monks)
83. P. Sanctorum Petri et Pauli de Coinciaco	Coincy, Aisne (prior and 35 monks)
84. Decanatus[1] Sancti Petri de Lehuno in sanguine terso	Lihons-en-Santerre, Somme (decanus and 25 monks)

[1] The title of decanatus was given in 1291 to Lihons-en-Santerre, Nogent-le-Rotrou, Gassicourt, Gaye, Vergy, Vendœuvre, Tours-sur-Marne, Carennac, Moirax, Ronsenac, Saint-Côme, Marmesse and Montrot; it was only a nominal change.

85.	P. Sancti Petri Abbatisvillae	Abbeville, Somme (prior and 24 monks)
86.	P. Sancti Lupi de Asserento	Saint-Leu-d'Esserent, Oise (prior and 25 monks)
87.	P. Sancti Arnulphi de Crispeio	Crépy-en-Valois, Oise (prior and 27 monks)
88.	Decanatus B. Mariae de Gaya	Gaye, Marne (decanus and 20 monks)
89.	P. B. Mariae de Longo-ponte	Longpont, Seine-et-Oise (prior and 22 monks)
90.	Decanatus Sancti Dyonisii, de Nogento Retrodi	Nogent-le-Rotrou, Eure-et-Loir (prior and 27 monks)
91.	P. Sancti Salui de Valenciniis	Saint-Saulve, Valenciennes, Nord (prior and 28 monks)
92.	P. B. Mariae de Nantolio	Nanteuil-le-Haudoin, Oise (prior and 12 monks)
93.	P. B. Mariae de Autolio in Valesia	Autheuil-en-Valois, Oise (prior and 2 monks)
94.	P. Sanctae Margaretae de Elincuria	Élincourt-Sainte-Marguerite, Oise (prior and 12 monks)
95.	P. Sancti Nicolai de Monte Vineo (alias de Vingtmont)	Vignemont, Oise (prior and 2 monks)
96.	P. Sanctae Margaretae de Mergerye in Campania	Margerie-Hancourt, Marne (prior and 8 monks)
97.	P. Sancti Stephani, Nivernensis Diocesis	Saint-Étienne-de-Nevers, Nièvre (prior and 12 monks)
98.	P. Sancti Reueriani	Saint-Révérien, Nièvre (prior and 12 monks)
99.	P. B. Mariae de Prato Donziaci (alias Donzi-le-Pré)	Donzy-le-Pré, Nièvre (prior and 12 monks)
100.	P. B. Mariae de Petra Solari, alias de Pierre Solaire	Pierre Solaire, Calvados
101.	P. B. Mariae Montisdesiderii	Montdidier, Somme (prior and 12 monks)
102.	P. Sancti Petri de Donna petra	Dompierre, Oise (prior and 2 monks)
103.	Decanatus Sancti Petri de Turribus	Tours-sur-Marne, Marne (decanus and 2 monks)
104.	P. Sancti Theobaldi, de Vitriaco Castro	Saint-Thibault, Vitry-en-Perthois, Marne (prior and 2 monks)
105.	Decanatus Sancti Georgii de Vendopera	Vendœuvre-sur-Barse, Aube (decanus and 4 monks)
106.	P. Sanctae Eulaliae d'Oruille	Sainte-Eulalie-d'Orville, Bligny, Aube (prior and 1 monk)
107.	P. Sancti Ioannis Baptistae de Colombeyo	Colombey-les-deux-Églises, Haute-Marne (prior and 2 monks)
108.	Decanatus Sancti Martini de Marmessa	Marmesse, Haute-Marne (sacristan and 2 monks)
109.	[Decanatus] Sancti Petri de Mo[n]streto	Montrot, Haute-Marne (decanus and 2 monks)
110.	P. Sancti Petri de Romiliaco Comite	Rumilly-le-Comte, Pas-de-Calais (prior and 4 monks)
111.	P. Sanctorum Petri et Pauli de Burgo sanguinum	Beussent, Pas-de-Calais
112.	P. Sancti Stephani de Namescha	Namèche, Belgium (prior and 2 monks)
113.	P. Sancti Seuerini in Condrom	Saint-Séverin-en-Condroz, Belgium (prior and 3 monks)
114.	P. B. Mariae de Bertreia	Bertrée, Belgium (prior and 4 monks)

115. P. Monialium Sancti Victoris de Ceyo iuxta Huy — Huy, Belgium (2 monks and over 30 nuns)

116. Domus de Aunayo — Aulnay-lès-Bondy, Seine-et-Oise (prior and 2 monks)

117. P. B. Mariae de Grandi-Campo — Grandchamp, Seine-et-Marne (prior and 3 monks)

118. P. Sanctorum Geruasii et Prothasii de Luperciaco burgo, vulgo Leurcy-le-bourg — Lurcy-le-Bourg, Nièvre (prior and 4 monks)

119. P. Sancti Odomari, de Beurgissant (Bougesaut) in Picardia — ? Beussent, Pas-de-Calais (prior and 2 monks)

120. P. Sancti Michaëlis de Wasto — Le Wast, Pas-de-Calais (prior and 4 monks)

121. Decanatus Sancti Cosmae in monte — Saint-Côme-du-Mont, Manche (decanus and 4 monks)

122. D. Sancti Sulpitii de Gassicuria — Gassicourt, Seine-et-Oise (decanus and 8 monks)

123. P. de Donna Maria — Dammarie-sur-Saulx, Meuse (prior and 3 monks)

124. P. Sancti Christophori de Castro-canino (de Chateau-Chino[n]) — Châteauchinon, Nièvre (prior and 3 monks)

124a. P. Sancti Hieronymi de Ponte Monachorum — Pont-aux-Moines, Loiret (prior and 3 monks)

125. P. Sancti Petri de Abbatia, in suburbio de Pithiueriis — Pithiviers, Loiret (prior and 4 monks)

126. P. de Alneto — Annet-sur-Marne, Seine-et-Marne (prior and 2 monks)

127. P. Sancti Saluatoris, Niuernensis dioecesis — Saint-Sauveur, Nevers, Nièvre (prior and 4 monks)

128. P. de Tota-villa — Étouteville, Seine-Inférieure

129. P. de Mortuo-mari — Mortemer, Seine-Inférieure

130. P. Sancti Petri de Aqualia — See no. 62

131. P. de Mechi — ? See no. 112

Dependent on La Charité-sur-Loire

132. P. Sanctae Fidis de Longa-villa — Sainte-Foy-de-Longueville, Seine-Inférieure (36 monks)

133. P. B. Mariae de Bellomon[n]te Petroso — Beaumont-le-Perreux, Eure

134. P. Sanctorum Petri et Pauli de Ruello siue Rodolio, Ruel, prope la Ferté-sur-Iouarre — Reuil, Seine-et-Marne (25 monks)

135. P. Sanctorum Petri et Pauli de Bonyaco — Bonny-sur-Loire, Loiret (sacristan and 12 monks)

136. P. Sanctorum Petri et Pauli de Cortenayo — Courtenay, Loiret (8 monks)

137. P. B. Mariae de Charnerio, Senonensis dioecesis — Notre-Dame-du-Charnier, Sens, Yonne (8 monks)

138. P. Apostolorum Simonis et Judae de Sancti Rancone prope muros Eduenses — Saint-Racho, dans le faubourg Saint-André, Autun, Saône-et-Loire

139. P. Brayciaci   Brassy, Nièvre
140. P. Vallis-noxiae   Vanoise, La Roche-Millay, Nièvre
141. P. Sancti Honorati   Saint-Honoré, Nièvre
142. P. B. Mariae de Colongiis   Colonges, Nièvre (6 monks)
143. P. Sancti Sulpitii   Saint-Sulpice, Nièvre (prior and 1 monk)
144. P. de Bichiis   Biches, Nièvre
145. P. Ialliaci   Jailly, Nièvre
146. P. Sancti Aniani de Albiniaco supra   Aubigny-sur-Loire, Cher (4 monks)
     Ligerim
147. P. de Sanconio (alias Sancoin)   Sancoins, Cher (2 monks)
148. P. B. Mariae de Valligniato   Valigny, Allier (2 monks)
149. P. de Oratorio   Louroux-Hodemont, Allier
150. P. B. Mariae Berruati vulgo Berij   Berry, Cher
151. P. Sancti Celsi, vulgo Saint-Ceaulx   Saint-Céols, Cher
152. P. B. Mariae de Monesto-rastelli, vulgo de   Menetou-Ratel, Cher (3 monks)
     Montonrateau
153. P. Sancti Aniani de Conada, vulgo Cone-   Cosne, Nièvre
     sur-Loire
154. P. Sancti Petri de Monte-Hu[m]berto   Montambert, Nièvre
155. P. Sancti Nicolai de Castroregnardi   Châteaurenard, Loiret
156. P. Sancti Sebastiani de Diziaco (d'Issy)   Dicy, Charny, Yonne
     inter Castrum Regnardum et Ioignia-
     cum
157. P. Sancti Michaelis de Guerchia   Saint-Michel-de-la-Guerche, Tours, Indre-et-
                                                     Loire
158. P. Sancti Nicolai supra pontes de Charitate   La Charité-sur-Loire, Nièvre
159. P. Sancti Victoris, Niuernensis dioecesis   Saint-Victor-de-Nevers, Nièvre
160. P. Sancti Iuliani de Sezana   Sézanne, Marne (8 monks)
161. P. Sancti Martini de Patingiis (Patinges)   Patinges, Cher
162. P. Sancti Victoris   See no. 159
163. P. B. Mariae de Joigniaco supra Yonne   Joigny, Yonne (4 monks)
164. P. Sancti Sidronii   Saint-Cydroine, Yonne
165. P. Sancti Laurentii, Aurelianensis dioe-   Saint-Laurent-des-Orgerils, Orléans, Loiret (3
     cesis   monks)
166. P. B. Mariae Mo[n]tis-Mauri, vulgo   Montmort, Marne
     Mo[n]tmore
167. P. Sancti Sepulchri Tricassinensis siue   Villacerf, Aube (3 monks)
     Trecensis diœcesis
168. P. B. Mariae Magdalenes de paruo Bello   Beaulieu-le-Petit, Chartres, Eure-et-Loir
     loco
169. P. Sancti Petri de Montigny   Montigny-l'Engrain, Aisne
170. P. Sancti Petri de Veniziaco (alias de   Venizy, Yonne (prior, 1 monk and 2 novices)
     Venisi)
171. P. Sancti Yonii   Saint-Yon, Seine-et-Oise
172. P. B. Mariac de Ouana (vulgo Oueine)   Ouanne, Yonne (4 monks)
173. P. Iulliaci (alias Iully)   Jeuilly, Yonne

174. P. Sancti Remigii de Braina — Braisne-sur-Vesle, Aisne (6 monks)
175. P. Sancti Quintini de Villiers — Villiers-sur-Fère, Aisne
176. P. Sancti Christophori in Halata — Saint-Christophe-en-Halatte, Oise (prior and 7 monks)

Dependencies of La Charité in England

177. P. de Bermondeste — Bermondsey (Saint Saviour's) (prior and 24 monks)
178. P. Sancti Milburgis, de Vanneloch — Much Wenlock, Salop (over 40 monks)
179. P. Sancti Ioannis Evangelistae de Ponte-fracto — Pontefract, Yorks. (prior and 22 monks)
180. P. de Arenthona — Arthington, Yorks. (30 monks)

In Portugal

181. P. B. Mariae de Ratis — Rates (15 monks)

Dependencies of Saint-Arnoul-de-Crépy-en-Valois

182. P. Sancti Petri de Morando Monasterio — Marestmoutiers, Somme (prior and 2 monks)
183. P. Sancti Michaelis de Fronceriis — Froncières, Oise (prior and 1 monk)
184. P. B. Mariae de Vernellis — Vernelles, Seine-et-Oise (prior and 1 monk)
185. P. Sanctae Agathae, prope Crispeiam — Sainte-Agathe-de-Crépy-en-Valois, Oise (prior and 1 monk)

Dependencies of Saint-Martin-des-Champs

186. P. B. Mariae de Gornayo ad Matronam fluviu[m] — Gournay-sur-Marne, Seine-et-Oise (prior and 24 monks)
187. P. B. Mariae de Grosso-bosco — Grosbois, Claye-Souilly, Seine-et-Marne (prior only)
188. P. Sancti Nicolai de Acy — Acy-en-Multien, Oise (prior and 8 monks)
189. P. Sanctorum Geruasii et Prothasii de Encra — Albert (formerly called Encre), Somme (prior and 8 monks)
190. P. Sancti Dionysii de Carcere, Parisiensis dioecesis — Saint-Denis-de-la-Chartre, Paris (prior and 4 monks)
191. P. Sancti Petri de Cannis — Cannes, Seine-et-Marne (prior and 5 monks)
192. P. Sancti Medardi de Capiaco — Cappy, Somme (prior and 5 monks)
193. P. Sanctorum Viti et Modesti, de Ligniaco ad Canchiam fluuiolum — Ligny-sur-Canche, Pas-de-Calais (prior and 3 monks)
194. P. Sancti Martini de Passu — Pas-en-Artois, Pas-de-Calais (prior and 2 monks)
195. P. Sanctae Oportunae de Moussiaco-novo — Moussy-le-Neuf, Seine-et-Marne (prior and 5 monks)
196. P. Sancti Arnulphi de Marroliis — Marolles-en-Brie, Seine-et-Oise (prior and 4 monks)
197. P. Sancti Georgii de Roinuilla in Belsia — Roinville, Seine-et-Oise (prior and 2 monks)
198. P. Sancti Germani de Aneto — See no. 126

199. P. B. Mariae de Hyenuilla in Belsia — Hienville, Eure-et-Loir (prior and 3 monks)
200. P. Sancti Petri de Choisiaco — Choisy-en-Brie, Seine-et-Marne (prior and 3 monks)
201. P. Sancti Martini de Crecyaco in Bria — Crécy-en-Brie, Seine-et-Marne (prior and 2 monks)
202. P. Sancti Simphoriani de Bonnella in Belsia — Bonnelles, Seine-et-Oise (prior and 1 monk)
203. P. Sancti Leonorii de Bellomonte ad Ysaram fluuium — Beaumont-sur-Oise, Seine-et-Oise (prior and 6 monks)
204. P. B. Mariae de Dolomonte — Domont, Seine-et-Oise (prior and 6 monks)
205. P. B. Mariae de Pringiaco (en Gastinois) — Pringy, Seine-et-Marne (prior and 2 monks)
206. P. B. Mariae de Insula-Adae — L'Isle Adam, Seine-et-Oise (prior and 3 monks)
207. P. B. Mariae de Arenis — Airaines, Somme (prior and 4 monks)
208. P. Sancti Nicolai de Marnoa — Marnoue, Seine-et-Marne (prior and 2 monks)
209. P. Sancti Martini de Cresson-essart — Cressonsacq, Oise (prior and 2 monks)
210. P. Sancti Ioannis Baptistae de Malo-respectu — Mauregard, Seine-et-Marne (prior and 3 monks)
211. P. Sanctae Gemmae — Sainte-Gemme, Seine-et-Oise (prior and 4 monks)
212. P. B. Mariae de Baillon — Baillon, Seine-et-Oise (prior and 1 monk)

Dependencies of Saint-Martin-des-Champs in England

213. P. Sanctae Mariae Magdalenes de Barna-stapoli — Barnstaple, Devon (prior and 1 monk)
214. P. Sancti Iacobi, iuxta Oxoniam (sic: lege Exoniam) — Saint James's, Exeter, Devon (prior and 1 monk)
215. P. Sanctae Clare, in Wallia — Saint Clear's, Carmarthen (prior and 1 monk)

(Prebends, Cures and Chapelries of Saint-Martin omitted.)

Dependencies of Coincy

216. P. B. Mariae Montis-Heliae (alias Mo[n]t-hellan) — Monthellan, Marne (sacristan and 5 monks)
217. P. Sancti Fidelii (Saint Fal) — Saint-Phal, Aube (sacristan and 4 monks)
218. P. Montis-mirabilis (alias Mont-mireil) — Montmirail, Marne
219. P. Sancti Petri de Buissono (alias du Buisson) in Bria, prope Castilione[m] supra Matronam — Binson, Marne
220. P. Sancti Petri de Calce (alias de la Chaulx), Suessionens. dioecesis — Saint-Pierre-à-la-Chaux, Soissons, Aisne
221. P. Sanctae Crucis de Turpiniaco — Tupigny, Aisne
222. P. S. Germani de Roncheriis — Ronchères, Aisne
223. P. B. Mariae de Fossa, in Bria, supra Matronam — Notre-Dame-de-la-Fosse, Saint-Guiffort, Marne

Dependencies of Lihons-en-Santerre

224.	Decanatus Sancti Martini de Quirisiaco	Quierzy, Aisne (decanus and 2 monks)
225.	D. Sancti Petri de Bretigniaco	Brétigny, Oise (decanus and 4 monks)
226.	D. Sancti Taurini	Saint-Aurin, Somme (decanus and 2 monks)
227.	D. B. Mariae de Dauenescuria	Davenescourt, Somme (decanus and 4 monks)
228.	D. Sancti Osberti de Boua	Boves, Somme (decanus and 2 monks)
229.	D. B. Mariae de Merincuria	Méricourt, Somme (decanus and 1 monk)
230.	D. B. Mariae de Fayo	Fay, Pierpont-en-Laonnais, Aisne (decanus only)
231.	P. de Roquemore	Not identified

Dependencies of Saint-Pierre-d'Abbeville

232.	P. seu Hospitale Sancti Spiritus in Abbatis-villa	Abbeville, Somme (prior only)
233.	P. Sancti Praiecti de Bethune	Béthune, Pas-de-Calais
234.	P. Sancti Petri de Dourlens	Doullens, Somme

Dependencies of Gaye

235.	Decanatus Sancti Sulpitii de Regiis	Rhèges, Aube (decanus and 1 monk)
236.	D. Sancti Iacobi. . .in suburbio Trecensi	Troyes, Aube
237.	D. B. Mariae de Tullo	Le Thoult, Marne

Dependencies of Longpont

238.	P. Sancti Iuliani Pauperis	Saint-Julien-le-Pauvre, Paris
239.	P. Sancti Laurentij de Monteleherico (de Montlhery)	Montl'héry, Seine-et-Oise
240.	P. Sancti Martini de Orseyo	Orsay, Seine-et-Oise
241.	P. Sancti Arnulphi supra Touquam	Saint-Arnoult-sur-Touques, Calvados
242.	P. de Forgiis	Forges, Corbeil, Seine-et-Oise
243.	P. Sancti Laurentij, prope Milliacum	Saint-Laurent, Milly-en-Gâtinais, Seine-et-Oise

Dependencies of Nogent-le-Rotrou

244.	Decanatus Sancti Sepulchri Castriduni (de Chasteaudun)	Saint-Sépulcre-de-Châteaudun, Eure-et-Loir
245.	D. B. Mariae de Cetonio	Céton, Orne
246.	P. Sancti Ulphali (Ulphacii)	Saint-Ulphace, Sarthe
247.	D. de Chaurrond (Cha[m]prond)	Champrond-en-Gâtine, Sarthe
248.	D. de Pont-villiers	Happonvillers, Eure-et-Loir
249.	D. de Ponte novo	Pontneuf, Beaumont-le-Vicomte, Sarthe
250.	D. de Flace	Flacey, Eure-et-Loir
251.	P. Sancti Saluatoris de campo-rotundo	See no. 247

PROVINCE OF PROVENCE, TARENTAISE, DAUPHINÉ AND VIENNE

252. P. Sancti Saturnini de Portu — Saint-Sernin-du-Port (Pont-Saint-Esprit), Gard (prior, 4 officers and 24 monks)
253. P. de Tornaco — Tornac, Anduze, Gard (prior and 12 monks)
254. P. de Rampone — Rompon, Ardèche (prior and 12 monks)
255. P. Sancti Marcelli Diensis — Saint-Marcel-de-Die, Drôme (prior and 12 monks)
256. P. de Ganagobia — Ganagobie, Basses-Alpes (prior and 12 monks)
257. P. de Domena — Domène, Isère (prior and 12 monks)
258. P. de Falli-foco — Faillefeu, Bleziers, Basses-Alpes (prior and 9 monks)
259. P. Sancti Victoris, Gebennensis diœcesis — Saint-Victor-de-Genève, Switzerland (prior and 9 monks)
260. P. Sancti Marcelli de Sauzeto — Saint-Marcel-lès-Sauzet, Drôme (prior and 6 monks)
261. P. Sancti Petri de Me[n]thula — Manthes, Drôme (prior and 3 monks)
262. P. B. Mariae de Tincto — Tain-l'Hermitage, Drôme (prior and 4 monks)
263. P. de Bousal — Boze, Ardèche (united with last)
264. P. Sancti Baudili de Allesio — Allex, Drôme (prior and 3 monks)
265. P. Sancti Andreae de Rosanis — Saint-André-de-Rosans, Hautes-Alpes (prior and 6 monks)
266. P. Sancti Sebastiani in Triuiis — Saint-Sébastien-de-Cordiac, Morges, Mens, Isère (prior, 3 monks and priest)
267. P. Vallis-bonesii — Valbonnais, Isère (prior and 6 monks)
268. P. Sancti Petri de Aluardo — Saint-Pierre-d'Allevard, Isère (prior, 4 monks and priest)
269. P. Sancti Petri de Ternayo — Ternay, Isère (prior and 4 monks)
270. P. Sancti Petri de Artasio — Artas, Isère (prior and 3 monks)
271. Decanatus de Valenssoliis — Valensole, Basses-Alpes (decanus, 4 monks and priest)
272. P. Sancti Andreae, Vapincensis diœcesis — Saint-André-de-Gap, Hautes-Alpes (prior and 1 monk)
273. P. Sancti Georgii de Musaco — Saint-Georges-de-Musac, Saint-Georges-les-Bains, Ardèche (prior and 1 monk)
274. P. Sancti Petri de Fontibus, alias de Roquemoreta — Les Fonts-de-Rochemaure, Drôme (prior and 1 monk)
275. P. Sancti Amantii — Saint-Amand, Ardèche
276. P. Sancti Petri de Urro — Eurre, Drôme (prior and 1 monk)
277. P. de Beluana — Barnave, Drôme (prior and 1 monk)
278. P. de Vigilia — Vizille, Isère (prior and 2 monks)
279. P. de Claussone, alias de Chaudiaco — Chosséon, Drôme (prior, 1 monk and priest)
280. P. de Aualone — Avallon, Isère (prior and 2 monks)
281. P. de Burgeto — Le Bourget-du-Lac, Savoie (prior and 4 monks)

282.	P. de Contiaco	Conzieu, Ain (prior and 1 monk)
283.	P. de Ymmonte	Innimont, Ain (prior and 2 monks)
284.	P. de Auditu	Oyeu, Isère (prior and 1 monk)
285.	P. de Gigorcio	Gigors, Drôme (prior, 1 monk and priest)
286.	P. B. Mariae de Ulmatis	Notre-Dame-des-Aumades, Caseneuve, Vaucluse (prior and 2 monks)
287.	P. B. Mariae de Thesa	Thèze, Basses-Alpes (prior and 2 monks)
288.	P. de Pintenco, alias de Prolento	? See no. 291; dioc. Gap
289.	P. de Ripperiis	Ribiers, Hautes-Alpes (prior and 2 monks)
290.	P. Sanctae Helenae	Sainte-Hélène-du-Lac, Montmélian, Savoie (prior and 2 monks)
291.	P. Sancti Ioannis Baptistae, de Podiolano, alias Piolenc	Piolenc, Vaucluse (prior and 3 monks)
292.	P. de Alesio	See no. 264
293.	Domus de Condiaco	See no. 282
294.	D. Sancti Vincentii d'Orpierre	Orpierre, Hautes-Alpes (prior and 1 monk)
295.	P. Aregrandis	Lagrand, Hautes-Alpes (prior and 11 monks)
296.	P. Sancti Ioannis Doureau	Not identified; dioc. Valence (prior and 3 monks)

Dependencies of Pont-Saint-Esprit (Saint-Sernin-du-Port)

297.	P. Sancti Petri de Ryonis	Ruoms, Ardèche (prior and 3 monks)
298.	P. de Bello-monte	Not identified
299.	P. B. Mariae Rosariarum, alias Ioieuse	Rozières, Joyeuse, Ardèche (prior and 1 monk)
300.	P. B. Mariae de Vulgorio, alias de Volgüel	Vogüé, Ardèche (prior and 1 monk)
301.	P. de Castellione	Castillon-du-Gard, Gard (prior and 1 monk)
302.	P. de Connatio, alias Conau	Connaux, Gard (prior and 1 monk)
303.	P. B. Mariae de Ioffa	Notre-Dame-de-Jouffe, Montmirat, Gard (prior and 1 monk)
304.	P. Sancti Ioannis de Carnasio	Saint-Jean-de-Carnas, Servas, Gard (prior and 1 monk)
305.	P. Sancti Ioannis de Silua	? Selves, Gard (prior and 1 monk)
306.	P. de Pontellis	Potellières, Gard (prior and 1 monk)
307.	P. de Todonis, alias de Bolacio	Todouse or Boulas, now Saint-Jean-de-Rousigo, Gard (prior and 1 monk)
308.	P. de Meranis	Meyrannes, Gard (prior and 1 monk)
309.	P. Sancti Panthaleonis	Saint-Pantaléon, Drôme (prior and 2 monks)
310.	P. de Roseto	Rousset, Drôme (united to last)
311.	P. de Caderossa	Caderousse, Vaucluse (prior and 2 monks)
312.	P. Sancti Ioannis de Vallasolis	Saint-Jean-de-Vassols, Vaucluse (prior and 2 monks)
313.	Decanatus de Crouselles	Colonzelle, Drôme (prior and 1 monk)
314.	P. de Gardapariolis	La Garde-Paréol, Vaucluse (prior and 1 monk)
315.	P. de Ancona supra Rodanum	Ancone, Drôme (prior and 1 monk)
316.	P. Sancti Blasii de Monte-brissono	Montbrison, Drôme (prior and 1 monk)

317. P. Sancti Saluatoris de Ripa-alta   Saint-Sauveur-de-Ribaute, Anduze, Gard (prior and 1 monk)
318. P. Sancti Andreae de Plano de Monte-dracono   Saint-André-du-Plan, Mondragon, Vaucluse
319. P. Sancti Raphaelis   Saint-Raphael, Vaucluse
320. P. Interaquarum   Entraigues, Vaucluse
321. [P.] de Broscto   Brouzet-lès-Alais, Gard
322. P. Sancti Torquati   Saint-Turquoît, Suze-la-Rousse, Drôme
323. P. de Auisiano   Visan, Drôme (prior and 1 monk)
324. Domus de Sariano   Sarrians, Vaucluse (decanus, sacristan and prior of next house)
325. [P.] de Meratio   Not identified; near Sarrians
326. Domus de Tuleta   Tulette, Drôme

[Cures of Saint-Sernin-du-Port omitted.]

Dependencies of Tornac

327. P. de Andusia   Anduze, Gard
328. P. Sancti Nazarii de Gardiis   Saint-Nazaire-des-Gardies, Gard
329. P. de Colomberiis   Colombiers, Boisset, Gard
330. P. de Buxeriis   Boisset, Gard
331. P. de Soca   Not identified
332. P. de Vabres   Vabres, Gard

Dependencies of Ganagobie

333. P. B. Mariae Bellio-iacqueti   Beaujeu, Basses-Alpes
334. P. Sancti Petri de Albera   Not identified; dioc. Die
335. P. Sancti Michaelis   Saint-Michel, Basses-Alpes
336. P. Sancti Petri de Lausardo   Not identified; dioc. Gap
337. Domus Sancti Albani   Saint-Auban, Buis-les-Baronnies, Drôme
338. P. Sancti Petri de Bona-fossa   Bonnefosse, Basses-Alpes
339. P. B. Mariae de Bethleem, seu Sanctae Eusemiae de Nogeris   Sainte-Marie-de-Bethléem, Noyers-sur-Jabron, Basses-Alpes
340. P. Sancti Petri de Viseriis   Saint-Pierre-de-Viziers, Basses-Alpes
341. Domus Sancti Marcellini   Saint-Marcellin, Niozelles, Basses-Alpes

Dependencies of Saint-Victor-de-Genève

342. P. de Vallibus   Vaulx, Haute-Savoie
343. P. de Bella-gaieta   Bonneguête, Haute-Savoie
344. P. de Drulenis   Draillant, Haute-Savoie
345. P. Sanctae Helenae   See no. 290

Dependencies of Manthes

346. P. de Prolego seu Pelgio (de Peulgre)   Peaugres, Ardèche
347. P. Montis-castanei (de Mont-chataux)   Montchatain, Drôme
348. Domus de Charrere   Charrière, Châteauneuf-de-Galaure, Drôme

Dependencies of Saint-Marcel-de-Die

349.	P. de Chabolio	Chabeuil, Drôme
350.	P. de Mota	La Motte-Chalançon, Drôme
351.	P. de Petra	Notre-Dame-de-la-Pierre, Serres, Hautes-Alpes
352.	[P.] de tribus moeniis	Not identified; dioc. Die
353.	P. de Bello-monte	Beaumont, Drôme
354.	[P.] de Persico	Le Percy, Clelles, Isère
355.	P. de Beluana	? Beluy, Bouches-du-Rhône

(Cures omitted.)

Dependencies of Saint-Marcel-lès-Sauzet

356.	P. Sancti Martini de Alpibus	Aps, Ardèche
357.	P. Sancti Priuati de Roinaco	Roynac, Drôme
358.	P. de Antichant	Antichamp, Drôme
359.	P. B. Mariae de Banio in montibus	Plan-de-Baix, Drôme
360.	P. B. Mariae de Spelluchia (Espeluche)	Espeluche, Drôme
361.	P. Sancti Boniti de Podio Girono	Puygiron, Drôme

Dependencies of Saint-André-de-Gap

362.	P. de Podio Loutherii	Pelleautier, Hautes-Alpes
363.	P. de Pilloterio	See no. 362

Dependencies of Lagrand

364.	P. de Gigorciaco	See no. 285
365.	P. Sanctae Gallac	Sainte-Jalle, Drôme (prior and 1 monk)
366.	P. de Monte-fionco	Montfroc, Drôme
367.	P. de Spina	L'Épine, Hautes-Alpes
368.	P. de Calma	Lachau, Drôme
369.	P. de Serris	Serres, Hautes-Alpes
370.	Domus de Ceno	Not identified
371.	P. de Aymanis	Eyguians, Hautes-Alpes
372.	P. Sancti Mauri	Not identified

Dependencies of Sainte-Jalle

373.	Domus Sanctae Luciae	Sainte-Lucie, Bésignan, Drôme
374.	P. de Condorseyo	Condorcet, Drôme (prior and 1 monk)

Other dependent priories

375.	P. Sancti Stephani de Sors, dep. Piolenc	Saint-Étienne-des-Sorts, Gard
376.	P. de Villa-perdis, dep. Saint-Amand	Villeperdrix, Drôme
377.	P. de Treffortio, dep. Domène	? See no. 38
378.	P. de Toneto, dep. Allevard	Le Touvet, Isère
379.	Domus de Combonio, dep. Chosséon	Combovin, Drôme

380. P. de Francilione, dep. Rompon — Francillon, Drôme
381. P. Sancti Petri de Marsanis, dep. Rompon — Marsanne, Drôme
382. P. de Remello, dep. Rompon — Ravel, Drôme
383. Domus Sorgiae, dep. Saint-Martial, Avignon — Sorgues, Vaucluse

PROVINCE OF POITOU AND SAINTONGE

384. Abbatia Sanctorum Ioannis Euangelistae et Andreae Monasterii-noui — Montierneuf, Poitiers, Vienne (abbot and 40 monks)
385. P. Sancti Eutropii Santonensis diocesis — Saint-Eutrope-de-Saintes, Charente-Inférieure (prior and 12 monks)
386. Decanatus Sancti Ioannis de Roncenaco — Ronsenac, Charente (decanus and 8 monks)
387. P. de Villagarda — Villegarde, Charente
388. P. Insulae Aquensis (de l'Isle d'Aix) — Île d'Aix, Charente-Inférieure (prior and 12 monks)
389. P. Sancti Mauricii Montis Berulphi (alias de Mo[n]tbrun) — Montbron, Charente (prior and 6 monks)
390. P. Sancti Ioannis Baptistae de Mongonio — Mougon, Deux-Sèvres (prior and 6 monks)
391. P. Sancti Georgii de Dydonia — Saint-Georges-de-Didonne, Charente-Inférieure (prior and 6 monks)
392. P. B. Mariae de Barbesillo (alias Barbesieux) — Barbezieux, Charente (prior and 12 monks)
393. P. de Conciaco — Concié, Charente-Inférieure (prior and 1 monk)
394. P. de Castellario (alias de Chastellard) — Chastellard, Charente (prior and 1 monk)
395. P. de Cartalenca (Catheloges) — Cartelègue, Gironde (prior and 1 monk)
396. P. de Brulleto — Breuillet, Charente-Inférieure (prior and 1 monk)
397. P. Sancti Medardi — Saint-Médard-des-Prés, Vendée (prior and 1 monk)
398. P. Sancti Gelasii — Saint-Gelais, Deux-Sèvres (prior and 1 monk)
399. P. Sancti Pauli in Gastina — Saint-Paul-en-Gâtine, Deux-Sèvres (prior and 1 monk)
400. P. Sancti Nicolai de Grauia — Graves, Charente (prior and 1 monk)
401. P. Sancti Laurentij — Saint-Laurent, Charente (prior and 1 monk)
402. P. de Bersegolio (Bercegol) — Bersol, Gironde (prior and 1 monk)
403. P. de Brogliaco, alias Brogiaco — Breuil-la-Réorte, Charente-Inférieure
404. P. de Montonis — Mouton, Charente
405. Abbatia Sancti Ioannis Angeliacensis — Saint-Jean-d'Angely, Charente-Inférieure
406. P. de Brosiliis — Les Brousils, Saint-Fulgent, Vendée
407. P. de Aunessa — Anais, Charente-Inférieure
408. [P.] de Villa-gardelli — See no. 387
409. [P.] de Cuciaco — Cussac, Gironde
410. [P.] de Cordaus — Île de Cordouan, Gironde
411. [P.] de Manomena — Not identified

Dependencies of Montierneuf

412. P. de Faya-monachalis (alias de la Foy moneau) — La Foy-Mongault, Deux-Sèvres (prior and 1 monk)
413. P. de Marneyo (alias Marinier) — La Marinière, Vendée
414. P. de Lulayo (alias de Loulay) — Loulay, Charente-Inférieure
415. Domus Sancti Gerardi de Amberia — Saint-Genest-d'Ambière, Vienne (prior and 1 monk)
416. P. Sancti Laurentii de Breto — Saint-Laurent-de-Bret, Deux-Sèvres (prior and 1 monk)
417. P. Sancti Nicolai des Issars — Not identified; dioc. Saintes
418. P. de Bernayo (alias Benet-soubs-les-Noyers) — Bernay, Charente-Inférieure
419. P. B. Mariae de Podio — Le Puy-Notre-Dame, Maine-et-Loire
420. P. Sancti Saturnini de Bosco (alias Saint-Sourlin-des-Boys) — Saint-Sornin, Charente-Inférieure
421. P. Sanctae Mariae Magdalenae de Molieres — La Chapelle-Moulière, Poitiers, Vienne
422. P. Sancti Nicolai, Pictauiensis diocesis — Saint-Nicolas-de-Poitiers, Vienne
423. P. de Capella Monstro-Monbonis (alias la Chapelle-de-Monstreul-bouyn) — La Chapelle-Montreuil, Montreuil-Bonnin, Vienne
424. P. de Berugiis — Béruges, Vienne
425. P. de Andilliaco leuiaco (alias d'Andilliers-les-Maretz) — Andilly, Charente-Inférieure
426. P. de Sancto Sepulchro — Saint-Sépulcre, Charente-Inférieure
427. P. de Artisiis (alias l'isle de Medocq) — Île de Médoc, Gironde
428. P. de Canta-luppe — Chanteloup, Deux-Sèvres
429. P. de Laniaco-bosco (alias de Lany-les-Bois) — Leignes, Vienne
430. P. de Aubigniaco, prope Chestonne — Aubigné, Deux-Sèvres

Dependencies of Saint-Eutrope-de-Saintes

431. P. Sancti Petri de Torciaco — Torsac, Charente
432. P. de Grezaco — Grézac, Charente-Inférieure (8 monks)
433. [P. de] Sancto Simphoriano — Saint-Symphorien, Charente-Inférieure
434. P. Sancti Genesii de Geneyraco in Placiaco — Saint-Genis-d'Hiersac, Charente
435. P. Sancti Albini de Iarniaco (alias Iarnac) — Jarnac, Charente
436. P. Sancti Petri de Mediis — Médis, Charente-Inférieure
437. P. de Brolio-Monachorum — Le Breuil-aux-Moines, Charente-Inférieure
438. P. Sancti Palladij — Saint-Palais, Charente
439. P. Sancti Michaelis de Onziliaco — Ouzilly, Charroux, Vienne
440. P. de Neamia — Not identified; dioc. Saintes (prior and 1 monk)
441. [P.] de Roenne (alias du Rosne) — Roenne, Torsac, Charente (prior and 1 monk)
442. P. B. Mariae de Campiment — Campillan, Gironde
443. P. Sancti Eutropii de Allodio — Les Alleuds, Deux-Sèvres (prior and 4 monks)
444. P. Sancti Eutropii de Lande — Saint-Eutrope-de-la-Lande, Montmoreau, Charente
445. P. Sancti Martini de Molio — Meux, Charente

Dependencies of Saint-Georges-de-Didonne

446. P. de Meschio   Meschers, Charente-Inférieure
447. Domus Sancti Andreae de Olorono   Île d'Oleron, Charente-Inférieure
     (Oleron)

Dependencies of Aix

448. P. de Rez   Île de Ré, Charente-Inférieure
449. P. Sancti Viviani de Vulgorio   Saint-Vivien-du-Vergeroux, Charente-Infé-
                                                rieure (2 monks)
450. P. de Cormes   Cormes, Charente-Inférieure
451. P. de Allodio   ? See no. 443 (1 monk)
452. P. de Salles   Salles-lès-Aulnay, Charente-Inférieure

Other dependencies

453. Monachale de Vileboys, dep. Ronsenac   Villebois, Charente (nuns)
454. Domus de Anixa, dep. Ronsenac   ? See no. 407
455. Domus de Longa-sagerosa, dep. Saint-Paul- ? La Loge Fougereuse, Vendée (2 monks)
     en-Gâtine

PROVINCE OF AUVERGNE

456. Abbatia Mauziacensis   Mozac, Puy-de-Dôme (abbot and 50 monks)
457. Abbatia Thiernensis   Le Moûtier-de-Thiers, Puy-de-Dôme (abbot and
                                                14 monks)
458. P. Sancti Maioli de Sylviniaco   Souvigny, Allier (prior and 50 monks)
459. P. Celsiniarum (alias Soulcilanges)   Sauxillanges, Puy-de-Dôme (40 monks)
460. P. Sanctae Crucis de Volta   La Voulte-Chilhac, Haute-Loire (25 monks)
461. P. de Riuis   Ris, Puy-de-Dôme (20 monks)
462. P. de Gumeriis   Gumières, Loire
463. P. de Bacheleto   Bachelet, Puy-de-Dôme
464. P. de Venna (alias Auennes)   Laveine, Puy-de-Dôme (80 nuns, 20 domicellae
                                                and 4 monks)
465. P. de Borlo   Bort, Corrèze (prior and 1 monk)
466. P. de Gresiaco   Grazac, Haute-Loire (prior, 2 monks and priest)

Dependencies of Souvigny

467. P. de Firmitate (alias de la Ferté)   La Ferté-sur-Allier, Allier (2 monks)
468. P. de Champtenay   Chantenay, Nièvre (prior and 1 monk)
469. P. de Vuldres   Vaudres, Cher (prior and 3 monks)
470. P. de Campouoto   Champvoux, Nièvre (prior and 3 monks)
471. P. de Capis   Chappes, Allier (prior and 3 monks)
472. P. de Columbano   Colombier, Commentry, Allier (prior and 3
                                                monks)
473. P. de Gensiaco   Jenzat, Allier (prior and 3 monks)
474. P. de Brocco   Brout-Vernet, Allier (4 monks)

475.	Domus de Flabines	Not identified (prior and 2 monks)
476.	Domus de Chirac	Chirat-l'Église, Allier (prior and 1 monk)
477.	Domus de Bernoelleto	Vernouillet, Allier (prior and 1 monk)
478.	Domus de Sintriaco	Not identified (prior and 1 monk)
479.	Domus Sancti Fiacrii	Not identified
480.	P. de Martio (alias de Mars)	Mars, Nièvre (prior and 1 monk)
481.	P. de Mainsono	Mainsat, Creuse (prior and 1 monk)
482.	P. de Monte-podio (alias de Montepuy)	Montempuis, Dornes, Nièvre (prior and 2 monks)

Dependencies of Mozac

483.	P. Sancti Germani de Fossatis	Saint-Germain-des-Fossés, Allier (prior and 3 monks)
484.	P. Sancti Boniti de Monte-penserio	Montpensier, Puy-de-Dôme (prior and 2 monks)
485.	P. Marziaci	Marsat, Puy-de-Dôme (50 nuns)
486.	P. de Brentauuers	Not identified (prior and 2 monks)
487.	P. de Bredonio	Bredons, Cantal (prior and 2 monks)
488.	P. Sanae-culturae, prope villam Rionii	Not identified
489.	P. Sancti Martini de Allochiis	Saint-Martin-d'Alloches, Pont-du-Château, Puy-de-Dôme
490.	P. Sancti Hilarii	Saint-Hilaire-Château, Pontarion, Creuse
491.	P. Capellac de Rupcforte, in montibus	Rochefort-Montagne, Puy-de-Dôme
492.	P. Sancti Georgii in montibus	Saint-Georges-de-Mons, Puy-de-Dôme
493.	P. Sancti Boniti	Saint-Bonnet-de-Clermont, Puy-de-Dôme
494.	P. Sancti Ambrosii	Not identified
495.	P. de Graco	Graix, Loire
496.	P. Sancti Petri de Castro	Saint-Pierre-le-Châtel, Puy-de-Dôme
497.	P. Sancti Viti	Not identified

Dependencies of Sauxillanges

498.	P. de Choriaco	Chauriat, Puy-de-Dôme (4 monks)
499.	P. de Bonnaco	Bonnac, Cantal (prior and 2 monks)
500.	P. de Monte-acuto	Montaigut, Puy-de-Dôme (prior and 4 monks)
501.	P. de Caluo-monte	Chaumont, Puy-de-Dôme (prior and 4 monks)
502.	P. de Boisson	Boisson, Aurillac, Cantal *or* Saint-Cernin-du-Cantal (prior and 1 monk)
503.	P. de Bermoncle	Bournoncles, Cantal (prior and 1 monk)
504.	P. de Brennac	Brenat, Issoire, Puy-de-Dôme (prior and 1 monk)
505.	P. de Charnac	Charnat, Lezoux, Puy-de-Dôme (prior and 1 monk)
506.	P. de Londa	Lempdes, Haute-Loire (prior and 1 monk)
507.	P. de Chatal	Châtel, Cleppé, Loire (prior and 1 monk)
508.	P. Sancti Gervasii	Saint-Gervais, Gannat, Puy-de-Dôme (prior and 1 monk)

509. P. de Taluis — Tauves, Puy-de-Dôme (prior and 3 monks)
510. P. Sancti Hilarii — Saint-Alyre, Puy-de-Dôme (prior and 2 monks)
511. P. de Guignac — Not identified (prior and 1 monk)
512. P. de Vinarolis — Viverols, Puy-de-Dôme (prior and 2 monks)
513. P. Sancti Marcelli — Not identified (prior and 1 monk)
514. P. Sancti Perdulphi — Saint-Pardoux, Puy-de-Dôme

Dependencies of Thiers

515. P. de Culta-petra — Courpière, Puy-de-Dôme (20 nuns)
516. P. de Ioux — ? Joux, Rhône
517. P. de Landoso — Landos, Haute-Loire

Dependencies of Cluny

518. P. Sancti Petri de Moustier, de Ve[n]ta-doro — Moustier-Ventadour, Corrèze (6 monks)
519. P. de Castro in montanis — Châtelmontagne, Allier (prior and 4 monks)
520. P. de Nigro-stabulo — Noirétable, Loire (prior and 3 monks)
521. P. de Ageroliis — Augerolles, Puy-de-Dôme (4 monks)
522. P. de Saltu de Cosano — See no. 13
523. P. Sancti Blasii de Roseriis — Rosiers-Côtes-d'Aurec, Haute-Loire (prior and 2 monks)

Dependencies of La Voulte

524. P. de Rupe-forti — Rochefort, Saint-Poncy, Cantal (prior and 4 monks)
525. P. de Salgues — Sauges, Le Puy, Haute-Loire (prior and 2 monks)
526. P. de Alairac — Alleyras, Haute-Loire (prior and 1 monk)
527. P. de Calmo — Saint-Jean-Lachalm, Haute-Loire (prior and 1 monk)
528. P. Sancti Pauli frigidi — Saint-Paul-le-froid, Lozère

PROVINCE OF GASCONY

529. Abbatia Moysiace[n]sis — Moissac, Tarn-et-Garonne (80 monks)
530. Abbatia Sancti Petri Lezatensis, alias de Pede-laxato — Lézat, Ariège (25 monks)
531. P. Sancti Licerii — Saint-Lézer-sur-l'Adour, Hautes-Pyrénées (prior and 8 monks)
532. Abbatia Sancti Petri de Campo-Rotundo in Cathalonia — Camprodon, Catalonia (abbot and 12 monks)
533. Abbatia Sanctae Mariae Arullarum in Cathalonia — Arles-sur-Tech, Pyrénées-Orientales (20 monks)
534. Abbatia Sancti Geruasii et Prothasii Exiensis — Eysses, Lot-et-Garonne (22 monks)

535. P. de Emal   Eymet, Dordogne
536. Abbatia Figiacensis   Figeac, Lot (40 monks)
537. P. Sancti Orientij Auscensis   Saint-Orens-d'Auch, Gers (25 monks)
538. P. Sancti Martini de Aleyraco   Layrac, Lot-et-Garonne (prior and 16 monks)
539. P. de Pluuia   Laplume, Lot-et-Garonne
540. P. Sancti Luperci de Elizona   Éauze, Gers (8 monks)
541. P. Sanctae Fidis de Morlanis   Morlaas, Basses-Pyrénées (3 monks)
542. P. Sancti Ioannis de Mezin   Mezin, Lot-et-Garonne (9 monks)
543. P. Sancti Ioannis de Sancto-Monte   Saint-Mont, Gers (7 monks)
544. P. Sanctae Catherinae de Rombien   Rombœuf, Fourcès, Gers
545. Decanatus Sancti Petri de Carennaco   Carennac, Lot (12 monks)
546. P. Sancti Liseri   See no. 531
547. P. Sancti Leuberthi d'Heouse seu Ge[n]se See no. 540
548. Domus B. Mariae de Moyracho   Moirax, Lot-et-Garonne (4 monks)

Dependencies of Moissac

549. P. de sede Leyaco   Not identified (prior and 1 monk)
550. P. B. Mariae de Aurense   La Daurade, Toulouse, Haute-Garonne (25
                                               monks)
551. P. de Castro-sarraceno   Castelsarrasin, Tarn-et-Garonne (prior and 1
                                               monk)
552. P. de Similiaco   Sedilhac, Dordogne (prior and 4 monks)
553. P. de Rabasteins   Rabastens, Tarn
554. P. de Mirello   Not identified (prior and 4 monks)

Dependencies of Saint-Orens-d'Auch

555. P. Sancti Martini de Togeto   Touget, Gers (prior and 4 monks)
556. P. Sancti Orientij de Lauedano   Saint-Orens-de-Lavédan, Villelongue, Hautes-
                                               Pyrénées (6 monks)
557. P. Sancti Mamerti de Petrusia magna   Peyrusse-Grande, Gers (prior and 1 monk)
558. P. de Monte-Alto   Montaut, Gers (prior and 4 monks)

Dependencies of Carennac

559. P. de Monte-caluo   Not identified (nuns)
560. Domus Sancti Ioannis   Mont-Saint-Jean, Gourdon, Lot

PROVINCE OF GERMANY, LORRAINE
AND THE COUNTY OF BURGUNDY

561. Abbatia Balmensis (Baulme)   Baume-les-Messieurs, Jura (40 monks)
562. P. Paterniaci   Payerne, Vaud, Switzerland (30 monks)
563. P. Romani-Monasterij (Romanmonstier)   Romainmôtier, Switzerland (prior and 21
                                               monks)
564. P. de Vallibus (de Vaulx) supra Pollinia- Vaux-sur-Poligny, Jura (prior and 15 monks)
       cum

565. P. Sancti Albani Basiliensis diocesis — Saint-Alban-de-Bâle, Switzerland (prior and 11 monks)
566. P. de Verpaco — Feldbach, Haut-Rhin (prior and 3 monks)
567. P. de Sardone — Sölden, Baden (prior, 1 monk and 15 nuns)
568. P. de Mortua-aqua (Mortault) — Morteau, Doubs (prior and 3 monks)
569. P. Insulae-medij-lacus — Île Saint-Pierre, Lac de Bienne, cn. Berne, Switzerland (prior and 5 monks)
570. P. de Sella, alias Sancti Ulrici in nigra silua — Sankt Ulrich, Zell, Baden (prior and 6 monks)
571. P. de Frigido-fonte (Froide-fontaine) — Froidefontaine, terr. de Belfort (prior and 2 monks)
572. P. de Loco-Dei — Lieudieu, Doubs (prior and 1 monk)
573. P. de monte-Richerio — Rueggisberg, cn. Berne, Switzerland (prior and 4 monks)
574. P. de Villario-Monachorum — Münchenwiler (Villars-les-moines), cn. Berne, Switzerland (prior and 3 monks)
575. P. Sancti Nicolai de Salinis (Saint-Nicolas de Salins) — Salins, Jura (prior and 1 monk)
576. P. de Calce (de la Chaux) — Chaux-lès-Clerval, Doubs (prior and 2 monks)
577. P. de Alta-petra (de Haulte-pierre) — Mouthier-Hautepierre, Doubs (prior and 6 monks)
578. P. de Megiis — Mièges, Jura (prior and 2 monks)
579. P. de Fontenayo — Frontenay, Jura (prior and 1 monk)
580. P. de Tyrambech — Thierenbach, Haut-Rhin (prior and 1 monk)
581. P. de Relangiis — Relanges, Vosges (prior and 6 monks)
582. P. de Vendopera (Vendoeuure) propè Nancy — Vendœuvre, Meurthe-et-Moselle (prior and 2 monks)
583. P. de Frovilla — Froville, Meurthe-et-Moselle (prior and 4 monks)
584. P. B. Mariae de Bosco — Sainte-Marie-aux-Bois, Meurthe-et-Moselle (prior and 2 monks)
585. P. de Porta supra Sagonam — Port-sur-Saône, Haute-Saône
586. P. de Thiescourt — Thicourt, Moselle (prior and 2 monks)
587. P. de Beynes — Bevais, Neufchâtel, Switzerland
588. P. Sancti Morandi de Alta-cliqua — Altkirch, Haut-Rhin (prior and 5 monks)
589. P. de Ysteim — Isthein, Baden (prior, 1 monk and 7 nuns)
590. P. de Valle-clusa (Vaucluse) — Vaucluse, Doubs (prior and 5 monks)
591. P. de Ortho-villarij — Hettiswyl, cn. Berne, Switzerland (prior and 1 monk)

Dependencies of Baume

592. P. de Landi-sanerio, Sancti Desiderati (de Lyon-Saulnier) Saint-Desiré — Lons-le-Saunier, Jura
593. P. de Ioya (Ioue) — Jouhe, Jura
594. P. de Dolla — Dôle, Jura
595. P. Sancti Lauteni (Saint-Louthein) — Saint-Lothain, Jura

596.	P. de Poligniaco	Poligny, Jura
597.	P. de Insano Monte	Jussanmouthier, Besançon, Doubs
598.	P. de Monasterio in Bressia	Mouthiers-en-Bresse, Saône-et-Loire
599.	P. de Mostereto	Moutherot, Doubs
600.	P. de Bonneuent	Bonnevent, Gy, Haute-Saône
601.	P. de Capella	Not identified
602.	P. de Coye	Not identified
603.	P. de Sancto Ramberto	Saint-Rambert-en-Bugey, Ain
604.	P. de Listance	Lantenot, Haute-Saône
605.	P. de Salmasia	Salmaise, Côte-d'Or

Other dependencies

606.	P. de Colomberiis, dep. Payerne	Colmar, Haut-Rhin
607.	P. de Balmis, dep. Payerne	Baulmes, Switzerland
608.	P. de Baya, dep. Payerne	Léaz, Ain
609.	P. de Rubeo-monte, dep. Romainmôtier	Rougemont, Switzerland
610.	P. de Luzinges, dep. Hettiswyl	Luizigen, cn. Berne, Switzerland
611.	P. de Frouilla-bosco, dep. Froville	Not identified; near Froville
612.	P. Lacus Domini Walterii, dep. Romain-môtier	Lay-Damp-Waultier, lac de Saint-Point, Doubs
613.	P. Vallorbis, dep. Romainmôtier	Vallorbe, Switzerland
614.	P. de Monte-rotundo, dep. Vaux-sous-Poligny	Montrond, Jura
615.	Domus de Scambech, dep. Altkirch	Steinach, Haut-Rhin

PROVINCE OF LOMBARDY

616.	Abbatia Sancti Benedicti super Padum	Padilorone, nr. Mantua (abbot and 12 monks)
617.	Abbatia Monialium de Canturio	Cantù, prov. Como (80 nuns and 1 monk)
618.	P. Sancti Jacobi de Pontida	Pontida, Bergamo (30 monks)
619.	P. Sancti Maioli, Papiensis diocesis	Pavia (12 monks and prior)
620.	P. Sancti Nicolai de Payona	Not identified; dioc. Como (8 monks and prior)
621.	P. Sancti Pauli de Argono	Argano (6 monks and prior)
622.	P. B. Mariae de Cernobio	Cernobbio, prov. Como (prior, 2 monks, 10 nuns and priest)
623.	P. Sancti Marci de Laude	Lodi (prior and 4 monks)
624.	P. Sancti Nicolai de Signia	Signa (prior and 2 monks)
625.	P. B. Mariae de Caluenzano	Calvenzano; dioc. Milan (prior and 2 monks)
626.	P. Sancti Petri de Magdaniano	Not identified; dioc. Crema (prior and 1 monk)
627.	P. Sancti Nicolai de Verziano	Not identified; dioc. Brescia (prior and 2 monks)
628.	P. Sancti Nicolai de Rodingio	Rodigo (prior and 3 monks)
629.	P. Sancti Egidii de Fontanella	Fontanella (prior and 5 monks)
630.	P. Sancti Valeriani de Rondolio	Rodobbio, nr. Vercelli (prior and 2 monks)
631.	P. Sancti Vitalis de Vrsiniaco (alias de Arciniaco)	Not identified (prior and 1 monk)

632.	P. Sancti Gabrielis de Cremona	Cremona (prior and 3 monks)
633.	P. de Proualio	Provaglio d' Iseo, dioc. Brescia (prior, priest and 2 monks)
634.	P. Sancti Petri de Castelleto	Castelletto del Cerro, dioc. Vercelli (prior and 6 monks)
635.	P. Sancti Ioannis de Bayna	? Bagnaia; dioc. Vercelli (prior and 2 monks)
636.	P. de Burgo de Ultimano	Not identified; dioc. Vercelli (prior and 1 monk)
637.	P. Sancti Saluatoris de Thigiis	Not identified; dioc. Brescia (prior and 1 monk)
638.	P. Sancti Benedicti de Portesano	San Benedetto de Portesana (prior and 1 monk)
639.	P. de Vlzato	Not identified
640.	P. Sanctorum Nazarii et Celsi de Gercola	Not identified
641.	P. de Othigniaco	Not identified
642.	P. Sanctae Iuliae de Cazago	Not identified

Dependencies in Lombardy

643.	Abbatia Monialium Sancti Columbani, dep. Pontida	San Colombano, Vaprio d' Adda
644.	P. de Gerula, dep. Puntido	Not identified
645.	P. Sancti Gregorij de Placentia, dep. Saint Nicholas of Pavia	Piacenza
646.	P. Sancti Ypoliti de Cremona, dep. Saint Gabriel of Cremona	Cremona
647.	P. Sancti Pauli de Lacu, dep. Argano	Not identified
648.	P. de Quinsano, dep. Versano	Not identified; dioc. Brescia (prior and 1 monk)
649.	P. de Cluzanis, dep. Provaglio d' Iseo	Not identified; dioc. Brescia (prior and 1 monk)
650.	P. Sancti Benedicti de Cousano, dep. "P. de Vismano alias Arciniaco"	Not identified (prior and 1 monk)
651.	P. Sancti Ioannis de Vercemate, dep. Cernobbio	Badia di Vertemate (prior and 5 monks)

PROVINCE OF SPAIN

652.	P. B. Mariae de Nagera	Najera (30 monks)
653.	P. Sancti Pili de Carrione	San Zoil de Carrión, Carrión de los Condes (prior and 24 monks)
654.	P. Sancti Ysidori	San Isidro de Dueñas, Pisuerga (prior and 12 monks)
655.	P. Sancti Banduli de Pinal	Not identified; dioc. Segovia (prior and 2 monks)
656.	P. Sancti Vincentij de Salamantica	Salamanca (prior and 4 monks)
657.	P. Sanctae Agathae, civitatis Roderici	Ciudad Rodrigo (prior and 1 monk)
658.	P. Sancti Romani des Paignez	Entrapeñas (prior and 2 monks)
659.	P. Sancti Saluatoris de Villa-viridi	Villaverde (prior and 2 monks)
660.	P. Sanctae Columbae de Burgis	Burgos (prior only)
661.	P. B. Mariae de Cluniaco, de Villa-francha, alias de Valla-carceris	Villafranca de Valcárcel (8 monks and 3 chaplains)
662.	P. de Valle-viridi	See no. 659 (prior, 1 monk and 2 chaplains)

663. P. Sancti Vincentij de Palumberiis in Galicia — San Vicente de Pombeiro, ayuntamiento de Pantón, prov. Lugo (12 monks)
664. P. Sancti Saluatoris de Bondino in Gallicia — San Salvador de Budiño, ayunt. de Porriño (prior, 8 monks and chaplain)
665. P. Sancti Martini de Iuina in Gallicia — San Martín de Jubia, ayunt. de Naron (prior, 6 monks and chaplain)
666. P. de Vmbreriis in Portugalia — Ombres, Portugal (prior and 1 monk)
667. P. B. Mariae de Ratis — See no. 181 (15 monks)
668. P. Sancti Michaelis de Zemora, dep. Marcigny — See no. 60 (prior and 2 monks)
669. Abbatia quae vocatur Corneliana, in Asturia — Not identified; dioc. Oviedo
670. Decanatus Sancti Adriani de Sarragosse — Saragossa (6 monks)
671. P. Sancti Christophori de Layre in Nauarra prope Sarragosse — Not identified (abbess and 16 nuns)
672. P. Sancti Petri de Casseris — Sant Pere de Casseres (10 monks)
673. P. Sancti Petri de Clarano, dep. Sant Pere de Casseres — Not identified; dioc. Barcelona
674. P. Sancti Pontij de Corbaria, dep. Sant Pere de Casseres — Not identified; dioc. Barcelona
675. P. Sancti Petri de Campo rotundo — See no. 532 (abbot and 14 monks)
676. Abbatia Sanctae Mariae Arularum — See no. 533 (20 monks)
677. Domus de Tauro — Not identified
678. P. Sancti Martini dc Formeston, dep. San Zoil de Carrión — San Martín de Fromista

PROVINCE OF ENGLAND AND SCOTLAND

679. Abbatia de Passeleto — Paisley, Renfrewshire (25 monks)
680. Abbatia de Crossagnier, dep. Paisley — Crossraguel, Ayrshire (10 monks). (1405)
681. P. Sancti Pancratii Leluensis (Leuuensis) — Lewes, Sussex (40–50 monks)
682. P. Montis acuti — Montacute, Somerset (24 monks)
683. P. de Lenthona, in honorem Sancti Trinitatis — Lenton, Notts. (22 monks)
684. P. de Bermondeste — See no. 177 (24 monks)
685. P. Sancti Milburgis de Vanneloch, dep. La Charité — See no. 178 (40 monks)
686. P. Sancti Ioannis Evangelistae de Ponte-fracto, dep. La Charité — See no. 179 (22 monks)
687. P. de Cathelacra, dep. Lewes — Castleacre, Norfolk (26 monks)
688. P. de Pitorella, dep. Lewes — Prittlewell, Essex (14 monks)
689. P. B. Mariae Magdalenae de Farleya, dep. Lewes — Farleigh, Wilts. (20 monks)
690. P. B. Mariae de Cliffort, dep. Lewes — Clifford, Herefordshire (11 monks)
691. P. de Mendhray, dep. Castleacre — Mendham, Suffolk (9 monks)

692. P. Sancti Iacobi, iuxta Oxoniam (*sic*), dep. Saint-Martin-des-Champs — See no. 214 (prior and 1 monk)

693. P. B. Mariae Magdalenes, alias Sanctae Clari in Wallis, dep. Saint-Martin-des-Champs — See no. 215 (prior and 1 monk)

694. P. de Hortanna, dep. Lewes — Monk's Horton, Kent (8–13 monks)

695. P. de Vangeforti, dep. Thetford — Wangford, Suffolk (4–5 monks)

696. P. de Brumoulh, dep. Castleacre — Bromholm, Norfolk (prior and 15 monks)

697. P. de Arenthona, dep. La Charité — See no. 180 (25 monks)

698. P. Herkele siue Horkeselle, dep. Thetford — Little Horkesley, Essex (2–4 monks)

699. P. de Stangathe, dep. Lewes — Stanesgate, Essex (2–3 monks)

700. P. Sanctae Mariae de Tetford — Thetford, Suffolk (22 monks)

701. P. de Broholme, alias de Bremel — See no. 694 (16 monks)

702. P. de Malopassu, dep. Montacute — Malpas, Cheshire

703. P. de Allodio, subditus P. Sancti Eutropii — (? Not in England: see no. 443)

704. P. de Memurchin — Witchingham, Norfolk

705. P. de Oncholme — East Holme, Dorset

706. P. de Diomholim — ? See no. 694

707. P. Sancti Woldi, Nonhimpten, dep. La Charité — ? Saint Andrew, Northampton (18 monks)

708. P. de Regnam, alias de Reychin, dep. Castleacre — Not identified (prior and 2 monks)

709. P. de Slenchin — Slevesholm, Methwold, Norfolk (prior and 1 monk)

710. P. de Rupe, dep. Lenton — Not identified (2 monks)

711. P. de Cerbeye — Kirkby, Yorks. (prior and 1 monk)

712. P. de Dudeleye — Dudley, Worcs. (4 monks)

713. P. de Carsnelle, dep. Montacute — Kerswell, Devon (prior and 3–6 monks)

714. P. Sanctae Mariae de Alna, dep. Montacute — ? East Holme, otherwise Holne, Dorset: see no. 703 (prior and 2 monks)

715. P. Sancti Iacobi de Derbi, dep. Bermondsey — Derby (prior and 2 monks)

716. P. de Treffort, dep. Lewes — Trafford (22 monks)

APPENDIX B

PARISH CHURCHES OF THE ORDER OF CLUNY

Marrier's *Catalogus* includes (col. 1721) lists of the "Praebendae, Curae et Capellaniae" dependent on Saint-Martin-des-Champs, Saint-Nicolas-d'Acy, Saints-Gervais-et-Protais-d'Encre (Albert), Ligny, Cappy and Saint-Sernin-du-Port (col. 1731) and (col. 1753) on those near Cluny or its granges dependent on the abbey itself. I have omitted the prebends and the "capellae" (usually Chantries) in larger churches, but give the remainder. The sources for other dependencies will be found in the footnotes. I have omitted fractional possession (unless nearly total). The churches of the Romanesque period known to me as surviving are in italics.

Dependent on Cluny

Ecclesia parrochialis B. Mariae Cluniacensis	Cluny, Saône-et-Loire[1]
Capella Sancti Odilonis	Cluny, Saône-et-Loire
Ecclesia parrochialis Sancti Mayoli Clun.	Cluny, Saône-et-Loire[1]
Ecclesia parrochialis Sancti Marcelli Clun.	*Cluny, Saône-et-Loire*[1]
Capella sanctae Radegundis Montismedii	(Is this a separate church?) ? *Sainte-Radegonde, Saône-et-Loire*
Capella Sancti Saluatoris prope Sanuigne	Sanvignes, Saône-et-Loire
Capella Sancti Ioannis fundata in fortalitio de Saluamento	Le Sauvement, Saône-et-Loire
Ecclesia parrochialis de Campoloco, Cabilonensis dioecesis	*Champlieu, Saône-et-Loire*[2]
Ecclesia Sancti Ioannis Estrigniaci, Cabilonensis dioecesis	Étrigny[3], Saône-et-Loire

Through Paray-le-Monial (and see later under *Paray-le-Monial*)

Ecclesia beatae Mariae de Paredo	*Paray-le-Monial, Saône-et-Loire*
Ecclesia Sancti Benigni subtus Sanuigne	Saint-Bérain-sous-Sanvignes, Saône-et-Loire
Ecclesia de Tholono	*Toulon-sur-Arroux, Saône-et-Loire*
Ecclesia de Melli	*Millay, Saône-et-Loire*
Ecclesia Sancti Leodegarij	Saint-Léger-sous-Beuvray, Saône-et-Loire
Ecclesia Vallis de Bere	Vaudebarrier, Saône-et-Loire
Ecclesia de Barono	Baron, Saône-et-Loire
Ecclesia de Bosco	Not identified
Ecclesia de Mediolatio (corr. Medrolatio)	Meulin, Saône-et-Loire
Ecclesia de Columberiis	*Colombier-en-Brionnais, Saône-et-Loire*[4]
Ecclesia Sancti Symphoriani	Saint-Symphorien-des-Bois, Saône-et-Loire

[1] Given to Cluny in 972. Charmasse, p. 84.
[2] Given to Cluny in 983–4. See Dickson, p. 120.
[3] Given to Cluny by Bernard de Glane. Pignot, I, 207.
[4] Given to Cluny in 955. See Dickson, p. 137.

Ecclesia de Curbiniaco	*Corbigny, Nièvre*
Ecclesia de Oratorio	*Ouroux-sous-le-Bois-Sainte-Marie, Saône-et-Loire*
Ecclesia de Digonio	Digoin, Saône-et-Loire[1]
Ecclesia de Rigniaco	Rigny-sur-Arroux, Saône-et-Loire
Ecclesia de Vitriaco	Vitry-en-Charollais, Saône-et-Loire
Ecclesia de Poissons	Poisson, Saône-et-Loire
Ecclesia de Nochisis (corr. Nochesiis)	Nochize, Saône-et-Loire
Ecclesia de Prisiaco	Prizy, Saône-et-Loire
Ecclesia de Lurciaco (corr. Larciaco)	? Lurcy, Ain (see under *Limans*)
Ecclesia Sancti Ioannis de veteri Macello Cabilonens.	Chalon-sur-Saône, Saône-et-Loire
Domus Dei de Tholono	*Toulon-sur-Arroux, Saône-et-Loire*
Capella Sancti Nicolai, quae est infra villam Paredi	Saint-Nicolas, Paray-le-Monial, Saône-et-Loire

Through Montberthoud

Ecclesia Montis-Berthodi et Sauigniaci	Montberthoud, Ain, and Savigneux, Ain
Ecclesia de Villa-nova	Villeneuve, Saint-Trivier-sur-Moignans, Ain
Ecclesia de Aiguegnens	Aignoz, Ain
Ecclesia de Amberiaco	Ambérieux-en-Dombes[2], Ain
Ecclesia de Montigniaco et Cha[n]tanis simul unita	? Montigny-sur-l'Ain, Jura, and Chanteins, Ain
Ecclesia Sancti Desiderij de Rugnone (corr. Rognone) (alias de Plantain)	Renon-en-Lyonnais, Loire
Ecclesia Sancti Germani de Rignone (corr. Rognone)	Renon-en-Lyonnais, Loire
Ecclesia de Moncellis	Montceaux (Saint-Andoche)[3], Ain
Ecclesia Sancti Nicolai de Monte-Merulo (corr. Meulo)	*Montmerle, Ain*
Ecclesia Sanctae Mariae de Faranis (corr. Saranis)	Fareins, Ain
Ecclesia de Rioterio	Riotier, Ain
Ecclesia Sancti Desiderii de Fermans	Saint-Didier-de-Formans, Ain
Ecclesia Polliaci in Dombis	Polliat, Ain

Through Limans

Ecclesia de Lurceaco extra Sagonam	Lurcy, Ain
Ecclesia de Vallibus	*Vaux[4], Saône-et-Loire*
Ecclesia de Limano (corr. Timano)	Limans, Limas, Rhône
Ecclesia de Polliaco castri	? Pollieu, Ain
Ecclesia Sancti Juliani subtus Mommelard	Montmélard, Saône-et-Loire[5]
Ecclesia Sancti Andreae Namorosi (corr. Memorosi)	? Saint-André-le-Bouchoux, Ain

[1] Given to Paray by the Bishop of Auxerre. Pignot, I, 419.
[2] Given to Cluny in 931. Pignot, I, 214.
[3] Given to Cluny by Letald II, Comte de Mâcon. Pignot, I, 218.
[4] Given to Cluny in 938. Pignot, I, 209.   [5] Given to Cluny in 1037. Pignot, I, 210.

Through Frontenay

Ecclesia de Fontenayo	*Frontenay, Jura*
Ecclesia Sancti Eligij de Liargue	? Saint-Ferréol-de-Liergues[1], Rhône

Through Lourdon

Ecclesia de Cota	Not identified
Ecclesia de Massiaco	*Massy, Saône-et-Loire*
Ecclesia de Taysiaco	*Taizé (Saint-Martin), Saône-et-Loire*[2]
Ecclesia de Prayes	*Prayes, Saône-et-Loire*[3]
Ecclesia de Blanosto (corr. Blanosco)	*Blanot (Saint-Martin), Saône-et-Loire*[4]

Through Saint-Gengoux and Maizeray

Ecclesia sancti Gengulphi	*Saint-Gengoux-le-National, Saône-et-Loire*[5]
Ecclesia Capellae de Bragny	*Bragny-en-Charollais, Saône-et-Loire*[6]
Ecclesia de Serciaco	Sercy, Saône-et-Loire
Ecclesia Belli-montis Cabilon. diœces.	*Beaumont-sur-Grosne, Saône-et-Loire*[7]

Through Jully-lès-Buxy

Ecclesia de Iulleyo	Jully-lès-Buxy, Saône-et-Loire[8]
Ecclesia de Siennes et de Charmeia sibi unita	Sienne, Saône-et-Loire, and Charmoy, Saône-et-Loire

Through Saint-Cosme, nr. Chalon

Ecclesia Sancti Cosmae prope Cabilonem	Saint-Cosme, Chalon-sur-Saône, Saône-et-Loire

Through Mazilles

Ecclesia de Masiliis	*Mazilles, Saône-et-Loire*
Ecclesia de Claromana	*Clermain, Saône-et-Loire*
Ecclesia de Bergascrena (corr. Bergaserena)	*Bergesserin, Saône-et-Loire*
Ecclesia de Tomy	Not identified
Ecclesia de Trambly	*Trambly, Saône-et-Loire*
Ecclesia de Miolano	Mioland, Rhône
Ecclesia de Dampierre	Dampierre-en-Bresse, Saône-et-Loire
Ecclesia de Varoura (corr. Veroura)	Verosvres, Saône-et-Loire
Capella de Buxeria	Bussières, Saône-et-Loire

[1] Bénet and Bazin give this as Cluniac.
[2] Given to Cluny in 916. Pignot, I, 206. The church is of the end of the tenth century.
[3] Belonged to Cluny by 940.
[4] Given to Cluny by Letbald de Brancion in 925. Pignot, I, 205.
[5] The church is first mentioned in 950 and became definitely Cluniac in 1020. *Millénaire*, II, 80.
[6] Given to Cluny in 942. Charmasse, p. 84.   [7] Given to Cluny in 980. Charmasse, p. 84.
[8] Given to Cluny by Manasses, Archbishop of Arles. Pignot, I, 220.

Through Chevignes

Ecclesia de Dauayaco	Davayé, Saône-et-Loire
Ecclesia Sancti Saturnini	Saint-Sorlin, Ain [1]
Ecclesia Secutriaci (corr. Solutriaci)	*Solutré, Saône-et-Loire* [2]

Through Laizé

Ecclesia de Laysiaco	*Laizé, Saône-et-Loire*
Ecclesia de Aula	Not identified
Ecclesia de Seneciaco (corr. Seueriaco)	*Sennecey-le-Grand (Saint-Cyr), Saône-et-Loire*
Ecclesia de Loysiaco ultra Sagonam prope Cuseriacum	Loisy (Saint-Martin), Saône-et-Loire, nr. Cuisery, Saône-et-Loire [3]

Through Péronne

Ecclesia de Perona et Sancti Petri de Lanques sibi unita	*Péronne* and Saint-Pierre-de-Lanques, Saône-et-Loire [4]
Ecclesia de Igiaco	*Igé, Saône-et-Loire*
Ecclesia Loysiaci Cabilon. diœces.	Loisy, Varennes-le-Grand, Saône-et-Loire

Through Saint-Martin-des-Vignes, nr. Mâcon

Ecclesia de Conciliis prope Pontem Belle	? Concize, Loire
Ecclesia de Nancellis	Nancelles, Saône-et-Loire [5]
Ecclesia de Boisseyo (corr. Boseya)	Boissey, Ain
Capella beatae Mariae de Vineis prope et extra muros Matiscon.	Nr. Mâcon, Saône-et-Loire

Through Bouttavent

Ecclesia de Cortembert (corr. Contembert)	Cortambert, Saône-et-Loire

Through Escurolles

Ecclesia Sancti Christophori in Monte	Saint-Christophe, Rhône
Ecclesia de Trades	Trades, Rhône
Ecclesia Sancti Leodegarii prope Buxeriam	Saint-Léger-sous-la-Bussière, Saône-et-Loire
Ecclesia de Mommelert (corr. Mominelard)	Montmélard, Saône-et-Loire
Ecclesia Sancti Petri veteris	*Saint-Pierre-le-Vieux, Saône-et-Loire*

Through Besornay

Ecclesia Sancti Hippolyti	*Saint-Hippolyte, Saône-et-Loire*
Ecclesia Vallis-Berjaci prope Cadrellas	
Ecclesia sanctae Colombae	Sainte-Colombe, Saône-et-Loire

[1] Given to Cluny in 960. Pignot, I, 223. [2] Given to Cluny in 931. Pignot, I, 213.
[3] Given to Cluny between 993 and 1032. Charmasse, p. 84.
[4] Given to Cluny by Letbald de Brancion in 925. Pignot, I, 205.
[5] Given to Cluny in 962. Charmasse, *loc. cit.*

Through Mont-Saint-Vincent

Ecclesia sanctae Crucis Montis sancti Vincentij   Mont-Saint-Vincent, Saône-et-Loire

Through Malay

Ecclesia de Maleto   *Malay, Saône-et-Loire*
Ecclesia Sauigniaci   Savigny, Saône-et-Loire

Through Berzé-la-Ville

Ecclesia Berziaci villae   *Berzé-la-Ville, Saône-et-Loire*[1]
Ecclesia Berziaci castri   Berzé-le-Châtel, Saône-et-Loire

Through Arpayé

Ecclesia Sancti Stephani de Emerangiis   Émeringes, Rhône
Ecclesia Sancti Georgij de Roignans   Saint-Georges-de-Reneins, Rhône
Ecclesia Sanctorum Petri et Pauli Iulliaci   *Jullié, Rhône*

Through Jalogny

Ecclesia de Iallogniaco   *Jalogny*[2], *Saône-et-Loire*
Ecclesia sancti Pontij   Saint-Point, Saône-et-Loire

Through Chazelles

Ecclesia de Chasellis   *Chazelles*[3], *Saône-et-Loire*

Through Blanzy

Ecclesia Blanziaci   Blanzy, Saône-et-Loire[4]

Through Monthélon

Ecclesia de Polligniaco prope quercu[m] Edue.   Not identified
  diœc.

Through Gevrey-en-Montagne (Gevrey-Chambertin)

Ecclesia de Barges   Barges, Côte-d'Or
Ecclesia de Feriaux prope Giueryum   Not identified
Ecclesia de Milleyo   Milly, Yonne

Through Chaveyriat

Ecclesia Chauariaci   Chaveyriat, Ain
Ecclesia de Perugiis   Pérouges, Ain
Ecclesia de Vendans   Vendeins, Ain
Ecclesia Maystriaci (corr. Maysiriaci)   Mazoire[5], Ain

Through Saint-Laurent-en-Brionnais

Ecclesia Sancti Laurentij Briennensis   *Saint-Laurent-en-Brionnais, Saône-et-Loire*

---

[1] It formerly belonged to Marcigny, but was exchanged in 1088 for Iguerande. See Virey, 2nd ed. p. 302.

[2] Given to Cluny in 927. Pignot, I, 218.   [3] A grange of the abbey by about 1040.

[4] Given to Cluny in 937. Pignot, I, 219.   [5] Given to Cluny in 938. Pignot, I, 209.

Through Escurolles

Ecclesia Excurolliarum (corr. Escurolliarum)	Escurolles, Allier
Ecclesia de Congnaco	*Cognat, Allier*
Ecclesia de Sauzeto	Saulzet, Allier
Ecclesia de Charmes	Charmes, Allier
Ecclesia de Bousaco (corr. Bienzaco)	Boussac, Allier

Through Chevroux, dioc. Clermont

Ecclesia de Chaueroux	Chevroux, Puy-de-Dôme
Ecclesia Sancti Ignacij (corr. Igniaci)	Saint-Ignat, Puy-de-Dôme
Ecclesia Sancti Hilarij	? Saint-Hilaire-près-Pionsat, Puy-de-Dôme
	? Saint-Hilaire-les-Monges, Puy-de-Dôme
Ecclesia de Allochiis	Saint-Martin-d'Alloches, Pont du Chateau, Puy-de-Dôme

Through Arronnes

Ecclesia de Aronna	*Arronnes, Allier*

Through Mons

Ecclesia de Montibus	Mons, Puy-de-Dôme
Ecclesia Sancti Preiecti	? Saint-Prix, Bourbon-Lancy, Allier (see below)
Ecclesia Sancti Siluestri Pregolin. (corr. Pregolij)	Saint-Sylvestre, Puy-de-Dôme

Through Langy

Ecclesia de Langiaco	Langy, Allier
Ecclesia Mauheti, alias Magny	Magny, Allier
Ecclesia de Crechio siue de Toux (corr. de Crechier siue de Frux)	Créchy, Allier
Ecclesia Sancti Giraudi le Puits	*Saint-Géraud-le-Puy, Allier*
Ecclesia Sancti Stephani prope Geranum in Podio	Saint-Étienne, Saint-Géraud-le-Puy, Allier

Through Pouilly-en-Forez

Ecclesia Polliaci	*Pouilly-lès-Feurs, Loire*
Ecclesia de Grandi-Riuo	Grandris, Rhône
Ecclesia de Neyronde	*Néronde, Loire* [1]
Ecclesia Sancti Pauli	Saint-Paul, Loire
Ecclesia de Vengniaco (corr. Bergniaco)	Not identified
Ecclesia de Barbigniaco	Balbigny, Loire
Ecclesia Sancti Croiaci (corr. Ciriaci)	? Saint-Cirgues, Haute-Loire
Ecclesia de Arthenno	Arthun, Loire

Through Aulnay

Ecclesia de Aunayo (alias de Alneto)	*Aulnay, Seine-et-Oise*
Capella beatae Mariae de Sauigny Parisiensis diœcesis prope villagium de Bondis	Savigny, Aulnay-lès-Bondy, Seine

[1] Given to Cluny in 938. Pignot, I, 209.

Through Saint-Médard-de-Croix-Chapeau

Ecclesia Sancti Medardi	Croix-Chapeau, Charente-Inférieure
Ecclesia Sanctae Annae de Mont-ray	Not identified

Through Saint-Martial-d'Avignon and Tain

Ecclesia de Gnasaco (corr. de Grassaco)	Grasac, Haute-Loire
Ecclesia Sancti Ioannis Baptistae	Not identified
Ecclesia de Rancolis	Raucoules-Brossettes, Haute-Loire
Capella Sancti Petri in villa Montis-falconis	*Montfaucon, Haute-Loire*
Ecclesia de Turnone	Tournon, Ardèche
Ecclesia de Tincto	Tain-l'Hermitage, Drôme
Ecclesia de Planis	Les Plans, Drôme
Ecclesia de Bosanis	Bosas, Ardèche
Ecclesia de Podulano (corr. Podiolano)	Not identified

Other churches dependent on Cluny

Ambierle (Saint-Martin-et-Saint-Abond)[1]
Ameugny, Saône-et-Loire[2]
Arpayé-en-Bresse (Saint-Laurent)[3]
Aynard, Saône-et-Loire[4]
Besornay, Saône-et-Loire[5]
Brey, Saône-et-Loire[6]
Chevignes (Saint-Taurin), Saône-et-Loire[7]
Cotte, Saône-et-Loire[8]
Cropte[9]
Domange, Saône-et-Loire[10]
Écussoles, Saône-et-Loire[11]
Fley, Saône-et-Loire[12]
Forests, dioc. Paris[13]
Geny, Aisne[13]
Iguerande, Saône-et-Loire[14]

Lacheron, Rhône[15]
Lesme, Saône-et-Loire[16]
Lionas, Rhône[15]
Lys, Saône-et-Loire[17]
Marols, nr. Roanne, Loire[18]
Ougy, Saône-et-Loire[19]
Romenay, Saône-et-Loire[16]
Saint-Martin-des-Champs, Saône-et-Loire[20]
Saint-Martin-du-Tartre, Seine-et-Loire[21]
Saules, Saône-et-Loire[22]
Trivy, Saône-et-Loire[16]
Verrières, Saône-et-Loire[16]
Ecclesia de Ponte Roso[23]

[1] Pignot, I, 220.
[2] Given in 927. Pignot, I, 218.
[3] Given in 936. Bernard and Bruel, I, 433.
[4] Charmasse, p. 84.
[5] A *decanatus* of Cluny. Virey, 2nd ed. p. 93.
[6] Acquired, *c.* 1236. Virey, 2nd ed. p.106.
[7] Bernard and Bruel, I, 733. Given in 950.
[8] Bernard and Bruel, I, 350; given in 929.
[9] Pignot, I, 218.
[10] Virey, 2nd ed. p. 278.
[11] Given in 937. Pignot, I, 206.
[12] Dickson, p. 147.
[13] Brugelès, *Grand Pouillé des Bénéfices de France*, 1626.
[14] Exchanged with Maragny for Berzé-le-Ville in 1088. Virey, 2nd ed. p. 302.
[15] Valous gives this as a priory.
[16] Charmasse, p. 84.
[17] Certainly Cluniac by 1513; and probably much earlier. Virey, 2nd ed. p. 318.
[18] Pignot, I, 414.
[19] Virey, 2nd ed. p. 347.
[20] Dickson, p. 273.
[21] *Ibid.* p. 269.
[22] *Ibid.* p. 298.
[23] Pignot, I, 414.

Capella Sancti Victoris de Alsgoia[1]	Not identified
Ecclesia in villa Lanco[2]	Not identified (? St Pierre-de-Lanques)
Ecclesia Sancti Benigni[2]	? Saint-Benigne, Ain
Ecclesia Sancti Romani[2]	? Saint-Romain, Saône-et-Loire
Ecclesia de Solubrense[3]	*Soluté, Saône-et-Loire*
Ecclesia de Evaranda[4]	Eurarde, Saône-et-Loire
Ecclesia in Villa Sevanis[5]	Uzès district
Ecclesia Sancti Saturnini in vicaria Kaxionensse[6]	Uzès district
Ecclesia Sancti Sulpitii in villa Laliaco	Laly, Saône-et-Loire
Capella Sancti Germani[7]	? Saint-Germain, Saint-Germain-du-Plain, Saône-et-Loire
Ecclesia de Finiciaco[8]	Not identified
Ecclesia in villa Marzoniaco[9]	Marsonnas, Ain
Ecclesia de Bosarreries[10]	Not identified
Ecclesia in villa Flagiaco[11]	Saint-Martin-de-Flagy-en-Chalonnais, Saône-et-Loire
Ecclesia Sancti Martini de Montiniaco[12]	? Montigny-sur-Aube, Côte-d'Or
Ecclesia in Bolinlaco[13]	Bouligneux, Ain
Ecclesia B. Mariae in Villa Pradilis[14]	In Mâconnais
Ecclesia Sanctae Mariae de Croquello[15]	Not identified
Ecclesia Sancti Petri ⎱ in villa Communiaco[16] Ecclesia Sancti Lazari ⎰	Communay, Isère
Ecclesia Sanctae Mariae in villa Salentiaco in loco qui vocatur Vererias[17]	? *Salency, Oise*
Ecclesia Sancti Johannis Bapt. Cavariensis[18]	? Chaveyriat, Ain
Capella Sanctae Mariae et Sancti Michaelis in urbe Ticinense[19]	Not identified
Capella Sancti Juliani in loco Montones[20]	In Viennois
Ecclesia Sancti Michaelis de Metono[21]	Mettonex, Ain
Ecclesia Sanctae Mariae de Cantamerulo[22]	Chantemerle, Puy-de-Dôme
Ecclesia Sancti Projecti martyris in Forez[23]	Saint-Prix-en-Forest, Loire
Ecclesia Sancti Pauli in villa Ladimiago[24]	In Auvergne (? Ladignac, Cantal or Ladignat, Haute-Loire)
Ecclesia Sancti Mauricii in villa Brengis[25]	*Branges, Saône-et-Loire*

[1] Bernard and Bruel, I, 356; acquired in 929.   [2] *Ibid.* I, 360.
[3] Bernard and Bruel, I, 369; in 930.   [4] *Ibid.* I, 457; in 937.
[5] *Ibid.* I, 647; in 946.   [6] *Ibid.* I, 677; in 948.
[7] *Ibid.* I, 727; in 950.   [8] *Ibid.* I, 506; *c.* 920.
[9] *Ibid.* I, 557; in 942.   [10] *Ibid.* I, 651; in 943.
[11] *Ibid.* I, 609; in 944.   [12] *Ibid.* I, 612; in 914.
[13] *Ibid.* I, 494; in 940.   [14] *Ibid.* I, 502; *c.* 940.
[15] *Ibid.* I, 741; *c.* 950.   [16] *Ibid.* I, 749; in 951.
[17] *Ibid.* I, 829; in 954.   [18] *Ibid.* II, 307; in 967.
[19] *Ibid.* II, 313; in 967.   [20] *Ibid.* II, 319; in 967.
[21] *Ibid.* II, 252; in 963–4.   [22] *Ibid.* II, 254; in 963.
[23] *Ibid.* II, 273; in 965–6.   [24] *Ibid.* II, 290; in 966.
[25] *Ibid.* II, 129; in 957.

Ecclesia Sancti Ursae in villa Guiarada[1]	In Mâconnais
Ecclesia in villa Maceriis[2]	Maizeray, Saône-et-Loire
Ecclesia in villa Pagiaco[2]	? Le Paget, Ain
Ecclesia in Nova Cella[2]	? Neuvecelle, Haute-Savoie
Ecclesia Sancti Genesii infra moenia urbis Viennae[3]	Vienne, Isère
Ecclesia in villa Canloco[4]	Champlieu, Saône-et-Loire
Ecclesia Sancti Sulpicii in villa Cavaniaco[5]	? Chavannes-sur-Ressouse or Chavannes-sur-Suran, Ain
Ecclesia in villa Combris[6]	In Mâconnais
Ecclesia Sancti Petri Candiacensis[7]	In Lyonnais: ? Chandée, Ain
Ecclesia Sancti Aunemundi[8]	?Saint-Ennemond,Allier,or Saint-Ennemond,Rhône
Ecclesia Sancti Johannis in villa Lazeniaco[9]	Saint-Jean-de-Lazimac, Saône-et-Loire
Ecclesia Sancti Ferreoli in villa Liergio[9]	Liergues, Rhône
Ecclesia Sancti Sulpitii in villa Ledemgiaco[10]	Not identified
Ecclesia B. Martini et Capella Sanctae Mariae in villa Enziaco super fluvium Arcuntiam[11]	Anzy-le-Duc, Saône-et-Loire
Ecclesia Sancti Juliani in villa Malekasali (Malecasa)[12]	Saint-Julien-de-Malcaze, Rhône
Ecclesia Sanctae Mariae in villa Celsiaco super Arderiam[13]	Not identified
Ecclesia Sanctae Mariae Belmontis[14]	Beaumont-sur-Grosne, Saône-et-Loire
Ecclesia Sancti Martini a Carconiaco[15]	Not identified
Ecclesia in villa Rofeio[16]	In Mâconnais
Ecclesia Sancti Petri in villa Curtilis[17]	Curtil-sous-Buffières, Saône-et-Loire
Ecclesia Sanctae Mariae in Arteuno[18]	Arthun, Loire[19]
Capella B. Martini in villa Vigoseto[20]	Vigousset, Saône-et-Loire
Ecclesia in villa Saraciaco[21]	Sarrat, Puy-de-Dôme
Capella Sancti Petri in villa Molinis[22]	Moulins, Allier
Capella Sanctae Mariae de Dueria[23]	In Mâconnais
Capella Sancti Desiderii[24]	
Ecclesia Sancti Johannis[25] ⎫	
Ecclesia Sancti Antonii[25] ⎬	*In territorio de Dimone in com. Vendascense*
Ecclesia Sancti Eleutherii[25] ⎭	

[1] Bernard and Bruel, II, 207; in 961–2.
[2] *Ibid.* II, 229.
[3] *Ibid.* II, 15; 954–93.
[4] *Ibid.* II, 82; 955–85.
[5] *Ibid.* II, 89; in 956.
[6] *Ibid.* II, 400; in 972.
[7] *Ibid.* II, 485; in 976.
[8] *Ibid.* II, 489; in 976.
[9] *Ibid.* II, 351; in 969.
[10] *Ibid.* II, 386; in 971–2.
[11] *Ibid.* II, 396; in 972.
[12] *Ibid.* II, 300; in 967.
[13] *Ibid.* II, 307; in 967.
[14] *Ibid.* II, 574; in 980.
[15] *Ibid.* II, 593; *c.* 980.
[16] *Ibid.* II, 600; in 981.
[17] *Ibid.* II, 622; in 981–2.
[18] *Ibid.* II, 623; in 981–2.
[19] Valous gives this as a priory dependent on Pouilly-lès-Feurs.
[20] *Ibid.* II, 755; in 978.
[21] *Ibid.* III, 82; in 990.
[22] *Ibid.* III, 97; in 990–1.
[23] *Ibid.* III, 152; 192–3.
[24] *Ibid.* III, 186; in 993–4.
[25] *Ibid.* III, 207; 993–1032.

EA

24

Ecclesia Sancti Dionysii in villa Crusilicas[1]	Crouzilhac, Haute-Loire
Ecclesia Sanctae Mariae in villa Quintiaco[2]	Quincié, Rhône
Ecclesia Sancti Martini in villa Vallis[3]	Vaux, Rhône
Ecclesia Sancti Prejecti in suburbio Borboni[4]	Bourbon-Lancy, Saône-et-Loire (Saint-Prix)
Ecclesia Sancti Martini in loco qui dictur Prodolgus[5]	In Viennois
Ecclesia de Campo[6]	Dioc. Grenoble. ? Les Champs, Isère
Ecclesia Sancti Dionysii[7]	? Saint-Denis, Ain
Ecclesia Sancti Petri en villa Marogliaco[8]	Marols, Loire
Ecclesia quae dictur de Oratorio[9]	Dioc. Lyons
Ecclesia Sancti Andeoli[9]	Saint-Andéol-le-Château, Rhône
Ecclesia de Vallibus[9]	? Vaux, Rhône (see above)
A church in Vienne[9]	Vienne, Isère
Ecclesia Monte Ison[9]	Dioc. Valence (? Innimont, Ain)
Ecclesia Sancti Juliani in vicaria Lescherias[10]	Leschères, Jura
Ecclesia Sancti Sulpitii in monte Caballicoda[11]	Not identified
Ecclesia Sancti Laurentii[12]	? Saint-Laurent-du-Pont, Isère
Ecclesia Sancti Stephani de Portu[13]	Not identified
Ecclesia Sancti Pauli in vicaria Marevenno[14]	Aquitaine (? Marennes, Charente-Inférieure)
Capella Sanctae Mariae de Roca in villa Quinciaco[15]	Quincié, Rhône
Ecclesia in villa Meissano[16]	Meysse, Ardèche, later exchanged for Saint-Vincent-de-Barrès, Ardèche
Ecclesia in villa que vocatur Testorius, in aice Subdionense[17]	Not identified
Ecclesia Sancti Germani in villa Pernando, in comitatu Belnensi[18]	Pernand, Côte-d'Or
Capella Sancti Salvatoris in villa Luviniaco[19]	Lévigny, Saône-et-Loire
Ecclesia Sancti Flori in monte Indiciaco[20]	In Auvergne
Ecclesia Sancti Germani in inter Bulburum et Carusiam sitam[21]	Isle d'Abeau, Isère
Ecclesia Sancti Petri de Juviliaco[22]	In Mâconnais
Ecclesia Sancti Cirici super Graonam[23]	In Chalonnais
Ecclesia Sanctae Mariae in loco Heron[21]	Saint-Jean-d'Herans, Isère

[1] Bernard and Bruel, III, 210; 993–1032.
[2] Ibid. III, 216; 993–1048.
[3] Ibid. III, 293; 993–1048.
[4] Ibid. III, 295; 993–1048.
[5] Ibid. III, 295; 993–1048.
[6] Ibid. III, 296; 993–1048.
[7] Ibid. III, 407; 994–1022.
[8] Ibid. III, 419; in 995.
[9] Ibid. III, 547; in 998.
[10] Ibid. III, 650; in 1004. Dickson, p. 181, identifies as Lancharre, Saône-et-Loire.
[11] Ibid. III, 661; in 1005.
[12] Ibid. III, 687.
[13] Ibid. III, 721; in 1015.
[14] Ibid. III, 739; in 1019.
[15] Ibid. III, 751; confirmed in 1020.
[16] Ibid. III, 769; c. 1020.
[17] Ibid. III, 786; in 1023.
[18] Ibid. III, 798; in 1023.
[19] Ibid. III, 800; in 1023.
[20] Ibid. III, 816; in 1025.
[21] Ibid. IV, 78; in 1032.
[22] Ibid. IV, 114; in 1037.
[23] Ibid. IV, 125; in 1037.
[24] Ibid. IV, 151; given in 1040. It probably depended on Domène, that had a cell in that place.

Ecclesia Sanctae Mariae	juxta	
Ecclesia Sancti Petri	Castrum	Nr. Valence
and three others	Ur[1]	

Ecclesia Sanctae Mariae in territorio nomine Vorzio[2] — Nr. Sisteron

Ecclesia Sancti Privati[3] — Nr. Roanne

Ecclesia Sancti Angeli[3] — Nr. Roanne

Ecclesia Sancti Lamberti[3] — Nr. Roanne

Ecclesia Sancti Stephani de Rocolis[3] — In Velay

Ecclesia Castri Clavazonis[3] — ? Claveisolles, Rhône

Ecclesia Sanctae Mariae de Monte Castaneo[3] — Montchâtain, Drôme

Ecclesia Sancti Johannis Baptistae[4] — Avallon, Isère

Capella in castello Avalonensi[4] — Avallon, Isère

Ecclesia in Mederio in pago Caturcino[5] — Nr. Cahors

Ecclesia Sancti Johannis in villa Calcedonense[6] — Not identified

Ecclesia Sancti Martini in villa Vals[7] — ? Vaux, Rhône (see above)

Ecclesia Sancti Stephani de Monte Reculato[8] — ?? Montrecoux, Haute-Loire *or* Montagna-le-Reconduit, Jura

Ecclesia qui appellatur ad Cuith[9] — Not identified

Capella Castri Saxole[9] — Not identified

Ecclesia Sancti Maurici in Castello Alesio[10] — Alais, Gard

Ecclesia in villa Frontenay[11] — ? Frontenas, Rhône (priory)

Ecclesia de Banols[11] — Bagnols, Rhône

Ecclesia B. Mauricii[12] — *In terra campi Sauri*, ? Saint-Maurice-en-Valgaudemar, Hautes-Alpes

Ecclesia Sancti Jacobi[13] — Saint-Jacques, Hautes-Alpes

Ecclesia B. Mariae[13] — Sainte-Marie, Hautes-Alpes

Ecclesia Sancti Viatoris (? Victoris)[13] — Dioc. Gap

Ecclesia Sancti Petri[13] — Saint-Pierre-Avez, Hautes-Alpes

Ecclesia Sancti Martini[13] — Saint-Martin, Hautes-Alpes

Ecclesia Sancti Eusebii[13] — Saint-Eusèbe, Hautes-Alpes

Ecclesia Sanctae Mariae prope Castellum[14] — In Auvergne

Ecclesia in Podio Sancti Martini[15] — Puy-Saint-Martin, Drôme

Ecclesia Sancti Johannis Baptistae in Meditiaco loco[16] — Not identified

Ecclesia Sancti Johannis in villa Alosio[17] — Dioc. Poitiers (? *Alloue, Charente*)

Ecclesia de Jussiaco[18] — Not identified

---

[1] Bernard and Bruel, IV, 191; in time of Hugh.
[2] *Ibid.* IV, 200; in time of Hugh.
[3] *Ibid.* IV, 205; in time of Hugh.
[4] *Ibid.* IV, 207; in time of Hugh.
[5] *Ibid.* IV, 218; in time of Hugh.
[6] *Ibid.* IV, 230; in time of Hugh.
[7] *Ibid.* IV, 233; in time of Hugh.
[8] *Ibid.* IV, 234; in time of Hugh.
[9] *Ibid.* IV, 236; in time of Hugh.
[10] *Ibid.* IV, 237; in time of Hugh.
[11] *Ibid.* IV, 241; in time of Hugh.
[12] *Ibid.* IV, 242; in time of Hugh.
[13] *Ibid.* IV, 242; in time of Hugh.
[14] *Ibid.* IV, 244; in time of Hugh.
[15] *Ibid.* IV, 247; in time of Hugh.
[16] *Ibid.* IV, 248; in time of Hugh.
[17] *Ibid.* IV, 318; in time of Hugh.
[18] *Ibid.* IV, 329; in time of Hugh.

Ecclesia Sancti Severini Burdegalensis[1]	Bordeaux, Gironde
Ecclesia de Renangis[2]	*? Relanges, Vosges*
Ecclesia Sanctae Mariae de Veteri Donziaco[3]	*? Donzy, Nièvre*
	? Donzy-le-National, Saône-et-Loire
Ecclesia de Vitriaco[4]	Dioc. Autun. *? Vitry-sur-Loire, Saône-et-Loire*
Ecclesia Sanctae Mariae de Luciaco[5]	Lucy, Saône-et-Loire
Ecclesia Sancti Johannis in villa Colnac, in territorio Caturcino[6]	Dioc. Cahors
Ecclesia B. Petri in villa Boeniaco[7]	Boën, Loire
Ecclesia Sancti Petri de Coona[8]	Cosne, Nièvre
Ecclesia Sancti Petri Ispacensis[9]	Dioc. Nevers
Ecclesia de Lodessa[10]	Loddes, Allier
Ecclesia Sancti Marci juxta civitatem Laudensem, in loco Credayo[11]	Not identified
Ecclesia Sanctae Mariae et Sancti Stephani in suburbio Nevernensis[12]	Nevers, Nièvre
Ecclesia de Sancta Speria[13]	Dioc. Cahors
Ecclesia de Sancto Sereno[13]	*Saint-Céré, Lot*
Ecclesia de Riniaco[13]	Dioc. Cahors (? Rignac, Lot)
Ecclesia de Vendrovia[14]	*In pago Tullensi*
Ecclesia Sancti Genesii apud Turres super Matronam[15]	Tours-sur-Marne, Marne
Ecclesia Sancti Marcelli in loco qui vocatur Alavardus[16]	Allevard, Isère
Ecclesia de Aqua pulchra[17]	Not identified
Ecclesia de Castro carbonario[17]	? Château-Chardon, Saône-et-Loire
Ecclesia de Monte Agindrico[17]	Not identified
Ecclesia in loco nomine Valaris[18]	In Valtellina
Ecclesia Sancti Prejecti in Cumbis[19]	?? Les Combes, Isère
Capella de Muratio[19]	Not identified
Ecclesia Sancti Dionysii in valle quae dictur Sesedana[20]	In Lombardy
Ecclesia Sancti Crucis de Vertemate[21]	? Dioc. Como
Ecclesia de Arcu[22]	Arc-en-Barrois, Haute-Marne
Capella Sancti Petri in loco de Casalello[23]	In Lombardy

[1] Bernard and Bruel, IV, 414; c. 1050.
[3] *Ibid.* IV, 444; in 1055.
[5] *Ibid.* IV, 449; 1055–98.
[7] *Ibid.* IV, 478; in 1062.
[9] *Ibid.* IV, 497; in 1063.
[11] *Ibid.* IV, 524.
[13] *Ibid.* IV, 530; in 1068–1112.
[15] *Ibid.* IV, 569; in 1074.
[17] *Ibid.* IV, 752; in 1082.
[19] *Ibid.* IV, 669; 1079.
[21] *Ibid.* IV, 765; in 1084.
[23] *Ibid.* IV, 771; in 1086.

[2] *Ibid.* IV, 406; 1050.
[4] *Ibid.* IV, 447; c. 1055.
[6] *Ibid.* IV, 464; 1060–1108.
[8] *Ibid.* IV, 484; 1062–96.
[10] *Ibid.* IV, 501; in 1064.
[12] *Ibid.* IV, 528; in 1068.
[14] *Ibid.* IV, 554; 1070–1107.
[16] *Ibid.* IV, 751; in 1082.
[18] *Ibid.* IV, 64; in 1078.
[20] *Ibid.* IV, 757; in 1083.
[22] *Ibid.* IV, 769; in 1085–6.

Ecclesia Sancti Dei genetricis in villa quae vocatur Allincurtis[1]	Elincourt-Sainte-Marguerite, Oise
Ecclesia de Monsterol[2]	Monsteroux, Isère
Ecclesia Sancti Salvatoris de Vineolis[3]	Les Vigneaux, Saône-et-Loire
Ecclesia Sancti Nicholai de Castello Murassalt[4]	Dioc. Autun: ? Meursault, Côte-d'Or
Ecclesia Sancti Pauli[5]	? In the Bresse
Ecclesia Sancti Samsonis inter Nantholium et Berronem sitam[6]	Nanteuil-le-Haudoin, Oise
Ecclesia Sanctae Mariae de Aguriaco apud montem Berulfum[7]	(? See Aigueguens)
Ecclesia Sancti Juliani in Briennensi territorio[8]	Saint-Julien, Saône-et-Loire
Ecclesia Quadrellae[9]	Charolles, Saône-et-Loire
Ecclesia Sanctae Mariae de Vedeneto[10]	Diod. Gap: ? Vedènes-Vaucluse
Ecclesia de Barbona[11]	Barbonne-Fayel, Marne
Ecclesia de Lintis[12]	Linthes, Marne
Ecclesia de Lintellis[12]	Linthelles, Marne
Ecclesia B. Mariae de Rochella[13]	La Rochelle, Charente-Inférieure
Felne en Masconnois[11]	Not identified
Genouilly en Masconnois	*Genouilly, Saône-et-Loire*
Notre Dame de Grandmont ou Montmajour (1157)	Not identified
Plusieves, dioc. Orléans	Not identified
La Roche Beaunecourt	? La Roche-Beaucourt, Dordogne
Romans (Chapel)	Romans, Ain
Saint Andoche en Autunois	Not identified
Saint Cassien d'Olhinthe	Not identified
Saint Vivien de Bollet	Not identified

Dependent on Acy[15]

Cura Sanctorum Geruasii et Prothasii de Curtolio, Siluanecten dioecesis	Courteuil, Oise
Cura Sancti Martini de Monteaspero, Bellouacensis dioecesis	Apremont, Oise
Cura de Noa Sancti Martini Suessionensis dioecesis	*Noël-Saint-Martin, Oise*
Cura de Noa Sancti Remigij Bellouacensis dioecesis	Noël-Saint-Remy, Oise
Cura Sancti Germani de Charrona Parisiensis dioecesis	Not identified

[1] Bernard and Bruel, IV, 807.
[2] *Ibid.* V, 23; in 1093.
[3] *Ibid.* V, 29; in 1094.
[4] *Ibid.* V, 31; in 1094.
[5] *Ibid.* V, 33; in 1094.
[6] *Ibid.* V, 153; c. 1100.
[7] *Ibid.* V, 162; in 1102–9.
[8] *Ibid.* V, 183; in 1105.
[9] *Ibid.* V, 184; in 1105.
[10] *Ibid.* V, 193; c 1105.
[11] *Ibid.* V, 371; in 1130–2.
[12] *Ibid.* V, 371; in 1130–2.
[13] *Ibid.* V, 517; in 1152.
[14] Bénet and Bazin, Inventaire Général.
[15] Marrier.

Cura de Drenciaco paruo, Parisiensis dioeces	Drancy, Seine
Cura Sancti Georgij de Brayo, Siluanectensis dioecesis	Bray, Oise
Cura B. Mariae de Oriaco, Siluanectensis dioecesis	*Orry-la-Ville, Oise*

Dependent on Airaines[1]

Cura parochialis B. Dionysii	Airaines, Somme
Cura parochialis Sancti Richarii de Dourrier	Douriez, Somme
Cura parochialis Sancti Michaelis de Quesnoy super Arenas	Quesnoy-sous-Airaines, Somme
Cura parochialis de Croque-oison	Croquoison, Somme
Cura parochialis Sancti Martini d'Estrujen	Not identified
Cuisnon[2]	Not identified
Fraittecuisse	Frettecuisse, Somme

Dependent on Ambierle[3]

Ecclesia de Torziaco	*? Torcy, Saône-et-Loire*
	? Torcieu, Ain
Ecclesia de Mabliaco	Mably, Loire
Ecclesia Sancti Abundi Vetuli	Not identified
Ecclesia Sancti Andreae	? Saint-André, Rhône
Ecclesia Sancti Germani	? Saint-Germain-la-Montagne, Loire
Ecclesia Sancti Ferreoli	Not identified
Capella de Espinatia	Espinasse, Loire
Ecclesia de Vivent	Vivans, Loire
Ecclesia de Arzu	? Ars, Ain; Ars, Puy-de-Dôme
Ecclesia de Changiaco	Changy, Loire
Ecclesia de Anda	Not identified
Capella de Bosco	Not identified

Dependent on Ancre. See Encre

Dependent on Saint-Cybard-d'Angoulême[4]

Champdeuil	? Champdeuil, Seine-et-Marne
Montabourlet, Dordogne	
Montignac-le-Coq, Charente	
Pompourn	? Pomport, Dordogne, *or* Pompougnac, Dordogne
Saint-Pierre-de-Sales	? Sales, Lot
Saint-Avit-de-Villars	? Saint-Avit-de-Vialard, Dordogne
Saint-Maxime Montmalignac	Not identified
Valère	Not identified

[1] Marchand, p. 543.

[2] These two churches are taken from Brugelès, *Grand Pouillé des bénéfices de France*, 1626.

[3] Bernard and Bruel, v, 573; by 1166.

[4] Abbé J. Nanglard, "Pouillé historique du diocèse d'Angoulême", in *Bull. et Mém. de la Soc. arch. et hist. de la Charente*, 6th series, III, 1893, p. 108.

Chapelle-de-Montaigut   ? Montaign, Charente-Inférieure
Saint-Yrieix, Charente
Bouëx, Charente
Tourriers, Charente
Vœuil-et-Giget, Charente
Jarnac (Saint-Cybard-du-Château), Charente
Verdilles   Verdilles, Charente
Orlut-en-Cherves, Charente
Saint-Maxence   *? Saint-Maixant, Gironde* (dioc. Agen)
Saint-Orient   Saint-Orens, Gers (dioc. Agen)
Strades (dioc. Agen)   ? Estrade, Lot-et-Garonne
Theyrac (dioc. Agen)   *? Tevrac, Lot-et-Garonne*
Fléac, Charente
Saint-Genis, Charente-Inférieure
Lanville, Charente
Nanclars, Charente
Rouillac, Charente
Roullet, Charente
Rougnac, Charente
Fleuriac   ? Fleurac, Charente
Bassac, Charente
Chassors, Charente
Saint-Martin-de-Noulette   Not identified
La Chapelle-de-la-Tour-Blanche, Dordogne

Dependent on Auch[1]

Ecclesia Sancti Saturnini de Castelle   ? Saint-Sernin, Gers
Ecclesia Sancti Petri de Manidvilla   Not identified
Ecclesia Sancti Martini de Toget   Touget, Gers
Ecclesia Sancti Salvii   Saint-Sauvy, Gers
Ecclesia Sancti Martini de Gallovico   Not identified
Ecclesia Sanctae Christinae   Sainte-Christie, Auch, Gers
Ecclesia Sancti Frisii   Saint-Frix de Bassoues, Bassoues-d'Armagnac,
                                                 Gers
Ecclesia Sancti Juliani de Monasterio   *Mouchès, Gers*
Capella Sancti Clari   Saint-Clair, Tarn-et-Garonne

Dependent on Saint-Germain-d'Auxerre[2]

Église de Sainct-Loup-d'Auxerre   Auxerre, Yonne
Église de Dige   *Diges, Yonne*
Église de l'Escano de Saint-Germain   ? Escamps, Yonne
Église de Perinnac   Not identified
Église de Bleneau   ? Blenay, Nièvre

[1] A. Lavergne, "Les couvents de Cluny en Gascogne", in *Revue de Gascogne*, XVIII, 1877, p. 438. Auch.
[2] Brugelès, *Grand Pouillé des bénéfices de France*, 1626, II, 570.

Église de Bayne	Not identified
Église de Venete	*? Venette, Oise*
Église des Prez	Not identified
Église de Frannace[1]	? Franay, Nièvre
Église d'Errace[1]	? Errey, Aube
Église de Senalay	? Senailly, Côte-d'Or
Église de Ronvet	Not identified
Église du Chasteau-Sainct-Ferrel, avec le doyenné, par Tourne; avec le sieur temporel du Chasteau de Saint-Ferrel	Not identified
Église de Saincts	Saints, Yonne
Église de Saint-Pierre-des-Monastères	? St Pierre-le-Moutier, Nièvre
Église de Saincte-Colombe	Sainte-Colombe-en-Puisaye, Yonne
Église de Sainct-Bonite	Saint-Bonnet, Nièvre
Église de Sainct-Amand	Saint-Amand-en-Puisaye, Nièvre
Église de Sainct-Jean-Baptiste de Sainct-Sauveur	*Saint-Sauveur-en-Puisaye, Nièvre*
Église de Chassy	Chassy, Yonne
Église d'Asgreis	Not identified
Chappelle de Nezone	Not identified
Chappelle de Sarieres	Not identified
Église de Villeneuve-Sainct-Fial	? Saint-Phal, Yonne

Dans l'archévesché de Sens

Église de Egryaco	Egry, Loiret
Église de Phenis	Not identified
Église de Sainte-Croix	Not identified
Église de Corbeye	? Corbet, Cher
Église de Senguase	? Sangué, Nièvre
Église de Vlirede	Not identified
Église de Haulterive	Hauterive, Yonne
Église du Mont-de-Sainct-Sulpice	Mont-Saint-Sulpice, Yonne
Église de Bodoly	Not identified
Chappelle du Vicomte au lieu de Saint-Florentin	Saint-Florentin, Yonne
Église de Coneso	? Cosne, Nièvre

Dans l'évesché de Troyes

Église de Bretigny	Not identified
Chappelle de Vallecaroy	Not identified

En l'évesché de Langres

L'Église de Notre-Dame au bourg de Saint-Leodegare	Not identified
Église de Montreuil avec la chapelle des Estives et de Ceres	? Montreuil-sur-Blaise, Haute-Marne

[1] Probably wrongly taken from a Latin list, "de Franacio", "de Erracio".

Église de Morny	Not identified
Église de Massilly	Not identified
Église de Vessenete	? Le Vesenay, Doubs
Église de Nicete[1]	Nicey, Aube
Église limine	Not identified
Église de Pontrac	Not identified
Église de Lignerolle	*Lignorolles, Yonne*
Église de la Dusac[1]	*Laduz, Yonne*
Église de Molan	
Église d'Amesco	

En l'évesché de...

Église de Pesmes	*Pesmes, Haute-Saône*
Église de Tumbey	

En l'évesché d'Autun

Église de Lisy	
Église de Vertigny	? Vertilly, Yonne
Église de Disangic	Dissangis, Yonne
Église de Maunay	Mauny, Yonne

En l'évesché de Nevers

La chappelle de Notre-Dame-de-Disy	Not identified
La chappelle de Saint-Martin-de-Disy	Not identified
La chappelle de Sainct-Mart	Not identified
L'Église de Sainct-Leodegare	? Saint-Léger, Nièvre
L'Église de Toricque	Thory, Nièvre
L'Église Verdpré	Not identified
L'Église de Montereau	*? Montereau, Loiret*
L'Église de Taye	Not identified
L'Église Vaudevesse	Vandenesse, Nièvre
L'Église de Sainct-Jacques	Not identified
L'Église d'Alme	Not identified
L'Église de Fraisnet	Not identified
L'Église de Chauvé	Not identified
L'Église de Notre-Dame-de-la-Chappelle	Not identified
L'Église de Catie	Not identified
Chapelle de Notre-Dame-de-Castillon	Not identified
Chapelle de Saincte-Cecille	Not identified
Chapelle de Saincte-Marie-Magdelaine	Not identified

[1] Probably wrongly formed from a Latin version, "de Niceto", "de Laduzaco".

Dependent on Baume

La Frette, Saône-et-Loire[1]

Ecclesia Sancti Johannis Balme[2]	*Baume, Jura*
Ecclesia Sancti Gervasii Victoris	Not identified
Ecclesia Sancti Nicholai Carneti	Charnet, Jura
Ecclesia Laviniaci	Lavigny, Jura
Ecclesia Montis Huin	Not identified
Ecclesia Caveriaci	? Chaveyriat, Ain
Ecclesia Kavaniaci	? Chavannes-sur-Ressaise *or* Chavannes-sur-Suran, Ain
Ecclesia Brariaci	Bréry, Jura
Ecclesia Sancti Desiderati Ledonis	Lons-le-Saulnier, Jura
Ecclesia Sisinciaci	Not identified
Ecclesia Larnaci	Larnaud, Jura
Ecclesia Desnensis	Desnes, Jura
Ecclesia Domblensem	Domblans, Jura
Ecclesia de Guars	Not identified
Ecclesia Montis Tolose	Not identified
Ecclesia Asnensis	Asnans, Jura
Ecclesia Montis Alacris	Montalègre, Jura
Ecclesia Neblensis	Not identified
Capella Crancet	Baume, Jura
Ecclesia Belle Vavre, Ciencis ville	Not identified
Ecclesia Sarmacie	Not identified
Ecclesia Sabonarie	? Savonnière, Ain
Ecclesia Alefracte	Not identified
Ecclesia Cortunne	Not identified
Ecclesia Ver	Not identified
Ecclesia Biviliaci	Not identified
Ecclesia Sancti Mauricii et Sancti Germani Grausonis	Granson, Switzerland
Ecclesia Baensis	Not identified
Ecclesia Bellimontis	Not identified
Ecclesia Montis Relenis	Not identified
Ecclesia Esciconis	Not identified
Ecclesia Rancinaci	Rancenay, Doubs
Ecclesia Gelerensis	Not identified
Ecclesia Beneventi	Not identified
Ecclesia Sancti Regneberti	*? Saint-Rambert, Ain*
Ecclesia Sancti Stephani de Ponte	Not identified
Ecclesia D. Petri de Arlico	Arlay, Jura
Ecclesia Wistrivici	Not identified

[1] Dickson, p. 152.
[2] The subsequent churches belonged to Baume by 1106; Bernard and Bruel, v, 197.

Ecclesia Poloniaci cum cap. Marriaci	Poligny, Jura
Ecclesia Poloniaci cum cap. Castri	
Ecclesia Poloniaci cum cap. Platani	
Ecclesia Poloniaci cum cap. Sancti Saviniani	
Ecclesia Aquensis	Not identified
Ecclesia Solciaci	Not identified
Ecclesia Spinctensis	Not identified

Dependent on Beaulieu[1]

Ecclesia de Chamairaco	Chamarat, Dordogne
Ecclesia de Condato	? Condat, Puy-de-Dôme
Ecclesia de Stranquillo	Strenquels, Lot

Dependent on Bourbon-Lancy[2]

Ecclesia Sancti Petri in villa Leemna	Not identified
Capella Sancti Prejecti	Saint-Prix, Bourbon-Lancy
Capella Sancti Baudili in Pistichiaco	Not identified

Dependent on Cappy[3]

Cura Sancti Nicolai eiusdem loci	*Cappy, Somme*
Capella Sancti Stephani in Nosocomio, seu morbidorum aede dicti loci	Cappy, Somme
Cura B. Mariae de Fontanis, prope Capiacum	Not identified
Cura Sancti Eligij de Wauuille et Santars	Not identified
Cura Sanctae Genouefae de Frammeruille	Framerville, Somme
Cura Sancti Martini de Neufville, prope Brayum	La Neuville-lès-Bray, Somme
Cura Sancti Martini de Maumés	Mametz, Somme
Cura Sancti Nicolai de Longueual	*Longueval, Aisne*
Cura B. Martini de Cleriaco, ad Somonam fluu. Picardiae	Cléry, Somme
Cura Sancti Medardi d'Estrepigny, prope Peronam	
	Wamuller[4]

Dependent on Carennac[5]

Alvignac, Lot	Miers, Lot

Dependent on Saint-Marcel-lès-Chalon

Bey, Saône-et-Loire[6]	*Savigny-sur-Seille, Saône-et-Loire*[7]
Saint-Julien-de-Sennecey, Saône-et-Loire[8]	

---

[1] Bernard and Bruel, IV, 96; *c.* 1030.
[2] *Ibid.* IV, 602; in 1076.
[3] Marrier.
[4] Brugelès, *Grand Pouillé des bénéfices de France*, 1626.
[5] G. V., *Prieuré doyenné de Carennac*, p. 2.
[6] Dickson, p. 80.
[7] Given to Saint-Marcel in 960. Dickson, p. 300.
[8] *Ibid.* p. 255.

Dependent on La Charité

Saint-Caprais, Cher [1]

Ecclesia de Aona [2]	?? Annoux, Yonne
Ecclesia de Beluciano	Bulcy (Saint-Martin)
Ecclesia Sancti Lupi	? Saint-Loup-des-Bois, Nièvre
Ecclesia de Cavarias	Not identified
Ecclesia de Brenca	Not identified
Ecclesia de Monteboio	Montbouy, Loiret
Ecclesia de Castellione	?? Châtillon-en-Bazois, Nièvre
Ecclesia de Contentione	? Contenson, Loire
Ecclesia de Orolio	Not identified
Capella de Monte Falconis	Not identified
Ecclesia de Fontiniaco castro	Not identified
Ecclesia de Nerunda	*Nérondes, Cher*
Ecclesia de Ulmeriaco	Not identified
Ecclesia de Coola	Not identified
Ecclesia Sanctae Montane	Sainte-Montaine, Cher
Ecclesia Sancti Victoris in suburbio	? Nevers, Nièvre
Ecclesia Sancti Rozzi	Dioc. Autun
Ecclesia Sancti Salvatoris in suburbio	La Charité, Nièvre
Ecclesia de Firmitate Ansculfi [3]	Dioc. Meaux
Ecclesia de Chailli	Chailly-en-Bière, Seine-et-Marne
Ecclesia de Chamini	*Chamigny, Seine-et-Marne*
Ecclesia de Bussei	Bussy-Saint-Georges, Seine-et-Marne
Ecclesia Sancti Christophori in suburbio	
Ecclesia de Narci	Narcy (Saint-Marcel), Nièvre
Ecclesia de Varenna	*Varennes-lès-Narcy (Saint-Martin), Nièvre*
Ecclesia de Domno Petro	Dompierre, Nièvre
Ecclesia de Murliaco	*Murlin (Saint-Martin), Nièvre*
Ecclesia de Bosco Britannie	Bois-Bretoux, Saône-et-Loire
Capella de Castronovo	Not identified
Capella de Suliaco	*Sully (Saint-Symphorien), Nièvre*
Capella de Manniaco	Not identified
Capella de Colungiis super jonium	Not identified
Capella de Namui	Not identified
Ecclesia Sancti Jacobi de Charitate [4]	La Charité-sur-Loire, Nièvre
Ecclesia Sancti Petri de Charitate	La Charité-sur-Loire, Nièvre
Ecclesia Sancti Petri de Polliaco	Pouilly-en-Auxois, Côte-d'Or
Ecclesia Sancti Juliani de Meva	Mesves-sur-Loire, Nièvre
Ecclesia Sancti Martini de Garchiaco	*Garchy, Nièvre*

[1] Deshoulières in *Bull. Mon.* xc, 1931, p. 8.
[2] For this and subsequent churches see Bernard and Bruel, v, 204.
[3] For this and subsequent churches, see Bernard and Bruel, v, 434.
[4] This and the subsequent churches are taken from R. de Lespinasse, *Cartulaire du prieuré de La Charité*, p. 424.

Ecclesia Sancti Symphoriani de castro novo	? Châteauneuf-Val-de-Bargis, Nièvre
Ecclesia Sancti Symphoriani de Chasneio	Chasnay, Nièvre
Ecclesia Sancti Aniani de Nannayo	Nannay, Nièvre
Ecclesia Sancti Germani de Vergeriis	Les Vergers, Nièvre
Ecclesia de Sancta Colomba	Sainte-Colombe, Nièvre
Ecclesia de Arida bursa	Arbourse, Nièvre
Ecclesia de Șella supra Niverim	La Selle-sur-Nièvre, Nièvre
Ecclesia Sancti Egidii de Ravello	Raveau, Nièvre
Ecclesia B. Mariae de Perroyo	Perroy, Nièvre
Ecclesia Sancti Sulpitii Montis Leonardi	La Chapelle-Montlinard, Cher
Ecclesia Sancti Leodegarii parvi	Saint-Léger-le-petit, Cher
Ecclesia de Argenveriis	Argenvières, Cher
Ecclesia Sancti Marcelli de Muneto	Munot, Nièvre
Ecclesia de Corvolio, alias Corvou Dambenard, Saint-Gengoulx	Corvol-d'Embernard, Nièvre
Ecclesia de Chavanna, alias Chaunes	*Chevannes, Nièvre*
Ecclesia Sancti Aniani de Sex campis	Sichamps, Nièvre
Ecclesia de Lady	Lady, Seine-et-Marne
Ecclesia Sancti Justi	Saint-Just-Sauvage, Marne
Ecclesia de Bagneux	Bagneux, Marne

Through Berry

Ecclesia de Berriaco	Berry, Cher
Ecclesia de Preciaco	Précy, Cher
Ecclesia de Sevriaco	Sévry, Cher
Ecclesia de Louroux	Not identified

Through Biches

Ecclesia de Bischiis	Biches, Nièvre
Ecclesia de Tinturiaco	*Tintury, Nièvre*
Ecclesia de Limentone	Limon, Nièvre
Ecclesia Sanctae Fidis de Pouilliaco	Pouilly-sur-Loire, Nièvre
Ecclesia de Royaco	Not identified

Through Orouer

Ecclesia de Oratorio	
Ecclesia Censellis	Not identified
Ecclesia Sancti Conis[1]	? At La Charité-sur-Loire
Capella Sanctae Annae	? At La Charité-sur-Loire
Ecclesia Sancti Vincanii	? At La Charité-sur-Loire
Ecclesia Sancti Nicasii	? At La Charité-sur-Loire
Ecclesia Sancti Andreae in vico ferrorum	? At La Charité-sur-Loire
Ecclesia Sancti Stephani in vico deliatorum	? At La Charité-sur-Loire
Ecclesia Sancti Petri	? At La Charité-sur-Loire
Ecclesia Sancti Conis in vico Pelliparuorum	? At La Charité-sur-Loire
Ecclesia Sancti Petri de Castro	? At La Charité-sur-Loire

[1] This and the subsequent churches are taken from Brugelès, *Grand Pouillé des bénéfices de France*, 1626.

Ecclesia Sancti Germani de Igneville	?? Ignauville, Seine-Inférieure
Ecclesia de Bauilla	?? Baville, Seine-et-Oise
Ecclesia in Homma	Not identified
Ecclesia Sancti Nicolai de Magno Alueto	Not identified
Ecclesia de Ampevilla qua dicitur du Plain Bost	Not identified
Ecclesia de Bondalle	Not identified
Ecclesia Sancti Andoeni supra Sigi	Not identified
Ecclesia de Moranuilla	? Moranville, Meuse, *or Morainville, Eure*
Ecclesia de Rocheillores supra vinarum	Not identified
Ecclesia de figiaco	Not identified
Ecclesia de Martinuilla	? Martainville, Calvados
Ecclesia de Pierreval	Pierreval, Seine-Inférieure
Ecclesia de Quinquam poist	Quincampoix, Seine-Inférieure
Ecclesia de Minospiolio	Not identified
Ecclesia de Calleyo	Not identified
Ecclesia de Altareriis	Not identified
Ecclesia Cantus Luppi	Canteleu, Seine-Inférieure
Ecclesia de Espinetto	Not identified
Ecclesia de Lerquint	Not identified
Ecclesia de Perolio	Not identified
Ecclesia de Manenio	Not identified
Ecclesia de Cassonuille	Not identified
Ecclesia de Piris	Not identified
Ecclesia de Cymarre	Not identified
Ecclesia de Crenonuilla	Not identified
Ecclesia de Ymouilla	? Ymonville, Eure-et-Loir
Ecclesia de Vaillette	Not identified
Ecclesia de Coruile	Corville, Eure
Ecclesia de Gallifontanis	Not identified
Ecclesia de Aquosis	Not identified
Ecclesia de Vachiaco	? Vachy, Yonne
Ecclesia de Voulleio	Not identified
Ecclesia de Frayo	Not identified
Ecclesia de Saldomonte	Not identified
Ecclesia Sancti Albini Desurba	Not identified
Ecclesia de Transieres	Transières, Eure
Ecclesia de Tresencurtis	? Le-Petit-Tressancourt, Seine-et-Oise
Ecclesia de Genovefa	Not identified
Ecclesia de Camaio	Not identified
Ecclesia de Garema	Not identified
Ecclesia de Villaribus	? Villars, Eure, *or* Villars, Eure-et-Loir
Ecclesia de Romilla	? Romilly, Eure
Ecclesia de Cambray	Cambray, Eure-et-Loir
Ecclesia Sancti Aquillini	Saint-Aquilin-d'Augerons, Eure, *or* Saint-Aquilin-de-Pacy, Eure
Ecclesia de Venon	Venon, Eure

Ecclesia de Albodio	Not identified
Ecclesia Sancti Desiderii	? Saint-Didier-des-Bois, Eure
Ecclesia de Monte Aureo	Not identified
Ecclesia de Leriaco	*Léry, Eure*
Ecclesia de Valolio	Not identified
Ecclesia Bellimontis in Algia	*Beaumont-en-Auge, Calvados*
Ecclesia Sancti Elodoaldi	Not identified
Ecclesia de Peimes de Pis	Not identified
Ecclesia de Ficquesflen	*Fiquefleur-Équainville, Eure*
Ecclesia de Trequeuille	Not identified
Ecclesia de Theeya	Not identified
Ecclesia B. Mariae de veteri Burgo	Not identified
Ecclesia de Sacrauilla	?? Sacquenville, Eure
Ecclesia de Orueto	? Orveau, Eure
Ecclesia de Mamilla	Not identified
Ecclesia de Boucheuilla	Bouchevilliers, Eure
Ecclesia de Rotz	Not identified
Ecclesia Sancti Martini de Bosco	? Saint-Martin-des-Bois, Loir-et-Cher
Ecclesia de Merillo Migerii	Not identified
Ecclesia de Condeto super Auxone	*Condé-sur-Aisne, Aisne*
Ecclesia de Sausiaco	? Saussy, Côte-d'Or

Dependent on Charlieu [1]

Saint-Bonnet-de-Cray, Saône-et-Loire	*Saint-Pierre-de-Thizy, Rhône*
Saint-Martin-de-Cublise, Rhône	Saint-Sulpice-de-Montagny, Loire

Dependent on Coincy

Binson [2], *Aisne*	Janvillers, Marne [6]
Breny, Aisne [3]	Joncourt, Aisne [5]
Breuil, Aisne [4]	Magny-la-fosse, Aisne [5]
Celles [2], Haute-Marne	Mesleroy, Marne [5]
Chartèves, Aisne [4]	Rocourt, Aisne [6]
Châtillon [2], Aisne	Ronchères, Aisne [5]
Condé-en-Brie [2] (Saint-Remi), Aisne	Saint-Eugène, Aisne [5]
Corrobert, Marne [4]	Saint-Léger, Aisne [5]
Crézancy [5] (Sainte-Marie), Aisne	Saponay, Aisne [5]
La Croix (Notre-Dame), Aisne [6]	*Sermoise, Aisne* [6]
Dormans, Marne [6]	Vauciennes [5], Marne, *or* Vauciennes, Oise
Épaux (Saint-Médard), Aisne [6]	Veuilly-la-Poterie, Aisne [6]
Etrepilly, Aisne [6]	

[1] Thiollier, *Art roman à Charlieu*, p. 22.
[2] A. Audry, "Coincy à travers les âges", in *Ann. de la Soc. hist. et arch. de Château-Thierry*, 1912, p. 1.
[3] Given to Coincy in 1180.
[4] E. Lefèvre-Pontalis, *Architecture religieuse de l'ancien diocèse de Soissons*, I, 18.
[5] Audry, *loc. cit.*   [6] Lefèvre-Pontalis, *loc. cit.*

Dependent on Saint-Arnoul-de-Crépy-en-Valois

Bonneuil-en-Valois[1], Oise
Garmegny[2] (not identified)
Largny[3], Aisne

Retheuil, Aisne[4]
Reynel[2], Haute-Marne
Villers-sous-Roye[2], Oise

Dependent on Élincourt[2]

Bolonia	Bologne, Haute-Marne
Hadinllier	Not identified
Waches	Not identified
Sancti Hilarij de Condun	Not identified
Loucquières	Not identified
B. Mariae de Conduno	Not identified
Marigny supra Mass:	Not identified
Vandelicourt	Vandélicourt, Oise
Brana	Not identified
Sancti Ammosii de Conduno	? Condun, Oise
Gardinis in Conduno	Not identified
Capella de Massa	Matz, Oise
Capella de Bellouisa	Not identified
Ressomo supra Mass:	*Réssons-sur-Matz, Oise*

Dependent on Encre (Albert)

Cura Sanctorum Geruasii et Prothasii ipsius loci	Albert, Somme
Cura Sancti Serrei, Episcopi et Confessoris, de Auelluis	Aveluy, Somme
Cura Sancti Martini de Wadencourt	Vadencourt, Somme
Cura Sancti Martini de Englesbermer, et Witermont	Englebelmer, Somme, and Vitermont, Somme
Cura Sancti Firmini de Milancourt	Millencourt, Somme
Cura Sanctorum Nicolai et Egidij de Mesnillo, et Martinssart	Mesnil-Martinsart, Somme
Cura Sancti Vedasti de Becordel et Becourt	Bécourt-Bécordel, Somme
Cura Sancti Honorati de Bouzincourt et Rancourt	Bouzincourt, Somme, and Rancourt, Somme
Cura Sancti Vincentij de Ouillé et Boisselle	Ovillers and La Boiselle, Somme
Cura B. Mariae de Beaumont et Hamel	Beaumont-Hamel, Somme
Quenillier[2]	? Quevilly, Seine-Inférieure
Bonsincourt[2]	
Malencourt[2]	? Malincourt, Nord
Vaudencourt[2]	*Vaudancourt, Oise*

[1] Given to Crépy in 1053. See E. Lefèvre-Pontalis, *Architecture religieuse de l'ancien diocèse de Soissons*, I, 11.
[2] Brugelès, *Grand Pouillé des bénéfices de France*, 1626.
[3] Given to Crépy in 1118. See E. Lefèvre-Pontalis, *op. cit.* II, 59.
[4] E. Lefèvre-Pontalis, *op. cit.* I, 219.

Dependent on Ganagobie[1]

Saint-Pierre, nr. Pierrerue, Basses-Alpes Saint-Michel, nr. Thoard, Basses-Alpes

Dependent on Gassicourt[2]

Ecclesia Soundrie *or* Soimdrie	Soindres, Seine-et-Oise
Ecclesia de Joyacho	Not identified
Ecclesia de Boneriis	Bonnières, Seine-et-Oise
Ecclesia de Salleio	La Sallée, Seine-et-Oise
Fontanetum mali vicini[3]	Fontenay Mauvoisin, Seine-et-Oise
Perdrenuilla[3]	Perdreauville, Seine-et-Oise

Dependent on Saint-Victor, Geneva

Ecclesia de Chisenai[4]

Dependent on Gigny[5]

Andelot, Jura	Joudes, Saône-et-Loire
Beaufort, Jura	Jouvençon, Saône-et-Loire[6]
La Boissière, Jura	Loyons (Saint-Julien), Ain
Chambéria, Jura	Loysia, Jura
La Chapelle-Naude, Saône-et-Loire	Louvenne, Jura
Chatonnay, Jura	La Madeleine-sous-Cuiseaux, Saône-et-Loire
Civria, Jura	
Condal, Saône-et-Loire	Malefreta (not identified)
Cousance, Jura	*Marigna, Jura*
Cressia, Jura	Monnetay, Jura
Cuiseaux, Saône-et-Loire	Montagna le Templier, Jura
Cuisia, Ain	Moutier-Hautepierre, Doubs
Cuisia, Jura	Nantey, Jura
Digna, Jura	Pressia, Ain
Dommartin, Ain	Pymorin (not identified)
Dramelay, Jura	Romonay, Saône-et-Loire
Épy, Jura	Rosay, Jura
Étrée (? Doubs)	Sainte-Croix, Saône-et-Loire
Foissia, Ain	Saint-Jean-des-Treux, Jura
Frontenaud, Saône-et-Loire	Saint-Julien-sur-Suran, Jura
Germagna, Ain	Saint-Maurice-près-Clairvaux, Jura
Graye, Jura	Saint-Remi-du-Mont, Ain

[1] C. Bernard, "Notice historique sur Ganagobie", in *Bull. de la soc. scient. et litt. des Basses-Alpes*, XIV, 1909–10, p. 134. Digne.
[2] Bernard and Bruel, v, 577; in 1168.
[3] Brugelès, *Grand Pouillé des bénéfices de France*, 1626.   [4] Bernard and Bruel, v, 730; in 1198.
[5] Gaspard, *Histoire de Gigny*, pp. 37, 510; *Supplément à l'Histoire de Gigny*, p. 18.
[6] Given to Gigny in 981. Charmasse, p. 84.

Dependent on Gigny (cont.)

Saint-Sulpice, Ain	Veria, Jura
Thoulonjon, Saône-et-Loire	Verjon, Ain
Varennes-Saint-Sauveur, Saône-et-Loire	Villechantria, Jura

Dependent on Gournay [1]

Cura sancti Arnulphi, dicti loci de Gornayo	Gournay-sur-Marne, Seine-et-Oise
Cura de Noisiello	Noisiel, Seine-et-Marne
Cura de Bercheriis	La Berchère, Seine-et-Oise
Cura de Pontels	Le Pontel, Seine-et-Oise
Cura de Essona	*Essonnes, Seine-et-Oise*
Cura de Roissiaco in Bria	Roissy, Seine-et-Oise
Cura de Oratorio, subtus montem Gayum	Montgé, Seine-et-Marne

Dependent on Innimont [2]

Conzieu, Ain	Prémillieu, Ain
Peyrieu, Ain	Rossillon, Ain
Prémeyzel, Ain	Saint-Baudil (Saint-Boys), Ain

Dependent on Layrac [3]

Ecclesia Sancti Saturnini	Layrac, Lot-et-Garonne
Ecclesia Sancti Petri de Cals (Casales)	Not identified
Ecclesia Sancti Vincentii de Avezag (Veziacus)	? Auzat, Ariège
Ecclesia Sancti Vincentii de Preissag (Pressiacus)	*Preyssas, Lot-et-Garonne*
Ecclesia Sanctae Marie de Manzovilla	*Mansonville, Tarn-et-Garonne*
Ecclesia Sancti Gervasii de Cirsol	Not identified
Ecclesia Sanctae Mariae et Sancti Saturnini in Siriniaco	Not identified
Ecclesia Sanctae Mariae in Silva	Not identified

Dependent on Lézat [4]

Saint-Christaud-de-Volvestre, Haute-Garonne

Dependent on Ligny

Cura Sanctorum Viti, Modesti atque Crescentiae, ipsius loci de Ligniaco	Ligny-sur-Canche, Pas-de-Calais
Cura Sancti Hilarij de Feruent, Morinen. seu Bolonien. dioecesis	Not identified
Cura sancti Martini de Vis, Ambianensis dioecesis	? Wismes or Wisques, Pas-de-Calais

[1] Marrier.
[2] L. Joly, "Le prieuré de Saint-Pierre-d'Innimont", in *Bull. de la Soc. Gorini*, x, 1913, pp. 15, 164. Bourg.
[3] Bernard and Bruel, iv, 481; in 1062; and 503, in 1064.   [4] Mortet, i, 178.

Dependent on Lihons [1]

Foncancourt	Foucaucourt, Somme
Hellenuille	Hellenvilliers, Eure
Chaignolles	Chaignolles, Eure
Prognost	Not identified
Boussieres	? Boussières, Nord
Harbonnieres	Harbonnières, Somme
Bethisi	Béthisy, Oise
Rembempie	? Rubempré, Somme
Halu	? Haloup, Aisne
Fonquecourt	See Foncancourt above
Cointenchy	Not identified
Foudramps	?? Fouencamps, Somme
Thory	Thory, Somme
Sanlis	Senlis, Somme
Thielval	Not identified
Gentelle	Gentelles, Somme
Cans	Not identified

Dependent on Longpont [2]

Auffargis, dioc. Chartres	Auffargis, Seine-et-Oise
Bondouste, dioc. Paris	? Bondoufle, Seine-et-Oise
Champlans	Champlans, Seine-et-Oise
Floriac	Not identified
Mont-hery	Not identified
Nogen	Nogent, Seine-et-Oise
Ecclesia de Pacquensiis	Not identified
Orcey	Orsay, Seine-et-Oise
Orengeac	Not identified

Dependent on Sainte-Foy-de-Longueville

Ancourteville-sur-Héricourt, Ourville, Seine-Inférieure [3]

Angiens (Saint-Martin), Fontaine-le-Dun, Seine-Inférieure [3]

Anquetierville, Seine-Inférieure [4]

Auppegard, Seine-Inférieure [3]

Beaumont, ? Beaumont-en-Auge, Calvados [3]

Blancmesnil, Seine-Inférieure [4] (chapel)

Bois Hulin, Seine-Inférieure [3]

Le Bosc-le-Hard (Saint-Jean), Seine-Inférieure [5]

Canteleu, Seine-Inférieure [3]

Colmesnil, Seine-Inférieure [3]

Croisy-sur-Andelle, Seine-Inférieure [3]

Équiqueville (Saint-Vaast), Seine-Inférieure [3]

Héberville, Seine-Inférieure [3]

Leure (Saint-Nicolas), Le Havre, Seine-Inférieure [3]

[1] Brugelès, *Grand Pouillé des bénéfices de France*, 1626.
[2] Brugelès, *op. cit.*
[3] P. le Cacheux.
[4] Brugelès, *op. cit.*
[5] Brugelès, *op. cit.*, gives this as Bois Ricard.

Dependent on Sainte-Foy-de-Longueville (cont.)

Manéglise, Seine-Inférieure[1]
Menonville, Seine-et-Oise[3]
Mesnil-Rury, Seine-Inférieure[2]
Neuville-lès-Dieppe, Seine-Inférieure[1]
Ocqueville, Seine-Inférieure[1]
Offranville, Dieppe, Seine-Inférieure[1]
Ouville-la-Rivière, Seine-Inférieure[1]
Petiville, Lillebonne, Seine-Inférieure[1]
La Prée, Saint-Martin-Osmonville, Saint-Saëns, Seine-Inférieure[1]

Sainte-Foy[1] (not identified)
Sainte-Geneviève[3] (not identified)
Saint-Jouin-sur-Mer, Criquetot l'Esneval, Seine-Inférieure[1]
Saint-Mards, Eure[1]
Saint-Pierre-en-Val, Seine-Inférieure[1]
Tôtes (Sainte-Geneviève), Seine-Inférieure[1]
Vamevilla[3] (not identified)
Vaudreville, Longueville, Seine-Inférieure[1]

In England

Horowldam	? Harrold, Beds.
Niwentonam	Newton Longueville, Bucks.
Wadona	Whaddon, Bucks.
Westona	Weston Longueville, Norfolk
Wichinghehan	Witchingham, Norfolk

Dependent on Marcigny

Ecclesia Sancti Petri	Marcigny, Saône-et-Loire
Ecclesia Sancti Nicetii	Marcigny, Saône-et-Loire
	Saint-Julien-de-Avry, Saône-et-Loire[4]
	Varennes l'Arconce, Saône-et-Loire

Dependent on Moirax[5]

Ecclesia de Albar	Not identified
Ecclesia Sancti Amancii ad portum de Agenno	Agen, Lot-et-Garonne
Ecclesia de Launiano	Not identified
Ecclesia Sancti Lupercii	In episcopatu Basatensi

Dependent on Moissac[6]

Ecclesia de Alcionis	Dioc. Lectoure
Ecclesia de Arduno	Ardus, Lamothe-Capdeville, Tarn-et-Garonne
Ecclesia de Auriols	Lauriol, Auvillar, Tarn-et-Garonne (destroyed)
Ecclesia de Besingis	Bessens, Castelsarrasin, Tarn-et-Garonne
Ecclesia Sancti Petri Biuli	Bioule, Negrepelisse, Tarn-et-Garonne
	Saint-Pierre-de-Blagnac, Toulouse, Haute Garonne
Ecclesia de Sancta de Blanqueto	Blanquet, Mouchan, Gers
Ecclesia Sancti Petri de Bodor	Bodor, Moissac, Tarn-et-Garonne
Ecclesia Sancti Petri de Brugariis	Bruyères, Cazes Mondenard, Tarn-et-Garonne
	Saint-Pierre-de-Burlats, Roquecombe, Tarn

[1] P. le Cacheux.
[3] Brugelès, op. cit.
[5] Bernard and Bruel, IV, 174; in 1049.

[2] Brugelès gives this as Mesnil Remy.
[4] Charmasse, p. 84.
[6] Rupin, p. 181 et seqq.

Ecclesia de Castro Mariano	Castelmayran, Saint-Nicolas-de-la-Grave, Tarn-et-Garonne
Ecclesia de Calsiada	Caussade, Montauban, Tarn-et-Garonne (Notre-Dame and Saint-Audouin, two churches)
Ecclesia Sancti Petri de Cazer	Cazes Mondenard, Tarn-et-Garonne
Ecclesia de Corduba	? Cordes, Tarn-et-Garonne
Ecclesia de Cogornaco	Cougournac, Puycornet, Molières, Tarn-et-Garonne
Ecclesia de Doma	Domme, Sarlat, Dordogne
	Endayssac, nr. Villeneuve-en-Rouergue, Aveyron
Ecclesia de Angarriaco	Engayrac, Beauville, Lot-et-Garonne
Ecclesia Sancti Juliani de Affiniano *or* Affiniaco	Finhan, Montech, Tarn-et-Garonne
Ecclesia de Flamalingis	Flamarens, Mauvezin, Gers
	Fromensal, Escatalens, Tarn-et-Garonne
	Gandalou, Castelsarrasin, Tarn-et-Garonne
Gavarzas	Not known
Ecclesia de Godorvilla	*Goudourville, nr. Moissac, Tarn-et-Garonne*
Ecclesia de Grata Cumba	Dioc. Cahors
Capella de Guilaran	Guileran, nr. Moissac, Tarn-et-Garonne
Ecclesia Sanctae Mariae de Erma	L'Herm, Catus, Lot
Ecclesia de Gardia	Lagarde-en-Calvère, Saint-Amans-de-Pellegal, Tarn-et-Garonne
	DEPENDENCY
	Saint-Mamet, Tarn-et-Garonne
Ecclesia de Livro	Livran, Caylus, Tarn-et-Garonne
Ecclesia Sancti Stephani de Liciaco, de Lezico	Lizac, nr. Moissac, Tarn-et-Garonne
Ecclesia de Loparecas	Not known
Ecclesia Sancti Lupi de Malause	Malause, Moissac, Tarn-et-Garonne
Ecclesia Sancti Saturnini de Mansionis villa	*Mansonville, Tarn-et-Garonne*
Ecclesia de Marcels	Marcels, Saint-Amans-de-Pelligal, Tarn-et-Garonne
Ecclesia Sancti Johannis de Montalzat	Montalzat, Montpezat, Tarn-et-Garonne
Ecclesia de Monte Inciso, Incenso, *or* de Montrent	Montances, Montrem, Dordogne
Ecclesia de Monte Bertrios, de Monte Berterio, de Montanerio	Montebartier, Tarn-et-Garonne
Ecclesia Sancti Stephani de Montescor	Montescot, Moissac, Tarn-et-Garonne
Ecclesia de Monte ricozo	Montricoux, Nègrepelisse, Tarn-et-Garonne
Ecclesia Sancti Petri de Murato	Murat, Cantal
	La Rode, an oratory in Moissac
Ecclesia de Rupercarazera de Rupeceyseria	Roqueserière, Montastruc, Haute-Garonne
Ecclesia Sancti Amantii de Larcisvade	Saint-Amans-de-Lourcinade, Moissac, Tarn-et-Garonne
Capella et Ecclesia Sancti Ansberti	Saint-Ansbert, Moissac, Tarn-et-Garonne
Ecclesia Sancti Christophori	Saint-Christophe, Moissac, Tarn-et-Garonne

Ecclesia Sancti Quiriaci	*Saint-Cirice, Auvillar, Tarn-et-Garonne*
Ecclesia Sancti Clari	Saint-Clair, Valence, Tarn-et-Garonne
Ecclesia Sancti Clari de Varennis	Saint-Clar-de-Varennes, Lectoure, Gers
Ecclesia Saint-Fructueux	Probably Fronton, Haute-Garonne
	Saint-Germain-de-Moissac, Tarn-et-Garonne
	Saint-Germain-sur-Garonne, in Villelongue (Castelsarrasin), Tarn-et-Garonne
Ecclesia Sancti Hilarii	Probably Allanche, Mauriac, Cantal
Ecclesia Sancti Hilarii	Another, prob. dep. Saint-Cirice, Tarn-et-Garronne
	Saint-Jacques-de-Moissac, Tarn-et-Garonne
Ecclesia Sancti Johannis de Pertica, de Pergica	Saint-Jean-de-Perges, Labarthe, Tarn-et-Garonne
	Saint-Jean-du-Désert, Segur, Tarn
	Saint-Laurent, Moissac, Tarn-et-Garonne
Ecclesia Sancti Lupi	Saint-Loup, Auvillar, Tarn-et-Garonne
	DEPENDENCIES
	Cristinag (not identified)
	Casterex *or* Castellus (not identified)
	Saint-Martial, Lizac, Moissac, Tarn-et-Garonne
Ecclesia Sancti Martini	Saint-Martin, uncertain
Ecclesia Sancti Martini	Another, Mauroux, Saint-Clar, Gers
Ecclesia Sancti Mauricii	Saint-Maurice, Lafrançaise, Tarn-et-Garonne
	Saint-Michel-de-Moissac, Tarn-et-Garonne
	Saint-Michel-du-Château, Toulouse, Haute-Garonne
Ecclesia Sancti Petri de Tissaco et Sancti Saturnini	Saint-Pierre-de-Tissac et de-Saint-Sernin, Cazes Mondenard, Tarn-et-Garonne
	Saint-Romain, Fauroux, Tarn-et-Garonne
	Saint-Cyprien, Fauroux, Tarn-et-Garonne
Ecclesia Sancti Saturnini de Bosco	Saint-Sernin-de-Bosc, Lauzerte, Tarn-et-Garonne
	Saint-Sernin-de-Sieurac, Tarn
	Saint-Séverin-de-Moissac, Tarn-et-Garonne
	Saint-Séverin-de-Mesme, Cognac, Charente
Ecclesia Sancti Urcisini	Saint-Urcisse, Tréjouls, Tarn-et-Garonne
Ecclesia Sancti Vincentii de Antejaco	Saint-Vincent-d'Antejac, Caussade, Tarn-et-Garonne
Ecclesia Sanctae Liberatae	Sainte-Livrade, Lafrançaise, Tarn-et-Garonne
	Sainte-Marie-de-Laclive, Moissac, Tarn-et-Garonne
	Sainte-Marie-de-Nogarède, Revel, Villefranche
	Sainte-Marie-du-Port, oratory in Moissac, Tarn-et-Garonne
Ecclesia de Sarraciago	Uncertain
Ecclesia de Salx	*Saux, Sauveterre, Tarn-et-Garonne*

Ecclesia Sanctae Mariae Delseffoniac	Senouillac, Caillac, Tarn
Ecclesia Sancti Amantii de Tarrago	*Tayrac, Beauville, Lot-et-Garonne*
Ecclesia de Titiaco	Tissac, Cazes Mondenard, Tarn-et-Garonne
Ecclesia de Verdageria	Verdegas, Brugnac, Lot-et-Garonne
Ecclesia Sancti Johannis de Biarosa	Viarose, Moissac, Tarn-et-Garonne
Ecclesia de Villarich	Villariès, Fronton, Haute-Garonne
Ecclesia dicta de Verrangas	Virangues *or* Virargues, Murat, Cantal

Dependent on Montdidier[1]

Hangest	Hangest-en-Santerre, Somme
Contoirre	Contoire, Somme
Brach	Braches, Somme
Dommerolieu	? Domeliers, Oise
Dompierre	Dompierre, Somme
Herelle	La Hérelle, Oise
Neufville	Not identified
Estaillefay	Not identified
Fresloy	Not identified
Ferrieres	Ferrières, Somme
Ambouiller	? Ambonville, Haute-Marne
Courdemanches	Courdimanche, Seine-et-Oise
Doulencourt	Doulaincourt, Haute-Marne
Saint-Martin, Montdidier	
Saint-Sépulcre, Montdidier	
Saint-Pierre, Montdidier	
Saint-Marc, Montdidier	
Notre-Dame, Montdidier	

Dependent on Nantua[2]

Ecclesia Engiaci	Not identified
Ecclesia Giniaci	
Ecclesia Moies	? Moye, Haute-Savoie
Ecclesia Annisiaci	Annecy, Haute-Savoie
Ecclesia Viriaci parvi	Viry, Haute-Savoie
Ecclesia de Chavornac	Chavornay, Ain
Ecclesia de Paissins	? Les Paissons, Savoie
Ecclesia de Alberjamont	Not identified
Ecclesia de Corcellos	Corcelles, Ain
Ecclesia de Chantre	?? Chindrieux, Savoie
Ecclesia de Sorreires	Not identified
Ecclesia Darlon	?? Ardon, Ain
Ecclesia Doche	Not identified
Ecclesia Biliadi	Not identified
Ecclesia de Chasnas	?? Chêne-en-Semine, Haute-Savoie

[1] Brugelès, *Grand Pouillé des bénéfices de France*, 1626.
[2] Bernard and Bruel, v, 730; in 1198.

Dependent on Nogent-le-Rotrou

Ecclesia Sancti Hylarii super Ioginiae fluvium[1]	? Saint-Hilaire-sur-Yerre, Eure-et-Loir
Boisvillette[2]	Boisvillette, Eure-et-Loir
Condrecelle	Condreceau, Eure-et-Loir
Frazay	*? Frazé, Eure-et-Loir*
Margone	Margon, Eure-et-Loir
Membroles	Membrolles, Loir-et-Cher
Pierre-ficte	Pierrefixte, Eure-et-Loir
Saint-Jean, Nogent-le-Rotrou	
Saint-Hilaire, Nogent-le-Rotrou	
Saint-Laurent, Nogent-le-Rotrou	
Sainte-Marie, Nogent-le-Rotrou	
Saint-Hilaire-des-Noyers, Eure-et-Loir	

Dependent on Paray-le-Monial (and see under *Cluny*)

Curdins[4], Saône-et-Loire	Saint-Jean-de-Maizel-de-Chalon[4], Saône-et-Loire
Dyo[4], Saône-et-Loire	
Hôpital-le-Mercier[4], Saône-et-Loire	Saint-Léger-lès-Paray[4], Saône-et-Loire
Marly-sur-Arroux[4], Saône-et-Loire	*Sassangy (Chassengés), Saône-et-Loire*[3]

Dependent on Saint-Martin-des-Champs, Paris

Cura seu Vicaria perpetua Sancti Iacobi, vulgo de carnificeria, in urbe Parisiensi	Saint-Jacques-la-Boucherie, Paris
Cura Sancti Nicolai de Campis, in urbe Parisiensi, et in ambitu atque septis praefati Prioratus	Saint-Nicolas-des-Champs, Paris
Cura Sancti Laurentii, in suburbio Martiniano Parisiensi	Saint-Laurent, Paris
Cura Sancti Iodoci Parisiis	Saint-Josse, Paris
Cura Sanctorum Egidii et Lupi, in Prioratu sancti Dionysii de Carcere, in hac urbe Parisiensi	Saint-Denis-de-la-Chartre, Paris
Cura de Escouaco	Écos, Eure
Capella de Esanvilla	Essonville, Seine-et-Oise
Cura de Attinvilla	Attainville, Seine-et-Oise
Cura sancti Aquilini de Fontaneto	Fontenay-près-Louvres, Seine-et-Oise
Cura sancti Petri de Bungeiis (alias de Bondis)	Bondy, Seine
Cura Sancti Germani de Penthino	Pantin, Seine
Cura sancti Germani de Drenciaco Magno	Drancy, Seine
Cura sancti Martini de Casteneto	Castenet, Seine

[1] Bernard and Bruel, IV, 698; *c.* 1080.
[2] This and the subsequent churches are from Brugelès, *Grand Pouillé des bénéfices de France*, 1626.
[3] Dickson, p. 293.   [4] Charmasse, p. 84.

Cura de Confluentio	*Conflans-Sainte-Honorine, Seine-et-Oise*
Cura de Clamardo	Clamart, Seine
Cura de Liuryaco	Livry, Seine-et-Oise
Cura de Seuranno	Sevran, Seine-et-Oise
Cura sancti Martini de Nosiaco magno	*Noisy-le-Grand, Seine-et-Oise*
Cura de Balbiniaco	Bobigny, Seine
Cura Sancti Saturnini de Campiniaco	Champigny, Seine
Capellania B. Mariae de Groleyo	Groslay, Seine-et-Oise
Cura de Maroliis	*Marolles, Seine-et-Oise*
Cura de Limogiis	Limoges-Fourches, Seine-et-Marne
Cura de Chalioto	*Châlo-Saint-Mars, Seine-et-Oise*
Cura de Dolomonte	*Domont, Seine-et-Oise*
Cura Sancti Ioannis Baptistae, de Nonuilla	Nonville, Seine-et-Marne
Cura sancti Germani de Erinniaco	Éragny, Seine-et-Oise
Cura sancti Dionysii de Ermenonuilla	Ermenonville, Oise
Cura sancti Iustini de Luperiis	*Louvres, Seine-et-Oise*
Capella Castri de Liuriaco	Livry, Seine-et-Oise
Capella de Condiel	Not identified
Cura de Milliaco	*Milly, Seine-et-Oise*
Cura de Nosiaco Sicco	Noisy-le-Sec, Seine
Cura de Sauigniaco	? Savigny, Aulnay-lès-Bondy, Seine-et-Oise
Cura de Francoruilla	Franconville-la-Garenne, Seine-et-Oise
Cura de Praeriis, Beluacensis dioecesis	Not identified
Cura de Wirma, Bellouacensis dioecesis	? Wismes, Pas-de-Calais
Cura sancti Luciani de Meruaco, Bellouacensis dioecesis	*Méru, Oise*
Capella de Lardieres	Lardières, Oise
Cura de Cresperiis, Carnotensis dioecesis	*Crespières, Seine-et-Oise*
Cura sancti Andreae de Orsonuilla, Carnotensis dioecesis	Orsonville, Seine-et-Oise
Cura B. Mariae de Goullons, Carnotensis dioecesis	Gouillons, Eure-et-Loir
Cura de Roinuilla, Carnotensis dioecesis	*Roinville, Eure-et-Loir*
Cura Sanctorum Gerivasii et Prothasii de Bonnellis, Carnoten. dioec.	Bonnelles, Seine-et-Oise
Cura sancti Hilarii de Behoust, Carnotensis dioecesis	Behoust, Seine-et-Oise
Cura de Hienuilla, Aurelianensis dioecesis	Hienville, Eure-et-Loir
Cura Sancti Simphoriani de Noua-villa Aurelia-nensis dioeces.	Neuville, Loiret
Cura de Bazochiis Galerandis Aurel. dioecesis	*Bazoches-les-Gallerandes, Loiret*
Cura de Fontanis-portu, Senonensis dioecesis	Fontaine-le-Port, Seine-et-Marne
Cura de Cona (seu de Canis), Senonensis dioecesis	Cannes-Écluse, Seine-et-Marne
Cura de Flagiaco, Senonensis dioecesis	*Flagy, Seine-et-Marne*

EA

Cura Sancti Martini de Dormellis, Senonensis dioecesis	*Dormelles, Seine-et-Marne*
Capella de Bellofonte	? Belfonds, Orne; ? *Bellefontaine, Oise*
Cura de Sorde-Villari, Siluanectensis dioecesis	
Cura beatae Mariae de Choisiaco, Meldensis dioecesis	*Choisy-en-Brie, Seine-et-Marne*
Cura de Carnetain, Meldensis dioecesis	Carnetin, Seine-et-Marne
Cura de Malo-respectu, Meldensis dioecesis	Mauregard, Seine-et-Marne
Cura sancti Germani de Aneto, Meldensis dioecesis	Annet, Seine-et-Marne
Cura de Lerniaco, Suessionensis dioecesis	Not identified
Cura Sanctae Gemmae, Suessionensis dioecesis	Sainte-Gemme, Marne
Cura de Gorencourt, prope sanctam Gemmam	
Cura de Nogent l'Artault	*Nogent-l'Artaud, Aisne*
Cura B. Mariae de Chevriaco	Chevry-en-Sereine, Seine-et-Marne
Ecclesia de Frevens[1]	Frévent, Seine-et-Marne
Beaubourg[2], dioc. Paris	Not identified
Lauric[2], dioc. Paris.	Not identified
Caprice[2], dioc. Paris.	Not identified
Chaillon[2]	Not identified
	Saint-Leufroid[2], Eure

Dependent on Payerne

Ecclesia de Terelai[3]	Not identified

Dependent on Peyrissas[4]

Saint-Pierre-d'Adeilhac	Saint-Michel, Obarcium

Dependent on Montierneuf, Poitiers[5]

Ecclesia Sancti Germani	? Poitiers
Capella leprosorum	? Poitiers
Ecclesia Sancti Eparci	? Poitiers
Ecclesia de Pectinaria	? Petignac, Charente
Ecclesia Sancti Pauli	St Paul, Charente
Ecclesia Sancti Nicolai	? St Nicolas, Charente-Inférieure
Ecclesia de Capella Mosterioli	*La Chapelle-Montreuil, Montreuil-Bonnin, Vienne*
Ecclesia de Chiric	Chirac, Charente
Ecclesia de Lerpina	Not identified
Ecclesia de Magnic	Not identified
Ecclesia de Benniaco	Not identified
Ecclesia de Marnic	? Margnac, Charente
Ecclesia de Cormeria	? *Cormery, Indre-et-Loire*
Ecclesia de Boeth	?? Boësse, Deux-Sèvres

[1] Bernard and Bruel, v, 254; in 1112. [2] Brugelès, *Grand Pouillé des bénéfices de France*, 1626.
[3] Bernard and Bruel, v, 730; in 1198.
[4] J. Dedieu, "Le Prieuré de Peyrissas", in *Revue de Comminges*, XXVIII, 1913, p. 65. Saint-Gaudens.
[5] Bernard and Bruel, v, 626; in 1179.

Ecclesia Sancti Vincentii	? Saint-Vincent, Charente
Capella Sepulchri	? Saint-Sépulchre, Charente-Inférieure
Ecclesia de Sartis	? Sart, Deux-Sèvres (and see Capella de Sart below)
Ecclesia de Banzac	Not identified
Ecclesia de Vinast	Vinax, Charente-Inférieure
Ecclesia de Ruella	Ruelle, Charente
Capella de Sart	? Sart, Deux-Sèvres

Dependent on Romainmôtier[1]

Agiez[2]	Not identified
Applez	Not identified
Arnex	Not identified
Ballens	Not identified
Bannens	Bannans, Doubs
Betuaci (? Bethusi)	Not identified
Brethonières	Not identified
Bursinel	Not identified
Cossonay	Not identified
Gimel	Gimel, Switzerland
Gumoens	Not identified
Mollens	Not identified
Sainte-Colombe, Doubs	
Saint-Léodegard, Lully, près Estavayer	
Senarclens	Not identified
Soulens	Not identified
Torclens	Not identified

Dependent on Saint-André-de-Rosans[3]

Ecclesia Sancti Arigii de Rosano	Rosans, Hautes-Alpes

Dependent on Saint-Aurin[4]

Allencourt (not identified)	La Chenale (not identified)
Dannierry (not identified)	

Dependent on Saint-Flour[5]

Bapaume, Haute-Loire	Gourdièges, Cantal
Brossadol (Saint-Georges), Cantal	Oradour (Saint-Étienne), Haute-Loire
Broussac, Cantal	Roueyre (Notre-Dame), Haute-Loire
Courtines, Cantal	*Tiviers, Cantal*
Cussac-en-Planèze, Cantal	

---

[1] F. de Charrière, *Recherches sur le couvent de Romainmôtier*, pp. 16, 210, 214. Lausanne, 1841.
[2] After 1228.
[3] Bernard and Bruel, v, 192; in 1105.
[4] Brugelès, *Grand Pouillé des bénéfices de France*, 1626.
[5] M. Bondet, *Cartulaire du Prieuré de Saint-Flour*, p. cxciv. Monaco, 1910.

Dependent on Saint-Jean-d'Angely[1]

Diocese of Saintes

Ecclesia parrochialis Sancti Petri de Porigniaco	*Pérignac, Charente-Inférieure*
Ecclesia B. Mariae de Louraco	Lonzac, Charente-Inférieure
Ecclesia Sancti Severi prope Tasiacum	? Saint-Sever, Charente-Inférieure
Ecclesia Sancti Radegondi de Talornone	*Talmont, Charente-Inférieure*
Ecclesia B. Mariae de Corma exclusa	*Corme-Écluse, Charente-Inférieure*
Ecclesia Sancti Andreae de Vallero	Not identified
Ecclesia de Campo Petro supra Corrahbonem	Not identified
Ecclesia Sancti Symphoriani de Zanto	Saintes, Charente-Inférieure
Ecclesia B. M. de Trischei	Not identified
Ecclesia Perigni	Périgny, Charente-Inférieure
Ecclesia Sancti Petri de Ucaroyo	Not identified
Ecclesia Sancti Saturnini de Caiboneriis	Cherbonnières, Charente-Inférieure
Ecclesia Sancti Petri de Manstacio	Not identified
Ecclesia Sancti Stephani de Sonaco	*Sonnac, Charente-Inférieure*
Ecclesia Sancti Martini de Esnoda	*Esnandes, Charente-Inférieure*
Ecclesia Sancti Stephani de Yves	Yves, Charente-Inférieure
Ecclesia Sancti Viviani de Bors	Bors, Charente
Ecclesia B. Mariae de Campodolenti	Champdolent, Charente-Inférieure
Ecclesia B. Mariae de Mazerio	? Mazières, Charente
Ecclesia Sancti Germani de Varezia	*Varaize, Charente-Inférieure*
Ecclesia Sancti Vincentii de Fonteneto	*Fontenet, Charente-Inférieure*
Ecclesia B. Mariae de Pricioso	Not identified
Ecclesia Sancti Georgii de Paille	Paillé, Charente-Inférieure
Ecclesia Sancti Joannis Angeriariosensis	Saint-Jean-d'Angely, Charente-Inférieure
Ecclesia Sancti Dionysii de Pinu	Le Pin, Charente-Inférieure
Ecclesia Sancti Nicolai de Courselles	Courcelles, Charente-Inférieure
Ecclesia Sancti Nazarei de Antexaux	Antezant, Charente-Inférieure
Ecclesia Sancti Paradulphi	Saint-Pardoult, Charente-Inférieure
Ecclesia Sancti Clementis de Capella Basen	? La Chapelle-Bâton, Charente-Inférieure
Ecclesia B. Mariae de Jarriis	? Les Jarris, Charente
Ecclesia Sancti Salvatoris de Loraio	*Lozay, Charente-Inférieure*
Ecclesia Sancti Petri de Insula	Saint-Pierre-de-l'Isle, Charente-Inférieure
Ecclesia Sancti Martialis prope Coycertun, alias de Valone	Not identified
Ecclesia Sancti Petri de Sansacc	Sansac, Charente
Ecclesia Reverentii de Corce de Comesissa	Not identified
Ecclesia B. Mariae de Poriciis	Not identified
Ecclesia Sancti Felicis	*Saint-Félix, Charente-Inférieure*
Ecclesia Sancti Xisti de Murone	Muron, Charente-Inférieure
Ecclesia B. Mariae de Charentonario	Charentenay, Charente-Inférieure
Ecclesia Sancti Eutropi de Voulfrion	Not identified

[1] Brugelès, *Grand Pouillé des bénéfices de France*, 1626.

Ecclesia Sancti Georgii de Coustaux	Coustand, Gironde
Ecclesia Sancti Petti (*sic*) de Virones	Not identified
Ecclesia Sancti Macubi extra maios (*sic*) Xantonensis	Saintes, Charente-Inférieure
Ecclesia de Lupi saltu	Dioc. Bordeaux
Ecclesia Sancti Laurentii Medullo.	Not identified

Dependent on Saint-Leu-d'Esserent[1]

Chapelle-Saint-Michel-aux-Bois	Andechy, Somme ⎫
Cauffrey, Oise	Figniéres, Somme ⎭ shared with Montdidier
Avrigny, Oise	

Dependent on Saint-Marcel-lès-Sauzet[2]

Ecclesia de Savatia	Savas, Ardèche

Dependent on Saint-Sernin-du-Port[3]

Cura Sancti Saturnini de Ventiani	Not identified
[Cura] de Salusiaco	*Saou, Drôme*
[Cura] B. Clementis, Uceticensis dioc.	Saint-Clément, Gard
[Cura] de Bastida, Viuariensis diocesis	La Bastide, Ardèche

Dependent on Souvigny

Ecclesia Sancti Pardulfi[4]	Saint-Pardoux, Puy-de-Dôme
Saint-Martin-de-Moyeau[5]	Not identified
Saint-Basolle-de-Chastillon	Châtillon, Allier
Saint-Julien-de-Crassange	Not identified
Saint-Pierre-de-Becay-le-Monial	Bessac-le-Monial, Allier
Saint-Martin-d'Igrande	*Ygrande, Allier*
Saint-Étienne-de-Francesches	*Franchesse, Allier*
Saint-Jacques-de-Lunoise	Not identified
Notre-Dame-de-Vieure	*Vieure, Allier*
Saint-Pierre-de-Vigenoulle	Not identified
Saint-Blaise-de-Vallon	*Vallon-en-Sully, Allier*
Notre-Dame-de-Chappes	*Chappes, Allier*
Saint-Martin-de-Sazeret	Sazeret, Allier
Saint-Maurice-de-Bruxiere	Not identified
Saint-Hilaire	*Saint-Hilaire, Allier*
Saint-Marcel	Saint-Marcel-en-Marcillat, *or* Saint-Marcel-en-Murat, Allier
Saint-Pierre-de-Hirac	Not identified
Saint-Patrocle-de-la-Selle	Not identified

[1] E. Muller, *Le Prieuré de Saint-Leu-d'Esserent; Cartulaire.* Pontoise, 1900–1.
[2] Bernard and Bruel, v, 460; in 1146. [3] Marrier.
[4] Bernard and Bruel, v, 63; in time of Hugh.
[5] This and the subsequent churches are taken from Brugelès, *Grand Pouillé des bénéfices de France*, 1626.

Saint-Hyppolite-dadueuldre	Not identified
Saint-Germain-de-Neuore	Not identified
Saint-Pierre-de-Treban	Treban, Allier
Saint-Pierre-de-Colombier	*Colombier, Allier*
Saint-Martin-de-Cerilly	*Cérilly, Allier*
Saint-Aubin	Saint-Aubin, Allier[1]
Saint-Romul-de-Mesangi	Not identified
Saint-Plaisir	*Saint-Plaisir, Allier*
Saint-Berthomier-de-Brenay	Bresnay, Allier
Saint-Vindrese-de-haute-Riue	*Hauterive, Allier*
Saint-Pierre-de-longe-pree	Longepré, Allier
Saint-Martin-de-Monestay	Monestier, Allier
Saint-Marcel-de-Contigny	Contigny, Allier
Saint-Martin-de-Meillard	Meillard, Allier
Sainte-Madelaine-de-Rougeret	Not identified
Saint-Julian-de-Montegu-le-blain	Montaigu-le-Blin, Allier
Saint-Julien-de-Vaux	Vaux, Allier
Saint-Pierre-de-Lonzac	Lonzat, Allier
Saint-Christophe-de-Soigny-le-Lyon	Not identified
Saint-Sylvain-de-Cour	Not identified
Saint-Pierre-de-Marcy	? Marcy, Nièvre
Notre-Dame-des-Souppes	*? Souppes, Seine-et-Marne*
Saint-Sauveur-de-Bressoles	Bressolles, Allier
Saint-Denis-de-Chemilly	*Chemilly, Allier*
Notre-Dame-de-la-Foy	Not identified
Saint-Martin-de-Cintrac	Cintrat, Allier
Saint-Nicolas-de-Souvigny	Souvigny, Allier
Saint-Pierre-de-Guise	Not identified
Saint-Martin-de-Vomas	Not identified
Haue-Roche	Not identified
Saint-Pierre-de-Sandré	Not identified
Saint-Germain-d'Entrevaux	
Saint-Martin-de-Chantenay	*Chantenay, Nièvre*
Notre-Dame-de-Mars	*Mars-sur-Allier, Nièvre*
Minsac	Mainsat, Creuse

Dependent on Sainte-Marie-de-la-Daurade, Toulouse[2]

Saint-Jacques, suburbs of Toulouse	Sainte-Marie-de-la-Grave, suburbs of Toulouse
Saint-Michel, suburbs of Toulouse	

Dependent on Tours-sur-Marne[3]

Saint-Pierre, Tours-sur-Marne	Sanctae Mariae de Bonzis

[1] Some capitals survive.
[3] Lahondès, *Monuments de Toulouse*, p. 112. Toulouse, 1920.
[2] Brugelès, *Grand Pouillé des bénéfices de France*, 1626.

Dependent on Trémolat[1]

Ecclesia Sancti Petri de Culiaco (? Cussaco)	Cussac, Dordogne
Ecclesia Sancti Medardi de Calesio	Calès, Dordogne
Ecclesia Sancti Petri de Colas	? Collas, Charente
Ecclesia Petri de Jorrefort	Not identified
Ecclesia Maximi de Mont-Malainac	Not identified
Ecclesia Sancti Cypriani	*? Saint-Cyprien, Dordogne*
Ecclesia Sancti Hilarii	? Saint-Hilaire, Dordogne
Ecclesia de Valaro	Not·identified
Ecclesia Sancti Aviti de Vilars	Not identified
Capella de Montcuq	Montcuq, Lot

Dependent on Vézelay[2]

Saint-Martin-de-Dornecy	Dornecy, Nièvre
Saint-Supplice-d'Asnières	Asnières, Yonne
Saint-Germain-de-Fontenay	*Fontenay-près-Vézelay, Yonne*
Saint-Audochene-de-Brosses	Brosses, Yonne
Saint-André-de-Voulteray	? Voutenay, Yonne
Prane	Not identified
Precy-le-Sec	*Précy-le-Sec, Yonne*
Saint-Adrian-de-Mailly-le-Chastel	Mailly-le-Château, Yonne
Saint-Adrian-de-Mailly-la-Ville	Mailly-la-Ville, Yonne
Saint-Guidon-de-Lery	? Léry, Côte-d'Or
Sainte-Marie-Magdelaine-de-Loblane	Dioc. Mâcon
Argenteuil	Argenteuil, Yonne
Saint-Étienne-de-Vézelay	Vézelay, Yonne
Saint-Pierre	Saint-Père-sous-Vézelay, Yonne
Aquien	Not identified
Montubert-de-Saint-Laurent	Not identified
Saint-Philippe	Not identified
Chapelle-de-Barraux	Not identified
Saint-Michel	Not identified
Saint-Liger-de-Forcheray	Saint-Léger-de-Foucherets, Yonne
Saint-Audomare	Not identified
Saint-Denis-de-Saisy	Saisy, Nièvre
Saint-Symphorien-de-Fley	Fley, Saône-et-Loire

BELGIUM

Dependent on Saint-Séverin-en-Condroz[3]

Mosen (not identified)   Herpinei (not identified)

[1] *Dictionnaire topographique de la Dordogne.*   [2] Brugelès, *Grand Pouillé des bénéfices de France*, 1626.
[3] J. Halkin, "Documents concernant le prieuré de Saint-Séverin-en-Condroz, de l'Ordre de Cluny", in *Compte rendu des séances de la Commission Royale d'Histoire*, 5th series, III, 1893, p. 169. Brussels.

ENGLAND

Dependent on Lewes[1]

Baldesdena	Balsdean, Sussex
Balecumba	Balcombe, Sussex
Bercamp	Barcombe, Sussex
Blachinton	West Blachington, Sussex
Bradewell	Not identified
Brittelmeston	Brighton, Sussex (2 churches)
Burgton	Kirkburton, Yorks.
Burneham	Eastbourne, Yorks. (2 churches)
Clayton	*Clayton, Sussex*
Cunningeburg	Conisborough, Yorks.
Dewesbiri	Dewsbury, Yorks.
Dicheling	Ditchling, Sussex
Dorgyng	Dorking, Surrey
Duninton	Dunnington, Yorks.
Erdingelega	Ardingly, Sussex
Feltewella	Feltwell, Norfolk
Fislac	Fislake, Yorks.
Fugeldon	Foulden, Norfolk (2 churches)
Gimmingeham	Gimmingham, Norfolk
Hadlega	*Hoathly, Sussex*
Halifax	Halifax, Yorks.
Hangelton	Hangleton, Sussex
Harpeleye	Harpley, Norfolk
Hertil	Harthill, Yorks.
Hertsueth	Hartshead, Yorks.
Hethfield	Heathfield, Yorks.
Horriby (chapel)	Horbury, Yorks.
Ifford	Iford, Sussex
Kanefelda	*Canfield, Essex*
Kiemera	Keymer, Sussex
Kukefeld	Cuckfield, Sussex
Kyngestona	Kingston by Lewes, Sussex
Lewes, Saint Andrew	Sussex
Lewes, Saint John	Sussex
Lewes, Saint Martin	Sussex
Lewes, Saint Mary	Sussex
Lewes, Saint Nicholas	Sussex
Lewes, Holy Trinity	Sussex
Mecinges	Not identified
Mertona	? Merton, Norfolk

[1] L. F. Salzman, "The Chartulary of the Priory of Saint Pancras of Lewes", *Sussex Record Society*, XXXVIII, 1932, pp. 20 *et seqq.* Lewes.

Niwica	Newick, Sussex
Pengedena	Pangdean, Sussex
Pidingeho	*Piddinghoe, Sussex*
Pincheam	Patcham, Sussex
Punyng	Poynings, Sussex
Radmelde	Rodmell, Sussex
Rising	Wood Rising, Norfolk
Ristona	Not identified
Roinges	High Roding, Essex
Rottingedena	*Rottingdean, Sussex*
Sandale	Sandal, Yorks.
Sireford	*Shereford, Norfolk*
Sotenebr.	Not identified
Stokes	Stokes, Guildford
Sudewerca	Saint Olave's, Southwark
Tetfordia	Thetford, Norfolk (2 chapels)
Thorn	Thorne, Yorks.
Toftes	Tofts, Norfolk
Wakefield	Wakefield, Yorks.
Westona	Weston Colville, Suffolk
Westute, Saint Peter	Saint Peter's, Lewes, Sussex
Westute, Saint Mary	*Saint Mary's, Lewes, Sussex*
Wiltona	Wilton, Norfolk
Wiuelesfeld	*Wivelsfield, Sussex*

Dependent on Montacute[1]

Altrenune	Alternon, Cornwall
Brimetune	Brimpton, Somerset
Clouesword	Not identified
Criche	*? Creech Saint Michael, Somerset*
⎰Gerlingstun	Not identified
⎱Gerlintune	Not identified
Gersich	?? Pengersick, Cornwall
Hunesberg	Not identified
Legh	Lee, Devon
Lerky	Cornwall
Melebire	Melbury, Dorset
Modiforde	Muddiford, Devon
Odecumb	Odcombe, Somerset
Pennard	Pennard, Somerset
Saint Carentoc	Cornwall
Saint Neots	Saint Neot's, Cornwall

[1] *Somerset Record Society*, "Two Cartularies of the Augustinian Priory of Bruton and the Cluniac Priory of Montacute", VIII, 1894, pp. 119 *et seq.*

Sennet	? Sennen, Cornwall
Tintenelle	Tintinhull, Somerset
Wermewell	Warmwell, Dorset

Dependent on Prittlewell[1]

Canewdon, Essex
Clavering, Essex
Eastwood, Essex (chapel)
Great Horkesley, Essex
Langley, Essex
East Mersea, Essex
Nayland, Suffolk (chapel)
Rawreth, Essex

Rayleigh, Essex
Great Shoebury, Essex
Little Shoebury, Essex
Stoke, Suffolk
Sutton, Essex (chapel)
Thundersley, Essex
Wickford, Essex

[1] Anon., "Prittlewell Priory and Museum", *History and Guide*.

PLATES

Fig. 21. Mouthiers, Charente. The Nave. Early twelfth century.

Fig. 20. Vianne, Lot-et-Garonne. The Nave. c. 1090.

Fig. 22. Champmillon, Charente. The Nave. *c.* 1100; the domes
added in the twelfth century.

Fig. 23. Saint-Séverin-en-Condroz, Belgium. The Nave.
Consecrated, 1091.

Fig. 25. Baume-les-Messieurs, Jura. The Nave. The lower part, middle of the eleventh century; the vaults added in the thirteenth century.

Fig. 24. Saint-Nazaire-de-Bourbon-Lancy, Saône-et-Loire. The Nave. *c.* 1040.

Fig. 26. Gassicourt, Seine-et-Oise. The Nave. End of eleventh century.

Fig. 27. Gigny, Jura. The Nave. Eleventh century.

Fig. 28. Saint-Béat, Haute-Garonne. The North Aisle. Late eleventh century.

Fig. 29. Pommiers, Loire. The Nave. Eleventh century.

Fig. 30. Châtelmontagne, Allier. The
Aisle Vault. *c.* 1100.

Fig. 31. Saint-Eutrope-de-Saintes, Charente-Inférieure.
The South Aisle of the Ambulatory 1081–96.

Fig. 32. Saint-Révérien, Nièvre. The Nave.
Early twelfth century.

Fig. 35. Champvoux, Nièvre. The Sanctuary. First half of eleventh century.

Fig. 36. Saint-Hilaire-de-Melle, Deux-Sèvres. The Nave. First half of twelfth century.

Fig. 37. Sémelay, Nièvre. The Nave.
Twelfth century.

Fig. 38 *a*. Cluny, Saône-et-Loire. The interior of the
Abbey Church. Begun in 1088.

Fig. 39. Vézelay, Yonne. The Nave. Begun in 1089.

Fig. 40. Saint-Lazare-d'Avallon, Yonne. The Nave. Consecrated, 1106.

Fig. 41. Saint-Maurice, Vienne. The Nave. *c.* 1100.

Fig. 42. Champdeniers, Deux-Sèvres. The Nave. *c.* 1100.

Fig. 43. Le Moûtier-de-Thiers, Puy-de-Dôme. The Nave. *c.* 1100.

Fig. 44. Moirax, Lot-et-Garonne. The Nave. End of eleventh century.

Fig. 45. Saint-Pierre-le-Moûtier, Nièvre. The Nave. *c.* 1100.

Fig. 46. Souvigny, Allier. The North Aisle. *c.* 1140.

Fig. 8. R. d. C. del Cássaro. Puy de Dôme. The Nave. Second

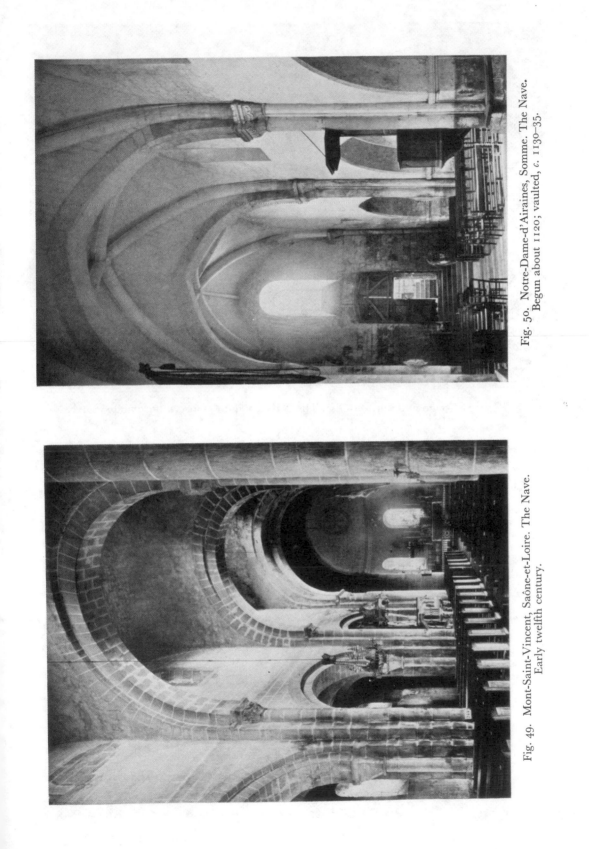

Fig. 50. Notre-Dame-d'Airaines, Somme. The Nave.
Begun about 1120; vaulted, c. 1130–35.

Fig. 49. Mont-Saint-Vincent, Saône-et-Loire. The Nave.
Early twelfth century.

Fig. 51. Longpont, Seine-et-Oise. The Nave. Begun before 1109; vaulted later.

Fig. 52. Marolles-en-Brie, Seine-et-Oise. The Interior. *c.* 1125.

Fig. 53. Beaulieu, Corrèze. The Nave. First half of twelfth century.

Fig. 54. Vézelay, Yonne. The South Aisle and Nave. Begun 1089.

Fig. 56. Saint-Étienne-de-Nevers, Nièvre.
The Nave. Consecrated, 1097.

Fig. 55. Nantua, Ain. The Nave. First half of
twelfth century.

Fig. 57. Saint-Marcel-lès-Chalon, Saône-et-Loire. The Nave. Second half of twelfth century.

Fig. 58. Moirax, Lot-et-Garonne. Pier
Base. Second half of eleventh century.

Fig. 59. Saint-Eutrope-de-Saintes, Charente-
Inférieure. Pier Base. 1081–96.

Fig. 60. Saint-Révérien, Nièvre. Column
Base. Early twelfth century.

Fig. 61. Charlieu, Loire. Column Base.
End of eleventh century.

Fig. 62. Saint-Étienne-de-Nevers,
Nièvre. Column Bases. End of
eleventh century.

Fig. 63. Saint-Marcel-lès-Sauzet, Drôme. Detail
of Pier Base. Second half of twelfth century.

Fig. 64. Castleacre, Norfolk. The West Wall
of the Nave. Consecrated, 1148.

Fig. 65. Souvigny, Allier. Detail of the
Wall of the North Aisle. *c.* 1140.

Fig. 66. Semur-en-Brionnais, Saône-et-Loire.
The West End. Middle of twelfth century.

Fig. 67. Semur-en-Brionnais, Saône-et-Loire. The Nave. Middle of twelfth century.

Fig. 68. Cluny, Saône-et-Loire. The Triforium and Clerestory of the Abbey Church in the surviving transept. Begun 1088.

Fig. 69. La Charité, Nièvre. False Triforium of the Nave. Early twelfth century.

Fig. 70. La Charité, Nièvre. False Triforium of the Nave. Late twelfth century.

Fig. 72. Saint-Sauveur-de-Figeac, Lot. The Nave. Late twelfth century.

Fig. 71. Châtelmontagne, Allier. The Nave. c. 1100.

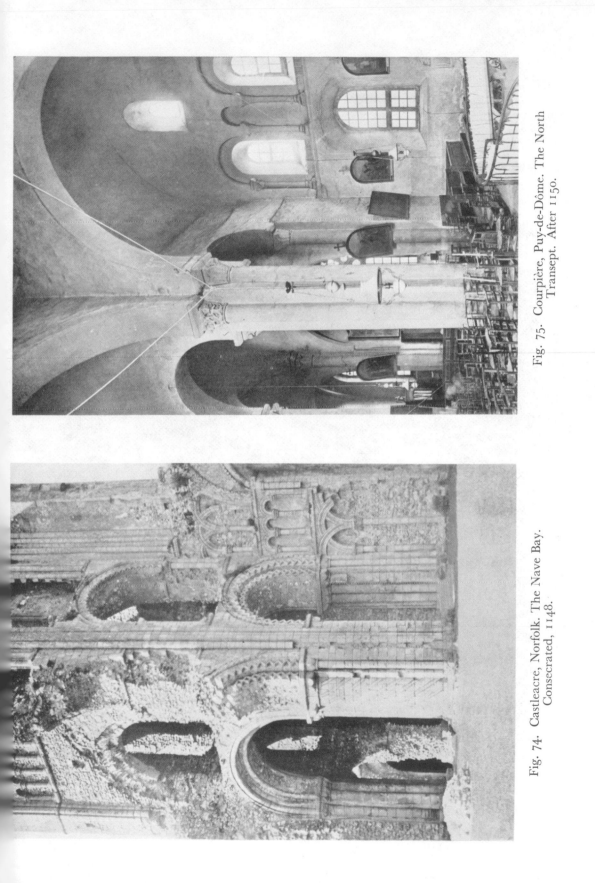

Fig. 75. Courpière, Puy-de-Dôme. The North Transept. After 1150.

Fig. 74. Castleacre, Norfolk. The Nave Bay. Consecrated, 1148.

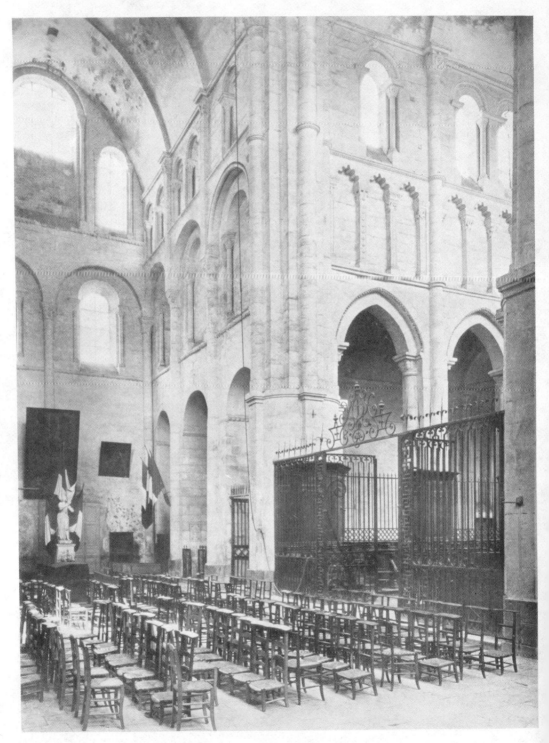

Fig. 76. La Charité, Nièvre. The North Transept. Consecrated, 1107.

Fig. 77. Montbron, Charente. Squinches of the Cupola.
Early twelfth century.

Fig. 78. Compains, Puy-de-Dôme. Squinch
of the Cupola. Twelfth century.

Fig. 79. Saint-Germain-les-Fossés, Allier.
Squinch of the Cupola. Eleventh century.

Fig. 81. Cluny. Section of the surviving Transept, from a drawing by Aymar Verdier, 1850.

Fig. 80. Cluny. The surviving Transept. c. 1100.

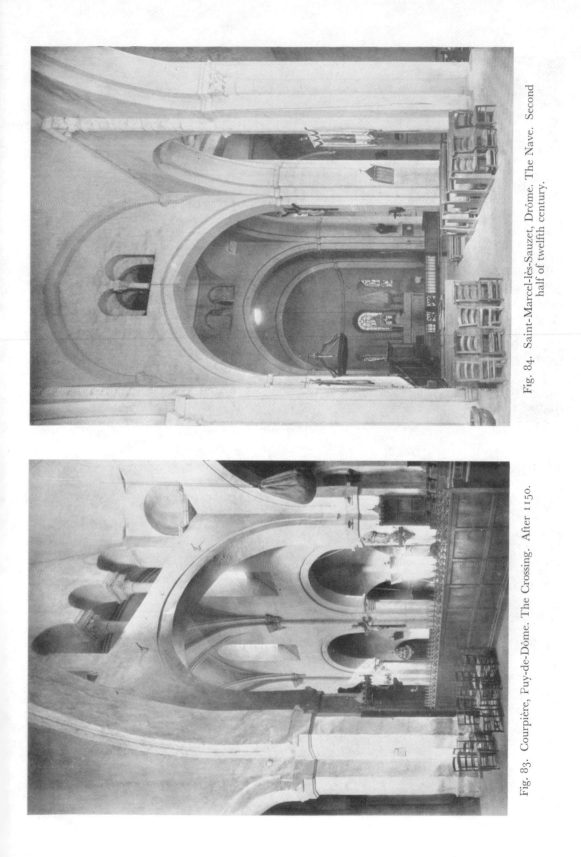

Fig. 84. Saint-Marcel-lès-Sauzet, Drôme. The Nave. Second
half of twelfth century.

Fig. 83. Courpière, Puy-de-Dôme. The Crossing. After 1150.

Fig. 86. Prahecc, Deux-Sèvres. The Crossing, looking north. Twelfth century.

Fig. 85. Nantua, Ain. The Crossing, looking south. Twelfth century.

Fig. 87. Mouchan, Gers. The Crossing Vault, looking east. First half of twelfth century.

Fig. 88. Saint-Sornin, Charente-Inférieure. The Crossing Vault, looking upwards. Early twelfth century.

Fig. 89. Semur-en-Brionnais, Saône-et-Loire. The Crossing, Choir and Apse. Middle of the twelfth century.

Fig. 91. Bourbon-Lancy, Saône-et-Loire. The Apse. *c.* 1040.

Fig. 90. Champvoux, Nièvre. The Apse. Eleventh century.

Fig. 93. Arnac-Pompadour, Corrèze. The Apse.
c. 1105.

Fig. 92. Rouy, Nièvre. The Apse. Middle of
twelfth century.

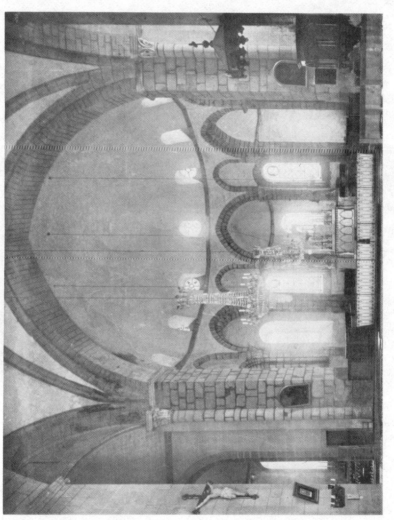

Fig. 94. Vigeois, Corrèze. The Apse. Middle of twelfth century.

Fig. 95. Ternay, Isère. The Apse. Twelfth century.

Fig. 96. Mouchan, Gers. The Arcade of the Choir.
Twelfth century.

Fig. 98. Mornac, Charente-Inférieure. The Choir and Apse. First half of twelfth century.

Fig. 97. Vaux-sur-Mer, Vienne. The Choir and Apse. First half of twelfth century.

Fig. 100. Volvic, Puy-de-Dôme. The Apse. *c.* 1100.

Fig. 99. Moirax, Lot-et-Garonne. The Choir
and Apse. *c.* 1100.

Fig. 101. Cénac, Dordogne. The Apse. *c.* 1090.

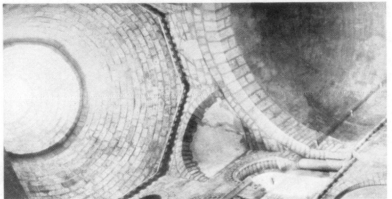

Fig. 103. Moirax, Lot-et-Garonne.
The Choir Vault. c. 1100.

Fig. 102. Mezin, Lot-et-Garonne. The Apse.
First half of twelfth century.

Fig. 105. Cluny. The Ambulatory. *c.* 1095.

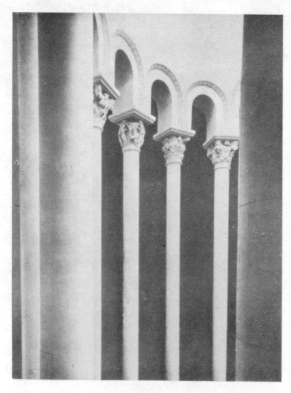

Fig. 106. Cluny. Reconstruction of the Apse.

Fig. 107. Paray-le-Monial, Saône-et-Loire. The Ambulatory.
Consecrated, 1104.

Fig. 108. La Charité, Nièvre. The Apse. Consecrated, 1107.

Fig. 109. Saint-Révérien, Nièvre. Early twelfth century.

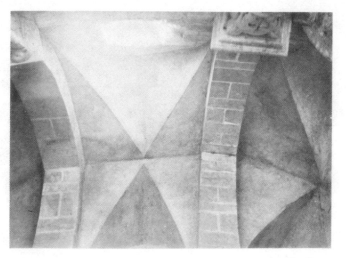

Fig. 110. Saint-Révérien, Nièvre. The Ambulatory Vault.
Twelfth century.

Fig. 112. Paray-le-Monial, Saône-et-Loire. The Ambulatory.
Consecrated, 1104.

Fig. 111. Uzerche, Corrèze. The Apse.
Consecrated, 1098.

Fig. 113. Dun-sur-Auron, Cher. The Ambulatory. Twelfth century.

Fig. 114. La Charité, Nièvre. The Ambulatory. Twelfth century.

Fig. 115. Saint-Martin-des-Champs, Paris. The Ambulatory,
Finished, 1140.

Fig. 116. Saint-Martin-des-Champs, Paris. The Choir.
Finished, 1140.

Fig. 117. Domont, Seine-et-Oise. The Choir. *c.* 1155.

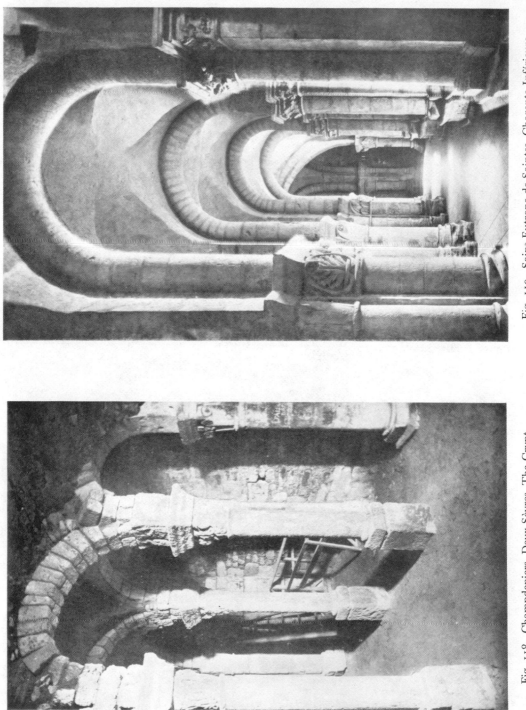

Fig. 119. Sain-Eutrope-de-Saintes, Charente-Inférieure. An Aisle of the Crypt. Dedicated, 1096.

Fig. 118. Champdeniers, Deux-Sèvres. The Crypt. Eleventh century.

Fig. 120. Saint-Eutrope-de-Saintes, Charente-Inférieure. The Crypt. Dedicated, 1096.

Fig. 121. Moissac, Tarn-et-Garonne. The Porch. 1120–25.

Fig. 122. Moissac, Tarn-et-Garonne. Room above the Porch.
1125–30.

Fig. 124. Vézelay, Yonne. The Narthex. Begun, *c.* 1120; dedicated, 1132.

Fig. 123. Romainmôtier, Switzerland. The Galilee, upper floor. *c.* 1100.

Fig. 125. Romainmôtier, Switzerland. The Galilee and Porch.
Twelfth century.

Fig. 126. Saint-Leu-d'Esserent, Oise. The Narthex from within. *c.* 1150.

Fig. 127. Châtelmontagne, Allier. The Façade
of the Narthex. Twelfth century.

Fig. 128. Moûtiers-en-Puisaye, Yonne. The Narthex.
Twelfth century.

Fig. 129. Charlieu, Loire. Room above the Narthex. *c.* 1130.

Fig. 130. Cluny. Marble Slab of the High Altar, dedicated by Pope Urban II, 1095.
(Cluny, Musée Ochier.)

Fig. 131. Notre-Dame-d'Airaines, Somme. Altar. *c.* 1130.

Fig. 133. Saint-Lothain, Jura. The Apse. Eleventh century.

Fig. 132. Champvoux, Nièvre. The Apse. Eleventh century.

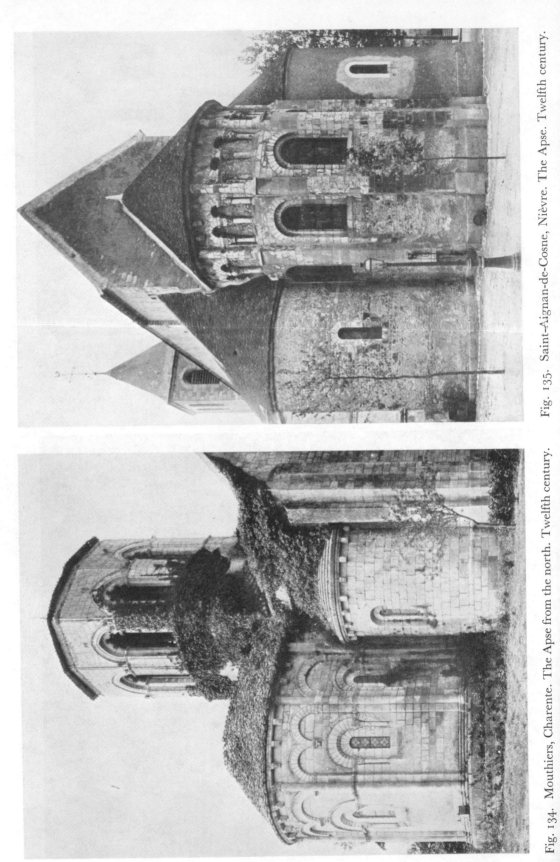

Fig. 135. Saint-Aignan-de-Cosne, Nièvre. The Apse. Twelfth century.

Fig. 134. Mouthiers, Charente. The Apse from the north. Twelfth century.

Fig. 136. Cénac, Dordogne. The Apse. *c.* 1090.

Fig. 137. Moirax, Lot-et-Garonne. The Choir and Apse. *c.* 1100.

Fig. 138. Payerne, Switzerland. The East End. Late eleventh century.

Fig. 139. Semur-en-Brionnais, Saône-et-Loire. The East End. Middle of twelfth century.

Fig. 140. La Charité, Nièvre. The East End. Consecrated, 1107; the lower chapels added later.

Fig. 141. Varaize, Charente-Inférieure. The Apses from the north.
Twelfth century.

Fig. 142. Saint-Maurice, Vienne. The Church from the north. *c.* 1100.

Fig. 143. Talmont, Gironde. The Church from the east. Twelfth century.

Fig. 144. Retaud, Charente-Inférieure. The Apse. Twelfth century.

Fig. 145. Saint-Étienne-de-Nevers, Nièvre. The East End. Before 1099.

Fig. 146. Châtelmontagne, Allier. The East End. *c.* 1100; modified later.

Fig. 147. Reconstruction of the East End of Abbot Hugh's Abbey Church at Cluny.
By Professor K. J. Konant.

Fig. 148. Cluny. The surviving Apsidiole.
c. 1090–*c.* 1105.

Fig. 149. Paray-le-Monial, Saône-et-Loire. The East End before restoration. *c.* 1100.

Fig. 150. Vigeois, Corrèze. The Apse. Twelfth century.

Fig. 151. Saint-Martin-des-Champs, Paris. Detail of the Apse.
Second quarter of twelfth century.

Fig. 152.   Saint-Eutrope-de-Saintes, Charente-Inférieure. The Apse, north side.   1081–96.

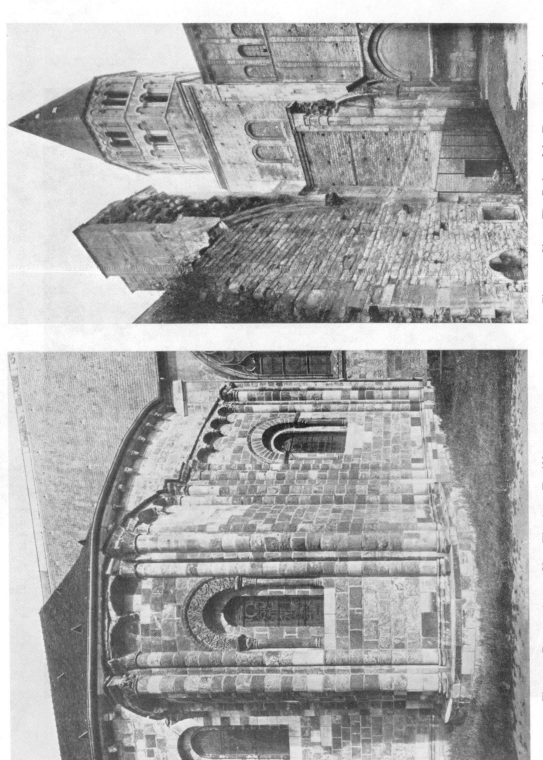

Fig. 154. Cluny. The Ruins of the Transept from the North Aisle. *c.* 1090–*c.* 1105.

Fig. 153. Dun-sur-Auron, Cher. The Apse. Twelfth century

Fig. 156. Chauriat, Puy-de-Dôme. The Transept from the south. Twelfth century.

Fig. 155. Saint-Étienne-de-Nevers, Nièvre. The Transept from the north. Before 1097.

Fig. 157. Paray-le-Monial, Saône-et-Loire. The Transept from the north.
Consecrated, 1104.

Fig. 158. Courpière, Puy-de-Dôme. The Transept from the east. After 1150.

Fig. 159. Noël-Saint-Martin, Oise. Exterior. *c.* 1100.

Fig. 160. Saint-Nazaire-de-Bourbon-Lancy, Saône-et-Loire. Exterior. *c.* 1040.

Fig. 161. Cluny. The Abbey Church. From the drawing made by the
Jesuit Father Martellange in 1617.

Fig. 162. La Souterraine, Creuse. The Exterior. *c.* 1150.

Fig. 163. Trémolac, Dordogne. Exterior. End of eleventh century.

Fig. 164. Payerne, Switzerland. Exterior of the Nave, south side. Eleventh century.

Fig. 156. Berzé-la-Ville, Saône-et-Loire.
St Hugh's Chapel c. 1103.

Fig. 165. Baume-les-Messieurs, Jura.
Exterior of the Nave. 1107–39.

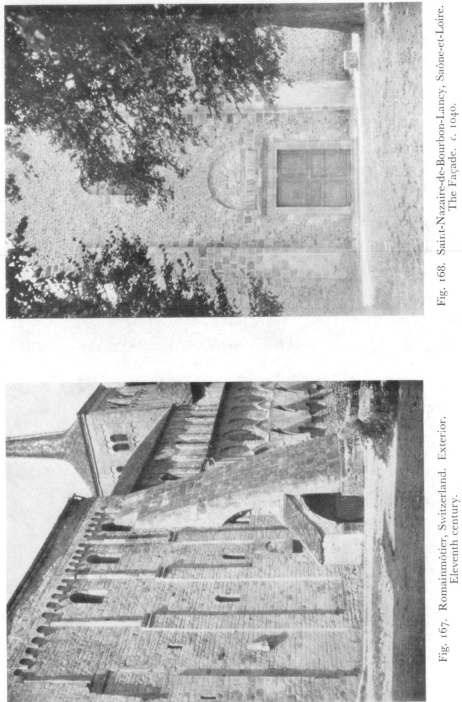

Fig. 168. Saint-Nazaire-de-Bourbon-Lancy, Saône-et-Loire.
The Façade. *c.* 1040.

Fig. 167. Romainmôtier, Switzerland. Exterior.
Eleventh century.

Fig. 170. Notre-Dame-d'Airaines, Somme. The West Front.
c. 1125.

Fig. 169. Saint-Étienne-de-Nevers, Nièvre. West Front.
Before 1097.

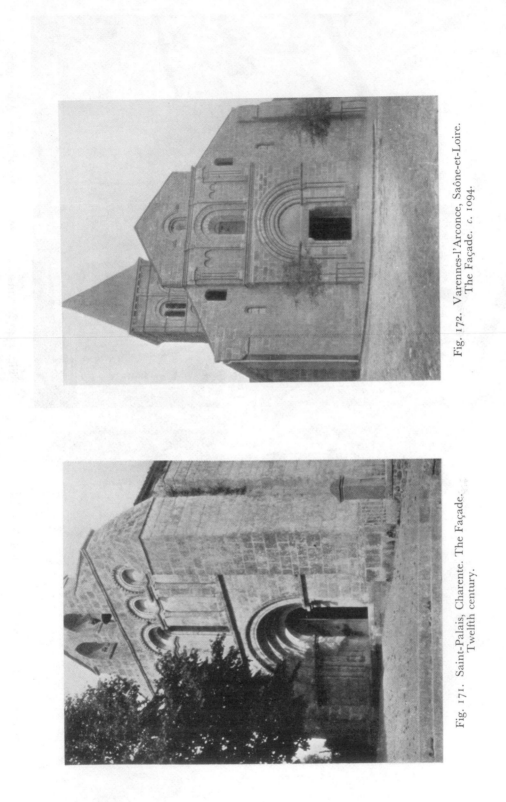

Fig. 172. Varennes-l'Arconce, Saône-et-Loire.
The Façade. c. 1094.

Fig. 171. Saint-Palais, Charente. The Façade.
Twelfth century.

Fig. 174. Meymac, Corrèze. The West Front. After 1085.

Fig. 173. Bellenaves, Allier. The Façade. Twelfth century.

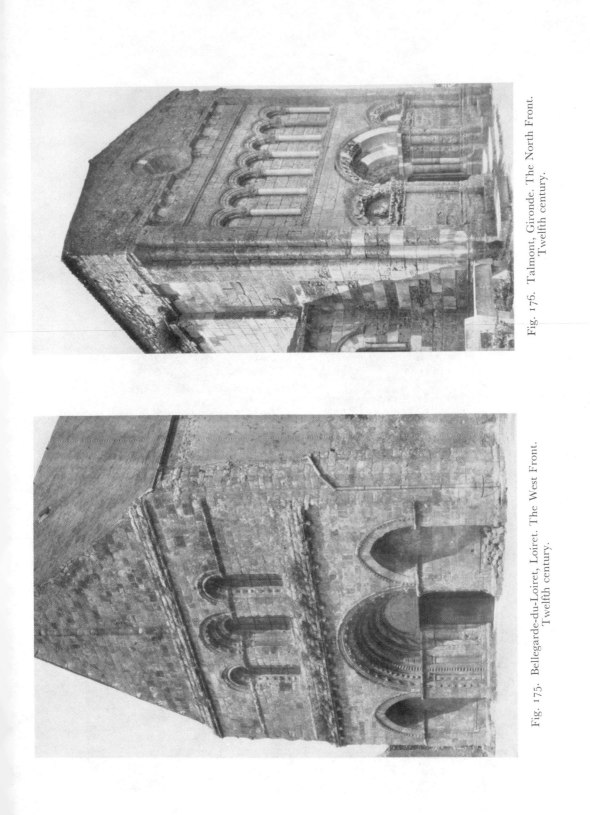

Fig. 176. Talmont, Gironde. The North Front.
Twelfth century.

Fig. 175. Bellegarde-du-Loiret, Loiret. The West Front.
Twelfth century.

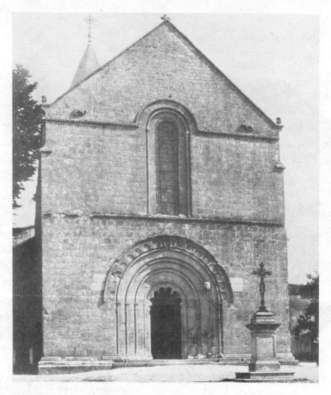

Fig. 177. Montbron, Charente. The West Front. Early twelfth century.

Fig. 178. Oulmes, Vendée. The West Front. End of eleventh century.

Fig. 179. Saint-Gilles, Gard. The Southern Half of the Portal. *c.* 1140.

Fig. 180. Le Douhet, Charente-Inférieure. The West Front. Twelfth century.

Fig. 181. Castleacre, Norfolk. The West Front. Consecrated, 1148.

Fig. 183. Fontaines, Vendée. The West Front.
Twelfth century.

Fig. 182. Corme-Écluse, Charente-Inférieure. The North Front.
Early twelfth century.

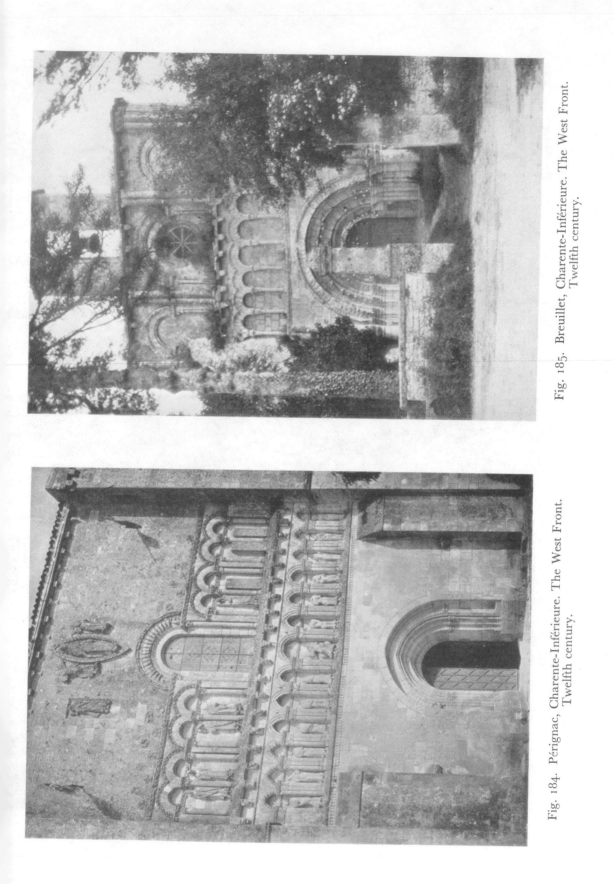

Fig. 185. Breuillet, Charente-Inférieure. The West Front.
Twelfth century.

Fig. 184. Pérignac, Charente-Inférieure. The West Front.
Twelfth century.

Fig. 186. Chalais, Charente. Remains of the West Front. Middle of twelfth century.

Fig. 187. Esnandes, Charente. Remains of the West Front. *c.* 1140.

Fig. 188. Gassicourt, Seine-et-Oise. The Church. End of eleventh century.

Fig. 189. Moirax, Lot-et-Garonne. The West Front, *c.* 1100.

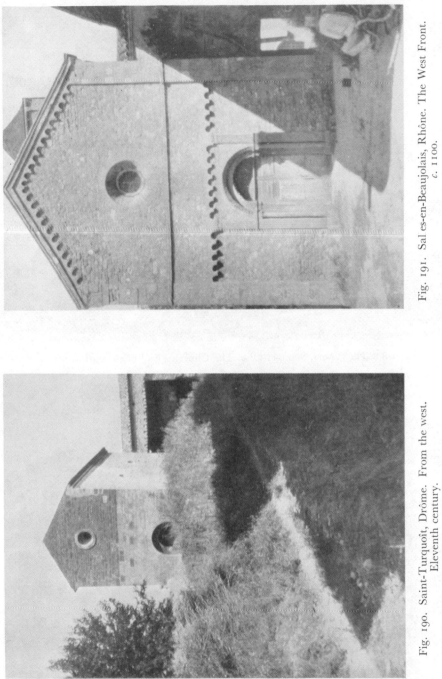

Fig. 191. Sal es-en-Beaujolais, Rhône. The West Front.
c. 1100.

Fig. 190. Saint-Turquoit, Drôme. From the west.
Eleventh century.

Fig. 193. Champmillon, Charente. The West Front. Twelfth century.

Fig. 192. Maillezais, Vendée. Parish Church. The West Front. Twelfth century.

Fig. 194. La Souterraine, Creuse. The Façade. *c.* 1150.

Fig. 195. Paray-le-Monial, Saône-et-Loire. Façade of the Narthex.
Eleventh century.

Fig. 196. Saint-Leu-d'Esserent, Oise. Façade. *c.* 1150.

Fig. 197. Charlieu, Loire. The Portal of
the Church. Consecrated, 1094.

Fig. 198. Marcigny, Saône-et-Loire.
The Portal. *c.* 1100.

Fig. 199. Fontenet, Charente-Inférieure. The Portal. Twelfth century.

Fig. 200. Château-Larcher, Vienne. The Portal. Twelfth century.

Fig. 201. Lurcy-le-Bourg, Nièvre.
The Portal. Twelfth century.

Fig. 202. Rouy, Nièvre. The Portal.
Second half of twelfth century.

Fig. 203. Le Breuil-sur-Couze, Puy-de-Dôme.
The Portal. Twelfth century.

Fig. 204. Bredons, Cantal. The Portal.
Consecrated, 1095.

Fig. 205. Semur-en-Brionnais, Saône-et-Loire. The Portal.
Twelfth century.

Fig. 207. Paray-le-Monial, Saône-et-Loire. The North Door.
Consecrated, 1104.

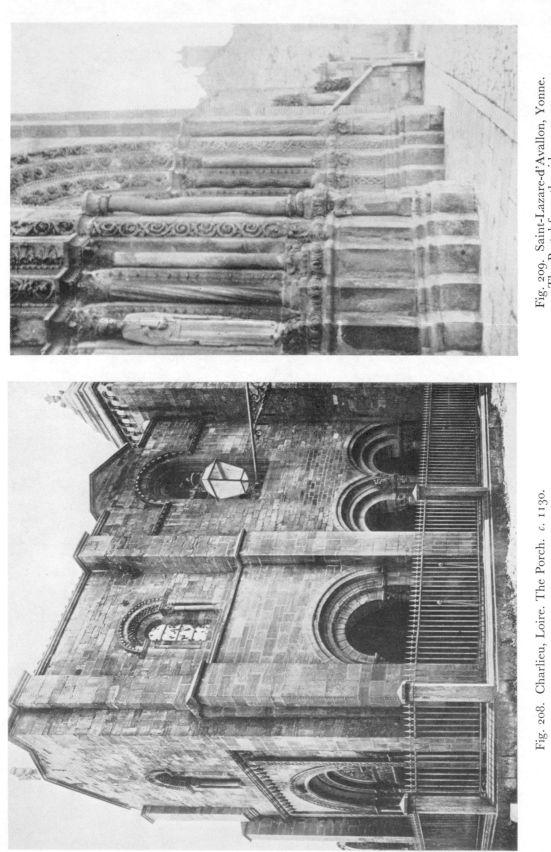

Fig. 209. Saint-Lazare-d'Avallon, Yonne. The Portal from the side. *c.* 1140.

Fig. 208. Charlieu, Loire. The Porch. *c.* 1130.

Fig. 210. Landos, Haute-Loire. The Portal.
Twelfth century.

Fig. 211. Semur-en-Brionnais, Saône-et-Loire.
The Side Door. Middle of twelfth century.

Fig. 212. Vigeois, Corrèze. Detail of the Door.
Twelfth century.

Fig. 213. Le Wast, Pas-de-Calais.
The Portal. Before 1099.

Fig. 214. Colombier, Allier. The Portal.
Twelfth century.

Fig. 215. Saint-Ybars, Ariège. The Portal.
Twelfth century.

Fig. 216. Tayac, Dordogne. The Portal.
Twelfth century.

Fig. 217. Condéon, Charente-Inférieure.
The Portal. Twelfth century.

Fig. 218. Ganagobie, Basses-Alpes. The Portal. Twelfth century.

Fig. 219. Cluny. The Second Abbey Church. Sketch reconstruction by Professor Kenneth Conant.

Needs revision (Conant 1965:163)

Fig. 220. Varennes-l'Arconce, Saône-et-Loire. The Church from the north-east. *c.* 1094.

Fig. 221. Massy, Saône-et-Loire. The Tower.
c. 1060.

Fig. 222. Blanot, Saône-et-Loire. The Tower.
c. 1050.

Fig. 223. Marcigny, Saône-et-Loire. The
West End of the Church. c. 1100.

Fig. 225. Moûtier-d'Ahun, Creuse. The Belfry. *c.* 1160.

Fig. 224. Saint-Hippolyte, Saône-et-Loire. The Church.
c. 1100; the Tower fortified before 1319.

Fig. 226. Salles-en-Beaujolais, Rhône.
Tower. *c.* 1100.

Fig. 227. Souvigny, Allier. The South-West
Tower. *c.* 1100.

Fig. 228. Saint-Germain-d'Auxerre, Yonne.
The Tower. Twelfth century.

Fig. 229. Uzerche, Corrèze. The Tower.
Second half of twelfth century.

Fig. 230. La Charité, Nièvre. La Tour-Sainte-Croix. Second half of twelfth century.

Fig. 232. Saint-Martin-des-Champs, Paris. The Tower on the south-west of the Choir. First quarter of the twelfth century.

Fig. 231. Vézelay, Yonne. The Transept Tower. c. 1160.

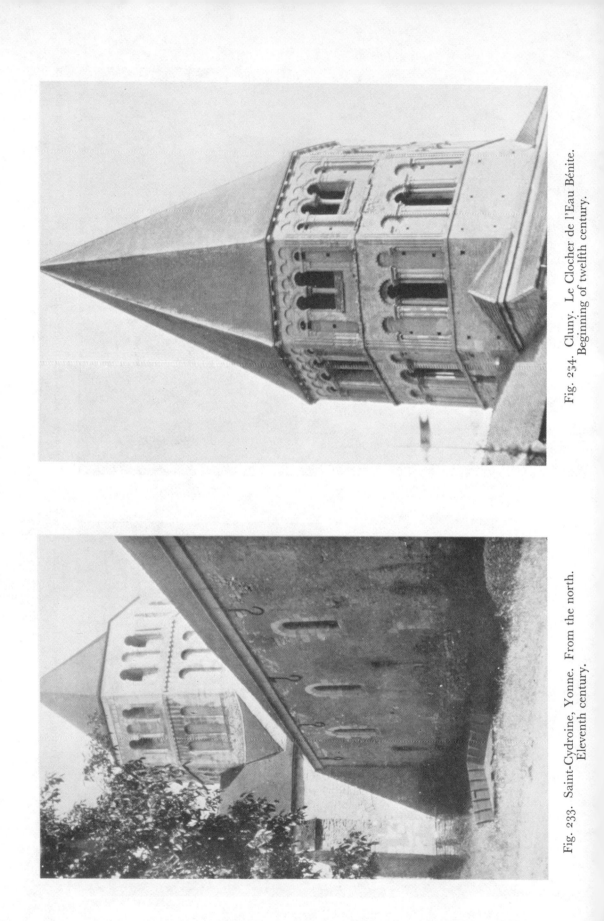

Fig. 234. Cluny. Le Clocher de l'Eau Bénite. Beginning of twelfth century.

Fig. 233. Saint-Cydroine, Yonne. From the north. Eleventh century.

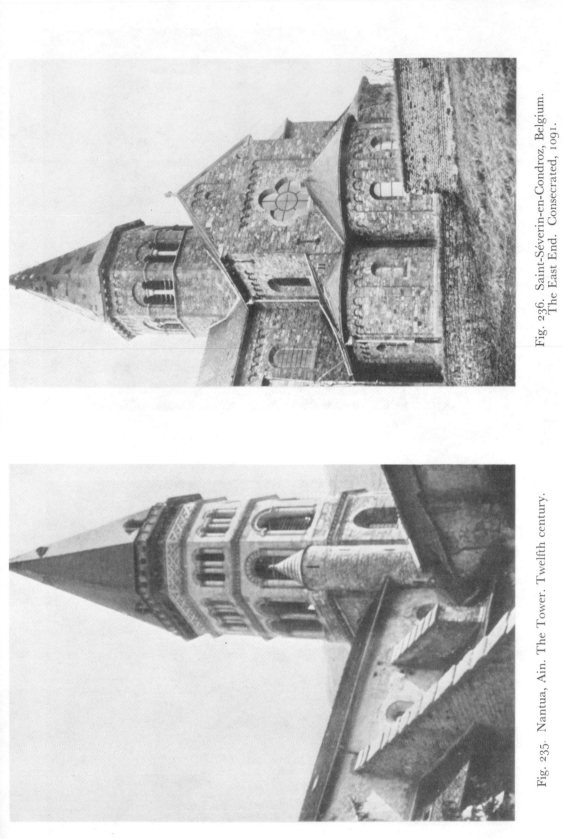

Fig. 236. Saint-Séverin-en-Condroz, Belgium.
The East End. Consecrated, 1091.

Fig. 235. Nantua, Ain. The Tower. Twelfth century.

Fig. 238. Caderousse, Vaucluse. The Belfry.

Fig. 237. Landos, Haute-Loire. The Belfry.

Fig. 239. Cluny. The Tower of Saint-Marcel. 1159; the steeple later.

Fig. 240. Charlieu, Loire. Arcade on the Inner Wall of the Cloister.
Eleventh century.

Fig. 241. Salles-en-Beaujolais, Rhône. The Remains of the Cloister.
c. 1100.

Fig. 242. Moissac, Tarn-et-Garonne. The Cloister. The capitals for the most part, *c.* 1100; re-used in the thirteenth century.

Fig. 243. Carennac, Lot. The Cloister. *c.* 1120.

Fig. 244. Ganagobie, Basses-Alpes. The Cloister. *c.* 1130.

Fig. 245. Beaulieu, Corrèze. The Entrance to the Chapter House. Early twelfth century.

Fig. 246. Marcilhac, Lot. The Entrance to the Chapter House. Early twelfth century.

Fig. 247. Vézelay, Yonne. The Chapter House. *c.* 1170.

Fig. 248. Much Wenlock, Shropshire. The Entrance to the
ruined Chapter House. *c.* 1140.

Fig. 249. Ganagobie, Basses-Alpes. The Entrance to the Refectory.
c. 1130.

Fig. 250. Much Wenlock, Shropshire. The Remains of the
Cloister Lavatory. End of the twelfth century.

Fig. 251. Much Wenlock, Shropshire. The Interior of the Chapter House. *c.* 1140.

Fig. 252. Ganagobie, Basses-Alpes. The Refectory.
Middle of twelfth century.

Fig. 253. Payerne, Switzerland. The Monastic Buildings. Late eleventh century.

Fig. 254. Payerne, Switzerland. Arcade on the Inner Wall of the former Cloister. Eleventh century.

Fig. 255. Cluny. The Abbey Gateway. *c.* 1100.

Fig. 256. Autun. The Porte-Saint-André. A.D. 69.

Fig. 257. Cluny. "Les Écuries de Saint-Hugues"(in background).
c. 1100.

Fig. 258. Charlieu, Loire. The Wall of the earlier monastic building
by the Prior's lodging.

Fig. 259. Château-Larcher, Vienne. *Lanterne des Morts*. Twelfth century.

INDEX

INDEX

Names of places that have not been identified are printed in italics.

Map 1

Cluniac Houses
of the
PROVINCE OF LYONS

Scale of Miles
0 5 10   20   30   40

'f the map: Mornay, Aube   Not located: Boisy, Loire
Fontaines d'Ozillac, Char.   Rosay, Savoie
Montausier, Charente   Clos St. Jean, Jura
Nevers: St. Loup, Nièvre   St. Hilaire, Jura
Moutiers en Torentaise   Grelonges, Ain

•Duesme

•Trouhaut

•St. Vivant de Vergy

Chambornay
lès Pin

Marny

Mont St. Jean

St. Jean de l'Osne

Chatelay

47

•Château sur Salins

Semelay   •Mesvres   •Pontoux
•St. Loup sur Abron   •St. Marcel lès Chalon   Cuiseaux   Frontenay
•Luzy   •Ruffey
Germagny.   Maynal
Mont St. Vincent   Cuisia   Flacey
•Bourbon Lancy   Poitte   St. Laurent
                        Dompierre   Clairvaux   du Roc
                        Chatelchevroux   Ilay
Paray le Monial   St. Nizier   Champagnat
            CLUNY   le Bouchoux   Montagna   Gigny
      •Charolles   Curciat   le Reconduit
•Varennes l'Arconce   Domsure   Louvenne
Marcigny   Mâcon: St. Laurent   Chazelles   •St. Laurent de Creux   Farges   Divonne
                  St. Martin lès Mâcon   Marboz   Asserans
•Fleury la Montagne   St. Jean   St. Martin
Charlieu Ajoux   •St. Mamert   de Larenay   Montfort
                  St. Nizier   Treffort
Ambierle   de l'Estra   Chaveyriat   Mornay
St. Nicolas   Renaison   Bohas   Ceyzériat   Nantua   Ville en   Ville la Grande
des Biefs   Cercié.   Valeins   Oussiat   St. Martin   Michaille   Viuz la Chiesaz
Villeret   Regny   Salles   en Dombes   St. Alban du Fresne   Ardon   •Contamine sur Arve
            St. Victor   Lurcy   Prin   Brenod   Thiez
      •Lay   sur Rhins   Montberthoud   Chindrieux
                  Limans   Villette   Chêne en Semine
      St. Véran   Frontenas   Sillingy
Pommiers   Montluel St. Germain de   St. Sorlin   St. Clair
Arthur   Villeneuve   Beynost.   de la Cluse   Rumilly
Sail sous Cousan   •Pouilly lès Feurs   Talissieu
                  Chandieu   Viuz Faverges
            Taluyers   •Bellevaux en Bauges

46

45

St. Martin

Oriol en Royans   Oulx

La Baume Cornillane

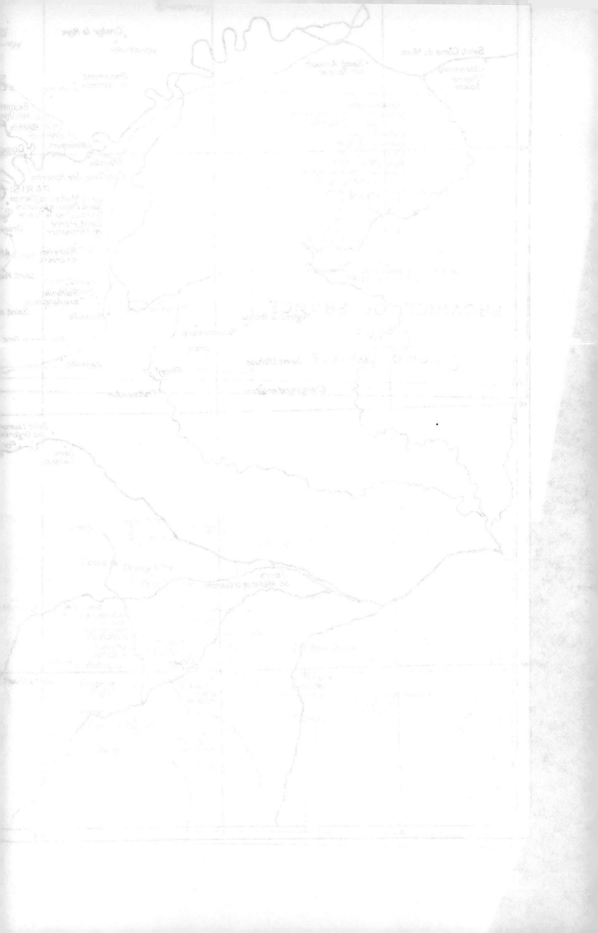

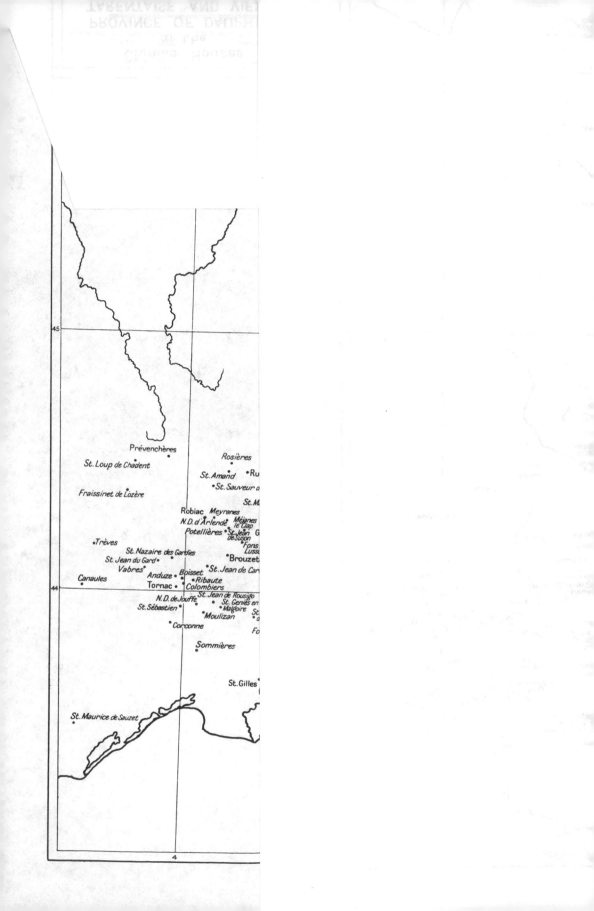

45

Prévenchères

St. Loup de Chadent

Rosières

St. Amand   •Ru

•St. Sauveur d

Fraissinet de Lozère

St. M.

Robiac   Meyranes
N.D. d'Arlende   Méjanes
le Clap
Potellières •St. Jean   G
de Suson

•Trèves   Fons
Lussa

St. Nazaire des Gardies   •Brouzet

St. Jean du Gard•   •St. Jean de Car

Vabres•   Anduze • Boisset
Canaules   •Ribaute
•   Tornac • Colombiers

44

St. Jean de Rousigo
N.D. de Jouffe   St. Geniès en
St. Sébastien•   •Malgoire   St.
•Moulizan   •

•Corconne   Fo

Sommières

St. Gilles•

St. Maurice de Sauzet
•

4

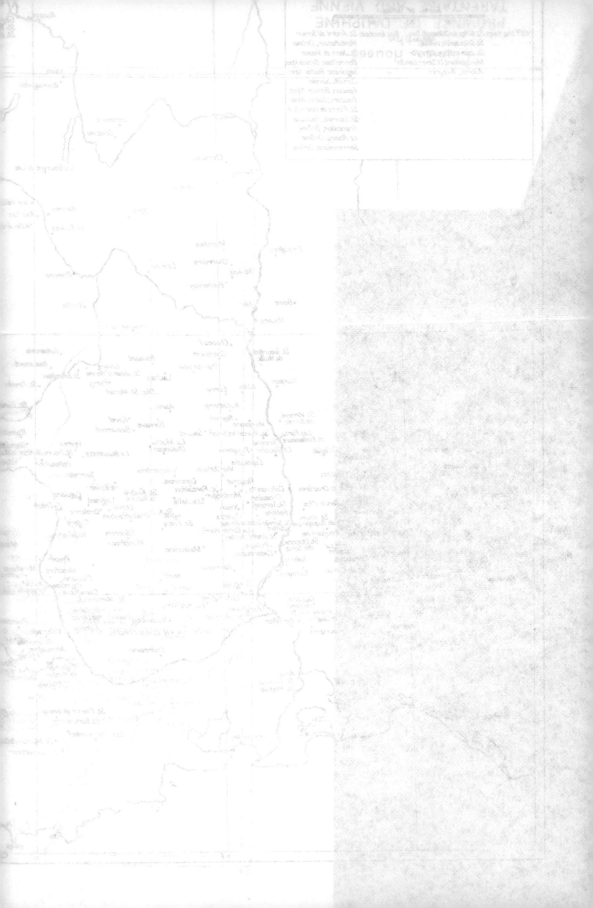

46

45

PR

Off

44

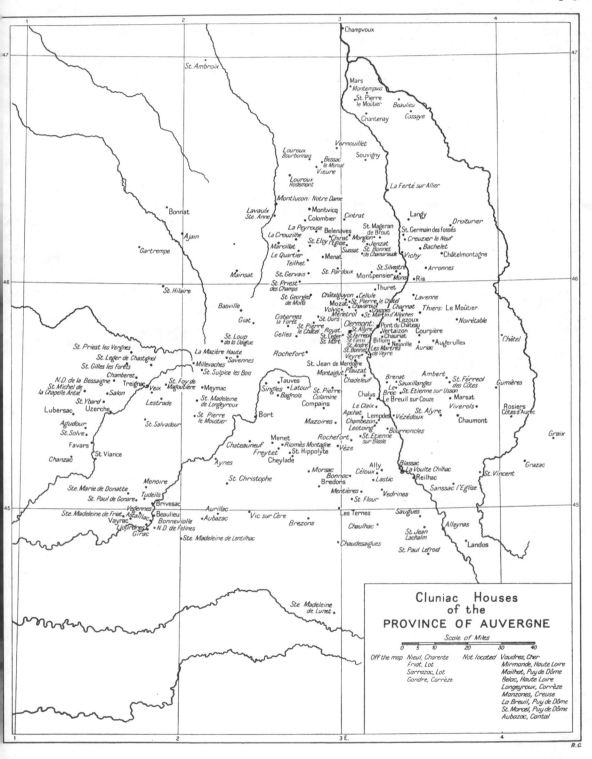

Cluniac Houses
of the
PROVINCE OF AUVERGNE

Scale of Miles

0 5 10 20 30 40

Off the map: Nieul, Charente
Friat, Lot
Sarrazac, Lot
Gondre, Corrèze

Not located: Vaudres, Cher
Mirmande, Haute Loire
Mailhat, Puy de Dôme
Belac, Haute Loire
Longeyroux, Corrèze
Manzanes, Creuse
La Breuil, Puy de Dôme
St. Marcel, Puy de Dôme
Aubazac, Cantal

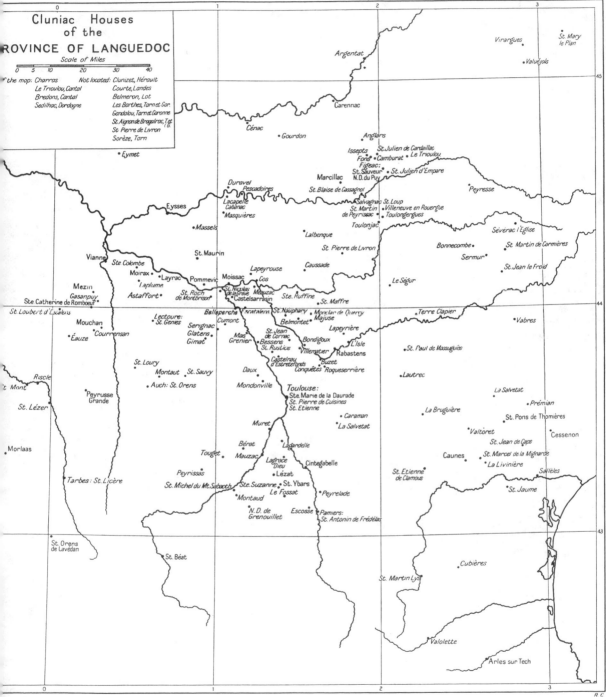

Map 6

St. Mary
le Plan

Virargues

Valuejols

Argentat

Carennac

Cénac

Gourdon

Anglars

Issepts   St. Julien de Cardaillac
Fons Camburat Le Trioulou
Figeac:
St. Sauveur   St. Julien d'Empare
N.D. du Puy

Peyresse

Duravel
Pescadoires
Lacapelle   St. Blaise de Cassagnol
Cabanac   Salvagnac St. Loup
Masquières   St. Martin Villeneuve en Rouergue
                   de Peyrisac Toulongergues

Eysses

Eymet

Massels

Toulonjac

Sévérac l'Eglise

Lalbenque

Bonnecombe   St. Martin de Cormières

St. Maurin

St. Pierre de Livron

Sermur

St. Jean le Froid

Vianne

Ste. Colombe

Moirax   Layrac   Pommevic Moissac
Mezin   Laplume   Cos
Gasanpuy   Astaffort   St. Nicolas Mauzac
Ste. Catherine de Romboeuf   de la Grave Castelsarrasin
St. Loubert d'Escalens   St. Roch
                               de Montbrison

Lapeyrouse

Caussade

Le Ségur

Le Segur

Mouchan
Lectoure:
St. Génies
Cumont
Balleperche Scatalens St. Nauphary
Mas   Belmontet   Monclar de Quercy
Éauze Courrensan Sérignac   Majuse
                 Glatens Mas   St. Jean Lapeyrière
                 Gimat   Grenier   de Cornac
                                   Bessens   Bondigoux   L'Isle
                                   St. Rustice Villematier Rabastens
St. Loury   Castelnau Buzet
Montaut   St. Sauvy   d'Estretefonds Conquètes Roqueserrière
Auch: St. Orens   Daux
                  Mondonville

Riscle

St. Mont

St. Lézer

Peyrusse
Grande

Toulouse:
Ste. Marie de la Daurade
St. Pierre de Cuisines
St. Etienne

Muret

Caraman
La Salvetat

Vabres

Terre Clapier

St. Paul de Massuguiès

Lautrec

La Salvetat

Prémian

La Bruguière

St. Pons de Thomières

Cessenon

Morlaas

Touget
Bérat   Lagardelle
Mauzac   Lézat
Peyrissas   Lagrace   Cintegabelle
            Dieu
St. Michel du Mt. Sabacch Ste. Suzanne St. Ybars
                           Le Fossat
Montaud
N.D. de   Escosse Pamiers:
Grenouillet   St. Antonin de Frédélas

Valtoret
St. Jean de Caps

Caunes   St. Marcel de la Mignarde
         La Livinière

Salléles

St. Etienne
de Clamous

St. Jaume

Tarbes: St. Licère

St. Orens
de Lavédan

St. Béat

Cubières

St. Martin Lys

Valolette

Arles sur Tech

R.C.

Map 7

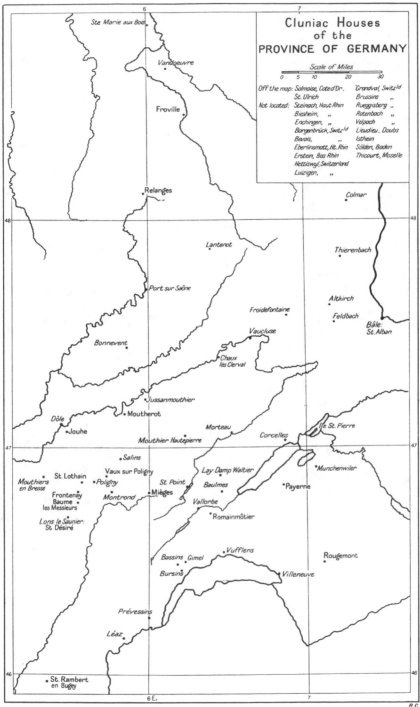

Cluniac Houses
of the
PROVINCE OF GERMANY

Scale of Miles
0   5   10   20   30

Off the map: Salmaise, Cote d'Or.
St. Ulrich
Not located: Steinach, Haut Rhin
Biesheim, „
Enchingen, „
Borgenbrück, Switz.ld
Bevois, „
Eberlinsmott, Ht. Rhin
Erstein, Bas Rhin
Hettiswyl, Switzerland
Luizigen, „

'Grandval, Switz.ld
Brussins „
Rueggisberg „
Rotenbach „
Velpach „
Lieudieu, Doubs
Isthein
Sölden, Baden
Thicourt, Moselle

Ste Marie aux Bois
Vandoeuvre
Froville
Relanges
Colmar
Lantenot
Thierenbach
Port sur Saône
Altkirch
Froidefontaine
Feldbach
Vaucluse
Bâle: St. Alban
Bonnevent
Chaux les Clerval
Jussanmouthier
Dôle · Moutherot
Jouhe
Morteau
Île St. Pierre
Mouthier Hautepierre
Corcelles
Salins
Vaux sur Poligny
Lay Damp Waltier
Munchenwiler
St. Lothain
St. Point
Mouthiers en Bresse · Poligny
Baulmes
Payerne
Frontenay
Montrond · Mièges
Baume les Messieurs
Vallorbe
Lons le Saunier: St. Désiré
Romainmôtier
Vufflens
Rougemont
Bassins · Gimel
Bursins
Villeneuve
Prévessins
Léaz
St. Rambert en Bugey

6 É.   7

R.C.